International Practitioner's Deskbook Series

The Foreign Corrupt Practices Act and the New International Norms

Stuart H. Deming

**Defending Liberty
Pursuing Justice**

ABA Section of
International Law
Your Gateway to International Practice

**Section of International Law and Practice
American Bar Association**

Cover design by ABA Publishing.

Printed in the United States of America.
09 08 07   5 4 3

Library of Congress Cataloging-in-Publication Data
Deming, Stuart H., 1951–
    Foreign Corrupt Practices Act and the new international norms / by
Stuart H. Deming.
        p. cm.—(International practitioner's deskbook series)
    Includes bibliographical references and index.
    ISBN 1-59031-326-7 (alk. paper)
    1. Corporations, American—Law and legislation—United
States—Criminal provisions. 2. Bribery—United States. 3. Disclosure
of information—Law and legislation—United States—Criminal provisions.
4. Foreign trade regulation—United States—Criminal provisions.
5. United States. Foreign Corrupt Practices Act of 1977. 6. Corporation
law—Criminal provisions. 7. International and municipal law—United
States. I. American Bar Association. Section of International Law and
Practice. II. Title. III. Series.

    KF9351.D46 2005
    345.73'02323—dc22
                                2005013059

Discounts are available for books ordered in bulk. Special consideration is given to state bars, CLE programs, and other bar-related organizations. Inquire at Book Publishing, ABA Publishing, American Bar Association, 321 N. Clark, Chicago, Illinois 60610-4714.

www.ababooks.org

In memory of my father,
Ned W. Deming

CONTENTS

PART III: COMPLIANCE

ABOUT THE AUTHOR

Stuart H. Deming is a principal with the law firm of Deming PLLC. He practices in its offices in Washington, D.C. and in his hometown of Kalamazoo, Michigan. Mr. Deming represents entities and individuals in a wide range of foreign business and investigatory matters. He provides advice on international transactions, develops and assists in the implementation of compliance programs, conducts internal investigations, and represents clients before federal and state agencies.

Mr. Deming began his legal career as an Assistant U.S. Attorney in Michigan where he managed a major grand jury investigation of kickbacks by a major German multinational corporation and litigated a landmark case requiring the production of foreign records by a major German bank. He later joined the Securities and Exchange Commission in Washington, D.C., where he managed the investigation of major corporations for violations of U.S. securities laws, including the successful investigation of a Fortune 500 company for accounting fraud. Before going into private practice, Mr. Deming prosecuted public figures, foreign nationals, and executives of major corporations at the Tax Division of the Department of Justice.

After joining the Washington, D.C. law firm of Steptoe & Johnson in 1987, Mr. Deming was directly involved in the representation of a major defense contractor. He later served for a brief period with the George H. W. Bush administration, first with the 1990 Economic Summit in Houston and later with the Department of Defense. In 1992 Mr. Deming was asked to return to the Department of Justice to serve as one of the special prosecutors in a highly sensitive and complex investigation involving many members of Congress of the United States and their use of the banking facility at the U.S. House of Representatives. In 1996 he was one of the founding partners of Inman Deming LLP, where he practiced in Washington and in Michigan until 2003.

Mr. Deming has written and spoken extensively in the United States and abroad on foreign corrupt practices issues. He for many years co-chaired the ABA's National Institutes on the Foreign Corrupt Practices Act; he was a founder and the Co-Chair of the ABA's Task Force on International Standards for Corrupt Practices, and he is a member of the Board of Editorial

Advisors to the *Foreign Corrupt Practices Act Reporter*. He has taught for several years a course on foreign corrupt practice issues as an adjunct professor at the John Marshall Law School Center for International Business and Trade Law in Chicago.

Mr. Deming has served in various capacities as an officer and member of the Council of the ABA's Section of International Law and Practice and as the Chair of the International Law Section of the State Bar of Michigan. He has served as an active member of the American Institute of Certified Public Accountant's Responsibilities in Tax Practice Committee and as the U.S. representative on the Transparency Committee of the Pacific Basin Economic Council. Mr. Deming received his B.A., M.B.A., and J.D. from the University of Michigan, and he has also been licensed as a Certified Public Accountant.

PREFACE

This deskbook is intended to provide practitioners, corporate counsel, accountants, compliance officials, and anyone engaged in international business with an overview of the Foreign Corrupt Practices Act (FCPA) as well as the new international norms that bear on the prohibition of payments to foreign officials. In this burgeoning area of law, no publication short of a treatise should be considered comprehensive. Yet, this deskbook, to the degree possible, seeks to provide insight into the range of considerations that need to be taken into account and to provide in one publication ready access to the key legal documents.

A range of experiences over many years serves as the basis for this deskbook. Very much part of these experiences has been the interaction with enforcement officials at programs sponsored by the American Bar Association's (ABA) Section of International Law and the Center for Legal Education. None of these programs would have been as beneficial to all concerned without the active participation of these officials. In this regard, special note should be made of the participation and efforts of Peter B. Clark, who, until recently, was the Deputy Chief of the Fraud Section of the U.S. Department of Justice (Justice Department). His help, guidance, and support over many years were critical to the success of these programs.

A number of other officials, many of whom are no longer serving in government, have also been critical to the success of the ABA's programs and activities. These other officials include Mark F. Mendelsohn and Philip E. Urofsky from the Justice Department; Linda Chatman Thomsen, Paul R. Berger, Meyer Eisenberg, Paul V. Gerlach, Richard W. Grime, Gregory S. Bruch, and Nancy Grunberg from the U.S. Securities and Exchange Commission; Eleanor Roberts Lewis, Arthur Aronoff, and Kathryn Helne Nickerson from the U.S. Department of Commerce; Thomas J. White from the U.S. Department of State; and Stephen D. Potts from the U.S. Office of Government Ethics. The thoughtful participation of Professor Mark Pieth and Professor Giorgio Sacerdoti from the Organization for Economic Cooperation and Development's Working Group on Bribery in International Business Transactions has also been particularly useful.

I am personally indebted to two of the most capable experts in this area of law for their comments and suggestions. Nicole M. Healy, who now practices with Wilson Sonsini Goodrich & Rosati in Palo Alto, California, and who investigated and prosecuted FCPA cases as a trial attorney with the Justice Department, and Margaret M. Ayres, who practices with Davis Polk & Wardwell in Washington, D.C. Both were most generous in making themselves available.

Special consideration should also be given to Don S. DeAmicis for inspiring this deskbook, to Salli A. Swartz for her instrumental support, and to Michael H. Byowitz and Darrell Prescott for their efforts behind the scenes. As is the case with so much of what takes place under the auspices of the ABA, the staff makes it all possible. In this regard, special note needs to be made of Richard G. Paszkiet and Barbara Leff and their staff. There are, of course, many others who have been very helpful over a number of years. Jennifer Dabson, Sushan Demirjian, Earnestine Murphy, and Virginia M. Russell are among these kind individuals.

And finally, there have been many colleagues who, over many years, have in their own way contributed to this deskbook. My former partner, Harry A. Inman, was a major source of encouragement as was Jacob A. Stein, a mentor in so many ways. But, as well, the perspective of A. Timothy Martin, one of the more thoughtful commentators in this area of law, played a significant role.

Many others have also provided useful insights over the years. These include, among others, Susan Rose-Ackerman, Lori B. Alexander, Stephen T. Black, Milos Barutciski, Stéphane Bonifassi, Nancy Zucker Boswell, John M. Bray, George Brown, H. Lowell Brown, Sharie A. Brown, J. Jerome Bullock, Charles E. Chamberlain, Jr., Bruno Cova, Thomas J. Crowley, Donald B. Cruver, Michael N. Davies, Eric A. Dubelier, David A. Gantz, Carl di Florio, Luis A. Garcia, Joseph P. Griffin, William M. Hannay III, Johnnie W. Hoffman, Jr., Nettie A. Horne, Bruce J. Horowitz, Cheryl Fackler Hug, Alfredo X. Jarrin, O. Thomas Johnson, Jr., James M. Klotz, Edward A. Krauland, Lisa M. Landmeier, John R. Liebman, David M. Luna, Jason P. Matechak, Andrew Josh Markus, Thomas F. McInerney, Obie L. Moore, Ramon Mullerat, Danforth Newcomb, William F. Pendergast, Rebekah J. Poston, Monty Raphael, Kenneth B. Reisenfeld, Jill Rhodes, Logan G. Robinson, Herbert T. Sears, Mary C. Spearing, Salli A. Swartz, Alexander Troller, Dale A. Turza, Laurence A. Urgensen, Howard O. Weissman, Jane L. Wexton, Roger M. Witten, Alexandra Wrage, Douglas R. Young, and Donald Zarin as well as my cochairs for many of these programs and activities with the ABA's Section of International Law, John A. Detzner, Timothy L. Dickinson, Lucinda A. Low, and Homer E. Moyer, Jr.

INTRODUCTION

The systemic character of illicit payments for the purpose of bribing officials of foreign countries in the context of international business has been known for years. These practices were implicitly permitted in spite of universal if often unstated agreement that the proliferation of this form of corruption threatens the proper functioning of democratic institutions and market economies, leads to serious misallocations of resources, and jeopardizes relations among nations. Yet, until the latter part of the twentieth century, prohibitions on the corruption of public officials were limited to a country's own officials and not officials of other countries or international organizations. Indeed, questionable payments to foreign officials, including what can only be described as bribes, were permitted as deductible business expenses for tax purposes.

In 1977, as an outgrowth of the Watergate scandal in the United States and a series of revelations associated with that period, the U.S. Congress adopted the Foreign Corrupt Practices Act (FCPA). For many years, it made the United States the only country to implement and actively enforce measures to prohibit its citizens, nationals, businesses, and, in some circumstances, foreign companies that enter its capital markets from bribing foreign officials. These prohibitions are no longer limited to the United States.

A convergence of factors ultimately led to a series of international initiatives, which are modeled on the FCPA, to prohibit improper inducements to foreign officials in connection with business transactions. Over the past ten years, a number of international conventions have been negotiated and entered into force. These, in turn, have led most developed countries to adopt domestic laws prohibiting improper inducements to foreign officials. Increasingly, less developed countries are implementing similar prohibitions as these initiatives have become more global in scope. And these initiatives are not limited to governments. They extend to international institutions, to nongovernmental organizations, and to corporate governance measures.

Conduct involving improper inducements to foreign officials can no longer be ignored. Nor can an individual or entity engaged in international business limit compliance concerns to the application and to the scope of the FCPA. There are ever-increasing obligations on businesses to detect and deter illegal conduct. The international developments are certain to continue to expand the breadth of the prohibitions of payments to foreign officials. They will also have the added effect of dramatically expanding the ability of U.S. enforcement officials to secure evidence from abroad.

An entity engaged in international business puts itself at significant risk by not taking steps to ensure that it has an effective system of internal controls that includes a compliance program. What appear to be short cuts or clever responses to these emerging international norms are dangerous and, over time, will be counterproductive. Entities, particularly publicly held entities, can no longer remain inert to the changing legal environment.

In counseling a client on issues relating to the FCPA and the new international norms, an earnest effort to comply is fundamental. By implementing and rigorously enforcing an effective compliance program and by undertaking carefully planned and thorough due diligence, an entity is most likely to avoid potential violations and, should the specter of a violation arise, to minimize the risk of an investigation.

PART I

THE FOREIGN CORRUPT PRACTICES ACT

CHAPTER I

OVERVIEW OF THE FOREIGN CORRUPT PRACTICES ACT

The Foreign Corrupt Practices Act (FCPA) is a statute designed to deter improper inducements to foreign officials in connection with business activities. It has two principal mechanisms for carrying out its purposes. One is a general prohibition on payments to foreign officials. This prohibition applies to U.S. nationals, U.S. businesses, publicly held companies, many foreign companies, and, in certain circumstances, almost anyone. The second mechanism imposes requirements on the accounting and record-keeping practices of the domestic and foreign operations of publicly held companies.

Initially enacted in 1977, and amended in 1988 and 1998, the FCPA plays a major role in legal jurisprudence in the United States and elsewhere. On a daily basis, it has a direct bearing on the foreign and domestic operations of publicly held entities. It also directly affects business practices of individuals and entities in international settings. Increasingly, often in unexpected ways, it is having an impact on litigation and arbitral proceedings.

Although the purpose and language of the FCPA appear to be straightforward in nature, the statute is much more nuanced than is generally recognized. Its scope and means of application can be complex and can lead to dramatically unexpected results. For example, the same set of facts in one setting can also lead to an entirely different result in another setting. And the same set of facts may constitute a violation of one part of the FCPA and, at the same time, may not be subject to the prohibitions in another part of the FCPA. Before rendering advice with respect to the FCPA, a thorough understanding is required. Otherwise, experts should be consulted.

❂ TWO MECHANISMS

Through the FCPA, the U.S. Congress sought to deter foreign corrupt practices, and specifically the offer or payment of anything of value to foreign officials in connection with business activities, through two principal mechanisms: the anti-bribery provisions and the accounting and record-keeping provisions. The two sets of provisions are conceptually different from each other. The former is proscriptive in orientation, and the latter is prescriptive. Their scope and application are also different.

Essential to any analysis of a situation that may involve an FCPA violation is the consideration of whether the anti-bribery provisions or the accounting and record-keeping provisions, or both, may be involved. A certain set of facts may suggest a violation of the anti-bribery provisions yet may not suggest a violation of the accounting and record-keeping provisions. Each set of provisions must be considered separately. While the anti-bribery provisions apply to issuers, domestic concerns, and foreign nationals while in the United States, the record-keeping provisions apply only to entities that are considered "issuers" under the U.S. securities laws. Neither provision should be considered alone. They were intended to work in tandem and thereby complement each other.

❂ LACK OF JUDICIAL REVIEW

Any analysis of the FCPA must begin with the understanding that its provisions have rarely been subject to judicial scrutiny. Although the FCPA has had, and will increasingly have, a major impact on how business is conducted, relatively few prosecutions have been brought under the anti-bribery provisions. Of these, most have resulted in the entry of a guilty plea or some sort of civil settlement. Far more prosecutions have been brought under the accounting and record-keeping provisions, but most have been in the context of civil proceedings and, even in that context, the vast majority of cases have resulted in settlements.

Because a multitude of legal issues associated with the FCPA have yet to be subject to judicial review, the anticipated upsurge in prosecutions can be expected to lead to rather extensive litigation both at the trial and appellate levels. Although entities are generally not inclined to contest enforcement actions, this will not be the case with individuals subject to imprisonment. This is especially so since the U.S. Federal Sentencing Guidelines have increasingly made incarceration more likely and more severe for white-collar crime. As a result, the basic underpinnings of the FCPA, as well as the application of its provisions, will be subject to more and more challenges with the anticipated increase in criminal prosecutions.

Situations are likely to arise where the courts interpret the FCPA differently from how it has been applied by the U.S. Department of Justice (Justice Department) and the U.S. Securities and Exchange Commission (SEC). However, in providing guidance, the prudent approach is to rely on historical interpretations as applied by U.S. enforcement officials. Conduct should always be avoided that might serve as a basis for the initiation of an investigation. If an investigation arises, and charges are brought, a host of legal issues can still be legitimately raised.

CHAPTER II

THE ANTI-BRIBERY PROVISIONS

The anti-bribery provisions come to mind first when reference is made to the FCPA. In terms of public interest, they serve as the focal point for most FCPA investigations. The anti-bribery provisions prohibit any promise, offer, or payment of anything of value if the offeror "knows" that any portion will be offered, given, or promised to a foreign official, foreign political party, or candidate for the purpose of influencing a governmental decision.

❂ SCOPE AND JURISDICTION

The jurisdiction of the anti-bribery provisions of the FCPA is broad. The anti-bribery provisions apply to what are known as "domestic concerns" and "issuers." They also apply to any person, including foreign individuals and entities, acting in furtherance of the improper inducement of a foreign public official while in the territory of the United States. The United States has generally followed the territorial principle in the application of most of its criminal laws. For the territorial principle to apply, some connection to the territory of the United States must exist in order for the prohibited activity to be subject to the laws of the United States. A common example of the territorial principle is where there is a requirement that there be the use of interstate or foreign commerce of the United States in order for jurisdiction to exist.

In implementing the Convention on Combating Bribery of Foreign Public Officials in International Business Transactions (OECD Convention), the U.S. Congress expanded the FCPA in 1998 to include the nationality principle as a basis for jurisdiction. For the nationality principle to apply, there is no requirement that there be any territorial connection to the United States. Jurisdiction is based solely on the status of an individual as a U.S. national or whether an entity was established under the laws of the United States or has its principal place of business in the United States. As a result, depending upon the circumstances, the jurisdiction of the anti-bribery provisions can be based upon principles of nationality or territoriality, or both.

The anti-bribery provisions include three distinct but essentially parallel sets of prohibitions. In general, each set prohibits improper inducements to officials, political parties, party officials, and political candidates of a foreign country. They differ in that each set addresses a separate category of inducers: issuers, domestic concerns, and any individual or entity acting within the territory of the United States in furtherance of a prohibited inducement.

Issuers

An issuer is any entity that is required under the Securities Exchange Act (Exchange Act) to register under Section 12 or to file reports under Section 15(d).[1] Issuers may be foreign companies, including a foreign company with American Depository Receipts (ADRs), that are registered pursuant to Section 12 or required to file reports pursuant to Section 15(d). ADRs represent an ownership interest in the securities of a foreign private issuer that are deposited, usually outside of the United States, with a financial institution as the depository. In general, publicly held companies with securities or ADRs listed on securities exchanges in the United States are issuers subject to the anti-bribery provisions.

Like domestic concerns, nationality principles of jurisdiction now apply to issuers.[2] There is no longer a jurisdictional requirement that there be the use of an instrumentality of interstate commerce in furtherance of a prohibited inducement. Officers, directors, employees, and agents of issuers who are subject to the anti-bribery provisions are also subject to nationality principles. For officers, directors, and employees of issuers and of domestic concerns and for individuals or entities acting as an agent for or on behalf of an issuer or a domestic concern, it does not matter whether they, in their own right, are issuers or domestic concerns under the anti-bribery provisions or whether an instrumentality of interstate commerce may be involved.

Foreign Subsidiaries

When the use of U.S. territory is not involved in furtherance of a prohibited inducement, foreign companies and foreign subsidiaries of an issuer are not subject to the anti-bribery provisions. It does not matter whether the foreign affiliate or subsidiary is wholly or partially owned by an issuer. Under agency principles, it is only when the foreign affiliate or subsidiary is acting as an agent of an issuer or domestic concern that the foreign affiliate or subsidiary would become subject to the anti-bribery provisions.

Domestic Concerns

The anti-bribery provisions extend to domestic concerns, which include U.S. individuals and entities.[3] Individuals who are nationals of the United States are subject to the terms of the anti-bribery provisions. The term "national" includes U.S. citizens as well as resident aliens and any other category of nationals of the United States under Section 101 of the Immigration and Nationality Act.[4]

Any juridical entity organized under U.S. law or with its principal place of business in the United States is a domestic concern. Juridical entities include corporations, partnerships, limited liability companies, and any other type of entity that might be established under U.S. law. Regardless of nationality, any officer, director, member, employee, agent, or stockholder of a domestic concern is also subject to the anti-bribery provisions. In this way, an individual who might not otherwise be a U.S. national and thus subject to the anti-bribery provisions of the FCPA can become subject to those provisions by his or her status or relationship with an entity of a domestic concern.

The anti-bribery provisions also apply to domestic concerns employed or retained by foreign entities and foreign subsidiaries that are not subject to the anti-bribery provisions. An individual's or entity's status as a domestic concern does not change with location or with business or employment relationships. A domestic concern can be employed by a foreign corporation that is not subject to the FCPA. That domestic concern, whether an individual or entity, is still barred from engaging in the conduct prohibited by the anti-bribery provisions. Depending upon whether, and to what degree, that domestic concern participates in the prohibited activity, an individual or entity can be subject to prosecution for violating the anti-bribery provisions.

Prior to the expansion of the jurisdictional bases of the anti-bribery provisions in 1998, the threshold for meeting the territorial nexus to the United States was easily reached. For domestic concerns, it no longer matters whether there is a territorial nexus to the United States through any means or instrumentality of interstate commerce. The nationality principle of jurisdiction can now be applied to improper inducements made by domestic concerns that take place wholly outside of the United States, regardless of whether an "instrumentality of interstate commerce" is used in furtherance of the prohibited conduct.

Any Other Person

When instrumentalities of interstate commerce are involved, any act in furtherance of the bribery of a foreign public official conducted in the territory of the United States provides a jurisdictional basis for an individual or entity to be subject to the anti-bribery provisions.[5] It does not matter whether the person is a domestic concern or an issuer. The critical requirement is that the act taken in furtherance of offering or making the prohibited inducement takes place within the territory of the United States. This may include situations when a foreign national or entity not otherwise subject to the anti-bribery provisions causes an act to be done within the territory of the United States by any individual or entity acting as an agent.

Historically, what includes the "territory" of the United States has been interpreted broadly. It includes the territorial boundaries of the 50 states as well as the territorial boundaries of the territories, possessions, and commonwealths of the United States. It also includes the territorial waters of the United States. Ships and aircraft operating under the auspices of the U.S. flag and aircraft en route to the United States have been considered to be within the territory of the United States.

How the phrase "while in the territory of the United States" will be interpreted has yet to be determined. With the critical role that facilities of the United States play in international commerce, such as the Internet, banking, and air travel, the implications could be dramatic if what constitutes "while in the territory of the United States" is interpreted broadly. In other contexts, U.S. courts have tended to interpret jurisdictional requirements of this nature very broadly in order to enable the prosecution of conduct perceived as being especially egregious. U.S. courts can be expected to take a similar approach in determining what constitutes the territory of the United States.

ESSENTIAL ELEMENTS

The anti-bribery provisions are expansive and designed to preclude any means of circumventing their terms. The anti-bribery provisions of the FCPA have been consistently applied in an expansive manner by the Justice Department to preclude unsanctioned means of avoiding their terms. The basic elements of the anti-bribery provisions are as follows:

- A payment, offer, or promise of;
- Anything of value;
- To any
  - foreign official,
  - any foreign political party or party official,
  - any candidate for foreign political office, or
  - any other person while knowing that all or part of the payment or promise to pay will be passed on to one of the foregoing;
- With corrupt intent;
- For the purpose of
  - influencing an official act or decision of the person;
  - inducing that person to do or omit to do any act in violation of his or her lawful duty;
  - inducing that person to use his influence with a foreign government to affect or influence any government act or decision; or
  - secure any improper purpose;
- To assist in obtaining or retaining business for or with, or directing business to, any person.

Payment, Offer, or Promise

Whether a payment is actually made is not critical. Any offer or promise that could reasonably be believed to be an inducement falls within the category of prohibited conduct. There is no requirement that the public official accept the bribe. There is also no requirement that anyone actually receive the bribe or that the object of the bribe actually be attainable. All that is required is that what is paid, offered, or promised be sufficient to form the basis for an inducement.

Consistent with the broad net that is cast by the anti-bribery provisions, the manner by which a payment is made, offered, or promised is not controlling. The manner or means by which a payment, promise, or offer is made can provide no safe harbor or the basis of a defense if the other elements of a violation of the anti-bribery provisions are met. No matter how attenuated, an offer, promise, or payment may be made or communicated to its intended recipient, any indirect means of making or communicating a prohibited inducement could conceivably fall within the ambit of the prohibitions of the anti-bribery provisions.

Anything of Value

As the phrase "anything of value" suggests, what is given or offered can be as broad and as esoteric as can be reasonably conceived. In addition to cash or some form of monetary instrument, almost any form of direct or indirect benefit could constitute something of value. This might include a benefit to a family member or a right or ability to designate to whom a benefit is directed. How a potential benefit is apt to be perceived by the intended recipient is critical to any analysis. In this regard, what might be perceived as inconsequential in one setting may be perceived as significant in other settings.

There are virtually no limitations on what can be construed as "anything of value." Among the benefits that have typically been viewed as falling within the prohibitions of the anti-bribery provisions are scholarships for family members, upgrades to first-class airfare, side trips to resorts, hiring a family member for a summer position, and permitting an official to designate to whom charitable contributions are directed.

What may be of value may depend upon the circumstances. For someone of limited means, what may be significant in terms of value could be perceived quite differently for someone of substantial means. Where certain national resources are limited, like access to water in an arid region, providing access to such limited resources could be of significant value. In other contexts, such as in a region with an abundance of water, providing access to water may not be of much significance. However, because the FCPA has no *de minimis* exception, the context in which the inducement is made may be determinative of what constitutes "anything of value."

Foreign Official

Who is considered a foreign official under the anti-bribery provisions should be presumed to have as broad an application as possible. Regardless of country, the prohibitions apply to officials of all branches of government as well as to all units of government. This includes civil service and political functions in countries where those functions are not unified. It does not matter whether the public official is a paid or an unpaid official. The critical factor is whether the inducement is in any way associated with influencing what an individual can do in his or her official capacity.

De Facto Members of Government

Within the context of the anti-bribery provisions, a "foreign official" can include *de facto* members of government. Political parties, party officials, or any candidate for political office are specifically included within the prohibitions of the anti-bribery provisions. A precise definition is not provided as to what constitutes a candidate for public office. Given the expansive manner in which the anti-bribery provisions have been applied, formalisms such as an announced candidacy should not be assumed to be a controlling factor.

Whether an individual actually holds a position as a party official also may not be controlling in terms of whether an investigation may be instigated. The practical realities of the particular individual's status with a political party may ultimately be more determinative. Perceptions of that individual's influence will be critical to any assessment as to whether there should be an inquiry. For example, a payment to a retired senior party leader may be sufficient because his or her real role behind the scenes may be equivalent to that of a party official.

The line between what does and does not constitute a foreign official can become especially blurred in parts of the world where there are royal families. The classic situation may be in the Middle East where, in some countries, the royal families are large and their unofficial roles in affairs of state can be significant. The Justice Department has taken the position that, depending upon the facts, members of a royal family may be considered "foreign officials" within the meaning of the anti-bribery provisions, regardless of whether the family members have official titles or positions.

Parastatals

The anti-bribery provisions apply to "instrumentalities" of foreign governments often referred to as parastatals, or state-owned enterprises. The result is that a foreign official under the anti-bribery provisions is not limited to someone who carries out traditional governmental roles. He or she can be someone who is employed by a commercial enterprise that is government-owned or operated. Depending upon a country, or even certain parts of a country, the services provided by government can vary quite dramatically. Traditionally, these services can extend to telecommunications, transportation, health care, and sanitation services. But the activities in which a parastatal may be engaged are unlimited.

There is no definitive test for determining what constitutes a parastatal. Factors that may bear upon such a determination include how the enterprise is characterized by its government and whether it prohibits and prosecutes bribery of the employees of state-owned enterprises as public corruption. Another factor may be the degree of control exercised by the government over the enterprise. While state ownership in an enterprise does not automatically make the enterprise a parastatal, the degree of ownership and control are some of the indicia that may lead to the conclusion that an entity is a parastatal.

The likelihood that an entity will be considered a parastatal increases with the degree to which a country is or has been socialized. As privatization takes place in various parts of the world, the likelihood that entities will be considered a parastatal will diminish. The incidence of parastatals will vary over time with the political dynamics of a country. Yet nothing should be assumed. What may appear to be a traditional commercial enterprise may in reality be a parastatal.

International Organizations

The definition of a foreign official in the anti-bribery provisions was expanded in 1998 to include any official or employee of a public international organization or any individual or entity acting on behalf of a public international organization. The public international organizations covered by the anti-bribery provisions are those organizations whose officials are accorded diplomatic immunity under U.S. law.

The mechanism by which organizations are accorded diplomatic immunity is by executive order pursuant to the International Organizations Immunities Act.[6] Organizations as diverse as the Organization of American States (OAS), the European Space Agency, and the Hong Kong Economic and Trade Offices are currently listed. Over time this list can be expected to grow. Prudence suggests that inducements to or for the benefit of any official or employee of any international organization, or any individual or entity acting on behalf of the international organization, should be considered presumptively prohibited.

Corrupt Intent

The anti-bribery provisions differ from most other fraud statutes in that they require that the intent be corrupt. The legislative history of the anti-bribery provisions makes clear that, like the domestic bribery statute,[7] the prohibited conduct occurs only when a payment or offer of payment is made to induce the intended beneficiary to in some way misuse his or her official position. This is consistent with the domestic bribery statute where the inducement must be intended in exchange or return for some official action, inaction, or violation of some official duty in order to be "corrupt."

Under the anti-bribery provisions, when an inducer intends to cause an official to misuse his official position, it is not relevant whether the official has the capacity to influence an official decision. Culpability is determined by the intent of the person making the inducement as opposed to the official's action, inaction, or capacity. There is no requirement that the bribe actually be paid. Nor does the intended beneficiary need to have the actual authority to make or influence the official decision.

It is also not relevant whether inducements are made directly or indirectly to a foreign government official. Any evidence of intent to influence a foreign official may be sufficient to constitute a violation of the anti-bribery provisions. The more dramatic the evidence of intent, the stronger the case from the perspective of an enforcement official. Trial and appellate courts typically provide a degree of flexibility in meeting the other elements of a crime if the requisite evidence of intent is present.

Influencing an Official Act

Official action or inaction that is sought to be induced to assist in obtaining or retaining business is known as the *quid pro quo* element of the anti-bribery provisions. The types of inducements that are sought to be prohibited fall into four categories:

1. Influencing the official's action in the context of the individual's official capacity;
2. Inducing the foreign official to do or not to do an act in violation of the individual's lawful duty;
3. Inducing the official to influence or affect an act or decision of his or her government; or
4. Securing any improper advantage.

It is not necessary that the action being induced relate to the foreign official's government. As long as the action being influenced relates to the official capacity of the individual being induced, the ultimate purpose need not relate to that official's government or to any government. The ultimate purpose can relate to influencing the U.S. government or to influencing private enterprise and still be improper. For example, inducing a foreign official to put in a "good word" with the U.S. government relative to a procurement by a U.S. firm has served as a basis for enforcement action.

Obtain or Retain Business

The anti-bribery provisions prohibit inducements to a foreign official in order to assist the individual or entity in obtaining or retaining business for or with, or directing business to, any individual or entity. The inducement must be intended to induce the official to act on the inducer's behalf to assist the individual or entity making the inducement in obtaining or retaining business. The anti-bribery provisions should be presumed to extend to official acts or inaction that indirectly assist the individual or entity making the inducement. Inducements seeking official action favorable to carrying on a business enterprise satisfy the business purpose element of the anti-bribery provisions. This includes making it easier to do more business.

The term "assist" in the anti-bribery provisions is relatively broad. Actions can assist a particular goal simply by making the eventual realization of that goal more likely. This might include payments to circumvent quotas, bypass licensing requirements, obtain concessions, or reduce taxes. In so doing, an improper inducement assists in obtaining or retaining business by increasing the amount of product available for sale or reducing an inducer's expenses of sale. This could extend, for example, to increasing or maintaining the quantity of its sales or other economic dealings.

There is no requirement that the foreign official be directly involved in awarding or directing the business. Nor is there a requirement that the inducement be limited to a certain kind of business or to a certain kind of customer. Retaining business is not limited to the renewal of contracts or other business. The prohibition extends to more than the renewal or award of a contract. It extends to corrupt payments related to the execution or performance of a contract or the carrying out of existing business. It also extends to payments to a foreign official for the purpose of obtaining more favorable treatment.

❸ EXCEPTIONS AND AFFIRMATIVE DEFENSES

Relief from the prohibitions of the anti-bribery provisions is limited. The anti-bribery provisions contain one category of exceptions and two categories of affirmative defenses. Each of these categories refers to circumstances in which inducements that are otherwise prohibited may be made. The practical effect is to provide a form of safe harbor where the particular inducement clearly falls within the terms of their provisions. However, the protection is afforded only if enforcement officials, or a judge or jury, are convinced that the inducement falls within the exception or affirmative defenses.

In addition, the Justice Department has developed an opinion procedure by which an individual or entity, in certain circumstances, can secure guidance and a limited form of protection from potential criminal prosecution and civil enforcement. The opinion procedure is available only for the anti-bribery provisions and not for the accounting and recording provisions. The SEC does not have a similar procedure for issuers.

Facilitating Payments

Through an exception, the anti-bribery provisions permit what are often commonly referred to as "facilitating," "expediting," or "grease" payments. These payments are made "to expedite or to secure the performance of a routine governmental action by a foreign official, political party, or party official."[8] Facilitating payments are given to secure or accelerate performance of a nondiscretionary act that an official is already obligated to perform.

Nondiscretionary Act

In concept, a facilitating payment relates to actions on the part of foreign officials that are not discretionary in nature. For example, if the issuance of a permit is deemed to be automatic or only a matter of time, it is not subject to discretion. A payment made to expedite the process, or move the issuance of the permit up in line, is likely to be considered a facilitating payment. Payments to a government-run telephone company to expedite installation of service are also apt to be considered a facilitating payment. There is not a question of whether one can get the telephone service; the payment is intended only to influence the timing.

The anti-bribery provisions define "routine governmental action" to include only action that is ordinarily and commonly performed by a foreign official.[9] It does not include any decision by a foreign official to award new business or to continue business. Facilitation payments can include payments made to obtain permits, licenses, or other official documents and to receive services such as police protection, mail, telephone, utilities, cargo handling, and protection of perishable products. They also include payments made in exchange for the processing of governmental papers, including visas and work orders; scheduling of inspections associated with contract performance or the transit of goods across country; and the expedition of shipments through customs.

Need for Caution

Determining what constitutes a facilitating payment can be extremely difficult as it is highly dependent upon the particular circumstances. What may be perceived as a facilitating payment under one set of circumstances may not be similarly perceived under another set of circumstances. The value of what is offered or paid is not necessarily determinative. Typically, facilitating payments are *de minimis* in terms of value. In theory, a large amount of money could still be determined to be a facilitating payment. However, the greater the value of a facilitating payment, the more likely it is that enforcement officials will become suspicious as to what is really intended.

Great caution needs to be exercised with respect to the use of facilitating payments. Although they are countenanced by the anti-bribery provisions, facilitating payments are seldom, if ever, countenanced by the written law of a host country. They present an inherent risk in the host country. The individual who makes the payment, as well as those who authorized it, could be subject to criminal liability in the host country. And, if not properly recorded, facilitating payments that may be permissible can still present problems for issuers under the accounting and record-keeping provisions.

There is also the obvious problem of where facilitating payments will ultimately lead. Without the exercise of care and adequate controls, facilitating payments that fall within the exception to the anti-bribery provisions can, in time, evolve to such a degree that they lead to the making of improper payments. The implications associated with starting down a slippery slope must always be kept carefully in mind when facilitating payments are made.

Bona Fide *Business Expenditures*

Through an affirmative defense, the anti-bribery provisions permit reasonable and *bona fide* expenditures.[10] To be permitted, the expenditures must directly relate to the promotion, demonstration, or explanation of products or services or to the execution or performance of a contract with a foreign government or agency. This seemingly reasonable and practical exception prompts the expenditure of an enormous amount of time and resources among entities seeking to comply with the prohibitions of the FCPA. When the very essence of these expenditures represents a form of promotion, the line can become extremely blurred as to what constitutes a *bona fide* expenditure and what may be perceived as an improper inducement.

Whether Permitted by Official's Government

At the outset of any determination of what constitutes a *bona fide* business expenditure, a threshold determination needs to be made concerning whether a government official or unit of government can be paid or reimbursed for expenses that may be incurred. In many countries, including the United States, there are limitations on what can be paid and, if so, how such payments are made. Similarly, there may be a need for prior approvals.

Reasonable Business Expenses

Care has to be exercised in determining whether an expenditure is legitimate. Unnecessary diversions to resorts and travel upgrades to first class can be cause for concern. It has not been considered a defense that all prospective customers, whether from the private or public sector, are treated the same way. The analysis must be focused upon whether the expenditures in each situation are necessary business expenditures and, if so, whether what is paid is reasonable under the circumstances. An expenditure that is out of proportion or unrelated to a legitimate business purpose can serve as a basis for concern.

With the radical differences in living standards in various parts of the world, there may be situations where relatively modest expenditures can be viewed as improper inducements. In those circumstances, there is a heightened need to be able to justify the legitimate basis for the expenditures that are made. What might be viewed as customary practices in certain parts of the world are apt to be viewed as once-in-a-lifetime opportunities in other parts of the world. A variety of perspectives must be kept in mind when determining whether a *bona fide* expenditure is proper.

Vetting of Offers or Payments

Although not required by the provisions of the anti-bribery provisions, even good faith offers to pay or reimburse reasonable expenses should be carefully documented and vetted as part of an entity's compliance program. The focus of any such determination is whether the expenditures

- are reasonable in terms of purpose and amount;
- are made in good faith; and
- relate *directly* to (1) the promotion, demonstration, or explanation of products or services or (2) the execution or performance of a contract with a foreign government or agency.

Local Law

An affirmative defense exists under the anti-bribery provisions for payments or offers that are lawful under the written laws and regulations of the country of the foreign official, political party, party official, or candidate.[11] It is a rare situation where a government would, as an official matter, permit payments or offers to violate a lawful duty. Recognized customs or practices within a particular country cannot form the basis of an affirmative defense. Nor is it a defense if "everyone does it." The sole basis is whether such a practice is permitted under the written laws of the relevant jurisdiction.

This affirmative defense has little practical relevance in most situations. It is most likely to be relevant in situations where contributions to political parties or candidates for public office are at issue. Yet even in those situations, special care needs to be exercised to ensure that the payments are clearly permitted by the written law of the country in question.

Opinion Procedure

There is a procedure, known as the Foreign Corrupt Practices Act Opinion Procedure, by which an issuer or a domestic concern can request an opinion of the Justice Department's enforcement intentions regarding proposed business conduct.[12] The opinion procedure provides a rebuttable presumption that the conduct that is the subject of the opinion does not violate the anti-bribery provisions. An opinion binds only the Justice Department and the parties to a request. It does not act as binding precedent with respect to anyone else. Reliance can be placed only on a written opinion and not on oral statements by Justice Department officials.

The SEC does not have an equivalent procedure. However, the SEC has taken the position that it will not take civil enforcement action under the anti-bribery provisions against a party that has obtained a favorable opinion from the Justice Department.[13] A favorable opinion also does not preclude action by the Justice Department or the SEC relative to the accounting and record-keeping provisions or to any other statutory or regulatory provisions.

The opinion request should focus only on well-defined issues involving prospective conduct. Neither historical nor hypothetical conduct can be reviewed. Yet the party making a request is not required to have entered into an agreement. Nor is there a need for the entire transaction or activity in question to be prospective. However, the Justice Department will opine only on those portions of the transaction or activity in question that remain prospective.

A request must "be specific and must be accompanied by all relevant and material information bearing on the conduct" for which the opinion is requested.[14] It should include the "circumstances of the prospective conduct, including background information, complete copies of all operative documents, and detailed statements of all collateral or oral understandings."[15] The identities of the parties as well as the particulars of a proposed transaction must be disclosed.

Disclosure must be full and entirely forthcoming once a party decides to make a request. Aside from impairing the likelihood of a favorable opinion, providing incomplete or inaccurate information can serve as an independent basis for prosecution. The Justice Department may request supplemental information and in some instances may seek certifications from other parties to the transaction. The Justice Department also has the power to conduct "whatever independent investigation it believes appropriate" in connection with a request.[16]

An opinion in response to a specific inquiry from an individual or entity is required to be issued within 30 days of the request. But the 30 days does not begin to run until the Justice Department has received all the information it requires. There have been occasions where the Justice Department has been able to render an opinion on an expedited basis. In those rare situations, a requestor must be extremely well-prepared.

Informal Discussions

The opinion procedure process should not be undertaken lightly. For requestors who are unprepared, the process can be lengthy and costly. To prevent this, Justice Department officials recommend that prospective requestors meet informally with them prior to making a formal request. These meetings can be helpful in determining whether a request for an opinion should be pursued and, if so, can aid in narrowing the issues and identifying the information that will need to be provided. A requestor is not required to complete the process. However, the Justice Department can retain a party's submission and use the information provided for governmental purposes.

Opinion Releases

Although the information provided by a requestor is exempt from disclosure through the Freedom of Information Act, the Justice Department reserves the right to issue a public release describing the requestor, identifying the country, summarizing the proposed conduct, and announcing the Justice Department's action. The names of the requestor and other parties often are not identified. But with the agreement of the requestor and the other parties, they may be identified. The opinion procedure releases are available on the Justice Department's Web site.[17] These can be very useful in providing guidance on structuring transactions and in determining how the Justice Department is likely to respond to certain factual situations.

NOTES

1. 15 U.S.C. §§ 78l, 78o(d).
2. *Id.,* § 78dd-1(g)(1).
3. 15 U.S.C. § 78dd-2(a)(1).
4. 8 U.S.C. § 1101.
5. 15 U.S.C. § 78dd-3(a)(1).
6. 22 U.S.C. § 288.
7. 18 U.S.C. § 201.

8. 15 U.S.C. §§ 78dd-1(b), -2(b), -3(b).

9. *Id.,* §§ 78dd-1(f)(3)(A), -2(h)(4)(A), -3(f)(4)(A).

10. *Id.,* §§ 78dd-1(c)(2), -2(c)(2), -3(c)(2).

11. *Id.,* §§ 78dd-1(c)(1), -2(c)(1), -3(c)(1).

12. *Id.,* §§ 78dd-1(e), -2(f); 28 C.F.R. §§ 80.1–.16. *See* Appendix I-C, *infra* at 71.

13. Exchange Act Release No. 34-18255, 4 FED. SEC. L. REP. (CCH) ¶ 26,629 (Nov. 12, 1981).

14. 28 C.F.R. § 80.6.

15. *Id.*

16. *Id.,* § 80.7.

17. Department of Justice, FCPA Opinion Procedure Releases, **http://www.usdoj.gov/criminal/ fraud/fcpa/opiindx.htm.**

CHAPTER III

THE ACCOUNTING AND RECORD-KEEPING PROVISIONS

One of the problems disclosed by the revelations of the Watergate era in the United States was the accounting and record-keeping practices that made improper payments possible. To address these practices, the FCPA placed new and significant obligations on issuers to maintain records that accurately reflect transactions and dispositions of assets and to maintain systems of internal accounting controls.

Known as the "accounting and record-keeping" provisions, these provisions constitute the second and less well-known mechanism to deter improper inducements to foreign officials. But they constitute a more potent mechanism that has implications far greater than simply deterring improper payments to foreign officials. The accounting and record-keeping provisions directly affect the worldwide operations of all issuers, including their majority-owned foreign subsidiaries and their officers, directors, employees, and agents acting on behalf of an issuer. These provisions also directly affect domestic practices, including practices wholly unrelated to the making of improper inducements in foreign settings.

 SCOPE AND JURISDICTION

The scope of the accounting and record-keeping provisions is more limited than the anti-bribery provisions. Specifically, these provisions apply only to issuers. Officers, directors, employees, and stockholders or agents of the issuer acting on its behalf are subject to the terms of the accounting and record-keeping provisions, regardless of whether they may be otherwise subject to the terms of the accounting and record-keeping provisions. Individuals and entities can also be subject to the accounting and record-keeping provisions to the extent that they may be accomplices to a violation of those provisions. In the latter set of circumstances, they are not required to be otherwise subject to the terms of the accounting and record-keeping provisions.

The accounting and record-keeping provisions require issuers to maintain accurate records of their transactions and of the disposition of their assets. Unlike the anti-bribery provisions, which apply only to transactions involving payments to foreign officials, the accounting and record-keeping provisions apply without regard to whether foreign conduct, foreign officials, or improper inducements are involved. They apply to an issuer's domestic and foreign operations, including domestic reporting and disclosure practices as well as practices involving foreign payments. They create an affirmative duty on the part of issuers and their officers, directors, employees, and agents or stockholders acting on behalf of the issuer.

The accounting and record-keeping provisions are not applicable to foreign subsidiaries if the U.S. issuer holds an interest of 50 percent or less in the foreign entity. Nevertheless, the issuer remains obliged to "proceed in good faith to use its influence to the extent reasonable under the circumstances to cause [the affiliate] to devise and maintain a system of internal accounting controls" consistent with the requirements of the accounting and record-keeping provisions.[1] What is reasonable depends primarily upon the practices governing the affiliate in the country where it is located. If the issuer demonstrates its good faith efforts to use its influence, it will be "conclusively presumed" to have fulfilled its statutory obligation.[2]

✪ THE RECORD-KEEPING PROVISIONS

The record-keeping provisions require an issuer to "make and keep books, records, and accounts which, in reasonable detail, accurately and fairly reflect the transactions and dispositions of the assets of the issuer."[3] An issuer's records should reflect transactions in conformity with accepted accounting standards and should be designed to prevent off-the-books transactions such as kickbacks and bribes. "Reasonable detail" is "such level of detail and degree of assurance as would satisfy prudent officials in the conduct of their own affairs."[4]

The accounting and record-keeping provisions apply to all payments, not merely sums that would be material in the traditional financial sense. Even if the amount of a payment would not affect the "bottom line" of an issuer in quantitative terms, it could still constitute a violation of the record-keeping provisions if not accurately recorded. This represented a dramatic departure from the traditional approach taken by U.S. securities laws. Historically, except for disclosures as to certain aspects of an issuer's activities, materiality was the overriding consideration as to what required disclosure and as to what constituted a violation. But as a result of the record-keeping provisions, relatively insignificant amounts of money, if not properly recorded, can have serious ramifications.

Falsification of Books and Records

The management of an issuer has the responsibility of ensuring that the issuer's books and records are accurate so that financial statements can be prepared in conformity with accepted procedures. But the accounting and record-keeping provisions did not expressly address the falsification of books and records and lying to auditors. This led the SEC to adopt two rules to ensure that the accounting books of original entry, ledgers, and other accounting data are maintained to the extent reasonably necessary to support the financial statements and to permit independent auditors to apply accepted audit procedures.

Rule 13b2-1 prohibits the falsification of books and records required to be kept under the record-keeping provisions.[5] It applies to "any person" and is not limited to officers and directors of an issuer. Consistent with the accounting and record-keeping provisions, Rule 13b2-1 contains no materiality requirement. Moreover, books and records are defined broadly to include "accounts, correspondence, memoranda, tapes, discs, papers, books, and other documents or transcribed information of any type, whether expressed in ordinary or machine language."[6] In combination with the statutory provisions of the FCPA, the manner in which information is entered into an issuer's records becomes very important under Rule 13b2-1.

Although the provisions of Rule 13b2-1 apply to all aspects of the books and records of an issuer, enforcement officials have less tolerance for inaccurate records that may bear on compliance obligations of an issuer. Manipulating books or records to mask transactions by characterizing them in some oblique way, or by actually falsifying a transaction, can lead to serious exposure for an issuer and those individuals involved. For example, placing a transaction into an abnormal category or "burying" it in some other way could serve as a basis for an enforcement action for a violation of Rule 13b2-1.

This is particularly so with respect to the anti-bribery provisions of the FCPA. In recent years, the SEC's posture has been described as one of "zero tolerance" for the falsification of records relating to an improper payment. In other words, the context in which a record may have been falsified, and whether the falsification was an isolated event, will be critical factors in a determination as to whether enforcement action will be taken for a violation of Rule 13b2-1.

Facilitating Payments

A related consideration is how facilitating payments are recorded. For example, facilitating payments, which are permitted under the anti-bribery provisions, could pose a problem if not accurately described. Clearly, an effort to conceal facilitating payments by placing them among other types of payments would be improper. Regulators prefer that such expenditures be set out in a separate line item. This reasoning is premised on the view that payments of a questionable nature are not apt to be disclosed. Thus the greater the degree to which facilitating payments are fully disclosed, the less likely they will be perceived as being suspect.

A separate line item may not be required as long as the line item in which a facilitating payment is incorporated is both logical and not calculated to conceal.

If, for example, the facilitating payment is a relatively small amount of money and has no relationship to any particular function of an entity, its inclusion in a category of miscellaneous items may not be inappropriate. Similarly, the degree to which the facilitating payments may be rolled up into larger line items and thereby hidden is not necessarily improper as long as the manner in which such payments are incorporated into a larger line item is logical and not for the purpose of concealing questionable transactions.

There are also internal accounting control considerations relating to facilitating payments. Consistent with maintaining a sound compliance program and the heightened obligations on auditors to plan audits so as to detect fraud, issuers need to be in a position to be responsive to inquiries and, if necessary, to quickly identify facilitating payments and to provide substantiating documentation. Greater segregation is more likely to enhance the adequacy of internal controls. Moreover, if the facilitating payments are not properly approved or recorded, an issuer opens itself up to possible allegations of inadequate internal controls.

The fundamental realities associated with facilitating payments must always be kept in mind. By their very nature, facilitating payments are illegal in the country of the intended recipient. Proper record-keeping is more likely to expose an entity to liability associated with an investigation by local authorities. This represents one of the potential trade-offs associated with facilitating payments.

Finally, still another consideration is the proper tax treatment of facilitating payments. "[D]eductions are not allowed for any payment made, directly or indirectly, to an official or employee of any government, or of any agency or instrumentality of any government, if the payment constitutes an illegal bribe or kickback or, if the payment is to an official or employee of a foreign government, the payment is unlawful under the [FCPA]."[7] "[L]awfulness, or unlawfulness of the payment under the laws of the foreign country is immaterial" under the U.S. tax code.[8]

Misrepresentations to Auditors

Rule 13b2-2 prohibits any officer or director from making materially false or misleading statements or omitting to state any material facts in the preparation of filings required by the Exchange Act. Although this rule applies only to officers and directors, it is very broad in terms of its coverage. It extends to internal auditors as well as to outside auditors. It also extends to "causing another person to make a material misstatement or make or cause to be made a materially false or misleading statement."[9] Not only are misrepresentations covered, but a material omission or failure to clarify a statement so as not to make it materially false or misleading can constitute a violation of Rule 13b2-2.

As a result of the adoption of the Sarbanes-Oxley Act of 2002 in the wake of recent corporate accounting scandals in the United States, Rule 13b2-2 was expanded to address a broader range of conduct than simply a material misstatement or omission. Officers and directors of an issuer, or anyone acting on their behalf, are prohibited from "taking any action to fraudulently influence, coerce, manipulate, or mislead any independent public or certified accountant engaged in the performance of an audit of the financial statements of that issuer for the purpose of rendering such financial statements materially misleading."[10]

❦ THE INTERNAL ACCOUNTING CONTROLS PROVISIONS

To enhance corporate accountability and ensure that boards of directors, officers, and shareholders of issuers are aware of and thus able to prevent the improper use of an issuer's assets, the accounting provisions require issuers to devise and maintain a system of internal accounting controls sufficient to provide reasonable assurance that

- transactions are executed in accordance with management's general or specific authorization;
- transactions are recorded as necessary to permit the preparation of financial statements in conformity with generally accepted accounting principles or any other criteria applicable to such statements, and to maintain accountability for assets;
- access to company assets is permitted only in accordance with management's general or specific authorization; and
- the recorded accountability for assets is compared with existing assets at reasonable intervals and appropriate action is taken with respect to any differences.[11]

"Reasonable assurance" of management control over an issuer's assets means "such level of detail and degree of assurance as would satisfy prudent officials in the conduct of their own affairs."[12] The "prudent man" standard is generally consistent with the expectations of management with respect to their oversight obligations under U.S. law. The accounting provisions do not mandate any particular kind of internal accounting controls. The standard for compliance is whether a system, taken as a whole, reasonably meets the statute's objectives.

Elements of an Internal Control System

The purpose of an accounting control system is to ensure that entities adopt accepted methods of recording economic events, protecting assets, and conforming transactions to management's authorization. No specific system of internal controls is required. The test is whether a system, taken as a whole, reasonably meets the statute's specified objectives. The SEC has identified elements of an adequate system of internal controls, which it will look for and evaluate when considering specific systems.

Controlling the Corporate Environment

It is important for boards of directors to oversee the establishment and maintenance of strong internal accounting controls. They should also put in place procedures for evaluating a system of internal accounting controls. An independent audit committee of the board of directors can play an important role in providing oversight to management's efforts to create effective internal accounting controls. Written policies and procedures are also important. Tests should be regularly planned and performed on the system of internal accounting controls. Those tests should be documented, and once identified, any necessary corrections or changes to the system of accounting controls should be made.

Reviewing Internal Accounting Controls

The effectiveness of control procedures should relate to the broad objectives of an internal accounting control system and to the circumstances of a particular issuer. Specific procedures and individual environmental factors should be identified and considered. The objective is to develop a method of analyzing the system of accounting controls that is effective within the context of each entity. Generally accepted auditing standards require auditors to understand an entity's internal control structure in planning and performing an audit. Auditors can also advise management regarding whether internal accounting controls are adequate.

Monitoring Compliance

Management should have reasonable assurance that the system of internal accounting controls is functioning as designed. A monitoring system is an integral part of the overall internal accounting control system. Compliance can be monitored by direct observation, by supervision, and by testing of the controls in place. An effective internal audit function plays an important role in monitoring compliance. The internal enforcement mechanism must be taken seriously by the management and personnel of each subsidiary, branch, and unit of an issuer.

Determining Reasonable Assurance

No internal accounting control system is without imperfections. Absolute assurance is not required. The test is reasonable assurance. The SEC recognizes that it is not in the interest of shareholders for the cost of internal accounting controls to exceed their benefits. There is no precise means of quantifying either benefits or costs. However, if management has documented the system of internal accounting controls and its ongoing review and evaluation of the system, the system is most likely to be perceived as being reasonable.

Heightened Obligations

At the core of the heightened obligations under Sarbanes-Oxley are those that relate to the accounting provisions of the FCPA. Issuers are required to include in their annual reports an internal control report expressing management's responsibility for establishing and maintaining adequate internal controls for financial reporting and assessing their effectiveness.[13] In addition, there is to be an attestation by an issuer's outside auditor as to management's assessment of the adequacy of the issuer's internal controls.

Broad Reach of Internal Accounting Control Provisions

The provisions of the FCPA relating to internal accounting controls provide an almost endless series of bases for the SEC to take action against an issuer. It must be kept in mind that the FCPA, and the internal control provisions in particular, will always be applied in hindsight. When fraud or other abuses are involved, especially relating to financial transactions, the question will arise as to whether the internal controls were adequate. In such situations, it will be a rare case where the internal controls will be found to be adequate.

Due in large part to their esoteric nature, the internal accounting control provisions are seldom the focus of criminal enforcement activity. But, in a civil enforcement context, these provisions are frequently used. The standard of proof is a preponderance of the evidence. In almost any after-the-fact analysis relating to financial irregularities, the SEC will be able to point to a breakdown of some sort associated with the internal accounting controls of an issuer. Whether the issuer had knowledge of a defect in the system of controls or improperly recorded transactions or other financial activity is irrelevant in the civil enforcement context with respect to the accounting and record-keeping provisions. No proof of intent is required.

Relationship with Compliance Programs

An issuer's anti-bribery compliance program should not necessarily be separate from its system of internal accounting controls. There is a natural and intended interplay between the anti-bribery and the accounting and record-keeping provisions. An effective system of internal accounting controls includes a range of review and approval guidelines designed to detect and deter questionable payments. Indeed, the planning, implementation, and monitoring of an issuer's compliance program should be closely linked, if not intertwined, with its system of internal accounting controls.

❦ NOTES

1. 15 U.S.C. § 78m(b)(6).
2. Id.
3. Id., § 78m(b)(2)(A).
4. Id., § 78m(b)(7).
5. 17 C.F.R. § 240.13b2-1.
6. 15 U.S.C. § 78c(a)(37).
7. 26 U.S.C. § 162(c)(1).
8. 26 C.F.R. § 1.162-18(a).
9. 17 C.F.R § 240.13b2-2.
10. 15 U.S.C. § 7242; 17 C.F.R. § 240.13b2-2(b).
11. Id., § 78m(b)(2)(B).
12. Id., § 78m(b)(7).
13. Id., § 7262.

CHAPTER IV

VICARIOUS LIABILITY

An individual or entity can be held vicariously liable for the conduct of a third party when the third party is acting for or on behalf of the individual or entity. Actions on the part of an agent, consultant, or representative can subject an individual or entity to liability. Even if a third party is not subject to the FCPA, an individual or entity can become subject to vicarious liability if the individual or entity authorizes, directs, or in some way ratifies activity that is prohibited by the FCPA. Depending upon whether the anti-bribery or the accounting or record-keeping provisions are involved and whether criminal or civil charges are brought, the knowledge requirement for establishing vicarious liability can vary dramatically.

There are two basic legal concepts for establishing the basis for imposing vicarious liability on an individual or entity for the conduct of a third party. One conceptual basis is premised on there being express provisions for vicarious liability as part of the statutory mandate. In a both a criminal and civil context, the anti-bribery provisions contain express provisions for vicarious liability. Implicitly, in a civil context, the accounting and record-keeping provisions provide for vicarious liability. The other conceptual basis is premised on legal principles associated with being an accomplice that are common to all U.S. statutory prohibitions. These principles apply to both the anti-bribery provisions and the accounting and record-keeping provisions.

❦ THE ANTI-BRIBERY PROVISIONS

The anti-bribery provisions specifically address the issue of vicarious liability of third parties. Offers or payments are expressly prohibited to "any person, while knowing that all or a portion of such money or things of value will be offered, given, or promised, directly or indirectly, to any foreign official, to any foreign political party or official thereof, or to any candidate for foreign political office."[1] These third-party payment provisions apply to anyone in the United States or abroad who acts on behalf of an individual or entity subject to the terms of the anti-bribery provisions. These could include consultants, distributors, joint venture partners, foreign subsidiaries or affiliates, contractors, or subcontractors.

In general, an offeror can be liable under the anti-bribery provisions with regard to improper payments made by or through a third party to obtain or retain business when

- anything of value is offered or paid to a third party knowing that all or a portion of such value is or will be offered, given, or promised, directly or indirectly, to a foreign official; or
- a third party is authorized to offer or pay anything of value to a foreign official.

In terms of the basis for vicarious liability, there is no fundamental difference between criminal and civil enforcement actions. The basic difference is the elevation of the standard of proof from a preponderance of evidence in a civil context to beyond a reasonable doubt in a criminal context.

Because of the third-party payment provisions, special care needs to be taken to avoid liability under the anti-bribery provisions for the improper conduct of a sales agent, consultant, foreign affiliate, or other third party. Frequently, an agent or consultant has no authority to bind the individual or entity. The role of the agent or consultant may simply be to advise on local customs and practices, to make introductions, and to otherwise assist and facilitate business. Yet often an individual or entity will learn that a third party with which the individual or entity has a relationship made an improper inducement on behalf of the individual or entity to advance the business interests of the individual or entity.

This type of situation presents the most difficulties because of the potential liability for actions that cannot be easily ascertained or controlled. Typically, suspicions or concerns are raised when allegations or incriminating information comes to the attention of those who have engaged the third party. The agent or consultant can be expected to deny the allegations. And it may be awkward and costly to sever the relationship. But that may be precisely what is required.

Requisite Knowledge

Activity prohibited by the anti-bribery provisions may not be undertaken in an indirect or circuitous manner. Promising or providing benefits to a third party is prohibited when the offeror knows that the benefits will be passed on by the third party to a foreign official. An individual or entity is responsible for the conduct of a third party when it "knew" that the money or thing of value given to the third party would be used, directly or indirectly, to make an improper payment. Even if the third party is, for example, a foreign affiliate not subject to the anti-bribery provisions, a U.S. parent corporation may be liable if it participates in, directs, authorizes, or acquiesces to the prohibited conduct.

Substantially Certain

When an individual or entity "is aware of a high probability of the existence of" activity prohibited by the anti-bribery provisions but does not have actual knowledge of the circumstance, the individual or entity is nonetheless deemed to "know" of the existence of the circumstance.[2] An individual or entity is deemed to have the requisite knowledge of an activity of a third party if the individual or entity (1) "is aware that such person is engaging in such conduct, that such circumstance exists, or that such result is substantially certain to occur" or (2) "has a firm belief that such circumstance exists or that such result is substantially certain to occur."[3]

Knowledge can be established under the anti-bribery provisions when it appears that the act is made with conscious disregard of or willful blindness to the evident purpose of the offer or payment. When confronted with circumstances that should raise suspicions, or what are often referred to as red flags, knowledge on the part of an individual or entity is more likely to be established. Classic examples include making a payment to someone who did not appear to perform a service or making a payment grossly disproportionate to the value of the services to be rendered. Yet another example is when the recipient volunteers that the payor will never need to know how the purpose of the payment is achieved. The possibilities can be almost endless when the nuances of a set of circumstances are taken into consideration.

1988 Amendments

Prior to the 1988 amendments to the FCPA, an individual or entity could, in theory, be held liable for a payment made to a third party while knowing or having reason to know that the payment would be given to a foreign official. The 1988 amendments eliminated what was termed the "reason to know" standard. The "reason to know" standard was never applied by the Justice Department. However, it was still viewed as possibly including situations where an individual or entity negligently disregarded the risk that a sales agent might use payments made to bribe a foreign official by an individual or entity subject to the anti-bribery provisions.

Through the 1988 amendments, the U.S. Congress removed the possibility that negligence could be a basis for criminal liability under the anti-bribery provisions. But the U.S. Congress still made it clear with the adoption of the following language that the knowledge standard did not necessarily require actual knowledge:

> (2)(A) A person's state of mind is "knowing" with respect to conduct, a circumstance, or a result if—
>
> (i) such person is aware that such person is engaging in such conduct, that such circumstance exists, or that such result is substantially certain to occur; or
>
> (ii) such person has a firm belief that such circumstance exists or that such result is substantially certain to occur.[4]

When knowledge of the existence of a particular circumstance is required for an offense, knowledge can be established if an individual or entity is aware of a high probability of the existence of such circumstance unless the individual or entity actually believes that the circumstance does not exist. The U.S. Congress intended that the knowledge standard continue to apply to situations where there was conscious disregard, willful blindness, or deliberate ignorance of circumstances that should alert one to the likelihood of a violation of the anti-bribery provisions.

> The Conferees intend that the requisite "state of mind" for this category of offense include a "conscious purpose to avoid learning the truth." Thus, the "knowing" standard adopted covers both prohibited actions that are taken with "actual knowledge" of intended results, as well as other actions that, while falling short of what the law terms "positive knowledge," nevertheless evidence a conscious disregard or deliberate ignorance of known circumstances that should reasonably alert one to the high probability of violations of the Act.
>
> . . . [T]he Conferees also agree that the so-called "head-in-the-sand" problem? variously described in the pertinent authorities as "conscious disregard," "willful blindness" or "deliberate ignorance"? should be covered so that management officials could not take refuge from the Act's prohibitions by their unwarranted obliviousness to any action (or inaction), language or other "signaling device" that should reasonably alert them of the "high probability" of an FCPA violation.
>
> . . . As such, it covers any instance where "any reasonable person would have realized" the existence of the circumstances or result and the defendant has "consciously chose[n] not to ask about what he had 'reason to believe' he would discover."[5]

In terms of how the anti-bribery provisions have been enforced, there is little practical difference between the current "knowledge" standard and the "reason to know" standard that existed prior to the adoption of the 1988 amendments. Although the 1988 amendments eliminated the possibility that negligence might be a basis for liability under the anti-bribery provisions, negligence on the part of an entity or individual had never been employed as a basis for prosecution under the anti-bribery provisions. But the definition of "knowing" under the anti-bribery provisions continued to be expansive. The 1988 amendments did not alter the necessity under the "reason to know" standard to follow up on red flags or evidence of possible wrongdoing that comes to the attention of an individual or entity.

Imputed Knowledge

The U.S. Congress intended that the "knowing" standard be consistent with the knowledge standard for criminal liability as developed by existing case law for other criminal statutes. Knowledge is accordingly imputed under the anti-bribery provisions to an individual or entity possessing information indicating a "high probability" that prohibited conduct may result. Knowledge can also be established if an individual or entity consciously disregards or deliberately ignores circumstances that should reasonably have alerted the individual or entity to a high probability of a violation. Actual knowledge is not required of an improper inducement being passed on to a foreign official. Circumstances may otherwise suggest that such an inducement was made or is likely to take place.

Failure to Inquire

The requirement of only an awareness of a high probability of prohibited conduct, combined with the imputation of knowledge to one who consciously disregards or deliberately ignores information, creates a standard of knowledge considerably broader than actual knowledge. One can be deemed to have knowledge that a payment to a third party will result in an improper payment if one consciously disregarded or deliberately ignored information that indicated a high probability that the third party would make an improper inducement.

It therefore follows that when an individual or entity becomes aware of questionable circumstances regarding the activities of a third party with whom a relationship may exist, diligence must be exercised in undertaking an inquiry. Otherwise, an individual or entity could be found to have consciously disregarded information that could have served as notice of the likelihood of a violation. Failure to inquire could result in the imputation to an individual or entity of knowledge regarding the prohibited conduct.

Authorization

The anti-bribery provisions not only prohibit an inducement to a foreign official, they also prohibit the "authorization" of an improper inducement to be made by another.[6] This includes, among others, sales representatives, consultants, and foreign subsidiaries. For example, the anti-bribery provisions apply in situations where an individual or entity "authorizes" a controlled foreign subsidiary to make an improper inducement through a third party.

The standard for authorization is not defined in the anti-bribery provisions. However, legislative history makes it clear that authorization can be either explicit or implicit. To "authorize" appears to mean approval or direction to carry out the conduct. Authorization in the form of acquiescence or direction can be implicit and can be derived from a course of conduct that conveys an intent that an improper inducement be made.

Implicit Authorization

Implicit authorization occurs when an individual or entity makes a payment to an agent "knowing" that all or a part may be used in violation of the anti-bribery provisions. In interpreting whether there may have been authorization, all of the surrounding circumstances must be taken into consideration. Accordingly, when an individual or entity becomes aware of possible improper payments made by third parties, it is critical that a record be established to demonstrate that the conduct was not authorized. An objection to the improper conduct must be clearly registered and, if at all possible, documented.

Acquiescence

In addition to knowing approval, authorization may also entail knowing acquiescence or tacit approval by individuals or entities that could have prevented the conduct that led to the making of an improper inducement. Ratification of conduct that leads to the making of improper inducements can also serve as a basis for vicarious liability. Depending upon the nature of the relationship between the individual or entity and the third party, and the surrounding circumstances, acquiescence can constitute authorization. For example, conscious acquiescence to a series of unauthorized acts could be found to constitute authorization to engage in similar acts in the future.

Foreign Partners

Depending upon the circumstances, if a foreign partner is a foreign government official, an initial capital contribution by a domestic concern or an issuer could be construed as an improper payment. Subsequent distributions by the joint venture could also be construed as constituting improper payments. The same set of considerations apply when a foreign joint venture partner is an enterprise owned by the foreign government and the officers or directors of the joint venture receive payments from the joint venture. In each of these situations, the joint venture serves in one way or another as a vehicle for funneling payments to foreign officials.

If a foreign partner has already made improper payments to government officials, capital contributions by a domestic concern or issuer could be regarded as a reimbursement of the improper payments. Distributions by the joint venture could also have the same effect. In both instances, the domestic concern or issuer would have had to know of the prior improper payments by the foreign partner. But actual knowledge is not necessarily required. For example, inadequate due diligence in entering into the joint venture could be used to establish willful blindness as to prohibited conduct on the part of a joint venture partner.

Registering Disapproval

All of these factors bear upon how a transaction should be structured to avoid the prospect or the perception of there being violations of the anti-bribery provisions. However, an individual or entity must not remain passive when circumstances arise that might suggest a violation of the anti-bribery provisions. A failure to affirmatively withdraw or disassociate from questionable conduct could serve as a basis for being implicated. An individual or entity should, in clear and unambiguous terms, express disapproval and repudiate the prohibited conduct. How the disapproval should be registered will be largely governed by the circumstances. But, to the extent possible, the disapproval should in some way be documented.

Control

Unless a foreign corporation is an issuer subject to the FCPA, the anti-bribery provisions do not generally apply to foreign corporations. This even includes controlled foreign affiliates of U.S. entities that are subject to the FCPA. An improper inducement made by a foreign subsidiary is not in itself a violation of the anti-bribery provisions unless an act in furtherance of the improper inducement takes place within the territory of the United States. For this same reason, officers, directors, employees, and agents of foreign affiliates are also not subject to the anti-bribery provisions if these individuals or entities are neither domestic concerns nor issuers. Yet an issuer of a domestic concern can be vicariously liable for the conduct of its foreign subsidiary if it in some way directs, authorizes, or knowingly acquiesces in the prohibited conduct on the part of the foreign subsidiary.

Under the anti-bribery provisions, whether an entity owns less than a controlling interest in a foreign affiliate is not determinative for establishing vicarious liability for the actions taken on the part of the foreign affiliate. The distinction between a controlled and noncontrolled affiliate relates only to the likelihood that an entity is apt to have knowledge of the prohibited conduct and to have been in a position to have authorized or acquiesced to it. Where the entity has a controlling interest, and is actively involved in the management of the affiliate, it is more likely to become aware of the prohibited conduct. In such a circumstance, if the parent fails to take immediate action to repudiate the prohibited conduct, the failure may be construed as an implicit authorization of the prohibited conduct.

Controlling Interest

If a foreign entity is deemed to be an agent of an individual or entity subject to the anti-bribery provisions, the individual or entity may also be vicariously liable for improper inducements by a foreign entity. Knowledge would still be required on the part of the principal. But common law agency principles will be critical in any determination as to whether an individual or entity has a legal right and effective ability to control the acts of its agent. Practical control will have much greater bearing than technical legal considerations. A number of factors can bear on this determination:

- The individual or entity owns all or a majority of the stock of the foreign entity or otherwise has effective control of the foreign entity;
- The entity and the foreign entity have common directors or officers;
- The foreign entity has grossly inadequate capital and the individual or entity provides financing for the foreign entity;
- The individual or entity incorporates the foreign entity;
- The individual or entity pays the salaries or expenses or covers the losses of the foreign entity;
- The foreign entity has substantially no business except with the individual or entity or no assets except those conveyed to it by the individual or entity;
- The entity formally refers to the foreign entity as a subsidiary, department, or division;
- The management of the foreign entity does not act independently in its interests but takes direction from the individual or entity, including seeking approvals or guidance;
- The entity is substantially involved in or directs the day-to-day activities of the foreign affiliate; and
- The foreign affiliate fails, or the degree to which the foreign affiliate fails, to observe a separate legal status.

An individual or entity that learns that a controlled foreign affiliate may have made an improper inducement has the same responsibilities as an individual or entity would have in learning of improper inducements by the individual's or entity's own employees. The questionable conduct must be repudiated and strong measures implemented to prevent its recurrence. An internal investigation, disciplinary action, and improved procedures that address the underlying problem should be expected. Absent a response that would be viewed by enforcement officials as effective, the controlling entity, and the personnel of that entity who may have interacted with the foreign entity, could well be charged with ratifying the prohibited conduct.

Noncontrolling Interest

The issues are more complicated if an entity subject to the anti-bribery provisions holds a minority interest in a foreign affiliate. An entity with a noncontrolling interest may become aware of the improper conduct on the part of its foreign affiliate. This is more likely to occur if the individual or entity represented on the board of directors of the affiliate is involved in the operations or activities of the affiliate. However, the extent of an individual's or entity's noncontrolling interest may bear on whether there was authorization.

If an individual or entity does not have a controlling interest and is without significant influence over the management or operations of a foreign affiliate, it is less likely that the individual or entity would be found to have implicitly authorized or ratified the prohibited conduct. This is particularly so if it can be shown that an individual or entity took all reasonable steps to prevent the prohibited conduct.

If a noncontrolling interest is represented on the board of directors, more affirmative steps may be required to distance the noncontrolling interest from the prohibited conduct and to undertake efforts to prevent its recurrence. At the very least, conduct that could be construed as direct participation in questionable conduct must cease. A formal protest should be made as well as a demand to prevent recurrence. And these steps should be carefully documented to avoid a charge of ratification or acquiescence.

If a foreign affiliate fails to take effective action, and questionable activities continue to take place, an individual or entity risks a charge that the continuing affiliation amounts to implicit authorization or acquiescence to the prohibited conduct. This prospect is enhanced if the entity holds considerable leverage over the affiliate such as holding a significant ownership interest or providing crucial financing. An individual or entity in these circumstances should seriously consider terminating the relationship with the foreign affiliate if questionable practices continue after all reasonable steps have been taken to end them.

THE ACCOUNTING AND RECORD-KEEPING PROVISIONS

In a civil enforcement context, issuers may be held strictly liable for the actions of controlled subsidiaries or foreign affiliates for violations of the accounting and record-keeping provisions. Civil liability may be established without the SEC having to prove that an issuer knew or even suspected wrongful conduct on the part of its controlled subsidiary or affiliate.

Criminal Liability

Consistent with the steps taken to avoid criminal liability for negligent conduct for a violation of the anti-bribery provisions, the U.S. Congress in 1988 also narrowed the knowledge requirement under the accounting and record-keeping procedures. Criminal liability may be established where an individual or entity subject to the accounting and record-keeping provisions knowingly circumvents or fails to implement a system of internal accounting controls or knowingly falsifies any book, record, or account.[7]

For criminal liability to be imposed for acts of third parties, an individual or entity must have knowledge that the third party has circumvented the internal controls or falsified books and records. As with the anti-bribery provisions and many other federal criminal statutes, proof of deliberate ignorance or knowing disregard can establish the requisite knowledge, especially when an individual or entity becomes aware of the existence of questionable circumstances.

Civil Liability

Unlike the anti-bribery provisions, in a civil enforcement action there is no knowledge requirement for a violation of the accounting and record-keeping provisions. In essence, issuers and others subject to their provisions can be held strictly liable for a violation of the accounting and record-keeping provisions. An entity subject to the accounting and record-keeping provisions can also be held vicariously liable for the conduct of a subsidiary or affiliate in which it has an interest greater than 50 percent. It makes no difference whether the controlling entity lacks knowledge of the conduct that serves as a basis for a violation.

OTHER FORMS OF VICARIOUS LIABILITY

In a criminal context, individuals and entities may also be secondarily liable under the federal conspiracy and aiding and abetting statutes for violations of the anti-bribery or the accounting and record-keeping provisions. In both instances, an individual or entity need not directly violate any of the provisions of the FCPA. Instead, the individual's or entity's knowledge coupled with either a conspiratorial agreement or actions that aid or abet a violation may lead to criminal liability in connection with prohibited conduct on the part of a third party.

Conspiracy

A conspiracy is established when two or more persons combine or agree to violate a federal statute. If one member takes an affirmative act in furtherance of the conspiracy before the other indicates withdrawal from the conspiracy, both can be held criminally liable for having entered into the conspiracy.[8]

When a conspiracy to violate the FCPA is involved, no offer or payment needs to be made, no record needs to be falsified, and no system of internal controls needs to be circumvented. It is the agreement to violate the anti-bribery provisions or the accounting and record-keeping provisions that serves as the basis for the criminal charge. The only additional evidence that is required is that there be an overt act by one of the coconspirators in furtherance of the conspiracy to violate the FCPA.

Aiding and Abetting

Vicarious liability can also arise out of an individual's or entity's involvement as an accomplice under the federal aiding and abetting statute.[9] To be liable as an accomplice, an individual or entity must act with intent that the offense be committed. But an individual or entity need not actually violate the anti-bribery or the accounting and record-keeping provisions. It is the conduct on the part of an individual or entity to assist another party's violation that serves as the basis for liability as an accomplice.

Implications

The implications for an individual or entity cannot be overstated. So long as the requisite knowledge exists, even casual discussions or interchanges or seemingly insignificant acts have the prospect of forming a basis for a conspiracy or an aiding and abetting charge. Relatively insignificant activity can constitute an overt act in furtherance of a conspiracy. For example, acquiescence combined with other affirmative acts of a very minor nature, like sending an e-mail, could form the basis for allegations of conspiring to violate the anti-bribery provisions.

The possibility that communications or actions can be misinterpreted so as to serve as a basis for an investigation and criminal charges heightens the degree of care that must be exercised when circumstances arise suggesting the prospect of a violation of the anti-bribery provisions or the accounting and record-keeping provisions. Clear and unequivocal objections must be registered and reasonable steps must be taken to prevent or deter a violation. To the degree possible, a record should be made of the manner and means by which objections are registered and other steps taken to prevent or deter a violation.

KNOWLEDGE OF A JURIDICAL ENTITY

The knowledge requirement under U.S. law for a juridical person or entity is distinctly different from that of a natural person. No one person within an entity has to have all of the requisite knowledge. Nor is there a requirement that there be knowledge on the part of senior members of management. Regardless of how disparate the knowledge may be within an entity, the collective knowledge of employees of the entity acting within the scope of their employment can serve as the basis for establishing knowledge under U.S. law.[10] In short, especially where

specific intent is not required, it is the sum of the knowledge of an entity's officers, directors, employees and agents, when acting within the scope of their
employment or responsibilities, that establishes knowledge on the part of an
entity.

The legal standard for establishing knowledge on the part of a juridical entity
differs among countries. In the United States, the threshold is, on a relative basis,
very low for an entity. In addition to issuers, this low threshold extends to privately held companies, limited liability companies, partnerships, and any other
juridical entity that is permitted by law to be established or that has its principal
place of business in the United States.

This is a critical factor in determining an entity's potential exposure. Actions
on the part of isolated members of management or on the part of low-level
employees could expose an entity to liability under the anti-bribery or the accounting and record-keeping provisions. Even more likely is the prospect of employees
or isolated members of management having knowledge of prohibited conduct
being undertaken by third parties on behalf of an entity. In such circumstances,
their failure to register an objection or to disavow the prohibited conduct has the
prospect of being interpreted as constituting an authorization or acquiescence on
the part of the entity.

❸ NOTES

1. 15 U.S.C. §§ 78dd-1(a)(3), -2(a)(3), -3(a)(3).
2. *Id.,* §§ 78dd-1(f)(2)(B); -2(h)(3)(B); -3(f)(3)(B).
3. *Id.,* §§ 78dd-1(f)(2)(A); -2(h)(3)(A); -3(f)(3)(A).
4. *Id.*
5. H.R. Conf. Rep. No. 576, 100th Cong., 2d Sess. (1988), *reprinted in* 1988 U.S.C.C.A.N. 1949, 1952–54.
6. 15 U.S.C. §§ 78dd-1(a), -2(a), -3(a).
7. *Id.,* § 78m(b)(4)-(5).
8. 18 U.S.C. § 371.
9. *Id.,* § 2.
10. *E.g.,* United States v. Bank of New England, N.A., 821 F.2d 844 (1st Cir. 1987).

CHAPTER V

ENFORCEMENT

Enforcement of the FCPA is divided between the Justice Department and the SEC. The Justice Department is responsible for investigating and prosecuting all criminal charges that are brought against an individual or entity for violations of the FCPA. The SEC cannot bring criminal charges. The SEC's civil enforcement authority is limited to issuers as well as their officers, directors, employees, and agents and stockholders acting on their behalf. All other civil enforcement of the FCPA is left to the Justice Department. This includes taking civil enforcement action against domestic concerns as well as anyone other than an issuer who may undertake action in furtherance of an improper inducement, or who may cause action to be undertaken by an agent, within the territory of the United States.

Historically, the Justice Department's focus has almost entirely been devoted to taking criminal enforcement action. But, on occasion, it has resorted to resolving matters in a civil context. Although relatively few cases have been brought by the Justice Department under the anti-bribery provisions, a far greater number of cases are always under active investigation. And the Justice Department's enforcement of anti-bribery provisions has not waned over time. It has remained remarkably consistent since the adoption of the FCPA.

Even though the SEC has been very aggressive in enforcing, in various contexts, the accounting and record-keeping provisions, its enforcement of the anti-bribery provisions waned for many years. This began to change in the latter part of the 1990s. Largely through applying the accounting and record-keeping provisions, the SEC is now very active in enforcing the anti-bribery provisions. In light of the developments following the Enron scandal, enforcement activity at the SEC is even more vigorous.

CRIMINAL INVESTIGATIONS

It is customary for the Justice Department and SEC to work together in coordinating their investigations and, to the extent possible, exchanging information. At times, attorneys from each agency are cross-designated to facilitate communications and minimize the duplication of resources. The agencies also typically work to coordinate parallel proceedings where the Justice Department and SEC are simultaneously conducting criminal and civil investigations. When the Justice Department is using a grand jury to facilitate an investigation, there are significant limitations on what can be disclosed to other units of government.

Although the investigation and trial of cases may be conducted by United States Attorneys and their staffs as well as attorneys with the Justice Department, authority to permit charges being brought under the anti-bribery provisions resides with the Fraud Section of the Criminal Division of the Justice Department. This does not necessarily mean that an FCPA case can be dismissed if the Fraud Section has not given authorization. But it does suggest that interaction, particularly on policy matters, needs to be directed to officials with the Fraud Section as well as the pertinent United States Attorney's office.

The Federal Bureau of Investigation (FBI) is charged with primary responsibility for the investigation of violations of the anti-bribery provisions. But whether the FBI is involved with an investigation is not determinative as to whether there may be violations of the anti-bribery provisions. It does not have exclusive jurisdiction. Other law enforcement agencies have been involved at one time or another in developing evidence and cases associated with violations of the anti-bribery provisions. The SEC's involvement or approval is also not required for the Justice Department to bring criminal charges under the accounting and record-keeping provisions.

Implications of the Record-Keeping Provisions

The record-keeping provisions provide an additional basis for prosecuting those involved with making improper inducements. An entity can face criminal charges for maintaining inaccurate records and for having inadequate internal accounting controls. At the very least, it could easily become embroiled in an SEC investigation where civil charges are actually filed and where proof of intent is not required.

The accounting and record-keeping provisions have also been used to buttress charges under the anti-bribery provisions. The critical factor with the accounting and record-keeping provisions is that the transaction need not be material. In almost every instance, it is unlikely that the making of improper payments will be accurately reported. Enforcement officials will almost always look to the accounting and record-keeping provisions when investigating violations of the anti-bribery provisions. In addition to the likelihood of the evidence being more readily available, proving a violation of the accounting and record-keeping provisions is more straightforward and more likely to succeed than proving a violation of the anti-bribery provisions.

Criminal liability for violations of the accounting and record-keeping provisions is limited to those who "knowingly circumvent" a system of internal accounting controls or "knowingly falsify" records"[1] An individual can be prosecuted regardless of whether the entity in question was actually involved or is convicted. Further, an entity's acquittal does not necessarily exonerate an individual who may be charged with the same offenses.

The record-keeping provisions can and do play a critical role in buttressing charges of violations of statutes other than the anti-bribery provisions. They are particularly used in buttressing charges of accounting and other forms of financial fraud involving the domestic operations of issuers. They have also been used in the context of public corruption within the United States where issuers are involved.

Penalties

Violations of the anti-bribery provisions can result in stiff penalties. A criminal violation may result in a fine of $2 million per violation for an entity.[2] An individual can face up to five years in prison or a fine of $100,000, or both, per violation. Criminal violations of the accounting and record-keeping provisions can lead to maximum sentences for an individual of up to 20 years in prison and fines up to $5 million, or both.[3] Entities can be assessed fines of up to $25 million. In addition, fines can be far greater under the alternative sentencing provisions.[4] A fine can be twice the gross gain or, if there is a pecuniary loss to an individual or entity other than the defendant, the fine can be the greater of twice the gross gain or twice the gross loss.

Regardless of the statutory provisions, an important consideration in terms of a likely criminal penalty will be the U.S. Federal Sentencing Guidelines.[5] A complex matrix is established by the U.S. Federal Sentencing Guidelines for determining fines based upon the culpability of the offender. The relevant factors in assessing culpability include the history of prior violations, the pecuniary gain obtained, and the steps taken by the offender to prevent violations.[6]

For individuals, the prospect of incarceration for a violation of the FCPA must be presumed. Although no one was subject to incarceration under the anti-bribery provisions until 1994, it is now commonplace for terms of incarceration to be imposed. The corporate scandals of the early 2000s now make incarceration under the U.S. Federal Sentencing Guidelines for a violation of the FCPA even more likely.[7]

Implications of Money Laundering Statutes

The provisions of the money laundering statutes should always be kept in mind relative to violations of the FCPA. A felony violation of the FCPA under the anti-bribery and the accounting and record-keeping provisions can serve as a predicate act under the money laundering provisions.[8] The money laundering statutes can also have the practical effect of extending the statute of limitations after the expiration of the statute of limitations for the underlying criminal violation.

Especially in the context of the anti-bribery provisions, the term of imprisonment would be raised from five to 20 years if an individual conducts, or attempts to conduct, a financial transaction with money derived from a felony violation of the FCPA.[9] The term of imprisonment would be ten years if the individual engages in a monetary transaction in criminally derived property.[10] In both instances, alternative fines could be imposed representing twice the value of the amount of the criminally-derived property involved in the transaction.

Forfeiture

Any real or personal property constituting or derived from proceeds traceable to a violation of the FCPA, or a conspiracy to violate the FCPA, may be forfeited. The Civil Asset Forfeiture Reform Act of 2000 (CAFRA) expanded the list of civil forfeiture predicates to include each offense listed as a specified unlawful activity in the Money Laundering Control Act (MLCA).[11] The FCPA is listed as specified unlawful activity in MLCA.[12] CAFRA further provides for criminal forfeiture for all offenses for which civil forfeiture is authorized.[13]

CIVIL ENFORCEMENT ACTIONS

The standard of proof in a civil enforcement action is a preponderance of evidence as opposed to the "beyond a reasonable doubt" standard applicable in a criminal enforcement context. This distinction represents a substantial reduction in the nature and quantum of evidence required to establish a violation of the anti-bribery and the accounting and record-keeping provisions. However, the penalties and sanctions associated with a civil violation are considerably less than those associated with a criminal conviction.

No "Knowing" Requirement under Accounting and Record-Keeping Provisions

There is no "knowing" requirement for civil liability under the accounting and record-keeping provisions. Strict liability is imposed upon issuers. Whether an action will be brought by the SEC rests largely upon the underlying circumstances. When a violation of the anti-bribery provisions may be involved, the SEC has "zero" tolerance when record-keeping violations are also involved. To the degree that discretion is apt to be exercised by the SEC, a declination is most likely in situations where prompt, effective, and comprehensive remedial measures are taken.

Recent actions by the SEC signal a renewed interest in focusing its investigatory efforts on the anti-bribery provisions of the FCPA. In these recent cases, the accounting and record-keeping provisions served as the critical link in addressing the underlying bribery that is alleged to have taken place. It would appear that this renewed interest is not likely to change.

Penalties

Violations of the anti-bribery and the accounting and record-keeping provisions are subject to the standard SEC enforcement consequences including injunctions, civil penalty actions involving substantial fines, and administrative proceedings.[14] The Justice Department can also seek injunctive relief and the imposition of civil penalties. Civil enforcement actions under the anti-bribery provisions are subject to a civil penalty of $10,000.[15]

STATUTES OF LIMITATIONS

As a general proposition, the statutes of limitations associated with the enforcement of the anti-bribery provisions and the accounting and record-keeping provisions are five years. This applies in both a criminal and a civil enforcement context.[16] However, reliance solely upon a five-year limitation as a basis for determining whether action will be taken can be misplaced. Capable enforcement officials can come up with legitimate ways of extending the five-year limitation period. The statute of limitations may have in some way been tolled;[17] evidence may be discovered suggesting an ongoing activity; and alternative legal theories may be employed.

NOTES

1. 15 U.S.C. § 78m(b)(4)-(5).
2. *Id.*, §§ 78dd-2(g), -3(e); 78ff(c)(1)(A)-(2)(A).
3. *Id.*, § 78ff(a).
4. 18 U.S.C. § 3571(d).
5. U.S.S.G. app. § 8A1.1.
6. *Id.*, app. § 8A1.2.
7. In light of the U.S. Supreme Court's recent decision in United States v. Booker, 543 U.S. ___, 160 L.Ed.2d 621, 125 S. Ct. 738 (2005), the U.S. Federal Sentencing Guidelines are to be treated as advisory by federal courts in the United States. Yet, even with the cessation of their mandatory status, the U.S. Federal Sentencing Guidelines can be expected to continue to play a very significant role in the sentencing process, especially with respect to organizations.
8. 18 U.S.C. §§ 1956(c)(7), 1957(f)(3).
9. *Id.*, § 1956.
10. *Id.*, § 1957.
11. *See* 18 U.S.C. § 981.
12. 18 U.S.C. § 1956(c)(7).
13. 28 U.S.C. § 2461(c).
14. 15 U.S.C. §§ 78u, 78u-3.
15. *Id.*, §§ 78dd-2(g)(1)(B), -2(g)(2)(B), -3(e)(1)(B), -3(e)(2)(B); 78ff(c)(1)(B), (c)(2)(B).
16. 18 U.S.C. § 3282; 28 U.S.C. § 2462.
17. A request for evidence from abroad can toll the statute of limitations. 18 U.S.C. § 3292. For an individual fleeing from justice, the statute of limitations does not apply. *Id.*, § 3290.

FOREIGN CORRUPT PRACTICES ACT*

§ 78M. PERIODICAL AND OTHER REPORTS

(a) Reports by issuer of security; contents

Every issuer of a security registered pursuant to section 78l of this title shall file with the Commission, in accordance with such rules and regulations as the Commission may prescribe as necessary or appropriate for the proper protection of investors and to insure fair dealing in the security—

(1) such information and documents (and such copies thereof) as the Commission shall require to keep reasonably current the information and documents required to be included in or filed with an application or registration statement filed pursuant to section 78l of this title, except that the Commission may not require the filing of any material contract wholly executed before July 1, 1962.

(2) such annual reports (and such copies thereof), certified if required by the rules and regulations of the Commission by independent public accountants, and such quarterly reports (and such copies thereof), as the Commission may prescribe.

Every issuer of a security registered on a national securities exchange shall also file a duplicate original of such information, documents, and reports with the exchange.

---

* 15 U.S.C. §§ 78m, 78dd-1, 78dd-2, 78dd-3, and 78ff.

(b) Form of report; books, records, and internal accounting; directives

★ ★ ★

(2) Every issuer which has a class of securities registered pursuant to section 78l of this title and every issuer which is required to file reports pursuant to section 78o(d) of this title shall—

(A) make and keep books, records, and accounts, which, in reasonable detail, accurately and fairly reflect the transactions and dispositions of the assets of the issuer; and

(B) devise and maintain a system of internal accounting controls sufficient to provide reasonable assurances that—

(i) transactions are executed in accordance with management's general or specific authorization;

(ii) transactions are recorded as necessary (I) to permit preparation of financial statements in conformity with generally accepted accounting principles or any other criteria applicable to such statements, and (II) to maintain accountability for assets;

(iii) access to assets is permitted only in accordance with management's general or specific authorization; and

(iv) the recorded accountability for assets is compared with the existing assets at reasonable intervals and appropriate action is taken with respect to any differences.

(3) (A) With respect to matters concerning the national security of the United States, no duty or liability under paragraph (2) of this subsection shall be imposed upon any person acting in cooperation with the head of any Federal department or agency responsible for such matters if such act in cooperation with such head of a department or agency was done upon the specific, written directive of the head of such department or agency pursuant to Presidential authority to issue such directives. Each directive issued under this paragraph shall set forth the specific facts and circumstances with respect to which the provisions of this paragraph are to be invoked. Each such directive shall, unless renewed in writing, expire one year after the date of issuance.

(B) Each head of a Federal department or agency of the United States who issues such a directive pursuant to this paragraph shall maintain a complete file of all such directives and shall, on October 1 of each year, transmit a summary of matters covered by such directives in force at any time during the previous year to the Permanent Select Committee on Intelligence of the House of Representatives and the Select Committee on Intelligence of the Senate.

(4) No criminal liability shall be imposed for failing to comply with the requirements of paragraph (2) of this subsection except as provided in paragraph (5) of this subsection.

(5) No person shall knowingly circumvent or knowingly fail to implement a system of internal accounting controls or knowingly falsify any book, record, or account described in paragraph (2).

(6) Where an issuer which has a class of securities registered pursuant to section 78l of this title or an issuer which is required to file reports pursuant to section 78o(d) of this title holds 50 per centum or less of the voting power with respect to a domestic or foreign firm, the provisions of paragraph (2) require only that the issuer proceed in good faith to use its influence, to the extent reasonable under the issuer's circumstances, to cause such domestic or foreign firm to devise and maintain a system of internal accounting controls consistent with paragraph (2). Such circumstances include the relative degree of the issuer's ownership of the domestic or foreign firm and the laws and practices governing the business operations of the country in which such firm is located. An issuer which demonstrates good faith efforts to use such influence shall be conclusively presumed to have complied with the requirements of paragraph (2).

(7) For the purpose of paragraph (2) of this subsection, the terms "reasonable assurances" and "reasonable detail" mean such level of detail and degree of assurance as would satisfy prudent officials in the conduct of their own affairs.

★ ★ ★

§ 78DD-1. PROHIBITED FOREIGN TRADE PRACTICES BY ISSUERS

(a) Prohibition

It shall be unlawful for any issuer which has a class of securities registered pursuant to section 78l of this title or which is required to file reports under section 78o(d) of this title, or for any officer, director, employee, or agent of such issuer or any stockholder thereof acting on behalf of such issuer, to make use of the mails or any means or instrumentality of interstate commerce corruptly in furtherance of an offer, payment, promise to pay, or authorization of the payment of any money, or offer, gift, promise to give, or authorization of the giving of anything of value to—

(1) any foreign official for purposes of—

(A) (i) influencing any act or decision of such foreign official in his official capacity, (ii) inducing such foreign official to do or omit to do any act in violation of the lawful duty of such official, or (iii) securing any improper advantage; or

(B) inducing such foreign official to use his influence with a foreign government or instrumentality thereof to affect or influence any act or decision of such government or instrumentality,

in order to assist such issuer in obtaining or retaining business for or with, or directing business to, any person;

(2) any foreign political party or official thereof or any candidate for foreign political office for purposes of—

(A) (i) influencing any act or decision of such party, official, or candidate in its or his official capacity, (ii) inducing such party, official, or candidate to do or omit to do an act in violation of the lawful duty of such party, official, or candidate, or (iii) securing any improper advantage; or

(B) inducing such party, official, or candidate to use its or his influence with a foreign government or instrumentality thereof to affect or influence any act or decision of such government or instrumentality,

in order to assist such issuer in obtaining or retaining business for or with, or directing business to, any person; or

(3) any person, while knowing that all or a portion of such money or thing of value will be offered, given, or promised, directly or indirectly, to any foreign official, to any foreign political party or official thereof, or to any candidate for foreign political office, for purposes of—

(A) (i) influencing any act or decision of such foreign official, political party, party official, or candidate in his or its official capacity, (ii) inducing such foreign official, political party, party official, or candidate to do or omit to do any act in violation of the lawful duty of such foreign official, political party, party official, or candidate, or (iii) securing any improper advantage; or

(B) inducing such foreign official, political party, party official, or candidate to use his or its influence with a foreign government or instrumentality thereof to affect or influence any act or decision of such government or instrumentality,

in order to assist such issuer in obtaining or retaining business for or with, or directing business to, any person.

(b) Exception for routine governmental action

Subsections (a) and (g) of this section shall not apply to any facilitating or expediting payment to a foreign official, political party, or party official the purpose of which is to expedite or to secure the performance of a routine governmental action by a foreign official, political party, or party official.

(c) Affirmative defenses

It shall be an affirmative defense to actions under subsection (a) or (g) of this section that—

(1) the payment, gift, offer, or promise of anything of value that was made, was lawful under the written laws and regulations of the foreign official's, political party's, party official's, or candidate's country; or

(2) the payment, gift, offer, or promise of anything of value that was made, was a reasonable and bona fide expenditure, such as travel and lodging expenses, incurred by or on behalf of a foreign official, party, party official, or candidate and was directly related to—

(A) the promotion, demonstration, or explanation of products or services; or

(B) the execution or performance of a contract with a foreign government or agency thereof.

(d) Guidelines by Attorney General

Not later than one year after August 23, 1988, the Attorney General, after consultation with the Commission, the Secretary of Commerce, the United States Trade Representative, the Secretary of State, and the Secretary of the Treasury, and after obtaining the views of all interested persons through public notice and comment procedures, shall determine to what extent compliance with this section would be enhanced and the business community would be assisted by further clarification of the preceding provisions of this section and may, based on such determination and to the extent necessary and appropriate, issue—

(1) guidelines describing specific types of conduct, associated with common types of export sales arrangements and business contracts, which for purposes of the Department of Justice's present enforcement policy, the Attorney General determines would be in conformance with the preceding provisions of this section; and

(2) general precautionary procedures which issuers may use on a voluntary basis to conform their conduct to the Department of Justice's present enforcement policy regarding the preceding provisions of this section.

The Attorney General shall issue the guidelines and procedures referred to in the preceding sentence in accordance with the provisions of subchapter II of chapter 5 of Title 5 and those guidelines and procedures shall be subject to the provisions of chapter 7 of that title.

(e) Opinions of Attorney General

(1) The Attorney General, after consultation with appropriate departments and agencies of the United States and after obtaining the views of all interested persons through

public notice and comment procedures, shall establish a procedure to provide responses to specific inquiries by issuers concerning conformance of their conduct with the Department of Justice's present enforcement policy regarding the preceding provisions of this section. The Attorney General shall, within 30 days after receiving such a request, issue an opinion in response to that request. The opinion shall state whether or not certain specified prospective conduct would, for purposes of the Department of Justice's present enforcement policy, violate the preceding provisions of this section. Additional requests for opinions may be filed with the Attorney General regarding other specified prospective conduct that is beyond the scope of conduct specified in previous requests. In any action brought under the applicable provisions of this section, there shall be a rebuttable presumption that conduct, which is specified in a request by an issuer and for which the Attorney General has issued an opinion that such conduct is in conformity with the Department of Justice's present enforcement policy, is in compliance with the preceding provisions of this section. Such a presumption may be rebutted by a preponderance of the evidence. In considering the presumption for purposes of this paragraph, a court shall weight all relevant factors, including but not limited to whether the information submitted to the Attorney General was accurate and complete and whether it was within the scope of the conduct specified in any request received by the Attorney General. The Attorney General shall establish the procedure required by this paragraph in accordance with the provisions of subchapter II of chapter 5 of Title 5 and that procedure shall be subject to the provisions of chapter 7 of that title.

(2) Any document or other material which is provided to, received by, or prepared in the Department of Justice or any other department or agency of the United States in connection with a request by an issuer under the procedure established under paragraph (1), shall be exempt from disclosure under section 552 of Title 5 and shall not, except with the consent of the issuer, be made publicly available, regardless of whether the Attorney General responds to such a request or the issuer withdraws such request before receiving a response.

(3) Any issuer who has made a request to the Attorney General under paragraph (1) may withdraw such request prior to the time the Attorney General issues an opinion in response to such request. Any request so withdrawn shall have no force or effect.

(4) The Attorney General shall, to the maximum extent practicable, provide timely guidance concerning the Department of Justice's present enforcement policy with respect to the preceding provisions of this section to potential exporters and small businesses that are unable to obtain specialized counsel on issues pertaining to such provisions. Such guidance shall be limited to responses to requests under paragraph (1) concerning conformity of specified prospective conduct with the Department of Justice's present enforcement policy regarding the preceding provisions of this section and general explanations of compliance responsibilities and of potential liabilities under the preceding provisions of this section.

(f) Definitions

For purposes of this section:

(1) (A) The term "foreign official" means any officer or employee of a foreign government or any department, agency, or instrumentality thereof, or of a public international organization, or any person acting in an official capacity for or on behalf of any such government or department, agency, or instrumentality, or for or on behalf of any such public international organization.

(B) For purposes of subparagraph (A), the term "public international organization" means—

(i) an organization that is designated by Executive Order pursuant to section 1 of the International Organizations Immunities Act (22 U.S.C. § 288); or

(ii) any other international organization that is designated by the President by Executive order for the purposes of this section, effective as of the date of publication of such order in the Federal Register.

(2) (A) A person's state of mind is "knowing" with respect to conduct, a circumstance, or a result if—

(i) such person is aware that such person is engaging in such conduct, that such circumstance exists, or that such result is substantially certain to occur; or

(ii) such person has a firm belief that such circumstance exists or that such result is substantially certain to occur.

(B) When knowledge of the existence of a particular circumstance is required for an offense, such knowledge is established if a person is aware of a high probability of the existence of such circumstance, unless the person actually believes that such circumstance does not exist.

(3) (A) The term "routine governmental action" means only an action which is ordinarily and commonly performed by a foreign official in—

(i) obtaining permits, licenses, or other official documents to qualify a person to do business in a foreign country;

(ii) processing governmental papers, such as visas and work orders;

(iii) providing police protection, mail pick-up and delivery, or scheduling inspections associated with contract performance or inspections related to transit of goods across country;

(iv) providing phone service, power and water supply, loading and unloading cargo, or protecting perishable products or commodities from deterioration; or

(v) actions of a similar nature.

(B) The term "routine governmental action" does not include any decision by a foreign official whether, or on what terms, to award new business to or to continue business with a particular party, or any action taken by a foreign official involved in the decision-making process to encourage a decision to award new business to or continue business with a particular party.

(g) Alternative jurisdiction

(1) It shall also be unlawful for any issuer organized under the laws of the United States, or a State, territory, possession, or commonwealth of the United States or a political subdivision thereof and which has a class of securities registered pursuant to section 12 of this title or which is required to file reports under section 15(d) of this title, or for any United States person that is an officer, director, employee, or agent of such issuer or a stockholder thereof acting on behalf of such issuer, to corruptly do any act outside the United States in furtherance of an offer, payment, promise to pay, or authorization of the payment of any money, or offer, gift, promise to give, or authorization of the giving of anything of value to any of the persons or entities set forth in paragraphs (1), (2), and (3) of this subsection (a) of this section for the purposes set forth therein, irrespective of whether such issuer or such officer, director, employee, agent, or stockholder makes use of the mails or any means or instrumentality of interstate commerce in furtherance of such offer, gift, payment, promise, or authorization.

(2) As used in this subsection, the term "United States person" means a national of the United States (as defined in section 101 of the Immigration and Nationality Act (8 U.S.C. § 1101)) or any corporation, partnership, association, joint-stock company, business trust, unincorporated organization, or sole proprietorship organized under the laws of the United States or any State, territory, possession, or commonwealth of the United States, or any political subdivision thereof.

§ 78DD-2. PROHIBITED FOREIGN TRADE PRACTICES BY DOMESTIC CONCERNS

(a) Prohibition

It shall be unlawful for any domestic concern, other than an issuer which is subject to section 78dd-1 of this title, or for any officer, director, employee, or agent of such domestic concern or any stockholder thereof acting on behalf of such domestic concern, to make use of the mails or any means or instrumentality of interstate commerce corruptly in furtherance of an offer, payment, promise to pay, or authorization of the payment of any money, or offer, gift, promise to give, or authorization of the giving of anything of value to—

(1) any foreign official for purposes of—

(A) (i) influencing any act or decision of such foreign official in his official capacity, (ii) inducing such foreign official to do or omit to do any act in violation of the lawful duty of such official, or (iii) securing any improper advantage; or

(B) inducing such foreign official to use his influence with a foreign government or instrumentality thereof to affect or influence any act or decision of such government or instrumentality,

in order to assist such domestic concern in obtaining or retaining business for or with, or directing business to, any person;

(2) any foreign political party or official thereof or any candidate for foreign political office for purposes of—

(A) (i) influencing any act or decision of such party, official, or candidate in its or his official capacity, (ii) inducing such party, official, or candidate to do or omit to do an act in violation of the lawful duty of such party, official, or candidate, or (iii) securing any improper advantage; or

(B) inducing such party, official, or candidate to use its or his influence with a foreign government or instrumentality thereof to affect or influence any act or decision of such government or instrumentality,

in order to assist such domestic concern in obtaining or retaining business for or with, or directing business to, any person;

(3) any person, while knowing that all or a portion of such money or thing of value will be offered, given, or promised, directly or indirectly, to any foreign official, to any foreign political party or official thereof, or to any candidate for foreign political office, for purposes of—

(A) (i) influencing any act or decision of such foreign official, political party, party official, or candidate in his or its official capacity, (ii) inducing such foreign official, political party, party official, or candidate to do or omit to do any act in violation of the lawful duty of such foreign official, political party, party official, or candidate, or (iii) securing any improper advantage; or

(B) inducing such foreign official, political party, party official, or candidate to use his or its influence with a foreign government or instrumentality thereof to affect or influence any act or decision of such government or instrumentality, in order to assist such domestic concern in obtaining or retaining business for or with, or directing business to, any person.

(b) Exception for routine governmental action

Subsections (a) and (i) of this section shall not apply to any facilitating or expediting payment to a foreign official, political party, or party official the purpose of which is to expedite or to secure the performance of a routine governmental action by a foreign official, political party, or party official.

(c) Affirmative defenses

It shall be an affirmative defense to actions under subsection (a) or (i) of this section that—

(1) the payment, gift, offer, or promise of anything of value that was made, was lawful under the written laws and regulations of the foreign official's, political party's, party official's, or candidate's country; or

(2) the payment, gift, offer, or promise of anything of value that was made, was a reasonable and bona fide expenditure, such as travel and lodging expenses, incurred by or on behalf of a foreign official, party, party official, or candidate and was directly related to—

   (A) the promotion, demonstration, or explanation of products or services; or

   (B) the execution or performance of a contract with a foreign government or agency thereof.

(d) Injunctive relief

(1) When it appears to the Attorney General that any domestic concern to which this section applies, or officer, director, employee, agent, or stockholder thereof, is engaged, or about to engage, in any act or practice constituting a violation of subsection (a) or (i) of this section, the Attorney General may, in his discretion, bring a civil action in an appropriate district court of the United States to enjoin such act or practice, and upon a proper showing, a permanent injunction or a temporary restraining order shall be granted without bond.

(2) For the purpose of any civil investigation which, in the opinion of the Attorney General, is necessary and proper to enforce this section, the Attorney General or his designee are empowered to administer oaths and affirmations, subpoena witnesses, take evidence, and require the production of any books, papers, or other documents

which the Attorney General deems relevant or material to such investigation. The attendance of witnesses and the production of documentary evidence may be required from any place in the United States, or any territory, possession, or commonwealth of the United States, at any designated place of hearing.

(3) In case of contumacy by, or refusal to obey a subpoena issued to, any person, the Attorney General may invoke the aid of any court of the United States within the jurisdiction of which such investigation or proceeding is carried on, or where such person resides or carries on business, in requiring the attendance and testimony of witnesses and the production of books, papers, or other documents. Any such court may issue an order requiring such person to appear before the Attorney General or his designee, there to produce records, if so ordered, or to give testimony touching the matter under investigation. Any failure to obey such order of the court may be punished by such court as a contempt thereof.

All process in any such case may be served in the judicial district in which such person resides or may be found. The Attorney General may make such rules relating to civil investigations as may be necessary or appropriate to implement the provisions of this subsection.

(e) Guidelines by Attorney General

Not later than 6 months after August 23, 1988, the Attorney General, after consultation with the Securities and Exchange Commission, the Secretary of Commerce, the United States Trade Representative, the Secretary of State, and the Secretary of the Treasury, and after obtaining the views of all interested persons through public notice and comment procedures, shall determine to what extent compliance with this section would be enhanced and the business community would be assisted by further clarification of the preceding provisions of this section and may, based on such determination and to the extent necessary and appropriate, issue—

(1) guidelines describing specific types of conduct, associated with common types of export sales arrangements and business contracts, which for purposes of the Department of Justice's present enforcement policy, the Attorney General determines would be in conformance with the preceding provisions of this section; and

(2) general precautionary procedures which domestic concerns may use on a voluntary basis to conform their conduct to the Department of Justice's present enforcement policy regarding the preceding provisions of this section.

The Attorney General shall issue the guidelines and procedures referred to in the preceding sentence in accordance with the provisions of subchapter II of chapter 5 of Title 5 and those guidelines and procedures shall be subject to the provisions of chapter 7 of that title.

(f) Opinions of the Attorney General

(1) The Attorney General, after consultation with appropriate departments and agencies of the United States and after obtaining the views of all interested persons through public notice and comment procedures, shall establish a procedure to provide responses to specific inquiries by domestic concerns concerning conformance of their conduct with the Department of Justice's present enforcement policy regarding the preceding provisions of this section. The Attorney General shall, within 30 days after receiving such a request, issue an opinion in response to that request. The opinion shall state whether or not certain specified prospective conduct would, for purposes of the Department of Justice's present enforcement policy, violate the preceding provisions of this section. Additional requests for opinions may be filed with the Attorney General regarding other specified prospective conduct that is beyond the scope of conduct specified in previous requests. In any action brought under the applicable provisions of this section, there shall be a rebuttable presumption that conduct, which is specified in a request by a domestic concern and for which the Attorney General has issued an opinion that such conduct is in conformity with the Department of Justice's present enforcement policy, is in compliance with the preceding provisions of this section. Such a presumption may be rebutted by a preponderance of the evidence. In considering the presumption for purposes of this paragraph, a court shall weigh all relevant factors, including but not limited to whether the information submitted to the Attorney General was accurate and complete and whether it was within the scope of the conduct specified in any request received by the Attorney General. The Attorney General shall establish the procedure required by this paragraph in accordance with the provisions of subchapter II of chapter 5 of Title 5 and that procedure shall be subject to the provisions of chapter 7 of that title.

(2) Any document or other material which is provided to, received by, or prepared in the Department of Justice or any other department or agency of the United States in connection with a request by a domestic concern under the procedure established under paragraph (1), shall be exempt from disclosure under section 552 of Title 5 and shall not, except with the consent of the domestic concern, by made publicly available, regardless of whether the Attorney General response to such a request or the domestic concern withdraws such request before receiving a response.

(3) Any domestic concern who has made a request to the Attorney General under paragraph (1) may withdraw such request prior to the time the Attorney General issues an opinion in response to such request. Any request so withdrawn shall have no force or effect.

(4) The Attorney General shall, to the maximum extent practicable, provide timely guidance concerning the Department of Justice's present enforcement policy with respect to the preceding provisions of this section to potential exporters and small businesses that are unable to obtain specialized counsel on issues pertaining to such provisions. Such guidance shall be limited to responses to requests under paragraph (1) concerning conformity of specified prospective conduct with the Department of Justice's

present enforcement policy regarding the preceding provisions of this section and general explanations of compliance responsibilities and of potential liabilities under the preceding provisions of this section.

(g) Penalties

(1) (A) Any domestic concern that is not a natural person and that violates subsection (a) or (i) of this section shall be fined not more than $2,000,000.

(B) Any domestic concern that is not a natural person and that violates subsection (a) or (i) of this section shall be subject to a civil penalty of not more than $10,000 imposed in an action brought by the Attorney General.

(2) (A) Any natural person that is an officer, director, employee, or agent of a domestic concern, or stockholder acting on behalf of such domestic concern, who willfully violates subsection (a) or (i) of this section shall be fined not more than $100,000 or imprisoned not more than 5 years, or both.

(B) Any natural person that is an officer, director, employee, or agent of a domestic concern, or stockholder acting on behalf of such domestic concern, who violates subsection (a) or (i) of this section shall be subject to a civil penalty of not more than $10,000 imposed in an action brought by the Attorney General.

(3) Whenever a fine is imposed under paragraph (2) upon any officer, director, employee, agent, or stockholder of a domestic concern, such fine may not be paid, directly or indirectly, by such domestic concern.

(h) Definitions

For purposes of this section:

(1) The term "domestic concern" means—

(A) any individual who is a citizen, national, or resident of the United States; and

(B) any corporation, partnership, association, joint-stock company, business trust, unincorporated organization, or sole proprietorship which has its principal place of business in the United States, or which is organized under the laws of a State of the United States or a territory, possession, or commonwealth of the United States.

(2) (A) The term "foreign official" means any officer or employee of a foreign government or any department, agency, or instrumentality thereof, or of a public international organization, or any person acting in an official capacity for or on behalf of any such government or department, agency, or instrumentality, or for or on behalf of any such public international organization.

(B) For purposes of subparagraph (A), the term "public international organization" means—

(i) an organization that has been designated by Executive order pursuant to Section 1 of the International Organizations Immunities Act (22 U.S.C. § 288); or

(ii) any other international organization that is designated by the President by Executive order for the purposes of this section, effective as of the date of publication of such order in the Federal Register.

(3) (A) A person's state of mind is "knowing" with respect to conduct, a circumstance, or a result if—

(i) such person is aware that such person is engaging in such conduct, that such circumstance exists, or that such result is substantially certain to occur; or

(ii) such person has a firm belief that such circumstance exists or that such result is substantially certain to occur.

(B) When knowledge of the existence of a particular circumstance is required for an offense, such knowledge is established if a person is aware of a high probability of the existence of such circumstance, unless the person actually believes that such circumstance does not exist.

(4) (A) The term "routine governmental action" means only an action which is ordinarily and commonly performed by a foreign official in—

(i) obtaining permits, licenses, or other official documents to qualify a person to do business in a foreign country;

(ii) processing governmental papers, such as visas and work orders;

(iii) providing police protection, mail pick-up and delivery, or scheduling inspections associated with contract performance or inspections related to transit of goods across country;

(iv) providing phone service, power and water supply, loading and unloading cargo, or protecting perishable products or commodities from deterioration; or

(v) actions of a similar nature.

(B) The term "routine governmental action" does not include any decision by a foreign official whether, or on what terms, to award new business to or to continue business with a particular party, or any action taken by a foreign official involved in the decision-making process to encourage a decision to award new business to or continue business with a particular party.

(5) The term "interstate commerce" means trade, commerce, transportation, or communication among the several States, or between any foreign country and any State or between any State and any place or ship outside thereof, and such term includes the intrastate use of—

(A) a telephone or other interstate means of communication, or

(B) any other interstate instrumentality.

(i) Alternative Jurisdiction

(1) It shall also be unlawful for any United States person to corruptly do any act outside the United States in furtherance of an offer, payment, promise to pay, or authorization of the payment of any money, or offer, gift, promise to give, or authorization of the giving of anything of value to any of the persons or entities set forth in paragraphs (1), (2), and (3) of subsection (a), for the purposes set forth therein, irrespective of whether such United States person makes use of the mails or any means or instrumentality of interstate commerce in furtherance of such offer, gift, payment, promise, or authorization.

(2) As used in this subsection, a "United States person" means a national of the United States (as defined in section 101 of the Immigration and Nationality Act (8 U.S.C. § 1101)) or any corporation, partnership, association, joint-stock company, business trust, unincorporated organization, or sole proprietorship organized under the laws of the United States or any State, territory, possession, or commonwealth of the United States, or any political subdivision thereof.

§ 78DD-3. PROHIBITED FOREIGN TRADE PRACTICES BY PERSONS OTHER THAN ISSUERS OR DOMESTIC CONCERNS

(a) Prohibition

It shall be unlawful for any person other than an issuer that is subject to section 30A of the Securities Exchange Act of 1934 or a domestic concern, as defined in section 104 of this Act), or for any officer, director, employee, or agent of such person or any stockholder thereof acting on behalf of such person, while in the territory of the United States, corruptly to make use of the mails or any means or instrumentality of interstate commerce or to do any other act in furtherance of an offer, payment, promise to pay, or authorization of the payment of any money, or offer, gift, promise to give, or authorization of the giving of anything of value to—

(1) any foreign official for purposes of—

(A) (i) influencing any act or decision of such foreign official in his official capacity, (ii) inducing such foreign official to do or omit to do any act in violation of the lawful duty of such official, or (iii) securing any improper advantage; or

(B) inducing such foreign official to use his influence with a foreign government or instrumentality thereof to affect or influence any act or decision of such government or instrumentality,

in order to assist such person in obtaining or retaining business for or with, or directing business to, any person;

(2) any foreign political party or official thereof or any candidate for foreign political office for purposes of—

(A) (i) influencing any act or decision of such party, official, or candidate in its or his official capacity, (ii) inducing such party, official, or candidate to do or omit to do an act in violation of the lawful duty of such party, official, or candidate, or (iii) securing any improper advantage; or

(B) inducing such party, official, or candidate to use its or his influence with a foreign government or instrumentality thereof to affect or influence any act or decision of such government or instrumentality,

in order to assist such person in obtaining or retaining business for or with, or directing business to, any person; or

(3) any person, while knowing that all or a portion of such money or thing of value will be offered, given, or promised, directly or indirectly, to any foreign official, to any foreign political party or official thereof, or to any candidate for foreign political office, for purposes of—

(A) (i) influencing any act or decision of such foreign official, political party, party official, or candidate in his or its official capacity, (ii) inducing such foreign official, political party, party official, or candidate to do or omit to do any act in violation of the lawful duty of such foreign official, political party, party official, or candidate, or (iii) securing any improper advantage; or

(B) inducing such foreign official, political party, party official, or candidate to use his or its influence with a foreign government or instrumentality thereof to affect or influence any act or decision of such government or instrumentality,

in order to assist such person in obtaining or retaining business for or with, or directing business to, any person.

(b) Exception for routine governmental action

Subsection (a) of this section shall not apply to any facilitating or expediting payment to a foreign official, political party, or party official the purpose of which is to expedite or to secure the performance of a routine governmental action by a foreign official, political party, or party official.

(c) Affirmative defenses

It shall be an affirmative defense to actions under subsection (a) of this section that—

(1) the payment, gift, offer, or promise of anything of value that was made, was lawful under the written laws and regulations of the foreign official's, political party's, party official's, or candidate's country; or

(2) the payment, gift, offer, or promise of anything of value that was made, was a reasonable and bona fide expenditure, such as travel and lodging expenses, incurred by or on behalf of a foreign official, party, party official, or candidate and was directly related to—

(A) the promotion, demonstration, or explanation of products or services; or

(B) the execution or performance of a contract with a foreign government or agency thereof.

(d) Injunctive relief

(1) When it appears to the Attorney General that any person to which this section applies, or officer, director, employee, agent, or stockholder thereof, is engaged, or about to engage, in any act or practice constituting a violation of subsection (a) of this section, the Attorney General may, in his discretion, bring a civil action in an appropriate district court of the United States to enjoin such act or practice, and upon a proper showing, a permanent injunction or a temporary restraining order shall be granted without bond.

(2) For the purpose of any civil investigation which, in the opinion of the Attorney General, is necessary and proper to enforce this section, the Attorney General or his designee are empowered to administer oaths and affirmations, subpoena witnesses, take evidence, and require the production of any books, papers, or other documents which the Attorney General deems relevant or material to such investigation. The attendance of witnesses and the production of documentary evidence may be required from any place in the United States, or any territory, possession, or commonwealth of the United States, at any designated place of hearing.

(3) In case of contumacy by, or refusal to obey a subpoena issued to, any person, the Attorney General may invoke the aid of any court of the United States within the jurisdiction of which such investigation or proceeding is carried on, or where such person resides or carries on business, in requiring the attendance and testimony of witnesses and the production of books, papers, or other documents. Any such court may issue an order requiring such person to appear before the Attorney General or his designee, there to produce records, if so ordered, or to give testimony touching the matter under investigation. Any failure to obey such order of the court may be punished by such court as a contempt thereof.

(4) All process in any such case may be served in the judicial district in which such person resides or may be found. The Attorney General may make such rules relating to civil investigations as may be necessary or appropriate to implement the provisions of this subsection.

(e) Penalties

(1) (A) Any juridical person that violates subsection (a) of this section shall be fined not more than $2,000,000.

(B) Any juridical person that violates subsection (a) of this section shall be subject to a civil penalty of not more than $10,000 imposed in an action brought by the Attorney General.

(2) (A) Any natural person who willfully violates subsection (a) of this section shall be fined not more than $100,000 or imprisoned not more than 5 years, or both.

(B) Any natural person who violates subsection (a) of this section shall be subject to a civil penalty of not more than $10,000 imposed in an action brought by the Attorney General.

(3) Whenever a fine is imposed under paragraph (2) upon any officer, director, employee, agent, or stockholder of a person, such fine may not be paid, directly or indirectly, by such person.

(f) Definitions

For purposes of this section:

(1) The term "person," when referring to an offender, means any natural person other than a. national of the United States (as defined in 8 U.S.C. § 1101) or any corporation, partnership, association, joint-stock company, business trust, unincorporated organization, or sole proprietorship organized under the law of a foreign nation or a political subdivision thereof

(2) (A) The term "foreign official" means any officer or employee of a foreign government or any department, agency, or instrumentality thereof, or of a public international organization, or any person acting in an official capacity for or on behalf of any such government or department, agency, or instrumentality, or for or on behalf of any such public international organization.

(3) For purposes of subparagraph (A), the term "public international organization" means—

(i) an organization that has been designated by Executive Order pursuant to Section 1 of the International Organizations Immunities Act (22 U.S.C. § 288); or

(ii) any other international organization that is designated by the President by Executive order for the purposes of this section, effective as of the date of publication of such order in the Federal Register.

(3) (A) A person's state of mind is "knowing" with respect to conduct, a circumstance, or a result if—

(i) such person is aware that such person is engaging in such conduct, that such circumstance exists, or that such result is substantially certain to occur; or

(ii) such person has a firm belief that such circumstance exists or that such result is substantially certain to occur.

(B) When knowledge of the existence of a particular circumstance is required for an offense, such knowledge is established if a person is aware of a high probability of the existence of such circumstance, unless the person actually believes that such circumstance does not exist.

(4) (A) The term "routine governmental action" means only an action which is ordinarily and commonly performed by a foreign official in—

(i) obtaining permits, licenses, or other official documents to qualify a person to do business in a foreign country;

(ii) processing governmental papers, such as visas and work orders;

(iii) providing police protection, mail pick-up and delivery, or scheduling inspections associated with contract performance or inspections related to transit of goods across country;

(iv) providing phone service, power and water supply, loading and unloading cargo, or protecting perishable products or commodities from deterioration; or

(v) actions of a similar nature.

(B) The term "routine governmental action" does not include any decision by a foreign official whether, or on what terms, to award new business to or to continue business with a particular party, or any action taken by a foreign official involved in the decision-making process to encourage a decision to award new business to or continue business with a particular party.

(5) The term "interstate commerce" means trade, commerce, transportation, or communication among the several States, or between any foreign country and any State or

between any State and any place or ship outside thereof, and such term includes the intrastate use of—

(A) a telephone or other interstate means of communication, or

(B) any other interstate instrumentality.

§ 78FF. PENALTIES

(a) Willful violations; false and misleading statements

Any person who willfully violates any provision of this chapter (other than section 78dd-1 of this title), or any rule or regulation thereunder the violation of which is made unlawful or the observance of which is required under the terms of this chapter, or any person who willfully and knowingly makes, or causes to be made, any statement in any application, report, or document required to be filed under this chapter or any rule or regulation thereunder or any undertaking contained in a registration statement as provided in subsection (d) of section 78o of this title, or by any self-regulatory organization in connection with an application for membership or participation therein or to become associated with a member thereof, which statement was false or misleading with respect to any material fact, shall upon conviction be fined not more than $5,000,000, or imprisoned not more than 20 years, or both, except that when such person is a person other than a natural person, a fine not exceeding $25,000,000 may be imposed; but no person shall be subject to imprisonment under this section for the violation of any rule or regulation if he proves that he had no knowledge of such rule or regulation.

(b) Failure to file information, documents, or reports

Any issuer which fails to file information, documents, or reports required to be filed under subsection (d) of section 78o of this title or any rule or regulation thereunder shall forfeit to the United States the sum of $100 for each and every day such failure to file shall continue. Such forfeiture, which shall be in lieu of any criminal penalty for such failure to file which might be deemed to arise under subsection (a) of this section, shall be payable into the Treasury of the United States and shall be recoverable in a civil suit in the name of the United States.

(c) Violations by issuers, officers, directors, stockholders, employees, or agents of issuers

(1) (A) Any issuer that violates subsection (a) or (g) of section 30A of this title [15 U.S.C. § 78dd-1] shall be fined not more than $2,000,000.

(B) Any issuer that violates subsection (a) or (g) of section 30A of this title [15 U.S.C. § 78dd-1] shall be subject to a civil penalty of not more than $10,000 imposed in an action brought by the Commission.

(2) (A) Any officer, director, employee, or agent of an issuer, or stockholder acting on behalf of such issuer, who willfully violates subsection (a) or (g) of section 30A of this title [15 U.S.C. § 78dd-1] shall be fined not more than $100,000, or imprisoned not more than 5 years, or both.

(B) Any officer, director, employee, or agent of an issuer, or stockholder acting on behalf of such issuer, who violates subsection (a) or (g) of section 30A of this title [15 U.S.C. § 78dd-1] shall be subject to a civil penalty of not more than $10,000 imposed in an action brought by the Commission.

(3) Whenever a fine is imposed under paragraph (2) upon any officer, director, employee, agent, or stockholder of an issuer, such fine may not be paid, directly or indirectly, by such issuer.

RECORD-KEEPING REGULATIONS*

§ 240.13B2-1 FALSIFICATION OF ACCOUNTING RECORDS.

No person shall directly or indirectly, falsify or cause to by falsified, any book, record, or account subject to Section 13(b)(2)(A) of the Securities Exchange Act.

§ 240.13B2-2 REPRESENTATIONS AND CONDUCT IN CONNECTION WITH THE PREPARATION OF REQUIRED REPORTS AND DOCUMENTS.

(a) No director or officer of an issuer shall, directly or indirectly:

  (1) Make or cause to be made a materially false or misleading statement to an accountant in connection with; or

  (2) Omit to state, or cause another person to omit to state, any material fact necessary in order to make statements made, in light of the circumstances under which such statements were made, not misleading, to an accountant in connection with:

    (i) Any audit, review or examination of the financial statements of the issuer required to be made pursuant to this subpart; or

    (ii) The preparation or filing of any document or report required to be filed with the Commission pursuant to this subpart or otherwise.

(b) (1) No officer or director of an issuer, or any other person acting under the direction thereof, shall directly or indirectly take any action to coerce, manipulate, mislead, or fraudulently influence any independent public or certified public accountant engaged in the performance of an audit or

---

* 17 C.F.R. §§ 240.13b1-2 to b2-2.

review of the financial statements of that issuer that are required to be filed with the Commission pursuant to this subpart or otherwise if that person knew or should have known that such action, if successful, could result in rendering the issuer's financial statements materially misleading.

(2) For purposes of paragraphs (b)(1) and (c)(2) of this section, actions that, "if successful, could result in rendering the issuer's financial statements materially misleading" include, but are not limited to, actions taken at any time with respect to the professional engagement period to coerce, manipulate, mislead, or fraudulently influence an auditor:

   (i)   To issue or reissue a report on an issuer's financial statements that is not warranted in the circumstances (due to material violations of generally accepted accounting principles, generally accepted auditing standards, or other professional or regulatory standards);

   (ii) Not to perform audit, review, or other procedures required by generally accepted auditing standards or other professional standards;

   (iii) Not to withdraw an issued report; or

   (iv) Not to communicate matters to an issuer's audit committee.

OPINION PROCEDURE REGULATIONS*

§ 80.1 PURPOSE.

These procedures enable issuers and domestic concerns to obtain an opinion of the Attorney General as to whether certain specified, prospective—not hypothetical—conduct conforms with the Department's present enforcement policy regarding the anti-bribery provisions of the Foreign Corrupt Practices Act of 1977, as amended, 15 U.S.C. § 78dd-1 and 78dd-2. An opinion issued pursuant to these procedures is a Foreign Corrupt Practices Act opinion (hereinafter FCPA Opinion).

§ 80.2 SUBMISSION REQUIREMENTS.

A request for an FCPA Opinion must be submitted in writing. An original and five copies of the request should be addressed to the Assistant Attorney General in charge of the Criminal Division, Attention: FCPA Opinion Group. The mailing address is P.O. Box 28188, Central Station, Washington, DC 20038. The address for hand delivery is Room 2424, Bond Building, 1400 New York Avenue, NW., Washington, DC 20005.

§ 80.3 TRANSACTION.

The entire transaction which is the subject of the request must be an actual—not a hypothetical—transaction but need not involve only prospective conduct. However, a request will not be considered unless that portion of the transaction for

---

* 28 C.F.R §§ 80.1–.16.

which an opinion is sought involves only prospective conduct. An executed contract is not a prerequisite and, in most—if not all—instances, an opinion request should be made prior to the requestor's commitment to proceed with a transaction.

§ 80.4 ISSUER OR DOMESTIC CONCERN.

The request must be submitted by an issuer or domestic concern within the meaning of 15 U.S.C. § 78dd-1 and 78dd-2, respectively, that is also a party to the transaction which is the subject of the request.

§ 80.5 AFFECTED PARTIES.

An FCPA Opinion shall have no application to any party which does not join in the request for the opinion.

§ 80.6 GENERAL REQUIREMENTS.

Each request shall be specific and must be accompanied by all relevant and material information bearing on the conduct for which an FCPA Opinion is requested and on the circumstances of the prospective conduct, including background information, complete copies of all operative documents, and detailed statements of all collateral or oral understandings, if any. The requesting issuer or domestic concern is under an affirmative obligation to make full and true disclosure with respect to the conduct for which an opinion is requested. Each request on behalf of a requesting issuer or corporate domestic concern must be signed by an appropriate senior officer with operational responsibility for the conduct that is the subject of the request and who has been designated by the requestor's chief executive officer to sign the opinion request. In appropriate cases, the Department of Justice may require the chief executive officer of each requesting issuer or corporate domestic concern to sign the request. All requests of other domestic concerns must also be signed. The person signing the request must certify that it contains a true, correct, and complete disclosure with respect to the proposed conduct and the circumstances of the conduct.

§ 80.7 ADDITIONAL INFORMATION.

If an issuer's or domestic concern's submission does not contain all of the information required by Section 80.6, the Department of Justice may request whatever additional information or documents it deems necessary to review the matter. The Department must do so within 30 days of receipt of the opinion request, or, in the case of an incomplete response to a previous request for additional information, within 30 days of receipt of such response. Each issuer or domestic concern requesting an FCPA Opinion must promptly provide the information requested.

A request will not be deemed complete until the Department of Justice receives such additional information. Such additional information, if furnished orally, shall be promptly confirmed in writing, signed by the same person or officer who signed the initial request and certified by this person or officer to be a true, correct, and complete disclosure of the requested information. In connection with any request for an FCPA Opinion, the Department of Justice may conduct whatever independent investigation it believes appropriate.

§ 80.8 ATTORNEY GENERAL OPINION.

The Attorney General or his designee shall, within 30 days after receiving a request that complies with the foregoing procedure, respond to the request by issuing an opinion that states whether the prospective conduct, would, for purposes of the Department of Justice's present enforcement policy, violate 15 U.S.C. § 78dd-1 and 78dd-2. The Department of Justice may also take such other positions or action as it considers appropriate. Should the Department request additional information, the Department's response shall be made within 30 days after receipt of such additional information.

§ 80.9 NO ORAL OPINION.

No oral clearance, release, or other statement purporting to limit the enforcement discretion of the Department of Justice may be given. The requesting issuer or domestic concern may rely only upon a written FCPA Opinion letter signed by the Attorney General or his designee.

§ 80.10 REBUTTABLE PRESUMPTION.

In any action brought under the applicable provisions of 15 U.S.C. §§ 78dd-1 and 78dd-2, there shall be a rebuttable presumption that a requestor's conduct, which is specified in a request, and for which the Attorney General has issued an opinion that such conduct is in conformity with the Department's present enforcement policy, is in compliance with those provisions of the FCPA. Such a presumption may be rebutted by a preponderance of the evidence. In considering the presumption, a court, in accordance with the statute, shall weigh all relevant factors, including but not limited to whether information submitted to the Attorney General was accurate and complete and whether the activity was within the scope of the conduct specified in any request received by the Attorney General.

§ 80.11 EFFECT OF FCPA OPINION.

Except as specified in Section 80.10, an FCPA Opinion will not bind or obligate any agency other than the Department of Justice. It will not affect the requesting issuer's or domestic concern's obligations to any other agency, or under any statutory or regulatory provision other than those specifically cited in the particular FCPA Opinion.

§ 80.12 ACCOUNTING REQUIREMENTS.

Neither the submission of a request for an FCPA Opinion, its pendency, nor the issuance of an FCPA Opinion, shall in any way alter the responsibility of an issuer to comply with the accounting requirements of 15 U.S.C. § 78m(b)(2) and (3).

§ 80.13 SCOPE OF FCPA OPINION.

An FCPA Opinion will state only the Attorney General's opinion as to whether the prospective conduct would violate the Department's present enforcement policy under 15 U.S.C. §§ 78dd-1 and 78dd-2. If the conduct for which an FCPA Opinion is requested is subject to approval by any other agency, such FCPA Opinion shall in no way be taken to indicate the Department of Justice's views on the legal or factual issues that may be raised before that agency, or in an appeal from the agency's decision.

§ 80.14 DISCLOSURE.

(a) Any document or other material which is provided to, received by, or prepared in the Department of Justice or any other department or agency of the United States in connection with a request by an issuer or domestic concern under the foregoing procedure shall be exempt from disclosure under 5 U.S.C. § 552 and shall not, except with the consent of the issuer or domestic concern, be made publicly available, regard-less of whether the Attorney General responds to such a request or the issuer or domestic concern withdraws such request before receiving a response.

(b) Nothing contained in paragraph (a) of this section shall limit the Department of Justice's right to issue, at its discretion, a release describing the identity of the requesting issuer or domestic concern, the identity of the foreign country in which the proposed conduct is to take place, the general nature and circumstances of the proposed conduct, and the action taken by the Department of Justice in response to the FCPA Opinion request. Such release shall not disclose either the identity of any foreign sales agents or other types of identifying information. The Department of Justice shall index such releases and place them in a file available to the public upon request.

(c) A requestor may request that the release not disclose proprietary information.

§ 80.15 WITHDRAWAL.

A request submitted under the foregoing procedure may be withdrawn prior to the time the Attorney General issues an opinion in response to such request. Any request so withdrawn shall have no force or effect. The Department of Justice reserves the right to retain any FCPA Opinion request, documents, and information submitted to it under this procedure or otherwise and to use them for any governmental purposes, subject to the restrictions on disclosures in Section 80.14.

§ 80.16 ADDITIONAL REQUESTS.

Additional requests for FCPA Opinions may be filed with the Attorney General under the foregoing procedure regarding other prospective conduct that is beyond the scope of conduct specified in previous requests.

SEC Staff Accounting
Bulletin: No. 99—Materiality*

AGENCY: Securities and Exchange Commission

ACTION: Publication of Staff Accounting Bulletin

SUMMARY: This staff accounting bulletin expresses the views of the staff that exclusive reliance on certain quantitative benchmarks to assess materiality in preparing financial statements and performing audits of those financial statements is inappropriate; misstatements are not immaterial simply because they fall beneath a numerical threshold.

DATES: Effective August 12, 1999.

FOR FURTHER INFORMATION CONTACT: W. Scott Bayless, Associate Chief Accountant, or Robert E. Burns, Chief Counsel, Office of the Chief Accountant (202-942-4400), or David R. Fredrickson, Office of General Counsel (202-942-0900), Securities and Exchange Commission, 450 Fifth Street, N.W., Washington, D.C. 20549-1103; electronic addresses: BaylessWS@sec.gov; BurnsR@sec.gov; FredricksonD@sec.gov.

SUPPLEMENTARY INFORMATION: The statements in the staff accounting bulletins are not rules or interpretations of the Commission, nor are they published as bearing the Commission's official approval. They represent interpretations and practices followed by the Division of Corporation Finance and the

---

* Staff Accounting Bulletin No. 99, Securities and Exchange Commission, Release No. SAB 99, 17 C.F.R. pt. 211.

Office of the Chief Accountant in administering the disclosure requirements of the Federal securities laws.

Jonathan G. Katz
Secretary
Date: August 12, 1999

Part 211—(AMEND) Accordingly, Part 211 of Title 17 of the Code of Federal Regulations is amended by adding Staff Accounting Bulletin No. 99 to the table found in Subpart B.

STAFF ACCOUNTING BULLETIN NO. 99

The staff hereby adds Section M to Topic 1 of the Staff Accounting Bulletin Series. Section M, entitled "Materiality," provides guidance in applying materiality thresholds to the preparation of financial statements filed with the Commission and the performance of audits of those financial statements.

STAFF ACCOUNTING BULLETINS

TOPIC 1: FINANCIAL STATEMENTS

★ ★ ★ ★ ★

M. Materiality

1. Assessing Materiality

Facts: During the course of preparing or auditing year-end financial statements, financial management or the registrant's independent auditor becomes aware of misstatements in a registrant's financial statements. When combined, the misstatements result in a 4% overstatement of net income and a $.02 (4%) overstatement of earnings per share. Because no item in the registrant's consolidated financial statements is misstated by more than 5%, management and the independent auditor conclude that the deviation from generally accepted accounting principles ("GAAP") is immaterial and that the accounting is permissible.[1]

Question: Each Statement of Financial Accounting Standards adopted by the Financial Accounting Standards Board ("FASB") states, "The provisions of this Statement need not be applied to immaterial items." In the staff's view, may a registrant or the auditor of its financial statements assume the immateriality of items that fall below a percentage threshold set by management or the auditor to determine whether amounts and items are material to the financial statements?

Interpretive Response: No. The staff is aware that certain registrants, over time, have developed quantitative thresholds as "rules of thumb" to assist in the preparation of their financial statements, and that auditors also have used these thresholds in their evaluation of whether items might be considered material to users of a registrant's financial statements. One rule of thumb in particular suggests that the misstatement or omission[2] of an item that falls under a 5% threshold is not material in the absence of particularly egregious circumstances, such as self-dealing or misappropriation by senior management. The staff reminds registrants and the auditors of their financial statements that exclusive reliance on this or any percentage or numerical threshold has no basis in the accounting literature or the law.

The use of a percentage as a numerical threshold, such as 5%, may provide the basis for a preliminary assumption that—without considering all relevant circumstances—a deviation of less than the specified percentage with respect to a particular item on the registrant's financial statements is unlikely to be material. The staff has no objection to such a "rule of thumb" as an initial step in assessing materiality. But quantifying, in percentage terms, the magnitude of a misstatement is only the beginning of an analysis of materiality; it cannot appropriately be used as a substitute for a full analysis of all relevant considerations.

Materiality concerns the significance of an item to users of a registrant's financial statements. A matter is "material" if there is a substantial likelihood that a reasonable person would consider it important. In its Statement of Financial Accounting Concepts No. 2, the FASB stated the essence of the concept of materiality as follows:

> The omission or misstatement of an item in a financial report is material if, in the light of surrounding circumstances, the magnitude of the item is such that it is probable that the judgment of a reasonable person relying upon the report would have been changed or influenced by the inclusion or correction of the item.[3]

This formulation in the accounting literature is in substance identical to the formulation used by the courts in interpreting the federal securities laws. The Supreme Court has held that a fact is material if there is—

> a substantial likelihood that the . . . fact would have been viewed by the reasonable investor as having significantly altered the "total mix" of information made available.[4]

Under the governing principles, an assessment of materiality requires that one views the facts in the context of the "surrounding circumstances," as the accounting literature puts it, or the "total mix" of information, in the words of the Supreme Court. In the context of a misstatement of a financial statement item, while the "total mix" includes the size in numerical or percentage terms of the misstatement, it also includes the factual context in which the user of financial statements would view the financial statement item. The shorthand in the accounting and auditing literature for this analysis is that financial management and the auditor must consider both "quantitative" and "qualitative" factors in assessing an item's materiality.[5] Court decisions, Commission rules and enforcement actions, and accounting and auditing literature[6] have all considered "qualitative" factors in various contexts.

The FASB has long emphasized that materiality cannot be reduced to a numerical formula. In its Concepts Statement No. 2, the FASB noted that some had urged it to promulgate quantitative materiality guides for use in a variety of situations. The FASB rejected such an approach as representing only a "minority view," stating—

> The predominant view is that materiality judgments can properly be made only by those who have all the facts. The Board's present position is that no general standards of materiality could be formulated to take into account all the considerations that enter into an experienced human judgment.[7]

The FASB noted that, in certain limited circumstances, the Commission and other authoritative bodies had issued quantitative materiality guidance, citing as examples guidelines ranging from one to ten percent with respect to a variety of disclosures.[8] And it took account of contradictory studies, one showing a lack of uniformity among auditors on materiality judgments, and another suggesting widespread use of a "rule of thumb" of five to ten percent of net income.[9] The FASB also considered whether an evaluation of materiality could be based solely on anticipating the market's reaction to accounting information.[10]

The FASB rejected a formulaic approach to discharging "the onerous duty of making materiality decisions"[11] in favor of an approach that takes into account all the relevant considerations. In so doing, it made clear that—

> [M]agnitude by itself, without regard to the nature of the item and the circumstances in which the judgment has to be made, will not generally be a sufficient basis for a materiality judgment.[12]

Evaluation of materiality requires a registrant and its auditor to consider *all* the relevant circumstances, and the staff believes that there are numerous circumstances in which misstatements below 5% could well be material. Qualitative factors may cause misstatements of quantitatively small amounts to be material; as stated in the auditing literature:

> As a result of the interaction of quantitative and qualitative considerations in materiality judgments, misstatements of relatively small amounts that come to the auditor's attention could have a material effect on the financial statements.[13]

Among the considerations that may well render material a quantitatively small misstatement of a financial statement item are—

- Whether the misstatement arises from an item capable of precise measurement or whether it arises from an estimate and, if so, the degree of imprecision inherent in the estimate[14]
- Whether the misstatement masks a change in earnings or other trends
- Whether the misstatement hides a failure to meet analysts' consensus expectations for the enterprise
- Whether the misstatement changes a loss into income or vice versa
- Whether the misstatement concerns a segment or other portion of the registrant's business that has been identified as playing a significant role in the registrant's operations or profitability
- Whether the misstatement affects the registrant's compliance with regulatory requirements
- Whether the misstatement affects the registrant's compliance with loan covenants or other contractual requirements

- Whether the misstatement has the effect of increasing management's compensation-for example, by satisfying requirements for the award of bonuses or other forms of incentive compensation
- Whether the misstatement involves concealment of an unlawful transaction.

This is not an exhaustive list of the circumstances that may affect the materiality of a quantitatively small misstatement.[15] Among other factors, the demonstrated volatility of the price of a registrant's securities in response to certain types of disclosures may provide guidance as to whether investors regard quantitatively small misstatements as material. Consideration of potential market reaction to disclosure of a misstatement is by itself "too blunt an instrument to be depended on" in considering whether a fact is material.[16] When, however, management or the independent auditor expects (based, for example, on a pattern of market performance) that a known misstatement may result in a significant positive or negative market reaction, that expected reaction should be taken into account when considering whether a misstatement is material.[17]

For the reasons noted above, the staff believes that a registrant and the auditors of its financial statements should not assume that even small intentional misstatements in financial statements, for example those pursuant to actions to "manage" earnings, are immaterial.[18] While the intent of management does not render a misstatement material, it may provide significant evidence of materiality. The evidence may be particularly compelling where management has intentionally misstated items in the financial statements to "manage" reported earnings. In that instance, it presumably has done so believing that the resulting amounts and trends would be significant to users of the registrant's financial statements.[19] The staff believes that investors generally would regard as significant a management practice to over- or understate earnings up to an amount just short of a percentage threshold in order to "manage" earnings. Investors presumably also would regard as significant an accounting practice that, in essence, rendered all earnings figures subject to a management-directed margin of misstatement.

The materiality of a misstatement may turn on where it appears in the financial statements. For example, a misstatement may involve a segment of the registrant's operations. In that instance, in assessing materiality of a misstatement to the financial statements taken as a whole, registrants and their auditors should consider not only the size of the misstatement but also the significance of the segment information to the financial statements taken as a whole.[20] "A misstatement of the revenue and operating profit of a relatively small segment that is represented by management to be important to the future profitability of the entity"[21] is more likely to be material to investors than a misstatement in a segment that management has not identified as especially important. In assessing the materiality of misstatements in segment information—as with materiality generally—situations may arise in practice where the auditor will conclude that a matter relating to segment information is qualitatively material even though, in his or her judgment, it is quantitatively immaterial to the financial statements taken as a whole.[22]

Aggregating and Netting Misstatements

In determining whether multiple misstatements cause the financial statements to be materially misstated, registrants and the auditors of their financial statements should consider each misstatement separately and the aggregate effect of all misstatements.[23] A registrant and its auditor should evaluate misstatements in light of quantitative and qualitative factors and "consider whether, in relation to individual line item amounts, subtotals, or totals in the financial statements, they materially misstate the financial statements taken as a whole."[24] This requires consideration of "the significance of an item to a particular entity (for example, inventories to a manufacturing company), the pervasiveness of the misstatement (such as whether it affects the presentation of numerous financial statement items), and the effect of the misstatement on the financial statements taken as a whole. . . ."[25]

Registrants and their auditors first should consider whether each misstatement is material, irrespective of its effect when combined with other misstatements. The literature notes that the analysis should consider whether the misstatement of "individual amounts" causes a material misstatement of the financial statements taken as a whole. As with materiality generally, this analysis requires consideration of both quantitative and qualitative factors.

If the misstatement of an individual amount causes the financial statements as a whole to be materially misstated, that effect cannot be eliminated by other misstatements whose effect may be to diminish the impact of the misstatement on other financial statement items. To take an obvious example, if a registrant's revenues are a material financial statement item and if they are materially overstated, the financial statements taken as a whole will be materially misleading even if the effect on earnings is completely offset by an equivalent overstatement of expenses.

Even though a misstatement of an individual amount may not cause the financial statements taken as a whole to be materially misstated, it may nonetheless, when aggregated with other misstatements, render the financial statements taken as a whole to be materially misleading. Registrants and the auditors of their financial statements accordingly should consider the effect of the misstatement on subtotals or totals. The auditor should aggregate all misstatements that affect each subtotal or total and consider whether the misstatements in the aggregate affect the subtotal or total in a way that causes the registrant's financial statements taken as a whole to be materially misleading.[26]

The staff believes that, in considering the aggregate effect of multiple misstatements on a subtotal or total, registrants and the auditors of their financial statements should exercise particular care when considering whether to offset (or the appropriateness of offsetting) a misstatement of an estimated amount with a misstatement of an item capable of precise measurement. As noted above, assessments of materiality should never be purely mechanical; given the imprecision inherent in estimates, there is by definition a corresponding imprecision in the aggregation of misstatements involving estimates with those that do not involve an estimate.

Registrants and auditors also should consider the effect of misstatements from prior periods on the current financial statements. For example, the auditing literature states,

Matters underlying adjustments proposed by the auditor but not recorded by the entity could potentially cause future financial statements to be materially misstated, even though the auditor has concluded that the adjustments are not material to the current financial statements.[27]

This may be particularly the case where immaterial misstatements recur in several years and the cumulative effect becomes material in the current year.

2. Immaterial Misstatements That Are Intentional

Facts: A registrant's management intentionally has made adjustments to various financial statement items in a manner inconsistent with GAAP. In each accounting period in which such actions were taken, none of the individual adjustments is by itself material, nor is the aggregate effect on the financial statements taken as a whole material for the period. The registrant's earnings "management" has been effected at the direction or acquiescence of management in the belief that any deviations from GAAP have been immaterial and that accordingly the accounting is permissible.

Question: In the staff's view, may a registrant make intentional immaterial misstatements in its financial statements?

Interpretive Response: No. In certain circumstances, intentional immaterial misstatements are unlawful.

Considerations of the Books and Records Provisions under the Exchange Act

Even if misstatements are immaterial,[28] registrants must comply with Sections 13(b)(2)–(7) of the Securities Exchange Act of 1934 (the "Exchange Act").[29] Under these provisions, each registrant with securities registered pursuant to Section 12 of the Exchange Act,[30] or required to file reports pursuant to Section 15(d),[31] must make and keep books, records, and accounts, which, in reasonable detail, accurately and fairly reflect the transactions and dispositions of assets of the registrant and must maintain internal accounting controls that are sufficient to provide reasonable assurances that, among other things, transactions are recorded as necessary to permit the preparation of financial statements in conformity with GAAP.[32] In this context, determinations of what constitutes "reasonable assurance" and "reasonable detail" are based not on a "materiality" analysis but on the level of detail and degree of assurance that would satisfy prudent officials in the conduct of their own affairs.[33] Accordingly, failure to record accurately immaterial items, in some instances, may result in violations of the securities laws.

The staff recognizes that there is limited authoritative guidance[34] regarding the "reasonableness" standard in Section 13(b)(2) of the Exchange Act. A principal statement of the Commission's policy in this area is set forth in an address given in 1981 by then Chairman Harold M. Williams.[35] In his address, Chairman Williams noted that, like materiality, "reasonableness" is not an "absolute standard of exactitude for corporate records."[36] Unlike materiality, however, "reasonableness" is not solely a measure of the significance of a financial statement item to investors. "Reasonableness," in this context, reflects a judgment as to whether an issuer's failure to correct a known misstatement implicates the purposes underlying the accounting provisions of Sections 13(b)(2)–(7) of the Exchange Act.[37]

In assessing whether a misstatement results in a violation of a registrant's obligation to keep books and records that are accurate "in reasonable detail," registrants and their auditors should consider, in addition to the factors discussed above concerning an evaluation of a misstatement's potential materiality, the factors set forth below.

- *The significance of the misstatement.* Though the staff does not believe that registrants need to make finely calibrated determinations of significance with respect to immaterial items, plainly it is "reasonable" to treat misstatements whose effects are clearly inconsequential differently than more significant ones.
- *How the misstatement arose.* It is unlikely that it is ever "reasonable" for registrants to record misstatements or not to correct known misstatements—even immaterial ones—as part of an ongoing effort directed by or known to senior management for the purposes of "managing" earnings. On the other hand, insignificant misstatements that arise from the operation of systems or recurring processes in the normal course of business generally will not cause a registrant's books to be inaccurate "in reasonable detail."[38]
- *The cost of correcting the misstatement.* The books and records provisions of the Exchange Act do not require registrants to make major expenditures to correct small misstatements.[39] Conversely, where there is little cost or delay involved in correcting a misstatement, failing to do so is unlikely to be "reasonable."
- *The clarity of authoritative accounting guidance with respect to the misstatement.* Where reasonable minds may differ about the appropriate accounting treatment of a financial statement item, a failure to correct it may not render the registrant's financial statements inaccurate "in reasonable detail." Where, however, there is little ground for reasonable disagreement, the case for leaving a misstatement uncorrected is correspondingly weaker.

There may be other indicators of "reasonableness" that registrants and their auditors may ordinarily consider. Because the judgment is not mechanical, the staff will be inclined to continue to defer to judgments that "allow a business, acting in good faith, to comply with the Act's accounting provisions in an innovative and cost-effective way."[40]

The Auditor's Response to Intentional Misstatements

Section 10A(b) of the Exchange Act requires auditors to take certain actions upon discovery of an "illegal act."[41] The statute specifies that these obligations are triggered "whether or not [the illegal acts are] perceived to have a material effect on the financial statements of the issuer. . . ." Among other things, Section 10A(b)(1) requires the auditor to inform the appropriate level of management of an illegal act (unless clearly inconsequential) and assure that the registrant's audit committee is "adequately informed" with respect to the illegal act.

As noted, an intentional misstatement of immaterial items in a registrant's financial statements may violate Section 13(b)(2) of the Exchange Act and thus be an illegal act. When such a violation occurs, an auditor must take steps to see that the registrant's audit committee is "adequately informed" about the illegal act. Because Section 10A(b)(1) is triggered regardless of whether an illegal act has a material effect on the registrant's financial statements, where the illegal act consists of a misstatement in the registrant's financial statements, the auditor will be required to report that illegal act to the audit committee irrespective of any "netting" of the misstatements with other financial statement items.

The requirements of Section 10A echo the auditing literature. See, for example, Statement on Auditing Standards No. ("SAS") 54, "Illegal Acts by Clients," and SAS 82, "Consideration of Fraud in a Financial Statement Audit." Pursuant to paragraph 38 of SAS 82, if the auditor determines there is evidence that fraud may exist, the auditor must discuss the matter with the appropriate level of management. The auditor must report directly to the audit committee fraud involving senior management and fraud that causes a material misstatement of the financial statements. Paragraph 4 of SAS 82 states that "misstatements arising from fraudulent financial reporting are intentional misstatements or omissions of amounts or disclosures in financial statements to deceive financial statement users."[42] SAS 82 further states that fraudulent financial reporting may involve falsification or alteration of accounting records; misrepresenting or omitting events, transactions or other information in the financial statements; and the intentional misapplication of accounting principles relating to amounts, classifications, the manner of presentation, or disclosures in the financial statements.[43] The clear implication of SAS 82 is that immaterial misstatements may be fraudulent financial reporting.[44]

Auditors that learn of intentional misstatements may also be required to (1) reevaluate the degree of audit risk involved in the audit engagement, (2) determine whether to revise the nature, timing, and extent of audit procedures accordingly, and (3) consider whether to resign.[45]

Intentional misstatements also may signal the existence of reportable conditions or material weaknesses in the registrant's system of internal accounting control designed to detect and deter improper accounting and financial reporting.[46] As stated by the National Commission on Fraudulent Financial Reporting, also known as the Treadway Commission, in its 1987 report, the tone set by top management—the corporate environment or culture within which financial reporting occurs—is the most important factor contributing to the integrity of the financial reporting process. Notwithstanding an impressive set of written rules and procedures, if the tone set by management is lax, fraudulent financial reporting is more likely to occur.[47]

An auditor is required to report to a registrant's audit committee any reportable conditions or material weaknesses in a registrant's system of internal accounting control that the auditor discovers in the course of the examination of the registrant's financial statements.[48]

GAAP Precedence over Industry Practice

Some have argued to the staff that registrants should be permitted to follow an industry accounting practice even though that practice is inconsistent with authoritative accounting literature. This situation might occur if a practice is developed when there are few transactions and the accounting results are clearly inconsequential, and that practice never changes despite a subsequent growth in the number or materiality of such transactions. The staff disagrees with this argument. Authoritative literature takes precedence over industry practice that is contrary to GAAP.[49]

General Comments

This SAB is not intended to change current law or guidance in the accounting or auditing literature.[50] This SAB and the authoritative accounting literature cannot specifically address all of the novel and complex business transactions and events that may occur. Accordingly, registrants may account for, and make disclosures about, these transactions and events based on analogies to similar situations or other factors. The staff may not, however, always be persuaded that a registrant's determination is the most appropriate under the circumstances. When disagreements occur after a transaction or an event has been reported, the consequences may be severe for registrants, auditors, and, most importantly, the users of financial statements who have a right to expect consistent accounting and reporting for, and disclosure of, similar transactions and events. The staff, therefore, encourages registrants and auditors to discuss on a timely basis with the staff proposed accounting treatments for, or disclosures about, transactions or events that are not specifically covered by the existing accounting literature.

✪ NOTES

1. American Institute of Certified Public Accountants ("AICPA"), Codification of Statements on Auditing Standards ("AU") § 312, "Audit Risk and Materiality in Conducting an Audit," states that the auditor should consider audit risk and materiality both in (a) planning and setting the scope for the audit and (b) evaluating whether the financial statements taken as a whole are fairly presented in all material respects in conformity with generally accepted accounting principles. The purpose of this Staff Accounting Bulletin ("SAB") is to provide guidance to financial management and independent auditors with respect to the evaluation of the materiality of misstatements that are identified in the audit process or preparation of the financial statements (i.e., (b) above). This SAB is not intended to provide definitive guidance for assessing "materiality" in other contexts, such as evaluations of auditor independence, as other factors may apply. There may be other rules that address financial presentation. See, e.g., Rule 2a-4, 17 C.F.R. 270.2a-4, under the Investment Company Act of 1940.

2. As used in this SAB, "misstatement" or "omission" refers to a financial statement assertion that would not be in conformity with GAAP.

3. FASB, Statement of Financial Accounting Concepts No. 2, *Qualitative Characteristics of Accounting Information* ("Concepts Statement No. 2")], ¶ 132 (1980). *See also* Concepts Statement No. 2, Glossary of Terms—Materiality.

4. TSC Industries v. Northway, Inc., 426 U.S. 438, 449 (1976). *See also* Basic, Inc. v. Levinson, 485 U.S. 224 (1988). As the Supreme Court has noted, determinations of materiality require "delicate assessments of the inferences a 'reasonable shareholder' would draw from a given set of facts and the significance of those inferences to him. . . ." TSC Industries, 426 U.S. at 450.

5. *See, e.g.,* Concepts Statement No. 2, 123–24; AU § 312.10 (". . . materiality judgments are made in light of surrounding circumstances and necessarily involve both quantitative and qualitative considerations."); AU § 312.34 ("Qualitative considerations also influence the auditor in reaching a conclusion as to whether misstatements are material."). As used in the accounting literature and in this SAB, "qualitative" materiality refers to the surrounding circumstances that inform an investor's evaluation of financial statement entries. Whether events may be material to investors for nonfinancial reasons is a matter not addressed by this SAB.

6. *See, e.g.,* Rule 1-02(o) of Regulation S-X, 17 C.F.R. 210.1-02(o); Rule 405 of Regulation C, 17 C.F.R. 230.405; Rule 12b-2, 17 C.F.R. 240.12b-2; AU §§ 312.10-.11, 317.13, 411.04 n. 1, and 508.36; *In re* Kidder Peabody Securities Litigation, 10 F. Supp. 2d 398 (S.D.N.Y. 1998); Parnes v. Gateway 2000, Inc., 122 F.3d 539 (8th Cir. 1997); *In re* Westinghouse Securities Litigation, 90 F.3d 696 (3d Cir. 1996); In the Matter of W.R. Grace & Co., Accounting and Auditing Enforcement Release No. ("AAER") 1140 (June 30, 1999); In the Matter of Eugene Gaughan, AAER 1141 (June 30, 1999); In the Matter of Thomas Scanlon, AAER 1142 (June 30, 1999); and *In re* Sensormatic Electronics Corporation, Sec. Act Rel. No. 7518 (March 25, 1998).

7. Concepts Statement No. 2, 131 (1980).

8. Concepts Statement No. 2, 131, 166.

9. Concepts Statement No. 2, 167.

10. Concepts Statement No. 2, 168-69.

11. Concepts Statement No. 2, 170.

12. Concepts Statement No. 2, 125.

13. AU § 312.11.

14. As stated in Concepts Statement No. 2, 130: Another factor in materiality judgments is the degree of precision that is attainable in estimating the judgment item. The amount of deviation that is considered immaterial may increase as the attainable degree of precision decreases. For example, accounts payable usually can be estimated more accurately than can contingent liabilities arising from litigation or threats of it, and a deviation considered to be material in the first case may be quite trivial in the second. This SAB is not intended to change current law or guidance in the accounting literature regarding accounting estimates. *See, e.g.,* Accounting Principles Board Opinion No. 20, Accounting Changes 10, 11, 31-33 (July 1971).

15. The staff understands that the Big Five Audit Materiality Task Force ("Task Force") was convened in March of 1998 and has made recommendations to the Auditing Standards Board including suggestions regarding communications with audit committees about unadjusted misstatements. *See generally* Big Five Audit Materiality Task Force, "Materiality in a Financial Statement Audit—Considering Qualitative Factors When Evaluating Audit Findings" (August 1998). The Task Force memorandum is available at **http://www.aicpa.org.**

16. *See* Concepts Statement No. 2, 169.

17. If management does not expect a significant market reaction, a misstatement still may be material and should be evaluated under the criteria discussed in this SAB.

18. Intentional management of earnings and intentional misstatements, as used in this SAB, do not include insignificant errors and omissions that may occur in systems and recurring processes in the normal course of business. *See* notes 38 and 50 *infra.*

19. Assessments of materiality should occur not only at year-end, but also during the preparation of each quarterly or interim financial statement. *See, e.g.,* In the Matter of Venator Group, Inc., AAER 1049 (June 29, 1998).

20. *See, e.g.,* In the Matter of W.R. Grace & Co., AAER 1140 (June 30, 1999).

21. AU § 326.33.

22. *Id.*

23. The auditing literature notes that the "concept of materiality recognizes that some matters, either individually or in the aggregate, are important for fair presentation of financial statements in conformity with generally accepted accounting principles." AU § 312.03. *See also* AU § 312.04.

24. AU § 312.34. Quantitative materiality assessments often are made by comparing adjustments to revenues, gross profit, pretax and net income, total assets, stockholders' equity, or individual line items in the financial statements. The particular items in the financial statements to be considered as a basis for the materiality determination depend on the proposed adjustment to be made and other factors, such as those identified in this SAB. For example, an adjustment to inventory that is immaterial to pretax income or net income may be material to the financial statements because it may affect a working capital ratio or cause the registrant to be in default of loan covenants.

25. AU § 508.36.

26. AU § 312.34

27. AU § 380.09.

28. FASB Statements of Financial Accounting Standards ("Standards" or "Statements") generally provide that "[t]he provisions of this Statement need not be applied to immaterial items." This SAB is consistent with that provision of the Statements. In theory, this language is subject to the interpretation that the registrant is free intentionally to set forth immaterial items in financial statements in a manner that plainly would be contrary to GAAP if the misstatement were material. The staff believes that the FASB did not intend this result.

29. 15 U.S.C. §§ 78m(b)(2)-(7).

30. 15 U.S.C. § 78l.

31. 15 U.S.C. § 78o(d).

32. Criminal liability may be imposed if a person knowingly circumvents or knowingly fails to implement a system of internal accounting controls or knowingly falsifies books, records or accounts. 15 U.S.C. §§ 78m(4) and (5). *See also* Rule 13b2-1 under the Exchange Act, 17 C.F.R. 240.13b2-1, which states, "No person shall, directly or indirectly, falsify or cause to be falsified, any book, record or account subject to Section 13(b)(2)(A) of the Securities Exchange Act."

33. 15 U.S.C. § 78m(b)(7). The books and records provisions of section 13(b) of the Exchange Act originally were passed as part of the Foreign Corrupt Practices Act ("FCPA"). In the conference committee report regarding the 1988 amendments to the FCPA, the committee stated,

> The conference committee adopted the prudent man qualification in order to clarify that the current standard does not connote an unrealistic degree of exactitude or precision. The concept of reasonableness of necessity contemplates the weighing of a number of relevant factors, including the costs of compliance.

CONG. REC. H2116 (daily ed. April 20, 1988).

34. So far as the staff is aware, there is only one judicial decision that discusses Section 13(b)(2) of the Exchange Act in any detail, SEC v. World-Wide Coin Investments, Ltd., 567 F. Supp. 724 (N.D. Ga. 1983), and the courts generally have found that no private right of action exists under the accounting and books and records provisions of the Exchange Act. *See, e.g.,* Lamb v. Phillip Morris Inc., 915 F.2d 1024 (6th Cir. 1990), and JS Service Center Corporation v. General Electric Technical Services Company, 937 F. Supp. 216 (S.D.N.Y. 1996).

35. The Commission adopted the address as a formal statement of policy in Securities Exchange Act Release No. 17500 (January 29, 1981), 46 Fed. Reg. 11,544 (February 9, 1981), 21 SEC Docket 1466 (February 10, 1981).

36. *Id.* at 46 Fed. Reg. 11,546.

37. *Id.*

38. For example, the conference report regarding the 1988 amendments to the FCPA stated, "The Conferees intend to codify current Securities and Exchange Commission (SEC) enforcement policy that penalties not be imposed for insignificant or technical infractions or inadvertent conduct. The amendment adopted by the Conferees [Section 13(b)(4)] accomplishes this by providing that criminal penalties shall not be imposed for failing to comply with the FCPA's books and records or accounting provisions. This provision [Section 13(b)(5)] is meant to ensure that criminal penalties would be imposed where acts of commission or omission in keeping books or records or administering accounting controls have the purpose of falsifying books, records or accounts, or of circumventing the accounting controls set forth in the Act. This would include the deliberate falsification of books and records and other conduct calculated to evade the internal accounting controls requirement." CONG. REC. H2115 (daily ed. April 20, 1988).

39. As Chairman Williams noted with respect to the internal control provisions of the FCPA, "[t]housands of dollars ordinarily should not be spent conserving hundreds." 46 Fed. Reg. 11,546.

40. *Id.* at 11,547.

41. Section 10A(f) defines, for purposes of Section 10A, an *illegal act* as "an act or omission that violates any law, or any rule or regulation having the force of law." This is broader than the definition of an "illegal act" in AU § 317.02, which states, "Illegal acts by clients do not include personal misconduct by the entity's personnel unrelated to their business activities."

42. AU § 316.04. *See also* AU § 316.03. An unintentional illegal act triggers the same procedures and considerations by the auditor as a fraudulent misstatement if the illegal act has a direct and material effect on the financial statements. *See* AU §§ 110 n. 1, 316 n. 1, 317.05, and 317.07. Although distinguishing between intentional and unintentional misstatements is often difficult, the auditor must plan and perform the audit to obtain reasonable assurance that the financial statements are free of material misstatements in either case. *See* AU § 316 note 3.

43. AU § 316.04. Although the auditor is not required to plan or perform the audit to detect misstatements that are immaterial to the financial statements, SAS No. 82 requires the auditor to evaluate several fraud "risk factors" that may bring such misstatements to his or her attention. For example, an analysis of fraud risk factors under SAS No. 82 must include, among other things, consideration of management's interest in maintaining or increasing the registrant's stock price or earnings trend through the use of unusually aggressive accounting practices, whether management has a practice of committing to analysts or others that it will achieve unduly aggressive or clearly unrealistic forecasts, and the existence of assets, liabilities, revenues, or expenses based on significant estimates that involve unusually subjective judgments or uncertainties. *See* AU §§ 316.17a and 316.17c.

44. AU §§ 316.34 and 316.35, in requiring the auditor to consider whether fraudulent misstatements are material, and in requiring differing responses depending on whether the misstatement is material, make clear that fraud can involve immaterial misstatements. Indeed, a misstatement can be "inconsequential" and still involve fraud. Under SAS No. 82, assessing whether misstatements due to fraud are material to the financial statements is a "cumulative process" that should occur both during and at the completion of the audit. SAS No. 82 further states that this accumulation is primarily a "qualitative matter" based on the auditor's judgment. AU § 316.33. The staff believes that in making these assessments, management and auditors should refer to the discussion in Part 1 of this SAB.

45. AU §§ 316.34 and 316.36. Auditors should document their determinations in accordance with AU §§ 316.37, 319.57, 339, and other appropriate sections.

46. *See, e.g.,* AU § 316.39.

47. Report of the National Commission on Fraudulent Financial Reporting at 32 (October 1987). *See also* Report and Recommendations of the Blue Ribbon Committee on Improving the Effectiveness of Corporate Audit Committees (February 8, 1999).

48. AU § 325.02. *See also* AU § 380.09, which, in discussing matters to be communicated by the auditor to the audit committee, states, "The auditor should inform the audit committee about adjustments

arising from the audit that could, in his judgment, either individually or in the aggregate, have a significant effect on the entity's financial reporting process. For purposes of this section, an audit adjustment, whether or not recorded by the entity, is a proposed correction of the financial statements. . . ."

49. *See* AU § 411.05.

50. The FASB Discussion Memorandum, Criteria for Determining Materiality, states that the financial accounting and reporting process considers that "a great deal of the time might be spent during the accounting process considering insignificant matters. . . . If presentations of financial information are to be prepared economically on a timely basis and presented in a concise intelligible form, the concept of materiality is crucial."

This SAB is not intended to require that misstatements arising from insignificant errors and omissions (individually and in the aggregate) arising from the normal recurring accounting close processes, such as a clerical error or an adjustment for a missed accounts payable invoice, always be corrected, even if the error is identified in the audit process and known to management. Management and the auditor would need to consider the various factors described elsewhere in this SAB in assessing whether such misstatements are material, need to be corrected to comply with the FCPA, or trigger procedures under Section 10A of the Exchange Act. Because this SAB does not change current law or guidance in the accounting or auditing literature, adherence to the principles described in this SAB should not raise the costs associated with record keeping or with audits of financial statements.

PART II

THE NEW INTERNATIONAL NORMS

CHAPTER VI

OVERVIEW OF THE NEW INTERNATIONAL NORMS

In the early 1970s, the international community began a serious examination of the incidence and consequences of corrupt practices in the conduct of international business. Much of the impetus came from revelations involving the foreign activities of U.S. companies. But there was considerable prompting by the United States for other nations to follow its lead in prohibiting the payment of bribes to foreign officials. The United Nations, the Organization for Economic Co-operation and Development (OECD), and the International Chamber of Commerce (ICC) were among the leaders of these efforts.

These initial efforts led to the creation in various international fora of "soft" law consisting of model laws, codes of conduct, and policy statements. Yet, other than what already existed in the United States in the form of the FCPA, no domestic legislation was ever adopted by any other country; no enforcement mechanisms were put in place; and no sanctions were imposed for a failure to abide by announced policies. The momentum associated with the promising efforts of the 1970s ultimately waned. In the 1990s, a multitude of factors, including the end of the Cold War, scandals in Europe, the Asian financial crisis, and U.S. efforts prompted by the legislation associated with the 1988 amendments to the FCPA, spawned a resurgence of international activity.

The resurgence of activity was reflected in a host of initiatives. At first, much of the resurgence followed the pattern of the 1970s, when policies were enunciated and positions taken without sanctions for a failure to carry out the commitments made. In time, this resurgence led to a rather dramatic evolution from "soft" to "hard" law. Foremost in this evolution was the work of the OECD. But the OECD was not alone. Among others, the Organization of American States

(OAS), the Council of Europe, the World Bank, and the United Nations have adopted significant measures.

These developments have now become so widespread that the international norms with respect to improper inducements to foreign officials increasingly resemble the anti-bribery provisions of the FCPA. Most developed countries have implemented legislation prohibiting their nationals from making improper inducements to foreign officials. It is only a matter of time before most of the world will have adopted legislation of a similar nature. And regardless of whether the anti-corruption conventions are actively enforced, the most immediate impact will be from the provisions requiring cooperation and mutual legal assistance.

Historically, many U.S. prosecutions under the anti-bribery provisions of the FCPA were hindered if not entirely precluded due to legal impediments to securing evidence from abroad. Bank secrecy laws in many countries posed a serious impediment. Another impediment was the requirement in many jurisdictions that there be dual criminality before evidence or assistance could be provided. Under dual criminality, the provision of evidence or assistance to another country is limited to situations where the conduct being investigated or for which charges have been brought could be subject to prosecution in the country receiving the request.

Directly as a result of these international developments, bank secrecy, dual criminality, and other impediments have been or are being removed relative to securing evidence or cooperation concerning violations of the anti-bribery provisions of the FCPA. Parties to these anti-corruption conventions will also have the opportunity to secure evidence and other assistance to aid their ability to prosecute individuals and entities subject to their jurisdiction for violations of domestic legislation, which has been implemented to prohibit improper inducements to foreign officials.

The enhanced ability to obtain evidence and to secure cooperation means, over time, a much broader net for investigators in the United States and elsewhere. Yet another result of these international agreements is the upsurge in prosecutions under the anti-bribery provisions of the FCPA. Indeed, countries that were previously limited as to what they could do have been in the forefront of bringing evidence of FCPA violations to the attention of U.S. authorities. This upsurge in enforcement activity can be expected to continue.

CHAPTER **VII**

THE OECD CONVENTION

The consideration of the criminalization of the bribery of foreign public officials was, in large part, led by the OECD Working Group on Bribery in International Business Transactions. Its work resulted in the adoption in 1994 of the first multilateral agreement among governments to combat the bribery of foreign officials. A year later, the OECD adopted a Recommendation on the Tax Deductibility of Bribes of Foreign Public Officials, which called on member countries to eliminate as a business expense the tax deductibility of bribes paid to foreign officials.[1] Prior to that time, bribes paid to foreign officials were treated in most countries as legitimate, deductible business expenses.

In adopting a Revised Recommendation of the Council on Combating Bribery in International Business Transactions (OECD Revised Recommendation), the OECD agreed to a firm time frame for developing a multilateral approach to criminalizing the bribery of foreign public officials.[2] But possibly the most important aspect of the OECD Revised Recommendation was the "Agreed Upon Common Elements of Criminal Legislation and Related Action" set forth in its Annex. These "common elements" were fundamentally in accord with the basic principles of the anti-bribery provisions of the FCPA. They served as the framework for the uniform autonomous standard ultimately adopted by the OECD Convention.

On November 21, 1997, members of the OECD and Argentina, Brazil, Bulgaria, Chile, and the Slovak Republic adopted the OECD Convention.[3] It entered into force in 1999. As of March 1, 2005, of the 36 countries that were signatories or that acceded to the OECD Convention, 35 have implemented legislation prohibiting the bribery of foreign officials.[4] All parties also no longer permit the tax deductibility of bribes paid to foreign officials.

OVERVIEW OF OECD CONVENTION

The OECD Convention requires parties to criminalize the bribery of foreign public officials and impose sanctions on a comparable basis to domestic bribery. It is unique among the anti-corruption conventions in that it is narrow in focus and premised upon an autonomous, agreed-upon standard. Parties are called upon to make it a criminal offense under their national laws for any person to intentionally offer, promise, or give any undue pecuniary or other advantage, directly or through intermediaries, to foreign public officials in order to obtain or retain business or to obtain any other improper advantage.

Like the FCPA's anti-bribery provisions, the OECD Convention applies only to the bribery of foreign officials, not to foreign commercial bribery, and focuses on the so-called "supply" side of such bribery. Similarly, complicity in the bribery of a foreign public official is prohibited. Broader than the FCPA in some respects, and narrower in others, on a few issues the impact of the OECD Convention is uncertain and will likely depend upon how it is implemented and enforced. Its other vital component is the obligation that is placed upon parties to cooperate in the investigation and in the enforcement of anti-bribery laws.

SCOPE AND JURISDICTION

Jurisdiction is established over offenses that are committed in whole or in part by "any person" acting within a party's territories.[5] This means that, regardless of citizenship, any individual or entity acting within a party's territory will be subject to its anti-bribery prohibitions. Each party is to apply its law extraterritorially in accordance with its own legal principles, whether they are nationality or territoriality principles, recognized by its legal system. The territorial basis for jurisdiction is to be interpreted broadly so that an extensive physical connection to the act of bribery is not required. Where more than one party has jurisdiction, the OECD Convention calls for consultation among the parties to determine the most appropriate jurisdiction for enforcement action.

FOREIGN OFFICIAL

Officials of any branch of government are covered by the OECD Convention. This includes part-time or unpaid officials, private individuals carrying out official functions, and officials of parastatals. Individuals who may not be considered public officials under the law of the country where the inducement is directed can still be treated as public officials under the terms of the OECD Convention. A "public official" under the OECD Convention is any person exercising a public function. A "public function" is any activity in the public interest delegated by a foreign country, such as a delegated task connected to public procurement.

Political Parties

Inducements to political parties, party officials, or candidates for political office are not specifically addressed by the OECD Convention. However, depending upon the legal principles of some parties to the OECD Convention, the prohibitions may apply in certain situations where political parties serve as intermediaries for inducements made to foreign public officials or where the officials of political parties are the ultimate recipients of inducements directed to them by public officials. In addition, for some parties to the OECD Convention, these types of inducements may already be covered through prohibitions on trading in influence.

Persons not formally designated as public officials but who perform a public function may also be considered a public official within the framework of the OECD Convention. An example could be political party officials in countries with single political parties. Depending upon the legal system, for some parties to the OECD Convention the prohibitions may also apply to inducements to a person in anticipation of becoming a public official.

Parastatals or State-Owned Enterprises

The OECD Convention introduces new considerations into the assessment of whether officials of parastatals are "public officials." Inducements to officials of parastatals and other government instrumentalities are covered by the OECD Convention. State ownership or control includes traditional indicia of control such as majority stock ownership, majority of directors, or appointing a majority of directors of the administrative body of an entity. Privately held companies can, under the terms of the OECD Convention, be treated as parastatals if they carry out public functions or receive government subsidies.

Yet not all parastatals necessarily carry out a public function. In relatively rare circumstances, parastatals that operate, without preferential subsidies or other privileges, on a normal commercial basis equivalent to that of a private enterprise may not be carrying out a public function. In those circumstances, an official of the parastatal may not be a public official according to the Commentaries to the OECD Convention (OECD Commentaries).[6]

TRANSFERS OF VALUE

Similar to the FCPA, transfers other than pecuniary payments are prohibited under the OECD Convention. No safe harbor for a *de minimis* amount is provided. Although facilitating or expediting payments are not expressly excluded, the OECD Commentaries indicate that "small 'facilitation' payments do not constitute payments made 'to obtain or retain business or other improper advantage' within the meaning of the OECD Convention."[7]

INTENT AND VICARIOUS LIABILITY

The conduct prohibited by the OECD Convention covers payments to obtain or retain business as well as those made to secure any "other improper advantage in the conduct of international business."[8] The prohibitions extend to a wide range of government activities including, for example, procurements, licenses, permits, exemptions, and incentives. This is functionally equivalent to how the anti-bribery provisions of the FCPA have been interpreted and applied by U.S. authorities.

Indirect as well as direct payments to public officials are covered by the OECD Convention. Like the FCPA's anti-bribery provisions, the OECD Convention's anti-bribery offense is made an "intent" crime. Although the FCPA establishes vicarious liability based on "knowledge," and includes "willful blindness" within that definition, the OECD Convention's standard is unclear as to whether intent will be found and liability vicariously imposed for payments by third parties in cases of "willful blindness" or in spite of knowledge of red flags or other indicia as to the likelihood of improper inducements being made. In the absence of an agreed-upon standard, vicarious liability can be expected to be addressed in a manner consistent with the domestic laws of each party.

An important factor when considering the culpability of legal entities will be how knowledge on the part of an entity is determined by each party. No autonomous standard was created by the OECD Convention. In the United States, knowledge of an entity is premised under federal law upon collective knowledge of those employed by or acting on behalf of an entity.[9] No single person or group of persons is required to have the requisite knowledge. It is a standard that can be easily met. In contrast, for many parties to the OECD Convention there is a requirement that a single person have the requisite knowledge. This represents a very important distinction. It is unlikely that many parties to the OECD Convention will have as low a threshold as exists under U.S. law to establish knowledge on the part of an entity.

❦ SANCTIONS AND CORPORATE CRIMINAL RESPONSIBILITY

The OECD Convention calls for parties to impose criminal penalties on violators comparable to those applicable to public officials in their respective jurisdictions. If a party's legal system does not provide for criminal sanctions against entities, then "effective, proportionate and dissuasive" noncriminal penalties, such as monetary sanctions, must be applied.[10] Parties are also required to institute measures that would permit the confiscation or forfeiture of an improper payment as well as the proceeds of an improper inducement. The proceeds can include the profits and other benefits derived by the individual or entity making the improper inducement.

❦ INTERNATIONAL COOPERATION

The OECD Convention requires members to give "prompt and effective" legal assistance to other parties in connection with investigations and proceedings brought by a party to the OECD Convention.[11] No longer can parties condition assistance on the existence of dual criminality. Dual criminality is deemed to exist for the offenses covered by the OECD Convention. Bank secrecy is also removed as a basis for declining to provide assistance. In addition, a party not recognizing corporate criminal responsibility must still provide assistance since the same assistance is required for noncriminal proceedings brought within the scope of the OECD Convention.

Although still leaving the question of extradition subject to the domestic laws and treaties of the parties, the OECD Convention seeks to facilitate it. The OECD Convention provides the treaty basis for extradition where a party from whom extradition is sought conditions its assistance on a treaty being in force with the requesting party as well as there being dual criminality. It also requires parties to follow the "extradite or prosecute" rule with respect to the nationals of other parties. Parties that decline an extradition request solely on the ground of nationality must prosecute that individual.

MONITORING AND FOLLOW-UP

Unlike many international conventions, a vital component of the OECD Convention is the requirement that parties cooperate in a follow-up program, within the framework of the OECD, to monitor and to promote full implementation and consistent enforcement of its provisions. The monitoring process has an implementation and an enforcement phase. Ultimately, much like the OECD's Financial Action Task Force for money laundering, the monitoring program is designed to ensure active and consistent implementation and enforcement by parties to the OECD Convention.

OUTSTANDING ISSUES

In order to reach consensus on the OECD Convention, the negotiators set aside a number of issues to be considered at a later point in time. The negotiators did agree to an accelerated work plan to address several outstanding issues, including acts of bribery relating to foreign political parties and candidates. Of the issues that continue to be considered by the OECD Working Group on Bribery, a number could have significant implications, including the following.

Books and Records

The OECD Convention does not contain prohibitions corresponding to the accounting and record-keeping provisions of the FCPA. Nor does it incorporate the expansive series of accounting and record-keeping procedures called for in the OECD Revised Recommendation. These procedures, oriented to deterring corrupt practices, would include heightened accounting requirements, independent external audits, and the imposition of internal controls.

Parties are required by the OECD Convention to take necessary measures, within the framework of their existing laws and regulations, to prohibit the establishment of off-the-books accounts and similar practices used to conceal the making of improper inducements to foreign public officials. No requirement was included to expand or to change the scope of individuals and entities subject to such laws and regulations. This means, for example, that for the United States the accounting and record-keeping provisions of the FCPA will continue to apply only to "issuers." For other parties to the OECD Convention, no change in their domestic law is required with respect to accounting and record-keeping practices.

Political Parties

The OECD Convention creates a narrower category of bribe recipients than the anti-bribery provisions of the FCPA. The OECD Convention's prohibitions do not extend to political parties, political candidates, or party officials. Given the important role that political parties and their officials play in many countries and in particular in parliamentary democracies, this narrower definition of a public official is viewed as constituting a major loophole in the OECD Convention. For many countries, depending upon the situation, a contribution to a political party has the prospect of having virtually the same impact as a payment to a public official.

Accession

Practical realities have served to raise concerns as to whether and, if so, how quickly and broadly accession to the OECD Convention should be permitted. Spreading resources too thin at these relatively early stages of the OECD Convention's existence is the source of these concerns. Limited resources are currently available for monitoring. The obvious benefit to broader accession is the facilitation of greater consistency in legal regimes and enhanced international cooperation. But without sufficient resources to ensure effective implementation and enforcement, the effectiveness of the OECD Convention, and ultimately its usefulness, will diminish over time.

◉ NOTES

1. OECD/C(96)27/FINAL (1996), *reprinted in* 35 I.L.M. 1311 (1996).
2. OECD/C(97)123/FINAL (1997), *reprinted in* 36 I.L.M. 1016 (1997).
3. OECD Doc. DAFFE/IME/BR(97)20, *reprinted in* 37 I.L.M. 1 (1998). The text of the OECD Convention is located at Appendix II-A: Part 1, *infra* at 131.
4. For the latest information relative to the status of ratification and implementation of the OECD Convention, *see* OECD Web site at **http://www.oecd.org/dataoecd/59/13/1898632.pdf.**
5. OECD Convention, art. 3, ¶ 1.
6. OECD Doc. DAFFE/IME/BR(97)20. The OECD Commentaries, which are located at Appendix II-A: Part 2, *infra* at 139, constitute a form of "legislative history" of the OECD Convention. They provide insight as to the intent of the negotiators with respect to a number of provisions. Most of the other international conventions that address issues relating to transnational bribery also have accompanying texts that explain their provisions.
7. OECD Commentaries, ¶ 9.
8. OECD Convention, art. 1, ¶ 1.
9. *E.g.,* United States v. Bank of New England, N.A., 821 F.2d 844 (1st Cir. 1987).
10. OECD Convention, art. 3, ¶ 2.
11. *Id.*, art. 9, ¶ 1.

CHAPTER **VIII**

INTER-AMERICAN CONVENTION
AGAINST CORRUPTION

In 1994, the General Assembly of the OAS adopted a resolution finding corrupt practices in international trade to be capable of frustrating development. In time, the resolution led to a series of initiatives within the OAS that culminated in 1996 in the approval of the Inter-American Convention Against Corruption (Inter-American Convention).[1] The Inter-American Convention was the first multilateral legal framework established to combat public corruption in international business transactions. The convention entered into force on March 6, 1997, and remains open for signature, ratification, and accession by any country. As of March 1, 2005, 33 countries have deposited their instruments of ratification of accession to the Inter-American Convention.[2]

⊘ OVERVIEW OF THE INTER-AMERICAN CONVENTION

The Inter-American Convention seeks to promote and strengthen cooperation to "prevent, detect, punish and eradicate corruption in the performance of public functions."[3] It calls for parties to criminalize in their domestic laws a number of acts of corruption. Much broader in scope than the OECD Convention, the Inter-American Convention, in addition to addressing the supply side of corruption, criminalizes the "demand" side of corruption, or what is often referred to as "passive" corruption in civil law countries. Provision is also made for the development of institutions to fight corruption and for the implementation of mechanisms to facilitate the enforcement of anti-corruption measures.

101

◉ PUBLIC OFFICIAL

Under the Inter-American Convention, all levels of civil servants, whether they are "governmental officials," "public servants," elected officials, appointed officials or employees, or others carrying out "public" functions, may be considered "public officials."[4] "[A]ny temporary or permanent, paid or honorary activity, performed by a natural person in the name of the State or in the service of the State or its institutions, at any level" is considered a "public function." Although not precluded, political parties, political candidates, and officials of political parties are not included in the definition of a public official.

What constitutes a public official appears to be more limited under the Inter-American Convention than under the OECD Convention. Officials or agents of a public international organization are not included. Officials or employees of parastatals covered by the OECD Convention may not be considered to be carrying out a public function.

◉ PASSIVE BRIBERY

The Inter-American Convention applies to the direct or indirect solicitation or acceptance by a public official of any article of monetary value or other benefit, whether for the public official or for another individual or entity, in exchange for any act or omission in the performance of his or her official functions. It extends to acts or omissions by a public official or by a person who performs a public function in order to obtain benefits. A benefit can include a gift, favor, promise, or advantage for the public official or for another individual or entity. The Inter-American Convention also extends to participation in a corrupt act and to the fraudulent use or concealment of property derived from a corrupt act.

◉ TRANSNATIONAL BRIBERY

Bribery of foreign officials is not listed as an act of corruption in the Inter-American Convention. Instead, it is treated in a separate article, which states that "subject to their Constitutions and the fundamental principles of their legal systems" the parties agree to prohibit and punish transnational bribery of foreign officials.[5] Once established as a criminal offense under the domestic laws of a party, transnational bribery is considered an act of corruption under the Inter-American Convention.

The basic contours of the transnational bribery provisions of the Inter-American Convention are consistent with the basic principles of the anti-bribery provisions of the FCPA. Both legal regimes are comparable in scope; both apply to payments made in seeking to obtain or retain business; and both focus on the giving of something of value for an official's act, omission, or exercise of influence in violation of his or her duties. The differences between the two legal regimes are matters of detail rather than fundamental concepts or principles.

The Inter-American Convention does not explicitly provide an exception for facilitating payments. However, the report of the OAS Juridical Committee on model elements for inclusion in domestic implementing legislation recognizes, at least implicitly, that parties may be able to exclude facilitating payments from their legislation. Although promises are not expressly addressed by the terms of the Inter-American Convention, offering a benefit, including a promise, to a foreign official in exchange for an act or omission is deemed an act of corruption.[6]

ILLICIT ENRICHMENT

Illicit enrichment is also not listed as an act of corruption under the Inter-American Convention. Illicit enrichment is defined as "a significant increase in the assets of a government official that he cannot reasonably explain in relation to his lawful earnings during the performance of his functions."[7] Parties to the Inter-American Convention are required to make illicit enrichment an offense under their laws unless it could contravene fundamental principles of their legal systems. Due to the presumption of innocence associated with their legal systems, the United States and Canada expressed an understanding or declaration in their instruments of ratification to the effect that they were not obligated to establish illicit enrichment as a crime in implementing the Inter-American Convention.

COOPERATION

The Inter-American Convention seeks to maximize cooperation among the parties. To the extent permitted by their laws, parties must cooperate and provide mutual legal assistance. This includes situations where transnational bribery or illicit enrichment may be involved, provided that such acts are crimes under a party's domestic laws. The Inter-American Convention precludes the use of bank secrecy laws and limits the use of the political offense exception as bases for refusing to cooperate.

Extradition treaties among the parties are, in effect, expanded to include the criminal offenses that are implemented in accordance with Inter-American Convention. The legal basis for extradition is also provided between parties that do not have an extradition treaty.

MONITORING

As originally written and adopted, the Inter-American Convention did not contain a monitoring mechanism comparable to that of the OECD Convention. However, the OAS adopted in June of 2001 the Mechanism for Follow-up of Implementation of the Inter-American Convention Against Corruption (Evaluation Mechanism).[8] The Evaluation Mechanism was designed to promote implementation and facilitate cooperation and harmonization among the parties to the

Inter-American Convention. At least 28 parties to the Inter-American Convention have now adopted the Evaluation Mechanism.[9]

⊕ NOTES

1. OAS Doc. B-58, *reprinted in* 35 I.L.M. 724 (1996).
2. For the latest information relative to signatories, accession, ratification, and reservations to the Inter-American Convention, *see* OAS, B-58: Inter-American Convention against Corruption, *at* **http://www.oas.org/juridico/english/Sigs/b-58.html.**
3. Inter-American Convention, art. I, ¶ 1.
4. *Id.*, art. I.
5. *Id.*, art. VIII.
6. *Id.*
7. *Id.*, art. IX.
8. AG/RES. 1784 (XXXI-O/01), *reprinted in* 41 I.L.M. 244 (2002).
9. For the latest information as to the parties that have adopted the Evaluation Mechanism, *see* OAS, Follow-up Signatories, Evaluation Mechanism, *at* **http://www.oas.org/juridico/english/followup_sigs.htm.**

CHAPTER IX

COUNCIL OF EUROPE
CRIMINAL LAW CONVENTION

On June 15, 1994, justice ministers from the Council of Europe adopted a program to combat corruption. The program established a multidisciplinary group on corruption (GMC) to address issues such as public and private codes of conduct, fines for illegal payments, ways to discourage corruption by foreign officials, and extradition and mutual legal assistance when corruption is involved. Central to the recommendations made in the GMC's initial report was the recommendation that domestic criminal legislation be revised along the lines of the anti-bribery provisions of the FCPA.

Consistent with the GMC's recommendations, the Council of Europe's Criminal Law Convention on Corruption (CoE Criminal Law Convention) was negotiated by the member states of the Council of Europe with the participation of observers, including the United States. It was adopted in 1998 by the Council of Ministers.[1] The CoE Criminal Law Convention entered into force on July 1, 2002. As of March 1, 2005, of the 46 signatories to the convention, 30 have ratified it.[2] The United States has signed but not yet ratified the CoE Criminal Law Convention.

🌐 OVERVIEW OF THE CoE CRIMINAL LAW CONVENTION

The CoE Criminal Law Convention addresses both the supply side and the demand side of corruption. Like the Inter-American Convention, parties are required to criminalize both the act of bribery (active bribery), and the act of soliciting or receiving a bribe (passive bribery). Like the OECD Convention and the Inter-American Convention, parties are required to criminalize the bribery of foreign officials and to cooperate with one another in the investigation and the prosecution of offenses implemented in accordance with the CoE Criminal Law Convention. The CoE Criminal Law Convention seeks to address a wider range of corrupt activities than the Inter-American Convention. It extends to private-sector bribery and "trading in influence." Like the other anti-corruption conventions, the CoE Criminal Law Convention calls for the implementation of mechanisms to facilitate the investigation and the prosecution of corruption offenses.

PUBLIC OFFICIAL

The CoE Criminal Law Convention does not have an autonomous standard for defining public officials like the OECD Convention. A party's national law governs the determination as to who is a public official. If a foreign public official would not be considered a public official within the context of a prosecuting party's national law, an inducement to that individual is not required to be prohibited by the terms of the CoE Criminal Law Convention. An individual who is considered a public official of another country is required to be considered a public official only to the extent that that country's definition is compatible with the national criminal law of the prosecuting party. However, consideration can be given to the national law of the public official's country as to the status of persons exercising public functions.

BRIBERY

Active bribery is defined as the intentional "promising, offering or giving by any person, directly or indirectly, of any undue advantage to any of its public officials . . . to act or refrain from acting in the exercise of his or her functions," whether the undue advantage accrues to the official or to a third party. Passive bribery is defined as the "request or receipt . . . or the acceptance of an offer or a promise of such an [undue] advantage" by a public official. "Undue" for purposes of the CoE Criminal Law Convention "should be interpreted as something that the recipient is not lawfully entitled to accept or receive."[3]

Transnational Bribery

The CoE Criminal Law Convention shares a basic definition of the offense of active bribery with the anti-bribery provisions of the FCPA, the OECD Convention, and the Inter-American Convention. All of these legal regimes prohibit improper inducements to or for an official to cause that person to misuse his or her office. Yet unlike the FCPA and the other anti-bribery conventions, which prohibit active transnational bribery only in a commercial context, the CoE Criminal Law Convention requires parties to criminalize both the active and passive bribery of foreign public officials whether or not the inducer's purpose relates to obtaining or retaining business.

Active or passive bribery is prohibited of foreign public officials, members of foreign public assemblies, officials of public international organizations, members of international assemblies, and judges and officials of international courts. However, the range of public officials is more limited than in the other anti-corruption conventions. The bribery of officials of public international organizations and members of international assemblies is required by the CoE Criminal Law Convention to be prohibited only where the intended recipient is an official or contracted employee of an organization or assembly of which a prosecuting party is also a member. Similarly, bribery of judges and officials of international courts is required to be prohibited only for courts whose jurisdiction has been accepted by a prosecuting party.

No specific exception appears to be provided for facilitating payments. However, without a separate autonomous standard setting forth the criteria for a violation of transnational bribery, no per se prohibition on facilitating payments appears to exist. Indeed, it is the position of the U.S. government that no implementing legislation would be required by the United States in order for it to ratify the CoE Criminal Law Convention. In addition, unlike the FCPA's anti-bribery provisions, the OECD Convention, and the Inter-American Convention, parties to the CoE Criminal Law Convention are required to adopt legislation or other measures to prohibit passive bribery by foreign officials.

Private-Sector/Commercial Bribery

Parties are required to criminalize the active and passive bribery of private individuals and entities "in the course of business activity."[4] Often referred to as commercial bribery and commonly exemplified in the form of kickbacks, neither the OECD Convention nor the Inter-American Convention addresses issues of bribery where no public officials are involved. Criminalizing active and passive bribery in non-public settings is the only part of the CoE Criminal Law Convention that requires the involvement of commercial activity in the conduct being prohibited.

⊕ TRADING IN INFLUENCE

Parties are required to adopt laws criminalizing the giving or receiving of "any undue advantage" in exchange for "improper influence" over the decisions of domestic or foreign officials, legislators, judges, or employees of international organizations. These prohibition apply to direct and indirect promises of "undue advantage" by an individual who "asserts or confirms" an ability to exert improper influence over a public official's decision-making functions. There is no requirement that the individual have the ability to do what is asserted or confirmed. Nor is there a requirement that the desired influence actually be exerted or that it lead to the intended result.

Although this provision has been drafted to address situations in which an individual or entity offers an improper inducement to a third party who claims to have sufficient influence over a decision maker to produce the sought-after result, its broad language could be interpreted to extend to activities considered to be lawful. Conceivably, unless the activity is expressly deemed to be legal under a party's legal regime, certain otherwise legal activities like lobbying or campaign contributions could fall within the prohibitions of the CoE Criminal Law Convention.

DERIVATIVE OFFENSES

The CoE Criminal Law Convention requires the adoption of laws covering acts intended to conceal or to launder the proceeds of bribery. Bribery offenses are to be treated as predicates for money laundering. To a certain degree, the CoE Criminal Law Convention may go further than the FCPA in imposing record-keeping standards on nonpublic entities. Yet the scope of activity covered is far more limited in nature. As opposed to prescribing comprehensive accounting and record-keeping practices, the requirement prohibits creating a document or failing to make a record in order to conceal or disguise activities prohibited by the CoE Criminal Law Convention for which a party has not made a reservation.

CORPORATE LIABILITY

The CoE Criminal Law Convention incorporates the legal concept of collective wrongdoing by requiring all parties to adopt measures to ensure that entities can be held liable, whether in a criminal, civil, or administrative context, for offenses committed for or on behalf of the entity by an individual with a "leading position" within the organization.[5] These offenses extend to accounting and record-keeping violations. Corporate liability is also mandated for failing to supervise or control an employee or other individual under the entity's authority or control who engages in the prohibited offenses for the benefit of the entity.

MONITORING

In its Programme of Action, the Council of Europe justice ministers directed the GMC to develop a follow-up mechanism to monitor the implementation of the Twenty Guiding Principles for the Fight Against Corruption adopted in 1997 by the Committee of Ministers, the CoE Criminal Law Convention, and any other international instruments that might be adopted. The monitoring mechanism that the GMC developed and proposed is called the Group of States against Corruption (GRECO).[6] GRECO's monitoring mechanisms rely primarily on first-hand evaluations by a peer-review investigative team. This process is similar to that implemented in Phase I by the parties to the OECD Convention. However, unlike the OECD, which makes public the country reports of parties, GRECO provides for confidential reporting. Enforcement is facilitated either through the European Committee on Crime Problems, a binding arbitral tribunal, or the International Court of Justice.

INTERNATIONAL COOPERATION

The CoE Criminal Law Convention does not require dual criminality as a basis for cooperation. Parties are required to adopt measures empowering the production of records for evidentiary purposes. Bank secrecy laws may not be used as a basis for prohibiting access to records. But parties are required to cooperate only to the extent of their "national law." Mutual legal assistance may be refused if compliance with the request would undermine a party's fundamental interests, national sovereignty, security, or public order. According to the Explanatory Report on the CoE Criminal Law Convention, "fundamental interests" could extend to human rights considerations as well as to cases in which the requested party has reasonable grounds to believe that the criminal proceedings instituted by the requesting party have been distorted or misused for purposes other than combating corruption.[7]

Offenses established under the CoE Criminal Law Convention are extraditable offenses under existing treaties between parties and are to be included in any future bilateral or multilateral extradition treaties between them. Parties without extradition treaties may consider the CoE Criminal Law Convention as a legal basis for extradition with respect to criminal offenses committed under the terms of the CoE Criminal Law Convention. If extradition is refused on nationality grounds, or where the requested party claims jurisdiction, the requested party is required to submit the case to its authorities for prosecution, unless otherwise agreed, and to report the outcome to the requesting party.

DECLARATIONS AND RESERVATIONS

The CoE Criminal Law Convention permits up to five reservations to certain portions of its provisions. The prospect of these reservations, the lack of autonomous definitions, and the reliance on national definitions may combine to promote inconsistency as opposed to consistency among parties. Yet a reservation cannot be taken with respect to the active transnational bribery of foreign officials, including officials of international organizations. A reservation can also not be taken with respect to the active or passive bribery of or by domestic public officials. Reservations can be taken with respect to some of the more controversial aspects of the CoE Criminal Law Convention, like trading in influence, other forms of passive bribery, and private-sector bribery.

ADDITIONAL PROTOCOL

In May of 2003, the Council of Europe adopted the Additional Protocol to the Criminal Law Convention on Corruption (Additional Protocol to the CoE Criminal Law Convention).[8] It entered into force on January 2, 2005. The United States is not among the 30 signatories to the additional protocol.[9] The Additional Protocol to the CoE Criminal Law Convention expands the scope of the CoE Criminal Law Convention to apply to arbitrators and to jurors. Monitoring and other mechanisms associated with the CoE Criminal Law Convention also apply to the additional protocol.

Active and passive bribery of domestic and foreign arbitrators is addressed by the Additional Protocol to the CoE Criminal Law Convention. The critical determination as to whether an arbitrator is covered by the additional protocol is whether the arbitration agreement is recognized by "the national law whereby the parties agree to submit a dispute for a decision by an arbitrator."[10] Any type of arbitration could conceivably be included. The limitation is based upon what types of arbitration are recognized by the national law of a party to the Additional Protocol to the CoE Criminal Law Convention.

The other expansion of the CoE Criminal Law Convention relates to the active and passive bribery of domestic and foreign jurors. There are two sets of criteria for determining who is a "juror" within the terms of the additional protocol. Reference to the national law of parties to the Additional Protocol to the CoE Criminal Law Convention represents one set of criteria. Jurors in a criminal context are covered regardless of the national laws of a party. If an individual is not a juror under a party's domestic law, autonomous criteria were established to apply to "a lay person acting as a member of a collegial body which has the responsibility of deciding on the guilt of an accused person in the framework of a trial."[11] However, in a civil context, who is a juror will depend upon the national laws of a party to the Additional Protocol to the CoE Criminal Law Convention.

❋ NOTES

1. ETS No. 173, *reprinted in* 38 I.L.M. 505 (1999). The text of the CoE Criminal Law Convention is located in Appendix II-C: Part 1, *infra* at 159.

2. For the latest information as to the parties, and the status of their ratification, to the CoE Criminal Law Convention, *see* Council of Europe at **http://conventions.coe.int,** then go to "Full List", then to No. "173", then to "Chart of signatures and ratifications".

3. Explanatory Report on the Criminal Law Convention (CoE Criminal Law Convention Explanatory Report), art. 3, ETS No. 173 (1991). The text of the CoE Criminal Law Convention Explanatory Report is located in Appendix II-C: Part 2, *infra* at 175.

4. CoE Criminal Law Convention, art. 8.

5. *Id.*, art. 18.

6. The GRECO Web site address is **http://www.greco.coe.int**.

7. CoE Criminal Law Convention Explanatory Report, art. 26, ¶ 125.

8. ETS No. 191 (2003). The text of the Additional Protocol to the CoE Criminal Law Convention is located at Appendix II-C: Part 3, *infra* at 215.

9. For the latest information as to the parties, and the status of their ratification, to the Additional Protocol to the CoE Criminal Law Convention, *see* Council of Europe at **http://conventions.coe. int**, then go to "Full List", then to No. "191", then to "Chart of signatures and ratifications".

10. Explanatory Report on the Additional Protocol to the Council of Europe Criminal Law Convention on Corruption, ¶ 11, ETS No. 191 (2003). The text of the Explanatory Report on the Additional Protocol is located in Appendix II-C: Part 4, *infra* at 221.

11. Additional Protocol to the CoE Criminal Law Convention, art. 1, ¶ 3.

CHAPTER **X**

COUNCIL OF EUROPE
CIVIL LAW CONVENTION

One of the 20 guiding principles adopted by the Council of Europe in 1997 for fighting corruption called for the civil law to take "into account the need to fight corruption and in particular provide for effective remedies for those whose rights and interests are affected by corruption"[1] This action led to the adoption by the Committee of Ministers of the Council of Europe Civil Law Convention on Corruption (CoE Civil Law Convention).[2] It opened for signature before the end of 1999, and it entered into force on November 1, 2003.[3] The United States is currently not a signatory to the CoE Civil Law Convention.

The CoE Civil Law Convention represents the first successful attempt to develop an international mechanism to address corruption by means of legal measures that are civil as opposed to criminal in nature. The parties to the CoE Civil Law Convention are required to provide in their domestic law "for effective remedies for persons who have suffered damage as a result of acts of corruption, to enable them to defend their rights and interests, including the possibility of obtaining compensation for damage."[4]

"Corruption" is defined by the CoE Civil Law Convention as "requesting, offering, giving or accepting, directly or indirectly, a bribe or any other undue advantage or prospect thereof, which distorts the proper performance of any duty or behaviour required of the recipient of the bribe, the undue advantage or the prospect thereof."[5] A broad definition was included to ensure that no matter would necessarily be excluded from the scope of the CoE Civil Law Convention. However, parties are not required to adopt this definition of corruption.

PRIVATE RIGHT OF ACTION

The primary purpose of the CoE Civil Law Convention is the requirement that each party provide for a private right of action for "full compensation" against an individual or entity that has committed or authorized an act of corruption or failed to take reasonable steps to prevent an act of corruption.[6] This private right of action is required to extend to the governments of parties and nonparties for an act of corruption by their public officials in the exercise of their functions. Provision is also required to enable the issuance of court orders to preserve the rights and interests of parties during the proceedings.

Contributory negligence is required to be taken into account in determining the amount of compensation. The compensation may extend to material damage or actual reduction in the economic situation, to loss of profits or what could reasonably have been expected, and to nonpecuniary losses such as loss of reputation.

STATUTE OF LIMITATIONS

The statute of limitations that applies to any action brought pursuant to the CoE Civil Law Convention is at least three years from knowledge of the act of corruption or knowledge of damage from the act of corruption and knowledge of the identity of the responsible individual or entity. Regardless of circumstances, no action is permitted ten years after the act of corruption.

VALIDITY OF CONTRACTS

Parties are required to provide in their domestic law for the nullification of "any contract or clause of a contract providing for corruption."[7] Similarly, provision is also required to be made to enable a party who entered into a contract as a result of an act of corruption to be able to apply to a court to have the contract voided without impairing the party's right to a claim for damages.

PROTECTION OF EMPLOYEES

Parties are required to provide in their domestic law protection against any unjustified sanction for employees who have reasonable grounds to suspect corruption and who report in good faith their suspicion to responsible persons or authorities. Reporting under these circumstances should not be considered as a breach of the duty of confidentiality. These protections should encourage employees to report their suspicions. Unjustified sanctions may include dismissal, demotion, or otherwise limiting the progress of a career.

ANNUAL ACCOUNTING AND AUDITS

The CoE Civil Law Convention requires parties to implement measures mandating that "companies" draw up "annual accounts" that provide a "true and fair view" of a company's financial position.[8] These annual accounts, which include statements of financial position and income statements, are required to be confirmed by auditors. Neither the language of the convention nor its explanatory report provide guidance as to whether these provisions are limited to publicly held companies. But no limitation is placed on the application of these provisions to privately held entities.

❸ COOPERATION

Parties are required to provide in their domestic law for effective procedures for the acquisition of evidence in civil proceedings arising from an act of corruption. They are also required to cooperate with one another concerning serving documents, obtaining evidence, determining jurisdiction, and recognizing and enforcing foreign judgments and litigation. However, cooperation may be subject to the provisions of relevant international instruments on international cooperation in civil and commercial matters to which a party is bound or to the limitations of a party's domestic law.

❸ RESERVATIONS, IMPLEMENTATION, AND MONITORING

No reservations to the CoE Civil Law Convention are permitted. However, parties may declare the territory or territories to which the implementation of its provisions applies. The CoE Civil Law Convention is not self-executing. It must be implemented by each of the parties, and GRECO is responsible for monitoring its implementation.

❸ NOTES

1. Explanatory Report on the Council of Europe Civil Law Convention on Corruption (Explanatory Report on CoE Civil Law Convention), ¶ 8, ETS No. 174 (1999). The text of the Explanatory Report on CoE Civil Law Convention is located in Appendix II-D: Part 2, *infra* at 241.
2. ETS No. 174 (1999). The text of the CoE Civil Law Convention is located in Appendix II-D: Part 1, *infra* at 233.
3. For updated information as to signatories and ratifications to the CoE Civil Law Convention, *see* Council of Europe, Treaty Office, *at* **http://conventions.coe.int/Treaty/EN/cadreprincipal.htm.**
4. CoE Civil Law Convention, art. 1.
5. *Id.*, art. 2.
6. *Id.*, art. 3, ¶ 1.
7. *Id.*, art. 8, ¶ 1.
8. *Id.*, art. 10, ¶ 1.

CHAPTER XI

UNITED NATIONS CONVENTION AGAINST CORRUPTION

Over the years the United Nations has sought to address the issue of corruption in various contexts. These efforts have largely taken the form of initiatives that were not mandatory in nature. One of these initiatives was pursued through the United Nation's Commission on International Trade Law ("UNCITRAL"). It led to the adoption in 1994 by UNCITRAL of a Model Law on Procurement of Goods, Construction, and Services.[1] This model law contains a provision requiring the rejection of a tender, proposal, offer, or quotation if there is an improper inducement from a supplier or contractor.

In 2000, a number of members of the United Nations signed the United Nations Convention against Transnational Organized Crime ("UN Organized Crime Convention").[2] Acts of corruption, including active and passive domestic bribery and corporate organized crime, were criminalized by the UN Organized Crime Convention. Though included, the bribery of foreign public officials was not made mandatory. In addition, parties committed themselves to taking steps to expedite and broaden extradition, prevent organized crime, and develop protocols containing measures to combat specific acts of transnational organized crime. The UN Organized Crime Convention entered into force in September of 2003. Though a signatory, the United States has yet to ratify the UN Organized Crime Convention.

Under the auspices of the United Nations, the various regional anti-corruption efforts culminated in the adoption in October of 2003 of the United Nations Convention against Corruption ("UN Convention").[3] It is the first globally negotiated anti-corruption convention to address the bribery of public officials in the conduct of international business. Many of the concepts and measures reflected in the OECD Convention, the Inter-American Convention, the CoE Criminal Law Convention, and the CoE Civil Law Convention have been incorporated into the UN Convention. However, the UN Convention is more comprehensive in scope than the other anti-corruption conventions. As of March 1, 2005, 118 countries had signed the UN Convention, and instruments of ratification were already being deposited.[4] The United States has signed but not yet ratified the UN Convention.

⊛ OVERVIEW

The UN Convention has as its primary objectives the criminalization of corrupt practices, the implementation of measures to prevent and to deter corruption, the establishment of legal mechanisms for recovering stolen assets, and the establishment of means of providing technical assistance. Both the public and private sectors are the focus of these objectives. While a number of provisions of the UN Convention are mandatory, most, in varying degrees, are optional, and a number are solely hortatory in nature.

⊛ PUBLIC OFFICIAL

The UN Convention looks to three factors in determining who is subject to its terms a "public official."[5] One is a semi-autonomous standard that is based on traditional considerations as to whether an individual holds a legislative, executive, administrative, or judicial office of a party.[6] Each party is to determine who is a member of these categories and how each category is to be applied.[7] However, it makes no difference whether the position is temporary or unpaid or what the seniority of the official might be.[8] Nor does it matter what unit or subunit of government may be involved.[9]

A second factor consists of a semi-autonomous standard associated with determining whether an individual performs a public function, including for a public agency or enterprise, or provides a public service.[10] What constitutes a public function or a public service is defined by the domestic law of a party. The third factor is whether an individual is otherwise defined as a "public official" in a party's domestic law.[11]

⊛ CORRUPTION OFFENSES

Parties are obligated to establish certain offenses within their domestic law as well as consider adopting other offenses. Basic forms of corruption such as active and passive bribery, embezzlement of public funds, laundering proceeds of crime, and obstruction of justice are required to be criminalized.[12] The other offenses to be considered but not required for adoption include trading in influence, abuse of public functions, illicit enrichment, private-sector or commercial bribery, the embezzlement of private property, and concealment of property.[13]

Transnational Bribery

The UN Convention follows the FCPA's anti-bribery provisions, the OECD Convention, and the Inter-American Convention in requiring that there be a commercial nexus to the prohibition against inducements to foreign officials. Parties are required to criminalize the "promise, offering or giving to a public official or an official of a public international organization, directly or indirectly, of an undue advantage, for the official himself or herself or another person or entity, in order that the official act or refrain from acting in the exercise of his or her official duties, in order to obtain or retain business or other undue advantage in relation to the conduct of international business."[14]

The UN Convention explicitly expands on what is customarily viewed as the definition of "international business" to include "the provision of international aid" within the meaning of conducting international business.[15] While the anti-bribery provisions of the FCPA have not been generally viewed as extending to the provision of international aid, the application of the anti-bribery provisions in the settlement reached in *Metcalf & Eddy* suggest that U.S. law, in its current form, could reach such a result in certain circumstances.[16] However, U.S. courts have yet to address this precise issue.

In contrast with the active component of transnational bribery, no commercial nexus is required for the passive component of transnational bribery under the UN Convention.[17] Nor is there a commercial nexus requirement for active or passive domestic bribery under the UN Convention.[18] This follows the legal regime in the United States,[19] and in most countries, where any form of bribery of its officials or any solicitation of bribes by its officials are prohibited.

Foreign Public Official

The UN Convention defines "foreign public official" in similar terms to that of the OECD Convention.[20] "Any person holding a legislative, executive, administrative or judicial office of a foreign country, whether appointed or elected, and any person exercising a public function for a foreign country, including for a public agency or public enterprise."[21] It extends to all "levels and subdivisions of government, from national to local" of the foreign country.[22]

Like the other international conventions, and unlike the anti-bribery provisions of the FCPA, the UN Convention does not extend its prohibitions to a candidate for public office, an official of a political party, or a political party. Consistent with the FCPA, the OECD Convention, and the CoE Criminal Law Convention, the UN Convention's definition of foreign public official extends to an "international civil servant or any person who is authorized by such organization to act on behalf of that organization."[23]

Autonomous Definition

Like the OECD Convention, the standard enunciated by the UN Convention is an autonomous standard.[24] Proof of the law or regulations of an official's country is not required.[25] This extends to situations where a party to the UN Convention has adopted a statute defining the offense of transnational bribery in terms of payments "to induce a breach of the official's duty" and where it is also understood that every public official has a duty to exercise judgment or discretion impartially.[26]

Facilitating Payments

No express exception was created for facilitating payments either in the UN Convention or in the interpretative notes to the UN Convention. It was the position of the United States in signing the UN Convention that no change in U.S. law would be required for its implementation. The United States government interprets facilitating payments under the FCPA as not being made for the purpose of obtaining or retaining business.

Money Laundering

As to property known to be the proceeds of crime, the UN Convention mandates the adoption of legislation and other measures to criminalize the conversion, transfer, acquisition, possession, use, or disguising the illicit origin of such property.[27] Criminal liability for a money laundering offense is also to extend to anyone who in some way facilitates the commission of the offense of money laundering. "[A] prior conviction for the predicate offence is not necessary to establish the illicit nature or origin of the assets laundered."[28]

In addition, the UN Convention mandates a much broader basis for invoking a party's money laundering statutes than is required under the CoE Criminal Law Convention.[29] The UN Convention requires the adoption of money laundering statutes whereby "the widest range of criminal offences" are to be used as predicate offenses.[30] At minimum, the range of criminal offenses must include criminal offenses established in accordance with the UN Convention.[31]

Knowledge

Where knowledge or intent is an element of an offense under the UN Convention, either can be inferred from objective factual circumstances.[32] In other words, the use of circumstantial evidence is expressly permitted. Parties are also required to make criminal the participation "in any capacity" in any of the offenses established under the UN Convention.[33] This would extend to accomplices, aiders and abettors, or others who instigate a money laundering offense. Parties are permitted but not required to distinguish among different degrees of participation.[34]

Liability of Entities

Each party is obligated to establish the liability of legal or juridical persons for offenses established in accordance with the UN Convention.[35] No requirement, like that of the CoE Criminal Law Convention, is placed on what must be known by any one person for there to be liability on the part of an entity. Like the OECD Convention, there is no requirement that the liability of juridical persons be criminal in nature as long as they are "subject to effective, proportionate and dissuasive criminal or non-criminal sanctions."[36]

Statutes of Limitations

In recognition of the inherent difficulties associated with investigating corruption, a long period for a statute of limitations is required for any offense established by the UN Convention. For anyone who has evaded the administration of justice, the imposition of a longer period for a statute of limitations or, in the alternative, the suspension of a statute of limitations is required.[37]

PRIVATE SECTOR

In addition to private-sector bribery and concealment,[38] the UN Convention addresses a number of aspects of corruption in the private sector. It seeks to enhance accounting and auditing standards through business codes of conduct, prevention of conflicts of interest, promoting transparency among private entities, and ensuring that private entities have sufficient internal auditing controls.[39]

Accounting Offenses

The parties are required to prohibit the following accounting and record-keeping practices that are carried out for the purpose of committing any of the offenses established in accordance with the UN Convention:

  (a) the establishment of off-the-books accounts;
  (b) the making of off-the-books or inadequately identified transactions;
  (c) the recording of non-existent expenditures;
  (d) the entry of liabilities with incorrect identification of their objects;
  (e) the use of false documents; and
  (f) the intentional destruction of bookkeeping documents earlier than foreseen by the law.[40]

The requirement that certain accounting offenses be adopted represents a significant advance over what has actually been required in the other anti-corruption conventions. The accounting offenses are not limited to publicly-held entities. Yet each requires a nexus to an offense established in accordance with the UN Convention. The UN Convention's accounting offenses therefore cannot, in their own right, have the same breadth of application or pervasive impact as the FCPA's accounting and record-keeping provisions. In many respects, the accounting offenses more closely resemble obstruction of justice and fraud statutes in the United States and elsewhere as they focus in various ways upon concealing criminal conduct.[41]

Tax Deductibility

The tax deductibility of bribes, whether paid in a domestic or foreign setting, is to be prohibited by parties to the UN Convention.[42] The UN Convention also calls, "where appropriate," for the elimination of the tax deductibility of "other expenses incurred in furtherance of corrupt conduct."[43]

Private Rights of Action

Similar to the CoE Civil Law Convention,[44] the UN Convention creates a private right of action. A right was established "to initiate legal proceedings against those responsible for that damage in order to obtain compensation."[45] States as well as legal and natural persons are to have this right.[46] While legal theories exist in the United States for victims of corruption to obtain compensation in certain circumstances, no private right of action is available for a violation of the provisions of the FCPA.[47] Nonetheless, it is the position of the U.S. government that this provision of the UN Convention will not require a change in U.S. law.

Also like the CoE Civil Law Convention,[48] the UN Convention provides that, in the context of civil proceedings, parties may "consider corruption a relevant factor in legal proceedings to annul or rescind a contract, withdraw a concession or other similar instrument or take any other remedial action."[49] This provision provides clear authority for what is arising increasingly in judicial and arbitral decisions where corruption has served as a basis for refusing to enforce a contract.[50]

🌐 PREVENTIVE MEASURES

The UN Convention requires parties to promote integrity, honesty, and responsibility among its public officials. Certain measures and policies oriented to achieving these goals are to be implemented. These include the implementation of comprehensive anti-money laundering practices and the establishment of systems of procurement based on transparency, competition, and objective criteria in decision-making.[51]

Public Officials

Parties are encouraged to adopt measures to facilitate the reporting by public officials of acts of corruption.[52] The establishment of systems and procedures are encouraged for public officials to declare outside activities, investments, assets, and substantial gifts or benefits that may result in conflicts of interest.[53] The UN Convention calls for the enforcement of codes of conduct applicable to public officials.[54]

Civil Society

The UN Convention expressly calls for the participation of civil society, including non-governmental organizations and community-based organizations.[55] Members of civil society are encouraged to contribute to the public decision-making process and to participate in educational programs.[56] Effective access to information is an important component of the measures designed to facilitate participation by civil society.[57]

ASSET RECOVERY

Asset recovery is one of the key components of the UN Convention.[58] A framework is established for parties to cooperate in recovering illicitly obtained assets. When embezzled public funds are involved, confiscated property is to be returned to the party requesting it.[59] Proceeds of any other offenses covered by the UN Convention are to be returned upon proof of ownership or recognition of the damage caused to a requesting party.[60] In all other contexts, priority consideration is to be given to the return of confiscated property to the requesting party, to the return of the confiscated property to the prior legitimate owners, or to the compensation of victims.[61]

COOPERATION

The UN Convention contains a very detailed and comprehensive set of provisions addressing mutual legal assistance, extradition, and other forms of international cooperation. Unlike most other parts of the UN Convention, the provisions relating to international cooperation are largely self-executing in nature. No need for implementing legislation is required. These provisions can therefore be expected to have the most immediate impact of any of the provisions of the UN Convention. Over time the significance of these provisions relating to international cooperation cannot be overstated as they can be expected to dramatically reduce and in large part eliminate barriers to mutual legal assistance, extradition, and other forms of international cooperation.

Parties are to cooperate in every aspect of the fight against corruption, including the investigation and the prosecution of offenders.[62] Parties "shall afford one another the widest measure of mutual legal assistance."[63] This extends to the tracing, freezing, seizure, and confiscation of the proceeds of corruption.[64] Parties are required to render specific forms of mutual legal assistance in gathering and in transferring evidence for use in legal proceedings and to extradite offenders.[65]

MONITORING

To promote implementation of the UN Convention, a "Conference of the States Parties" is to be established to meet regularly.[66] Like the monitoring mechanism associated with the OECD Convention,[67] the Conference is designed to serve as a mechanism for reviewing the status of implementation by the parties and for facilitating the progress of other obligations imposed by the UN Convention.[68] To assist in the "effective implementation of the [UN] Convention," the Conference is authorized to establish "any appropriate mechanism or body" it "deems necessary."[69]

NOTES

1. The UNCITRAL Web site where the Model Law on Procurement of Goods, Construction, and Services can be found is **http://www.uncitral.org/en-index.htm**.

2. The Convention against Transnational Organized Crime and its Protocols, U.N. Doc. A/55/383 (2000). The Web site for the UN Organized Crime Convention, its two protocols, and updates on the status of ratification can be found at **http://www.unodc.org/unodc/crime_cicp_convention.html**.

3. G.A. Res. 58/4, U.N. GAOR, 58th Sess., U.N. Doc. A/RES/58/4 (2003), *reprinted in* 43 I.L.M. 37 (2004). The text of the UN Convention is located at Appendix II-E: Part 1. *Infra* at 259.

4. The Web site for the latest information relative to signatories, accession, ratification, and reservations to the UN Convention can be found at **http://www.unodc.org/unodc/en/crime_signatures_corruption.html**.

5. UN Convention, art. 2, ¶ a.

6. *Id.*, art. 2, ¶ a(i). The "'executive' is understood to encompass the military branch." Report of the Ad Hoc Committee for the Negotiation of a Convention against Corruption on the work of its first to seventh sessions, Addendum, Interpretative notes for the official records (travaux préparatoires) of the negotiation of the United Nations Convention against Corruption, A/58/422/Add.1, note 2, 7 October 2003 ("Interpretive Notes to UN Convention"). The text of the Interpretive Notes to UN Convention is located at Appendix II-E: Part 2. *Infra* at 305.

7. *Id.*, note 4.

8. UN Convention, art. 2, ¶ a.

9. Interpretive Notes to UN Convention, note 3.

10. UN Convention, art. 2, ¶ a(ii).

11. *Id.*, art. 2, ¶ a(iii).

12. *Id.*, arts. 15-17, 23, 25.

13. *Id.*, arts. 18-22, 24.

14. *Id.*, art. 16, ¶ 1.

15. Interpretive Notes to UN Convention, note 25.

16. United States v. Metcalf & Eddy, Inc., No. 99CV12566NG, Consent and Undertaking (D.Mass., Dec. 14, 1999), *reprinted in* BUSINESS LAWS, INC. (FCPA) at § 699.749.

17. UN Convention, art. 16, ¶ 2.

18. *Id.*, art. 15.

19. *E.g.*, 18 U.S.C. § 201.

20. UN Convention, art. 2, ¶ b; OECD Convention, art. 1, ¶ 4(a).

21. UN Convention, art. 2, ¶ b.

22. Interpretive Notes to UN Convention, ¶ 5.

23. UN Convention, art. 2, ¶ c.

24. Interpretive Notes to UN Convention, note 24.

25. *Id.*

26. *Id.*

27. UN Convention, art. 23, ¶ 1.

28. Interpretive Notes to UN Convention, note 32.

29. CoE Criminal Law Convention, art. 13.

30. UN Convention, art. 23, ¶ 2(a).

31. *Id.*, art. 23, ¶ 2(b).

32. *Id.*, art. 28.

33. *Id.*. art. 27, ¶ 1.

34. Interpretive Notes to UN Convention, note 33.

35. UN Convention, art. 26, ¶ 1.

36. *Id.*, art. 27, ¶ 4.

37. This is consistent with the legal regime of the United States. *Supra* at 45.

38. UN Convention, arts. 21, 24.

39. *Id.*, art. 12, ¶¶ 1-2.

40. *Id.*, art. 12, ¶ 3.
41. *See, e.g.,* 18 U.S.C. §§ 1341, 1343, 1346, and 1519-1520.
42. U.N. Convention, art. 12, ¶ 4.
43. *Id.*
44. CoE Civil Law Convention, arts. 3-4.
45. UN Convention, art. 35.
46. Interpretive Notes to UN Convention, note 37.
47. Lamb v. Phillip Morris, Inc., 915 F.2d 1024, 1030 (6th Cir. 1990). *See infra* at 373.
48. CoE Civil Law Convention, art. 8.
49. UN Convention, art. 34.
50. *Infra* at 381.
51. UN Convention, arts. 9(1), 14(1).
52. *Id.*, art. 8, ¶ 4.
53. *Id.*, art. 8, ¶ 5.
54. *Id.*, arts. 8-10.
55. *Id.*, art. 13, ¶¶ 1-2.
56. *Id.*, art. 13, ¶ 1.
57. *Id.*
58. *Id.*, art. 51.
59. *Id.*, art. 57, ¶ 3(a).
60. *Id.*, art. 57, ¶ 3(b).
61. *Id.*, art. 57, ¶ 3(c).
62. *Id.*, art. 44.
63. *Id.*, art. 46, ¶ 1.
64. *Id.*, art. 55, ¶ 2.
65. *Id.*, art. 46.
66. *Id.*, art. 63, ¶¶ 1-2.
67. OECD Convention, art. 12.
68. U.N. Convention, art. 63, ¶ 4.
69. *Id.*, art. 63, ¶ 7.

CHAPTER XII

OTHER DEVELOPMENTS

Developments with respect to addressing foreign corrupt practices in the conduct of international business have continued to unfold in a number of ways. A number of organizations have established Web sites to track these developments.[1] Many of the ongoing developments represent different aspects of the implementation of measures associated with the new anti-corruption conventions. Others are reflective of efforts by nongovernmental organizations to assist countries and the private sector in adjusting their practices to the new international norms. Still others represent an expansion of regional efforts. A number of these noteworthy developments are described below.

 MULTILATERAL LENDING INSTITUTIONS

After years of disregarding the impediments to development posed by corruption, in the 1990s the World Bank and the regional development banks, including the European Bank for Reconstruction and Development, the African Development Bank, the Asian Development Bank, and the Inter-American Development Bank, began to address the issue of corruption and its relationship to development.[2] To take advantage of their virtually unmatched leverage with borrower governments and multinational corporations, these multilateral lending institutions looked to their own procurement practices as a means of deterring corruption.

The policies instituted by these multilateral lending institutions are intended to eliminate opportunities for corruption associated with the operations of each institution and to tie their lending to progress in combating corruption. The World Bank has added specific fraud and corruption language to its procurement rules and for the selection of consultants.[3] The regional development banks have, in large part, followed these same practices.

Among the key changes were explicit prohibitions on "corrupt" and "fraudulent" practices. "Corrupt practice" is defined as "the offering, giving, receiving or soliciting of anything of value to influence the action of a public official in the bidding process or in contract execution."[4] In addition, "fraudulent practice" is defined as

> a misrepresentation of facts in order to influence a bidding process or the execution of a contract to the detriment of the Borrower, and includes collusive practices among bidders (prior to or after bid submission) designed to establish bid prices at artificial, non-competitive levels and to deprive the Borrower of the benefits of free and open competition.[5]

A proposal will be rejected if it is determined that the bidder or consultant proposed for the award of a contract has engaged in corrupt or fraudulent activities in competing for the contract. The portion of a loan allocated to a contract for goods, works, or services can be cancelled if there is a determination that corrupt or fraudulent practices were engaged in by representatives of the borrower or executing agency during the procurement or selection process or the execution of the contract. The prospect of the rejection of a proposal or cancellation of a contract is reduced where timely and appropriate remedial action is taken and where that action is deemed to be satisfactory by the World Bank.

Among the most important of the new requirements is the provision that enables the World Bank to inspect the accounts and records of suppliers, contractors, or consultants related to the performance of the contract. This includes permitting the World Bank to appoint auditors to audit the accounts and records. In addition, the World Bank has instituted procedures for reporting allegations and protecting whistle blowers.

The World Bank will declare a firm or a consultant ineligible, either indefinitely or for a stated period of time, to be awarded a contract financed by it when there is a determination that the individual or entity has engaged in corrupt or fraudulent practices in competing for, or in executing, a contract financed by the World Bank. A number of individuals and entities have already been debarred or "blacklisted" from participation in contracts financed by the World Bank for a specific period or indefinitely.[6] Being debarred by the World Bank may also have implications in terms of being ineligible for procurements at other multilateral lending institutions as well as in some countries.

The World Bank has developed a series of procedures for the imposition of sanctions.[7] The process is prompted by a notice of debarment by the World Bank's Sanctions Committee. The notice will have been preceded by an investigation. The standard of proof is "reasonably sufficient" evidence that an individual or entity has engaged in corrupt or fraudulent practices. A hearing process has been established whereby an opportunity is afforded to challenge a notice of debarment. Formal rules of evidence do not apply in these proceedings.

The debarment process also permits the World Bank to make disclosures of evidence to other development institutions as well as to law enforcement agencies of governments that may be involved. This can take place prior to any determination that the World Bank may make with respect to an individual or entity. No prior notice is required. Nor is there a means of precluding such disclosures.

While the regional development banks are somewhat behind the World Bank in implementing policies and procedures to address corrupt and fraudulent practices, their policies and procedures can be expected to be modeled after those of the World Bank. Indeed, language relative to fraud and to corrupt practices has been added to their procurement guidelines. Hotlines and other means of reporting and investigating violations have also been instituted.

EUROPEAN UNION

In 1995, the European Union passed a Convention on the Protection of the Communities' Financial Interests (Convention on EU Financial Interests) obligating members of the European Union to impose criminal penalties in cases of serious fraud.[8] The First and Second Protocols to the Convention on Financial Interests (EU Corruption Protocols) were adopted, respectively, in 1996 and 1997. The Convention on the Fight Against Corruption Involving Officials of the European Communities or Officials of Member States of the European Union (EU Corruption Convention) was adopted in 1997.[9]

These conventions and protocols require member countries to impose criminal liability for corrupt acts, to punish corruption by "effective, proportionate and dissuasive" criminal penalties, and to create the obligation to extradite or prosecute an offender.[10] The focus is different between the EU Corruption Convention and the Convention on EU Financial Interests and EU Corruption Protocols. The EU Corruption Convention covers corruption by officials of the European Union or of European Union member countries whether or not the corruption involves the finances of the European Union. It does not cover or extend to officials of countries not members of the European Union.

The Convention on EU Financial Interests designates the types of conduct that constitute "fraud affecting the European Communities' financial interests."[11] The conduct prohibited includes, for example, the submission of false information to a public authority to induce it to pay funds or transfer property it would not otherwise have done. The EU Corruption Protocols address active and passive corruption, money laundering, and the confiscation of the proceeds of fraud and corruption. The forms of active and passive corruption that the EU Corruption Protocols address consist of bribery and similar conduct, in which some promise, benefit, or advantage is solicited, offered, or exchanged in return for undue influence on the exercise of a public duty.

After a considerable period of time, none of the conventions and protocols has obtained the necessary ratifications to enter into force. With ratification being unlikely in the near future, the European Commission proposed in 2001 the adoption of a directive to incorporate a large part of these two conventions and two protocols.[12] The proposal requires members of the European Union to make fraud, corruption, and money laundering affecting the financial interests of the European Union a criminal offense in their national law. European Union members are required to treat active and passive fraud and corruption committed by European Union officials in the same way as the same conduct would be treated if committed by their national officials.

OAU CORRUPTION CONVENTION

In July of 2003, the Organization of African Unity (OAU) adopted and opened for signature the Organization of African Unity Corruption Convention (OAU Convention).[13] Similar in a number of respects to the Inter-American and CoE Criminal Law Conventions, the OAU Convention seeks to address a range of issues relating to corruption. Provision is made for criminalizing active and passive bribery as well as illicit enrichment. No specific provision is included that addresses transnational bribery. However, international cooperation is an important component of the OAU Convention.

NON-GOVERNMENTAL ORGANIZATIONS

Much of the international activity to seek common means of deterring corrupt practices in the conduct of international business has been encouraged by nongovernmental organizations (NGOs). Many of these NGOs are business oriented and international in nature. Their prodding has played an important role in many of the initiatives to address foreign corrupt practices. Their active support and vigilance will also play a crucial role in the degree to which these anti-corruption conventions are fully implemented and actively enforced.

International Chamber of Commerce

In June of 1994, the Executive Board and Council of the International Chamber of Commerce (ICC) agreed to set up an Ad Hoc Committee on Extortion and Bribery in International Transactions to revise a 1977 ICC report on corrupt practices and to coordinate the ICC's participation in various forums on extortion and bribery issues. This led to the issuance of the ICC's Report on Extortion and Bribery in Business Transactions in 1996.

The 1996 report included recommendations to governments and to the private sector, including recommended rules of conduct for voluntary application by enterprises. The rules prohibit extortion and bribery for any purpose, not just to obtain or retain business, and cover extortion and bribery in judicial and legislative proceedings, tax matters, and environmental and other regulatory cases. In the 1999 "revised version" of the ICC's rules of conduct, no changes were made in the rules of conduct adopted in 1996.[14]

Some of the key provisions of the rules include:

- No enterprise may, directly or indirectly, offer or give a bribe, and any demands for such a bribe must be rejected;
- Enterprises should not kick back any portion of a contract payment to employees of the other contracting party;

- Enterprises should ensure that payments to agents represent no more than appropriate remuneration for legitimate services;
- All financial transactions must be properly recorded, with no off-the-books or secret accounts;
- Enterprises should draw up their own codes, consistent with ICC rules, to meet particular circumstances of their business; and
- Corporate governing bodies should establish control systems aimed at preventing payments that infringe ICC rules and take appropriate action against directors or employees who contravene the rules.[15]

Transparency International

In May of 1993, an international, nonprofit NGO known as Transparency International (TI) was established to curb corruption in international business transactions. TI is headquartered in Germany and has chapters all over the world. TI has played a very prominent and effective role in pressing governments, international organizations, and business entities to adopt measures designed to deter corruption in the conduct of international business. TI has also worked closely with the private sector to facilitate compliance as well as to develop mechanisms to assist entities subject to various forms of passive bribery.

NOTES

1. A number of these Web sites are included in Appendix II-H, *infra* at 333.
2. What is commonly referred to as the "World Bank" is officially known as the World Bank Group. The World Bank Group is comprised of five closely-associated institutions: the International Bank for Reconstruction and Development; the International Development Association; the International Finance Corporation; the Multilateral Investment Guarantee Agency; and the International Center for Settlement of Investment Disputes.
3. The new language is included in Appendix II-F, *infra* at 319.
4. World Bank Procurement Guidelines, § 1.14, ¶ a(i); World Bank Consultant Guidelines § 1.22, ¶ a(i).
5. World Bank Procurement Guidelines, § 1.14, ¶ a(ii); World Bank Consultant Guidelines § 1.22, ¶ a(ii).
6. An updated listing of individuals and entities debarred by the World Bank can be found at the World Bank's Web site, **http://www.worldbank.org.** In the search box, enter "List of Debarred Firms."
7. These procedures are included at Appendix II-G, *infra* at 323.
8. A summary of the Convention on EU Financial Interests and its two protocols can be found at **http://europa.eu.int/scadplus/leg/en/lvb/l33019.htm.**
9. A summary of the EU Corruption Convention can be found on the European Union's Web site at **http://europa.eu.int/scadplus/leg/en/lvb/l33027.htm.**
10. *Id.*
11. Summary of the Convention on EU Financial Interests.
12. The proposal can be found on the Web site of the European Union at **http://europa.eu.int/smartapi/cgi/sga_doc?smartapi!celexplus!prod!DocNumber&lg=en&type_doc=COMfinal&an_doc=2001&nu_doc=272.**

13. For the actual text of the OAU Convention and the list of countries that have signed and have ratified or acceded to the OAU Convention, *see* the OAU Web site at **http://www.africa-union.org.**

14. ICC, Extortion and Bribery in International Business Transactions, Part II—Rules of Conduct to Combat Extortion and Bribery, *at* **http://www.iccwbo.org/home/statements_rules/rules/1999/ briberydoc99.asp.**

15. *Id.*

CONVENTION ON COMBATING BRIBERY OF FOREIGN OFFICIALS IN INTERNATIONAL BUSINESS TRANSACTIONS*

Adopted by the Negotiating Conference on 21 November 1997

PREAMBLE

The Parties,

Considering that bribery is a widespread phenomenon in international business transactions, including trade and investment, which raises serious moral and political concerns, undermines good governance and economic development, and distorts international competitive conditions;

Considering that all countries share a responsibility to combat bribery in international business transactions;

Having regard to the Revised Recommendation on Combating Bribery in International Business Transactions, adopted by the Council of the Organisation for Economic Co-operation and Development (OECD) on 23 May 1997, C(97)123/ FINAL, which, *inter alia*, called for effective measures to deter, prevent and combat the bribery of foreign public officials in connection with international business transactions, in particular the prompt criminalisation of such bribery in an effective and coordinated manner and in conformity with the agreed common elements set out in that Recommendation and with the jurisdictional and other basic legal principles of each country;

Welcoming other recent developments which further advance international understanding and co-operation in combating bribery of public officials, including

---

* OECD Doc. DAFFE/IME/BR(97)20, *reprinted in* 37 I.L.M. 1 (1998).

actions of the United Nations, the World Bank, the International Monetary Fund, the World Trade Organisation, the Organisation of American States, the Council of Europe and the European Union;

Welcoming the efforts of companies, business organisations and trade unions as well as other non-governmental organisations to combat bribery;

Recognising the role of governments in the prevention of solicitation of bribes from individuals and enterprises in international business transactions;

Recognising that achieving progress in this field requires not only efforts on a national level but also multilateral co-operation, monitoring and follow-up;

Recognising that achieving equivalence among the measures to be taken by the Parties is an essential object and purpose of the Convention, which requires that the Convention be ratified without derogations affecting this equivalence;

Have agreed as follows:

ARTICLE 1

THE OFFENCE OF BRIBERY OF FOREIGN PUBLIC OFFICIALS

1. Each Party shall take such measures as may be necessary to establish that it is a criminal offence under its law for any person intentionally to offer, promise or give any undue pecuniary or other advantage, whether directly or through intermediaries, to a foreign public official, for that official or for a third party, in order that the official act or refrain from acting in relation to the performance of official duties, in order to obtain or retain business or other improper advantage in the conduct of international business.

2. Each Party shall take any measures necessary to establish that complicity in, including incitement, aiding and abetting, or authorisation of an act of bribery of a foreign public official shall be a criminal offence. Attempt and conspiracy to bribe a foreign public official shall be criminal offences to the same extent as attempt and conspiracy to bribe a public official of that Party.

3. The offences set out in paragraphs 1 and 2 above are hereinafter referred to as "bribery of a foreign public official".

4. For the purpose of this Convention:

    a. "foreign public official" means any person holding a legislative, administrative or judicial office of a foreign country, whether appointed or elected; any person exercising a public function for a foreign country, including for a public agency or public enterprise; and any official or agent of a public international organisation;

    b. "foreign country" includes all levels and subdivisions of government, from national to local;

    c. "act or refrain from acting in relation to the performance of official duties" includes any use of the public official's position, whether or not within the official's authorised competence.

ARTICLE 2

RESPONSIBILITY OF LEGAL PERSONS

Each Party shall take such measures as may be necessary, in accordance with its legal principles, to establish the liability of legal persons for the bribery of a foreign public official.

ARTICLE 3

SANCTIONS

1. The bribery of a foreign public official shall be punishable by effective, proportionate and dissuasive criminal penalties. The range of penalties shall be comparable to that applicable to the bribery of the Party's own public officials and shall, in the case of natural persons, include deprivation of liberty sufficient to enable effective mutual legal assistance and extradition.

2. In the event that, under the legal system of a Party, criminal responsibility is not applicable to legal persons, that Party shall ensure that legal persons shall be subject to effective, proportionate and dissuasive non-criminal sanctions, including monetary sanctions, for bribery of foreign public officials.

3. Each Party shall take such measures as may be necessary to provide that the bribe and the proceeds of the bribery of a foreign public official, or property the value of which corresponds to that of such proceeds, are subject to seizure and confiscation or that monetary sanctions of comparable effect are applicable.

4. Each Party shall consider the imposition of additional civil or administrative sanctions upon a person subject to sanctions for the bribery of a foreign public official.

ARTICLE 4

JURISDICTION

1. Each Party shall take such measures as may be necessary to establish its jurisdiction over the bribery of a foreign public official when the offence is committed in whole or in part in its territory.

2. Each Party which has jurisdiction to prosecute its nationals for offences committed abroad shall take such measures as may be necessary to establish its jurisdiction to do so in respect of the bribery of a foreign public official, according to the same principles.

3. When more than one Party has jurisdiction over an alleged offence described in this Convention, the Parties involved shall, at the request of one of them,

consult with a view to determining the most appropriate jurisdiction for prosecution.

4. Each Party shall review whether its current basis for jurisdiction is effective in the fight against the bribery of foreign public officials and, if it is not, shall take remedial steps.

ARTICLE 5

ENFORCEMENT

Investigation and prosecution of the bribery of a foreign public official shall be subject to the applicable rules and principles of each Party. They shall not be influenced by considerations of national economic interest, the potential effect upon relations with another State or the identity of the natural or legal persons involved.

ARTICLE 6

STATUTE OF LIMITATIONS

Any statute of limitations applicable to the offence of bribery of a foreign public official shall allow an adequate period of time for the investigation and prosecution of this offence.

ARTICLE 7

MONEY LAUNDERING

Each Party which has made bribery of its own public official a predicate offence for the purpose of the application of its money laundering legislation shall do so on the same terms for the bribery of a foreign public official, without regard to the place where the bribery occurred.

ARTICLE 8

ACCOUNTING

1. In order to combat bribery of foreign public officials effectively, each Party shall take such measures as may be necessary, within the framework of its laws and regulations regarding the maintenance of books and records, financial statement disclosures, and accounting and auditing standards, to prohibit the establishment of off-the-books accounts, the making of off-the-books or inadequately identified transactions, the recording of non-existent expenditures, the entry of liabilities with incorrect identification of their object, as

well as the use of false documents, by companies subject to those laws and regulations, for the purpose of bribing foreign public officials or of hiding such bribery.

2. Each Party shall provide effective, proportionate and dissuasive civil, administrative or criminal penalties for such omissions and falsifications in respect of the books, records, accounts and financial statements of such companies.

ARTICLE 9

MUTUAL LEGAL ASSISTANCE

1. Each Party shall, to the fullest extent possible under its laws and relevant treaties and arrangements, provide prompt and effective legal assistance to another Party for the purpose of criminal investigations and proceedings brought by a Party concerning offences within the scope of this Convention and for non-criminal proceedings within the scope of this Convention brought by a Party against a legal person. The requested Party shall inform the requesting Party, without delay, of any additional information or documents needed to support the request for assistance and, where requested, of the status and outcome of the request for assistance.

2. Where a Party makes mutual legal assistance conditional upon the existence of dual criminality, dual criminality shall be deemed to exist if the offence for which the assistance is sought is within the scope of this Convention.

3. A Party shall not decline to render mutual legal assistance for criminal matters within the scope of this Convention on the ground of bank secrecy.

ARTICLE 10

EXTRADITION

1. Bribery of a foreign public official shall be deemed to be included as an extraditable offence under the laws of the Parties and the extradition treaties between them.

2. If a Party which makes extradition conditional on the existence of an extradition treaty receives a request for extradition from another Party with which it has no extradition treaty, it may consider this Convention to be the legal basis for extradition in respect of the offence of bribery of a foreign public official.

3. Each Party shall take any measures necessary to assure either that it can extradite its nationals or that it can prosecute its nationals for the offence of bribery of a foreign public official. A Party which declines a request to extradite a person for bribery of a foreign public official solely on the ground that the person is its national shall submit the case to its competent authorities for the purpose of prosecution.

4. Extradition for bribery of a foreign public official is subject to the conditions set out in the domestic law and applicable treaties and arrangements of each Party. Where a Party makes extradition conditional upon the existence of dual criminality, that condition shall be deemed to be fulfilled if the offence for which extradition is sought is within the scope of Article 1 of this Convention.

ARTICLE 11

RESPONSIBLE AUTHORITIES

For the purposes of Article 4, paragraph 3, on consultation, Article 9, on mutual legal assistance and Article 10, on extradition, each Party shall notify to the Secretary-General of the OECD an authority or authorities responsible for making and receiving requests, which shall serve as channel of communication for these matters for that Party, without prejudice to other arrangements between Parties.

ARTICLE 12

MONITORING AND FOLLOW-UP

The Parties shall co-operate in carrying out a programme of systematic follow-up to monitor and promote the full implementation of this Convention. Unless otherwise decided by consensus of the Parties, this shall be done in the framework of the OECD Working Group on Bribery in International Business Transactions and according to its terms of reference, or within the framework and terms of reference of any successor to its functions, and Parties shall bear the costs of the programme in accordance with the rules applicable to that body.

ARTICLE 13

SIGNATURE AND ACCESSION

1. Until its entry into force, this Convention shall be open for signature by OECD members and by non-members which have been invited to become full participants in its Working Group on Bribery in International Business Transactions.

2. Subsequent to its entry into force, this Convention shall be open to accession by any nonsignatory which is a member of the OECD or has become a full participant in the Working Group on Bribery in International Business Transactions or any successor to its functions. For each such nonsignatory, the Convention shall enter into force on the sixtieth day following the date of deposit of its instrument of accession.

ARTICLE 14

RATIFICATION AND DEPOSITARY

1. This Convention is subject to acceptance, approval or ratification by the Signatories, in accordance with their respective laws.

2. Instruments of acceptance, approval, ratification or accession shall be deposited with the Secretary-General of the OECD, who shall serve as Depositary of this Convention.

ARTICLE 15

ENTRY INTO FORCE

1. This Convention shall enter into force on the sixtieth day following the date upon which five of the ten countries which have the ten largest export shares set out in (annexed),* and which represent by themselves at least sixty per cent of the combined total exports of those ten countries, have deposited their instruments of acceptance, approval, or ratification. For each signatory depositing its instrument after such entry into force, the Convention shall enter into force on the sixtieth day after deposit of its instrument.

2. If, after 31 December 1998, the Convention has not entered into force under paragraph 1 above, any signatory which has deposited its instrument of acceptance, approval or ratification may declare in writing to the Depositary its readiness to accept entry into force of this Convention under this paragraph 2. The Convention shall enter into force for such a signatory on the sixtieth day following the date upon which such declarations have been deposited by at least two signatories. For each signatory depositing its declaration after such entry into force, the Convention shall enter into force on the sixtieth day following the date of deposit.

ARTICLE 16

AMENDMENT

Any Party may propose the amendment of this Convention. A proposed amendment shall be submitted to the Depositary which shall communicate it to the other Parties at least sixty days before convening a meeting of the Parties to consider the proposed amendment. An amendment adopted by consensus of the Parties, or by such other means as the Parties may determine by consensus, shall enter into force sixty days after the deposit of an instrument of ratification, acceptance or approval by all of the Parties, or in such other

---

* The annex to the OECD Convention is not included in this appendix.

circumstances as may be specified by the Parties at the time of adoption of the amendment.

ARTICLE 17

WITHDRAWAL

A Party may withdraw from this Convention by submitting written notification to the Depositary. Such withdrawal shall be effective one year after the date of the receipt of the notification. After withdrawal, co-operation shall continue between the Parties and the Party which has withdrawn on all requests for assistance or extradition made before the effective date of withdrawal which remain pending.

Concerning Belgium-Luxembourg: Trade statistics for Belgium and Luxembourg are available only on a combined basis for the two countries. For purposes of Article 15, paragraph 1 of the Convention, if either Belgium or Luxembourg deposits its instrument of acceptance, approval or ratification, or if both Belgium and Luxembourg deposit their instruments of acceptance, approval or ratification, it shall be considered that one of the countries which have the ten largest exports shares has deposited its instrument and the joint exports of both countries will be counted towards the 60 percent of combined total exports of those ten countries, which is required for entry into force under this provision.

COMMENTARIES ON THE CONVENTION ON COMBATING BRIBERY OF FOREIGN OFFICIALS IN INTERNATIONAL BUSINESS TRANSACTIONS*

Adopted by the Negotiating Conference on 21 November 1997

General:

1. This Convention deals with what, in the law of some countries, is called "active corruption" or "active bribery", meaning the offence committed by the person who promises or gives the bribe, as contrasted with "passive bribery", the offence committed by the official who receives the bribe. The Convention does not utilise the term "active bribery" simply to avoid it being misread by the nontechnical reader as implying that the briber has taken the initiative and the recipient is a passive victim. In fact, in a number of situations, the recipient will have induced or pressured the briber and will have been, in that sense, the more active.

2. This Convention seeks to assure a functional equivalence among the measures taken by the Parties to sanction bribery of foreign public officials, without requiring uniformity or changes in fundamental principles of a Party's legal system.

ARTICLE 1

THE OFFENCE OF BRIBERY OF FOREIGN PUBLIC OFFICIALS

Re paragraph 1:

3. Article 1 establishes a standard to be met by Parties, but does not require them to utilise its precise terms in defining the offence under their domestic

---

* OECD Doc. DAFFE/IME/BR(97)20.

laws. A Party may use various approaches to fulfill its obligations, provided that conviction of a person for the offence does not require proof of elements beyond those which would be required to be proved if the offence were defined as in this paragraph. For example, a statute prohibiting the bribery of agents generally which does not specifically address bribery of a foreign public official, and a statute specifically limited to this case, could both comply with this Article. Similarly, a statute which defined the offence in terms of payments "to induce a breach of the official's duty" could meet the standard provided that it was understood that every public official had a duty to exercise judgement or discretion impartially and this was an "autonomous" definition not requiring proof of the law of the particular official's country.

4. It is an offence within the meaning of paragraph 1 to bribe to obtain or retain business or other improper advantage whether or not the company concerned was the best qualified bidder or was otherwise a company which could properly have been awarded the business.

5. "Other improper advantage" refers to something to which the company concerned was not clearly entitled, for example, an operating permit for a factory which fails to meet the statutory requirements.

6. The conduct described in paragraph 1 is an offence whether the offer or promise is made or the pecuniary or other advantage is given on that person's own behalf or on behalf of any other natural person or legal entity.

7. It is also an offence irrespective of, inter alia, the value of the advantage, its results, perceptions of local custom, the tolerance of such payments by local authorities, or the alleged necessity of the payment in order to obtain or retain business or other improper advantage.

8. It is not an offence, however, if the advantage was permitted or required by the written law or regulation of the foreign public official's country, including case law.

9. Small "facilitation" payments do not constitute payments made "to obtain or retain business or other improper advantage" within the meaning of paragraph 1 and, accordingly, are also not an offence. Such payments, which, in some countries, are made to induce public officials to perform their functions, such as issuing licenses or permits, are generally illegal in the foreign country concerned. Other countries can and should address this corrosive phenomenon by such means as support for programmes of good governance. However, criminalisation by other countries does not seem a practical or effective complementary action.

10. Under the legal system of some countries, an advantage promised or given to any person, in anticipation of his or her becoming a foreign public official, falls within the scope of the offences described in Article 1, paragraph 1 or 2. Under the legal system of many countries, it is considered technically distinct from the offences covered by the present Convention. However, there is a

commonly shared concern and intent to address this phenomenon through further work.

Re paragraph 2:

11. The offences set out in paragraph 2 are understood in terms of their normal content in national legal systems. Accordingly, if authorisation, incitement, or one of the other listed acts, which does not lead to further action, is not itself punishable under a Party's legal system, then the Party would not be required to make it punishable with respect to bribery of a foreign public official.

Re paragraph 4:

12. "Public function" includes any activity in the public interest, delegated by a foreign country, such as the performance of a task delegated by it in connection with public procurement.

13. A "public agency" is an entity constituted under public law to carry out specific tasks in the public interest.

14. A "public enterprise" is any enterprise, regardless of its legal form, over which a government, or governments, may, directly or indirectly, exercise a dominant influence. This is deemed to be the case, inter alia, when the government or governments hold the majority of the enterprise's subscribed capital, control the majority of votes attaching to shares issued by the enterprise or can appoint a majority of the members of the enterprise's administrative or managerial body or supervisory board.

15. An official of a public enterprise shall be deemed to perform a public function unless the enterprise operates on a normal commercial basis in the relevant market, i.e., on a basis which is substantially equivalent to that of a private enterprise, without preferential subsidies or other privileges.

16. In special circumstances, public authority may in fact be held by persons (e.g., political party officials in single party states) not formally designated as public officials. Such persons, through their *de facto* performance of a public function, may, under the legal principles of some countries, be considered to be foreign public officials.

17. "Public international organisation" includes any international organisation formed by states, governments, or other public international organisations, whatever the form of organisation and scope of competence, including, for example, a regional economic integration organisation such as the European Communities.

18. "Foreign country" is not limited to states, but includes any organised foreign area or entity, such as an autonomous territory or a separate customs territory.

19. One case of bribery which has been contemplated under the definition in paragraph 4.c is where an executive of a company gives a bribe to a senior official of a government, in order that this official use his office—though acting outside his competence—to make another official award a contract to that company.

ARTICLE 2

RESPONSIBILITY OF LEGAL PERSONS

20. In the event that, under the legal system of a Party, criminal responsibility is not applicable to legal persons, that Party shall not be required to establish such criminal responsibility.

ARTICLE 3

SANCTIONS

Re paragraph 3:

21. The "proceeds" of bribery are the profits or other benefits derived by the briber from the transaction or other improper advantage obtained or retained through bribery.

22. The term "confiscation" includes forfeiture where applicable and means the permanent deprivation of property by order of a court or other competent authority. This paragraph is without prejudice to rights of victims.

23. Paragraph 3 does not preclude setting appropriate limits to monetary sanctions.

Re paragraph 4:

24. Among the civil or administrative sanctions, other than non-criminal fines, which might be imposed upon legal persons for an act of bribery of a foreign public official are: exclusion from entitlement to public benefits or aid; temporary or permanent disqualification from participation in public procurement or from the practice of other commercial activities; placing under judicial supervision; and a judicial winding-up order.

ARTICLE 4

JURISDICTION

Re paragraph 1:

25. The territorial basis for jurisdiction should be interpreted broadly so that an extensive physical connection to the bribery act is not required.

Re paragraph 2:

26. Nationality jurisdiction is to be established according to the general principles and conditions in the legal system of each Party. These principles deal with such matters as dual criminality. However, the requirement of dual criminality should be deemed to be met if the act is unlawful where it occurred, even if under a different criminal statute. For countries which apply nationality jurisdiction only to certain types of offences, the reference to "principles" includes the principles upon which such selection is based.

ARTICLE 5

ENFORCEMENT

27. Article 5 recognises the fundamental nature of national regimes of prosecutorial discretion. It recognises as well that, in order to protect the independence of prosecution, such discretion is to be exercised on the basis of professional motives and is not to be subject to improper influence by concerns of a political nature. Article 5 is complemented by paragraph 6 of the Annex to the 1997 OECD Revised Recommendation on Combating Bribery in International Business Transactions, C(97)123/FINAL (hereinafter, "1997 OECD Recommendation"), which recommends, inter alia, that complaints of bribery of foreign public officials should be seriously investigated by competent authorities and that adequate resources should be provided by national governments to permit effective prosecution of such bribery. Parties will have accepted this Recommendation, including its monitoring and follow-up arrangements.

ARTICLE 7

MONEY LAUNDERING

28. In Article 7, "bribery of its own public official" is intended broadly, so that bribery of a foreign public official is to be made a predicate offence for money laundering legislation on the same terms, when a Party has made either active or passive bribery of its own public official such an offence. When a Party has made only passive bribery of its own public officials a predicate offence for money laundering purposes, this article requires that the laundering of the bribe payment be subject to money laundering legislation.

ARTICLE 8

ACCOUNTING

29. Article 8 is related to section V of the 1997 OECD Recommendation, which all Parties will have accepted and which is subject to follow-up in the OECD Working Group on Bribery in International Business Transactions. This paragraph contains a series of recommendations concerning accounting requirements, independent external audit and internal company controls the implementation of which will be important to the overall effectiveness of the fight against bribery in international business. However, one immediate consequence of the implementation of this Convention by the Parties will be that companies which are required to issue financial statements disclosing their material contingent liabilities will need to take into account the full potential liabilities under this Convention, in particular its Articles 3 and 8, as

well as other losses which might flow from conviction of the company or its agents for bribery. This also has implications for the execution of professional responsibilities of auditors regarding indications of bribery of foreign public officials. In addition, the accounting offences referred to in Article 8 will generally occur in the company's home country, when the bribery offence itself may have been committed in another country, and this can fill gaps in the effective reach of the Convention.

ARTICLE 9

MUTUAL LEGAL ASSISTANCE

30. Parties will have also accepted, through paragraph 8 of the Agreed Common Elements annexed to the 1997 OECD Recommendation, to explore and undertake means to improve the efficiency of mutual legal assistance.

Re paragraph 1:

31. Within the framework of paragraph 1 of Article 9, Parties should, upon request, facilitate or encourage the presence or availability of persons, including persons in custody, who consent to assist in investigations or participate in proceedings. Parties should take measures to be able, in appropriate cases, to transfer temporarily such a person in custody to a Party requesting it and to credit time in custody in the requesting Party to the transferred person's sentence in the requested Party. The Parties wishing to use this mechanism should also take measures to be able, as a requesting Party, to keep a transferred person in custody and return this person without necessity of extradition proceedings.

Re paragraph 2:

32. Paragraph 2 addresses the issue of identity of norms in the concept of dual criminality. Parties with statutes as diverse as a statute prohibiting the bribery of agents generally and a statute directed specifically at bribery of foreign public officials should be able to co-operate fully regarding cases whose facts fall within the scope of the offences described in this Convention.

ARTICLE 10

EXTRADITION

Re paragraph 2:

33. A Party may consider this Convention to be a legal basis for extradition if, for one or more categories of cases falling within this Convention, it requires an extradition treaty. For example, a country may consider it a basis for extradition of its nationals if it requires an extradition treaty for that category but does not require one for extradition of non-nationals.

ARTICLE 12

MONITORING AND FOLLOW-UP

34. The current terms of reference of the OECD Working Group on Bribery which are relevant to monitoring and follow-up are set out in Section VIII of the 1997 OECD Recommendation. They provide for:

    i) receipt of notifications and other information submitted to it by the [participating] countries;

    ii) regular reviews of steps taken by [participating] countries to implement the Recommendation and to make proposals, as appropriate, to assist [participating] countries in its implementation; these reviews will be based on the following complementary systems:

        — a system of self evaluation, where [participating] countries' responses on the basis of a questionnaire will provide a basis for assessing the implementation of the Recommendation;

        — a system of mutual evaluation, where each [participating] country will be examined in turn by the Working Group on Bribery, on the basis of a report which will provide an objective assessment of the progress of the [participating] country in implementing the Recommendation.

    iii) examination of specific issues relating to bribery in international business transactions;

        ...

    iv) provision of regular information to the public on its work and activities and on implementation of the Recommendation.

35. The costs of monitoring and follow-up will, for OECD Members, be handled through the normal OECD budget process. For non-members of the OECD, the current rules create an equivalent system of cost sharing, which is described in the Resolution of the Council Concerning Fees for Regular Observer Countries and Non-Member Full Participants in OECD Subsidiary Bodies, C(96)223/FINAL.

36. The follow-up of any aspect of the Convention which is not also follow-up of the 1997 OECD Recommendation or any other instrument accepted by all the participants in the OECD Working Group on Bribery will be carried out by the Parties to the Convention and, as appropriate, the participants party to another, corresponding instrument.

ARTICLE 13

SIGNATURE AND ACCESSION

37. The Convention will be open to non-members which become full participants in the OECD Working Group on Bribery in International Business Transactions. Full participation by non-members in this Working Group is

encouraged and arranged under simple procedures. Accordingly, the requirement of full participation in the Working Group, which follows from the relationship of the Convention to other aspects of the fight against bribery in international business, should not be seen as an obstacle by countries wishing to participate in that fight. The Council of the OECD has appealed to non-members to adhere to the 1997 OECD Recommendation and to participate in any institutional follow-up or implementation mechanism, i.e., in the Working Group. The current procedures regarding full participation by non-members in the Working Group may be found in the Resolution of the Council concerning the Participation of Non-Member Economies in the Work of Subsidiary Bodies of the Organisation, C(96)64/REV1/FINAL. In addition to accepting the Revised Recommendation of the Council on Combating Bribery, a full participant also accepts the Recommendation on the Tax Deductibility of Bribes of Foreign Public Officials, adopted on 11 April 1996, C(96)27/FINAL.

INTER-AMERICAN CONVENTION AGAINST CORRUPTION*

(Adopted at the third plenary session, held on March 29, 1996)

PREAMBLE

THE MEMBER STATES OF THE ORGANIZATION OF AMERICAN STATES,

CONVINCED that corruption undermines the legitimacy of public institutions and strikes at society, moral order and justice, as well as at the comprehensive development of peoples;

CONSIDERING that representative democracy, an essential condition for stability, peace and development of the region, requires, by its nature, the combating of every form of corruption in the performance of public functions, as well as acts of corruption specifically related to such performance;

PERSUADED that fighting corruption strengthens democratic institutions and prevents distortions in the economy, improprieties in public administration and damage to a society's moral fiber;

RECOGNIZING that corruption is often a tool used by organized crime for the accomplishment of its purposes;

CONVINCED of the importance of making people in the countries of the region aware of this problem and its gravity, and of the need to strengthen participation by civil society in preventing and fighting corruption;

RECOGNIZING that, in some cases, corruption has international dimensions, which requires coordinated action by States to fight it effectively;

CONVINCED of the need for prompt adoption of an international instrument to promote and facilitate international cooperation in fighting corruption

---

* OAS Doc. B-58, *reprinted in* 35 I.L.M. 724 (1996).

and, especially, in taking appropriate action against persons who commit acts of corruption in the performance of public functions, or acts specifically related to such performance, as well as appropriate measures with respect to the proceeds of such acts;

DEEPLY CONCERNED by the steadily increasing links between corruption and the proceeds generated by illicit narcotics trafficking which undermine and threaten legitimate commercial and financial activities, and society, at all levels;

BEARING IN MIND the responsibility of States to hold corrupt persons accountable in order to combat corruption and to cooperate with one another for their efforts in this area to be effective; and

DETERMINED to make every effort to prevent, detect, punish and eradicate corruption in the performance of public functions and acts of corruption specifically related to such performance,

HAVE AGREED to adopt the following

INTER-AMERICAN CONVENTION AGAINST CORRUPTION

ARTICLE I

DEFINITIONS

For the purposes of this Convention:

"Public function" means any temporary or permanent, paid or honorary activity, performed by a natural person in the name of the State or in the service of the State or its institutions, at any level of its hierarchy.

"Public official", "government official", or "public servant" means any official or employee of the State or its agencies, including those who have been selected, appointed, or elected to perform activities or functions in the name of the State or in the service of the State, at any level of its hierarchy.

"Property" means assets of any kind, whether movable or immovable, tangible or intangible, and any document or legal instrument demonstrating, purporting to demonstrate, or relating to ownership or other rights pertaining to such assets.

ARTICLE II

PURPOSES

The purposes of this Convention are:

1. To promote and strengthen the development by each of the States Parties of the mechanisms needed to prevent, detect, punish and eradicate corruption; and

2. To promote, facilitate and regulate cooperation among the States Parties to ensure the effectiveness of measures and actions to prevent, detect, punish and eradicate corruption in the performance of public functions and acts of corruption specifically related to such performance.

ARTICLE III

PREVENTIVE MEASURES

For the purposes set forth in Article II of this Convention, the States Parties agree to consider the applicability of measures within their own institutional systems to create, maintain and strengthen:

1. Standards of conduct for the correct, honorable, and proper fulfillment of public functions. These standards shall be intended to prevent conflicts of interest and mandate the proper conservation and use of resources entrusted to government officials in the performance of their functions. These standards shall also establish measures and systems requiring government officials to report to appropriate authorities acts of corruption in the performance of public functions. Such measures should help preserve the public's confidence in the integrity of public servants and government processes.

2. Mechanisms to enforce these standards of conduct.

3. Instruction to government personnel to ensure proper understanding of their responsibilities and the ethical rules governing their activities.

4. Systems for registering the income, assets and liabilities of persons who perform public functions in certain posts as specified by law and, where appropriate, for making such registrations public.

5. Systems of government hiring and procurement of goods and services that assure the openness, equity and efficiency of such systems.

6. Government revenue collection and control systems that deter corruption.

7. Laws that deny favorable tax treatment for any individual or corporation for expenditures made in violation of the anti-corruption laws of the States Parties.

8. Systems for protecting public servants and private citizens who, in good faith, report acts of corruption, including protection of their identities, in accordance with their Constitutions and the basic principles of their domestic legal systems.

9. Oversight bodies with a view to implementing modern mechanisms for preventing, detecting, punishing and eradicating corrupt acts.

10. Deterrents to the bribery of domestic and foreign government officials, such as mechanisms to ensure that publicly held companies and other types of associations maintain books and records which, in reasonable detail, accurately reflect the acquisition and disposition of assets, and have sufficient internal accounting controls to enable their officers to detect corrupt acts.

11. Mechanisms to encourage participation by civil society and nongovernmental organizations in efforts to prevent corruption.

12. The study of further preventive measures that take into account the relationship between equitable compensation and probity in public service.

ARTICLE IV

SCOPE

This Convention is applicable provided that the alleged act of corruption has been committed or has effects in a State Party.

ARTICLE V

JURISDICTION

1. Each State Party shall adopt such measures as may be necessary to establish its jurisdiction over the offenses it has established in accordance with this Convention when the offense in question is committed in its territory.

2. Each State Party may adopt such measures as may be necessary to establish its jurisdiction over the offenses it has established in accordance with this Convention when the offense is committed by one of its nationals or by a person who habitually resides in its territory.

3. Each State Party shall adopt such measures as may be necessary to establish its jurisdiction over the offenses it has established in accordance with this Convention when the alleged criminal is present in its territory and it does not extradite such person to another country on the ground of the nationality of the alleged criminal.

4. This Convention does not preclude the application of any other rule of criminal jurisdiction established by a State Party under its domestic law.

ARTICLE VI

ACTS OF CORRUPTION

1. This Convention is applicable to the following acts of corruption:
    a. The solicitation or acceptance, directly or indirectly, by a government official or a person who performs public functions, of any article of monetary value, or other benefit, such as a gift, favor, promise or advantage for himself or for another person or entity, in exchange for any act or omission in the performance of his public functions;
    b. The offering or granting, directly or indirectly, to a government official or a person who performs public functions, of any article of monetary value, or other benefit, such as a gift, favor, promise or advantage for himself or for another person or entity, in exchange for any act or omission in the performance of his public functions;
    c. Any act or omission in the discharge of his duties by a government official or a person who performs public functions for the purpose of illicitly obtaining benefits for himself or for a third party;

d. The fraudulent use or concealment of property derived from any of the acts referred to in this article; and

e. Participation as a principal, co-principal, instigator, accomplice or accessory after the fact, or in any other manner, in the commission or attempted commission of, or in any collaboration or conspiracy to commit, any of the acts referred to in this article.

2. This Convention shall also be applicable by mutual agreement between or among two or more States Parties with respect to any other act of corruption not described herein.

ARTICLE VII

DOMESTIC LAW

The States Parties that have not yet done so shall adopt the necessary legislative or other measures to establish as criminal offenses under their domestic law the acts of corruption described in Article VI(1) and to facilitate cooperation among themselves pursuant to this Convention.

ARTICLE VIII

TRANSNATIONAL BRIBERY

Subject to its Constitution and the fundamental principles of its legal system, each State Party shall prohibit and punish the offering or granting, directly or indirectly, by its nationals, persons having their habitual residence in its territory, and businesses domiciled there, to a government official of another State, of any article of monetary value, or other benefit, such as a gift, favor, promise or advantage, in connection with any economic or commercial transaction in exchange for any act or omission in the performance of that official's public functions.

Among those States Parties that have established transnational bribery as an offense, such offense shall be considered an act of corruption for the purposes of this Convention.

Any State Party that has not established transnational bribery as an offense shall, insofar as its laws permit, provide assistance and cooperation with respect to this offense as provided in this Convention.

ARTICLE IX

ILLICIT ENRICHMENT

Subject to its Constitution and the fundamental principles of its legal system, each State Party that has not yet done so shall take the necessary measures to establish under its laws as an offense a significant increase in the assets of a government official that he cannot reasonably explain in relation to his lawful earnings during the performance of his functions.

Among those States Parties that have established illicit enrichment as an offense, such offense shall be considered an act of corruption for the purposes of this Convention.

Any State Party that has not established illicit enrichment as an offense shall, insofar as its laws permit, provide assistance and cooperation with respect to this offense as provided in this Convention.

ARTICLE X

NOTIFICATION

When a State Party adopts the legislation referred to in paragraph 1 of articles VIII and IX, it shall notify the Secretary General of the Organization of American States, who shall in turn notify the other States Parties. For the purposes of this Convention, the crimes of transnational bribery and illicit enrichment shall be considered acts of corruption for that State Party thirty days following the date of such notification.

ARTICLE XI

PROGRESSIVE DEVELOPMENT

1. In order to foster the development and harmonization of their domestic legislation and the attainment of the purposes of this Convention, the States Parties view as desirable, and undertake to consider, establishing as offenses under their laws the following acts:
   a. The improper use by a government official or a person who performs public functions, for his own benefit or that of a third party, of any kind of classified or confidential information which that official or person who performs public functions has obtained because of, or in the performance of, his functions;
   b. The improper use by a government official or a person who performs public functions, for his own benefit or that of a third party, of any kind of property belonging to the State or to any firm or institution in which the State has a proprietary interest, to which that official or person who performs public functions has access because of, or in the performance of, his functions;
   c. Any act or omission by any person who, personally or through a third party, or acting as an intermediary, seeks to obtain a decision from a public authority whereby he illicitly obtains for himself or for another person any benefit or gain, whether or not such act or omission harms State property; and

d. The diversion by a government official, for purposes unrelated to those for which they were intended, for his own benefit or that of a third party, of any movable or immovable property, monies or securities belonging to the State, to an independent agency, or to an individual, that such official has received by virtue of his position for purposes of administration, custody or for other reasons.

2. Among those States Parties that have established these offenses, such offenses shall be considered acts of corruption for the purposes of this Convention.

3. Any State Party that has not established these offenses shall, insofar as its laws permit, provide assistance and cooperation with respect to these offenses as provided in this Convention.

ARTICLE XII

EFFECT ON STATE PROPERTY

For application of this Convention, it shall not be necessary that the acts of corruption harm State property.

ARTICLE XIII

EXTRADITION

1. This article shall apply to the offenses established by the States Parties in accordance with this Convention.

2. Each of the offenses to which this article applies shall be deemed to be included as an extraditable offense in any extradition treaty existing between or among the States Parties. The States Parties undertake to include such offenses as extraditable offenses in every extradition treaty to be concluded between or among them.

3. If a State Party that makes extradition conditional on the existence of a treaty receives a request for extradition from another State Party with which it does not have an extradition treaty, it may consider this Convention as the legal basis for extradition with respect to any offense to which this article applies.

4. States Parties that do not make extradition conditional on the existence of a treaty shall recognize offenses to which this article applies as extraditable offenses between themselves.

5. Extradition shall be subject to the conditions provided for by the law of the Requested State or by applicable extradition treaties, including the grounds on which the Requested State may refuse extradition.

6. If extradition for an offense to which this article applies is refused solely on the basis of the nationality of the person sought, or because the Requested State deems that it has jurisdiction over the offense, the Requested State shall

submit the case to its competent authorities for the purpose of prosecution unless otherwise agreed with the Requesting State, and shall report the final outcome to the Requesting State in due course.

7. Subject to the provisions of its domestic law and its extradition treaties, the Requested State may, upon being satisfied that the circumstances so warrant and are urgent, and at the request of the Requesting State, take into custody a person whose extradition is sought and who is present in its territory, or take other appropriate measures to ensure his presence at extradition proceedings.

ARTICLE XIV

ASSISTANCE AND COOPERATION

1. In accordance with their domestic laws and applicable treaties, the States Parties shall afford one another the widest measure of mutual assistance by processing requests from authorities that, in conformity with their domestic laws, have the power to investigate or prosecute the acts of corruption described in this Convention, to obtain evidence and take other necessary action to facilitate legal proceedings and measures regarding the investigation or prosecution of acts of corruption.

2. The States Parties shall also provide each other with the widest measure of mutual technical cooperation on the most effective ways and means of preventing, detecting, investigating and punishing acts of corruption. To that end, they shall foster exchanges of experiences by way of agreements and meetings between competent bodies and institutions, and shall pay special attention to methods and procedures of citizen participation in the fight against corruption.

ARTICLE XV

MEASURES REGARDING PROPERTY

1. In accordance with their applicable domestic laws and relevant treaties or other agreements that may be in force between or among them, the States Parties shall provide each other the broadest possible measure of assistance in the identification, tracing, freezing, seizure and forfeiture of property or proceeds obtained, derived from or used in the commission of offenses established in accordance with this Convention.

2. A State Party that enforces its own or another State Party's forfeiture judgment against property or proceeds described in paragraph 1 of this article shall dispose of the property or proceeds in accordance with its laws. To the extent permitted by a State Party's laws and upon such terms as it deems appropriate, it may transfer all or part of such property or proceeds to another State Party that assisted in the underlying investigation or proceedings.

ARTICLE XVI

BANK SECRECY

1. The Requested State shall not invoke bank secrecy as a basis for refusal to provide the assistance sought by the Requesting State. The Requested State shall apply this article in accordance with its domestic law, its procedural provisions, or bilateral or multilateral agreements with the Requesting State.

2. The Requesting State shall be obligated not to use any information received that is protected by bank secrecy for any purpose other than the proceeding for which that information was requested, unless authorized by the Requested State.

ARTICLE XVII

NATURE OF THE ACT

For the purposes of articles XIII, XIV, XV and XVI of this Convention, the fact that the property obtained or derived from an act of corruption was intended for political purposes, or that it is alleged that an act of corruption was committed for political motives or purposes, shall not suffice in and of itself to qualify the act as a political offense or as a common offense related to a political offense.

ARTICLE XVIII

CENTRAL AUTHORITIES

1. For the purposes of international assistance and cooperation provided under this Convention, each State Party may designate a central authority or may rely upon such central authorities as are provided for in any relevant treaties or other agreements.

2. The central authorities shall be responsible for making and receiving the requests for assistance and cooperation referred to in this Convention.

3. The central authorities shall communicate with each other directly for the purposes of this Convention.

ARTICLE XIX

TEMPORAL APPLICATION

Subject to the constitutional principles and the domestic laws of each State and existing treaties between the States Parties, the fact that the alleged act of corruption was committed before this Convention entered into force shall not preclude procedural cooperation in criminal matters between the States Parties. This provision shall in no case affect the principle of non-retroactivity in criminal law, nor shall application of this provision interrupt existing statutes of limitations relating to crimes committed prior to the date of the entry into force of this Convention.

ARTICLE XX

OTHER AGREEMENTS OR PRACTICES

No provision of this Convention shall be construed as preventing the States Parties from engaging in mutual cooperation within the framework of other international agreements, bilateral or multilateral, currently in force or concluded in the future, or pursuant to any other applicable arrangement or practice.

ARTICLE XXI

SIGNATURE

This Convention is open for signature by the Member States of the Organization of American States.

ARTICLE XXII

RATIFICATION

This Convention is subject to ratification. The instruments of ratification shall be deposited with the General Secretariat of the Organization of American States.

ARTICLE XXIII

ACCESSION

This Convention shall remain open for accession by any other State. The instruments of accession shall be deposited with the General Secretariat of the Organization of American States.

ARTICLE XXIV

RESERVATIONS

The States Parties may, at the time of adoption, signature, ratification, or accession, make reservations to this Convention, provided that each reservation concerns one or more specific provisions and is not incompatible with the object and purpose of the Convention.

ARTICLE XXV

ENTRY INTO FORCE

This Convention shall enter into force on the thirtieth day following the date of deposit of the second instrument of ratification. For each State ratifying or acceding to the Convention after the deposit of the second instrument of ratification, the Convention shall enter into force on the thirtieth day after deposit by such State of its instrument of ratification or accession.

ARTICLE XXVI

DENUNCIATION

This Convention shall remain in force indefinitely, but any of the States Parties may denounce it. The instrument of denunciation shall be deposited with the General Secretariat of the Organization of American States. One year from the date of deposit of the instrument of denunciation, the Convention shall cease to be in force for the denouncing State, but shall remain in force for the other States Parties.

ARTICLE XXVII

ADDITIONAL PROTOCOLS

Any State Party may submit for the consideration of other States Parties meeting at a General Assembly of the Organization of American States draft additional protocols to this Convention to contribute to the attainment of the purposes set forth in Article II thereof.

Each additional protocol shall establish the terms for its entry into force and shall apply only to those States that become Parties to it.

ARTICLE XXVIII

DEPOSIT OF ORIGINAL INSTRUMENT

The original instrument of this Convention, the English, French, Portuguese, and Spanish texts of which are equally authentic, shall be deposited with the General Secretariat of the Organization of American States, which shall forward an authenticated copy of its text to the Secretariat of the United Nations for registration and publication in accordance with Article 102 of the United Nations Charter. The General Secretariat of the Organization of American States shall notify its Member States and the States that have acceded to the Convention of signatures, of the deposit of instruments of ratification, accession, or denunciation, and of reservations, if any.

COUNCIL OF EUROPE CRIMINAL LAW CONVENTION ON CORRUPTION*

PREAMBLE

The member States of the Council of Europe and the other States signatory hereto,

Considering that the aim of the Council of Europe is to achieve a greater unity between its members;

Recognising the value of fostering co-operation with the other States signatories to this Convention;

Convinced of the need to pursue, as a matter of priority, a common criminal policy aimed at the protection of society against corruption, including the adoption of appropriate legislation and preventive measures;

Emphasising that corruption threatens the rule of law, democracy and human rights, undermines good governance, fairness and social justice, distorts competition, hinders economic development and endangers the stability of democratic institutions and the moral foundations of society;

Believing that an effective fight against corruption requires increased, rapid and well-functioning international co-operation in criminal matters;

Welcoming recent developments which further advance international understanding and co-operation in combating corruption, including actions of the United Nations, the World Bank, the International Monetary Fund, the World Trade Organisation, the Organisation of American States, the OECD and the European Union;

Having regard to the Programme of Action against Corruption adopted by the Committee of Ministers of the Council of Europe in November 1996 following the recommendations of the 19th Conference of European Ministers of Justice (Valletta, 1994);

---

* ETS No. 173, *reprinted in* 38 I.L.M. 505 (1999).

Recalling in this respect the importance of the participation of non-member States in the Council of Europe's activities against corruption and welcoming their valuable contribution to the implementation of the Programme of Action against Corruption;

Further recalling that Resolution No. 1 adopted by the European Ministers of Justice at their 21st Conference (Prague, 1997) recommended the speedy implementation of the Programme of Action against Corruption, and called, in particular, for the early adoption of a criminal law convention providing for the co-ordinated incrimination of corruption offences, enhanced co-operation for the prosecution of such offences as well as an effective follow-up mechanism open to member States and non-member States on an equal footing;

Bearing in mind that the Heads of State and Government of the Council of Europe decided, on the occasion of their Second Summit held in Strasbourg on 10 and 11 October 1997, to seek common responses to the challenges posed by the growth in corruption and adopted an Action Plan which, in order to promote co-operation in the fight against corruption, including its links with organised crime and money laundering, instructed the Committee of Ministers, *inter alia*, to secure the rapid completion of international legal instruments pursuant to the Programme of Action against Corruption;

Considering moreover that Resolution (97) 24 on the 20 Guiding Principles for the Fight against Corruption, adopted on 6 November 1997 by the Committee of Ministers at its 101st Session, stresses the need rapidly to complete the elaboration of international legal instruments pursuant to the Programme of Action against Corruption;

In view of the adoption by the Committee of Ministers, at its 102nd Session on 4 May 1998, of Resolution (98) 7 authorising the partial and enlarged agreement establishing the "Group of States against Corruption—GRECO", which aims at improving the capacity of its members to fight corruption by following up compliance with their undertakings in this field,

Have agreed as follows:

CHAPTER I—USE OF TERMS

Article 1

Use of terms

For the purposes of this Convention:

a   "public official" shall be understood by reference to the definition of "official", "public officer", "mayor", "minister" or "judge" in the national law of the State in which the person in question performs that function and as applied in its criminal law;

b   the term "judge" referred to in sub-paragraph a above shall include prosecutors and holders of judicial offices;

c   in the case of proceedings involving a public official of another State, the prosecuting State may apply the definition of public official only insofar as that definition is compatible with its national law;

d   "legal person" shall mean any entity having such status under the applicable national law, except for States or other public bodies in the exercise of State authority and for public international organisations.

CHAPTER II—MEASURES TO BE TAKEN AT NATIONAL LEVEL

Article 2

Active bribery of domestic public officials

Each Party shall adopt such legislative and other measures as may be necessary to establish as criminal offences under its domestic law, when committed intentionally, the promising, offering or giving by any person, directly or indirectly, of any undue advantage to any of its public officials, for himself or herself or for anyone else, for him or her to act or refrain from acting in the exercise of his or her functions.

Article 3

Passive bribery of domestic public officials

Each Party shall adopt such legislative and other measures as may be necessary to establish as criminal offences under its domestic law, when committed intentionally, the request or receipt by any of its public officials, directly or indirectly, of any undue advantage, for himself or herself or for anyone else, or the acceptance of an offer or a promise of such an advantage, to act or refrain from acting in the exercise of his or her functions.

Article 4

Bribery of members of domestic public assemblies

Each Party shall adopt such legislative and other measures as may be necessary to establish as criminal offences under its domestic law the conduct referred to in Articles 2 and 3, when involving any person who is a member of any domestic public assembly exercising legislative or administrative powers.

Article 5

Bribery of foreign public officials

Each Party shall adopt such legislative and other measures as may be necessary to establish as criminal offences under its domestic law the conduct referred to in Articles 2 and 3, when involving a public official of any other State.

Article 6

Bribery of members of foreign public assemblies

Each Party shall adopt such legislative and other measures as may be necessary to establish as criminal offences under its domestic law the conduct referred to in

Articles 2 and 3, when involving any person who is a member of any public assembly exercising legislative or administrative powers in any other State.

Article 7

Active bribery in the private sector

Each Party shall adopt such legislative and other measures as may be necessary to establish as criminal offences under its domestic law, when committed intentionally in the course of business activity, the promising, offering or giving, directly or indirectly, of any undue advantage to any persons who direct or work for, in any capacity, private sector entities, for themselves or for anyone else, for them to act, or refrain from acting, in breach of their duties.

Article 8

Passive bribery in the private sector

Each Party shall adopt such legislative and other measures as may be necessary to establish as criminal offences under its domestic law, when committed intentionally, in the course of business activity, the request or receipt, directly or indirectly, by any persons who direct or work for, in any capacity, private sector entities, of any undue advantage or the promise thereof for themselves or for anyone else, or the acceptance of an offer or a promise of such an advantage, to act or refrain from acting in breach of their duties.

Article 9

Bribery of officials of international organisations

Each Party shall adopt such legislative and other measures as may be necessary to establish as criminal offences under its domestic law the conduct referred to in Articles 2 and 3, when involving any official or other contracted employee, within the meaning of the staff regulations, of any public international or supranational organisation or body of which the Party is a member, and any person, whether seconded or not, carrying out functions corresponding to those performed by such officials or agents.

Article 10

Bribery of members of international parliamentary assemblies

Each Party shall adopt such legislative and other measures as may be necessary to establish as criminal offences under its domestic law the conduct referred to in Article 4 when involving any members of parliamentary assemblies of international or supranational organisations of which the Party is a member.

Article 11

Bribery of judges and officials of international courts

Each Party shall adopt such legislative and other measures as may be necessary to establish as criminal offences under its domestic law the conduct referred to in Articles 2 and 3 involving any holders of judicial office or officials of any international court whose jurisdiction is accepted by the Party.

Article 12

Trading in influence

Each Party shall adopt such legislative and other measures as may be necessary to establish as criminal offences under its domestic law, when committed intentionally, the promising, giving or offering, directly or indirectly, of any undue advantage to anyone who asserts or confirms that he or she is able to exert an improper influence over the decision-making of any person referred to in Articles 2, 4 to 6 and 9 to 11 in consideration thereof, whether the undue advantage is for himself or herself or for anyone else, as well as the request, receipt or the acceptance of the offer or the promise of such an advantage, in consideration of that influence, whether or not the influence is exerted or whether or not the supposed influence leads to the intended result.

Article 13

Money laundering of proceeds from corruption offences

Each Party shall adopt such legislative and other measures as may be necessary to establish as criminal offences under its domestic law the conduct referred to in the Council of Europe Convention on Laundering, Search, Seizure and Confiscation of the Products from Crime (ETS No. 141), Article 6, paragraphs 1 and 2, under the conditions referred to therein, when the predicate offence consists of any of the criminal offences established in accordance with Articles 2 to 12 of this Convention, to the extent that the Party has not made a reservation or a declaration with respect to these offences or does not consider such offences as serious ones for the purpose of their money laundering legislation.

Article 14

Account offences

Each Party shall adopt such legislative and other measures as may be necessary to establish as offences liable to criminal or other sanctions under its domestic law the following acts or omissions, when committed intentionally, in order to commit, conceal or disguise the offences referred to in Articles 2 to 12, to the extent the Party has not made a reservation or a declaration:

    a   creating or using an invoice or any other accounting document or record containing false or incomplete information;

    b   unlawfully omitting to make a record of a payment.

Article 15

Participatory acts

Each Party shall adopt such legislative and other measures as may be necessary to establish as criminal offences under its domestic law aiding or abetting the commission of any of the criminal offences established in accordance with this Convention.

Article 16

Immunity

The provisions of this Convention shall be without prejudice to the provisions of any Treaty, Protocol or Statute, as well as their implementing texts, as regards the withdrawal of immunity.

Article 17

Jurisdiction

1   Each Party shall adopt such legislative and other measures as may be necessary to establish jurisdiction over a criminal offence established in accordance with Articles 2 to 14 of this Convention where:

   a   the offence is committed in whole or in part in its territory;

   b   the offender is one of its nationals, one of its public officials, or a member of one of its domestic public assemblies;

   c   the offence involves one of its public officials or members of its domestic public assemblies or any person referred to in Articles 9 to 11 who is at the same time one of its nationals.

2   Each State may, at the time of signature or when depositing its instrument of ratification, acceptance, approval or accession, by a declaration addressed to the Secretary General of the Council of Europe, declare that it reserves the right not to apply or to apply only in specific cases or conditions the jurisdiction rules laid down in paragraphs 1 b and c of this article or any part thereof.

3   If a Party has made use of the reservation possibility provided for in paragraph 2 of this article, it shall adopt such measures as may be necessary to establish jurisdiction over a criminal offence established in accordance with this Convention, in cases where an alleged offender is present in its territory and it does not extradite him to another Party, solely on the basis of his nationality, after a request for extradition.

4   This Convention does not exclude any criminal jurisdiction exercised by a Party in accordance with national law.

Article 18

Corporate liability

1   Each Party shall adopt such legislative and other measures as may be necessary to ensure that legal persons can be held liable for the criminal offences

of active bribery, trading in influence and money laundering established in accordance with this Convention, committed for their benefit by any natural person, acting either individually or as part of an organ of the legal person, who has a leading position within the legal person, based on:

- a power of representation of the legal person; or
- an authority to take decisions on behalf of the legal person; or
- an authority to exercise control within the legal person;

as well as for involvement of such a natural person as accessory or instigator in the above-mentioned offences.

2   Apart from the cases already provided for in paragraph 1, each Party shall take the necessary measures to ensure that a legal person can be held liable where the lack of supervision or control by a natural person referred to in paragraph 1 has made possible the commission of the criminal offences mentioned in paragraph 1 for the benefit of that legal person by a natural person under its authority.

3   Liability of a legal person under paragraphs 1 and 2 shall not exclude criminal proceedings against natural persons who are perpetrators, instigators of, or accessories to, the criminal offences mentioned in paragraph 1.

Article 19

Sanctions and measures

1   Having regard to the serious nature of the criminal offences established in accordance with this Convention, each Party shall provide, in respect of those criminal offences established in accordance with Articles 2 to 14, effective, proportionate and dissuasive sanctions and measures, including, when committed by natural persons, penalties involving deprivation of liberty which can give rise to extradition.

2   Each Party shall ensure that legal persons held liable in accordance with Article 18, paragraphs 1 and 2, shall be subject to effective, proportionate and dissuasive criminal or non-criminal sanctions, including monetary sanctions.

3   Each Party shall adopt such legislative and other measures as may be necessary to enable it to confiscate or otherwise deprive the instrumentalities and proceeds of criminal offences established in accordance with this Convention, or property the value of which corresponds to such proceeds.

Article 20

Specialised authorities

Each Party shall adopt such measures as may be necessary to ensure that persons or entities are specialised in the fight against corruption. They shall have the necessary independence in accordance with the fundamental principles of the legal system of the Party, in order for them to be able to carry out their functions effectively and free from any undue pressure. The Party shall ensure that the staff of such entities has adequate training and financial resources for their tasks.

Article 21

Co-operation with and between national authorities

Each Party shall adopt such measures as may be necessary to ensure that public authorities, as well as any public official, co-operate, in accordance with national law, with those of its authorities responsible for investigating and prosecuting criminal offences:

a   by informing the latter authorities, on their own initiative, where there are reasonable grounds to believe that any of the criminal offences established in accordance with Articles 2 to 14 has been committed, or

b   by providing, upon request, to the latter authorities all necessary information.

Article 22

Protection of collaborators of justice and witnesses

Each Party shall adopt such measures as may be necessary to provide effective and appropriate protection for:

a   those who report the criminal offences established in accordance with Articles 2 to 14 or otherwise co-operate with the investigating or prosecuting authorities;

b   witnesses who give testimony concerning these offences.

Article 23

Measures to facilitate the gathering of evidence and the confiscation of proceeds

1   Each Party shall adopt such legislative and other measures as may be necessary, including those permitting the use of special investigative techniques, in accordance with national law, to enable it to facilitate the gathering of evidence related to criminal offences established in accordance with Articles 2 to 14 of this Convention and to identify, trace, freeze and seize instrumentalities and proceeds of corruption, or property the value of which corresponds to such proceeds, liable to measures set out in accordance with paragraph 3 of Article 19 of this Convention.

2   Each Party shall adopt such legislative and other measures as may be necessary to empower its courts or other competent authorities to order that bank, financial or commercial records be made available or be seized in order to carry out the actions referred to in paragraph 1 of this article.

3   Bank secrecy shall not be an obstacle to measures provided for in paragraphs 1 and 2 of this article.

4   Chapter III—Monitoring of implementation.

Article 24

Monitoring

The Group of States against Corruption (GRECO) shall monitor the implementation of this Convention by the Parties.

CHAPTER IV—INTERNATIONAL CO-OPERATION

Article 25

General principles and measures for international co-operation

1   The Parties shall co-operate with each other, in accordance with the provisions of relevant international instruments on international co-operation in criminal matters, or arrangements agreed on the basis of uniform or reciprocal legislation, and in accordance with their national law, to the widest extent possible for the purposes of investigations and proceedings concerning criminal offences established in accordance with this Convention.

2   Where no international instrument or arrangement referred to in paragraph 1 is in force between Parties, Articles 26 to 31 of this chapter shall apply.

3   Articles 26 to 31 of this chapter shall also apply where they are more favourable than those of the international instruments or arrangements referred to in paragraph 1.

Article 26

Mutual assistance

1   The Parties shall afford one another the widest measure of mutual assistance by promptly processing requests from authorities that, in conformity with their domestic laws, have the power to investigate or prosecute criminal offences established in accordance with this Convention.

2   Mutual legal assistance under paragraph 1 of this article may be refused if the requested Party believes that compliance with the request would undermine its fundamental interests, national sovereignty, national security or ordre public.

3   Parties shall not invoke bank secrecy as a ground to refuse any co-operation under this chapter. Where its domestic law so requires, a Party may require that a request for co-operation which would involve the lifting of bank secrecy be authorised by either a judge or another judicial authority, including public prosecutors, any of these authorities acting in relation to criminal offences.

Article 27

Extradition

1   The criminal offences established in accordance with this Convention shall be deemed to be included as extraditable offences in any extradition treaty existing

between or among the Parties. The Parties undertake to include such offences as extraditable offences in any extradition treaty to be concluded between or among them.

2   If a Party that makes extradition conditional on the existence of a treaty receives a request for extradition from another Party with which it does not have an extradition treaty, it may consider this Convention as the legal basis for extradition with respect to any criminal offence established in accordance with this Convention.

3   Parties that do not make extradition conditional on the existence of a treaty shall recognise criminal offences established in accordance with this Convention as extraditable offences between themselves.

4   Extradition shall be subject to the conditions provided for by the law of the requested Party or by applicable extradition treaties, including the grounds on which the requested Party may refuse extradition.

5   If extradition for a criminal offence established in accordance with this Convention is refused solely on the basis of the nationality of the person sought, or because the requested Party deems that it has jurisdiction over the offence, the requested Party shall submit the case to its competent authorities for the purpose of prosecution unless otherwise agreed with the requesting Party, and shall report the final outcome to the requesting Party in due course.

Article 28

Spontaneous information

Without prejudice to its own investigations or proceedings, a Party may without prior request forward to another Party information on facts when it considers that the disclosure of such information might assist the receiving Party in initiating or carrying out investigations or proceedings concerning criminal offences established in accordance with this Convention or might lead to a request by that Party under this chapter.

Article 29

Central authority

1   The Parties shall designate a central authority or, if appropriate, several central authorities, which shall be responsible for sending and answering requests made under this chapter, the execution of such requests or the transmission of them to the authorities competent for their execution.

2   Each Party shall, at the time of signature or when depositing its instrument of ratification, acceptance, approval or accession, communicate to the Secretary General of the Council of Europe the names and addresses of the authorities designated in pursuance of paragraph 1 of this article.

Article 30

Direct communication

1   The central authorities shall communicate directly with one another.

2   In the event of urgency, requests for mutual assistance or communications related thereto may be sent directly by the judicial authorities, including public prosecutors, of the requesting Party to such authorities of the requested Party. In such cases a copy shall be sent at the same time to the central authority of the requested Party through the central authority of the requesting Party.

3   Any request or communication under paragraphs 1 and 2 of this article may be made through the International Criminal Police Organisation (Interpol).

4   Where a request is made pursuant to paragraph 2 of this article and the authority is not competent to deal with the request, it shall refer the request to the competent national authority and inform directly the requesting Party that it has done so.

5   Requests or communications under paragraph 2 of this article, which do not involve coercive action, may be directly transmitted by the competent authorities of the requesting Party to the competent authorities of the requested Party.

6   Each State may, at the time of signature or when depositing its instrument of ratification, acceptance, approval or accession, inform the Secretary General of the Council of Europe that, for reasons of efficiency, requests made under this chapter are to be addressed to its central authority.

Article 31

Information

The requested Party shall promptly inform the requesting Party of the action taken on a request under this chapter and the final result of that action. The requested Party shall also promptly inform the requesting Party of any circumstances which render impossible the carrying out of the action sought or are likely to delay it significantly.

CHAPTER V—FINAL PROVISIONS

Article 32

Signature and entry into force

1   This Convention shall be open for signature by the member States of the Council of Europe and by non-member States which have participated in its elaboration. Such States may express their consent to be bound by:

    a   signature without reservation as to ratification, acceptance or approval; or

    b   signature subject to ratification, acceptance or approval, followed by ratification, acceptance or approval.

2   Instruments of ratification, acceptance or approval shall be deposited with the Secretary General of the Council of Europe.

3   This Convention shall enter into force on the first day of the month following the expiration of a period of three months after the date on which fourteen States have expressed their consent to be bound by the Convention in accordance with the provisions of paragraph 1. Any such State, which is not a member of the Group of States against Corruption (GRECO) at the time of ratification, shall automatically become a member on the date the Convention enters into force.

4   In respect of any signatory State which subsequently expresses its consent to be bound by it, the Convention shall enter into force on the first day of the month following the expiration of a period of three months after the date of the expression of their consent to be bound by the Convention in accordance with the provisions of paragraph 1. Any signatory State, which is not a member of the Group of States against Corruption (GRECO) at the time of ratification, shall automatically become a member on the date the Convention enters into force in its respect.

Article 33

Accession to the Convention

1   After the entry into force of this Convention, the Committee of Ministers of the Council of Europe, after consulting the Contracting States to the Convention, may invite the European Community as well as any State not a member of the Council and not having participated in its elaboration to accede to this Convention, by a decision taken by the majority provided for in Article 20d of the Statute of the Council of Europe and by the unanimous vote of the representatives of the Contracting States entitled to sit on the Committee of Ministers.

2   In respect of the European Community and any State acceding to it under paragraph 1 above, the Convention shall enter into force on the first day of the month following the expiration of a period of three months after the date of deposit of the instrument of accession with the Secretary General of the Council of Europe. The European Community and any State acceding to this Convention shall automatically become a member of GRECO, if it is not already a member at the time of accession, on the date the Convention enters into force in its respect.

Article 34

Territorial application

1   Any State may, at the time of signature or when depositing its instrument of ratification, acceptance, approval or accession, specify the territory or territories to which this Convention shall apply.

2   Any Party may, at any later date, by a declaration addressed to the Secretary General of the Council of Europe, extend the application of this Convention to any other territory specified in the declaration. In respect of such territory the Convention shall enter into force on the first day of the month following the expiration of a period of three months after the date of receipt of such declaration by the Secretary General.

3   Any declaration made under the two preceding paragraphs may, in respect of any territory specified in such declaration, be withdrawn by a notification addressed to the Secretary General of the Council of Europe. The withdrawal shall become effective on the first day of the month following the expiration of a period of three months after the date of receipt of such notification by the Secretary General.

Article 35

Relationship to other conventions and agreements

1   This Convention does not affect the rights and undertakings derived from international multilateral conventions concerning special matters.

2   The Parties to the Convention may conclude bilateral or multilateral agreements with one another on the matters dealt with in this Convention, for purposes of supplementing or strengthening its provisions or facilitating the application of the principles embodied in it.

3   If two or more Parties have already concluded an agreement or treaty in respect of a subject which is dealt with in this Convention or otherwise have established their relations in respect of that subject, they shall be entitled to apply that agreement or treaty or to regulate those relations accordingly, in lieu of the present Convention, if it facilitates international co-operation.

Article 36

Declarations

Any State may, at the time of signature or when depositing its instrument of ratification, acceptance, approval or accession, declare that it will establish as criminal offences the active and passive bribery of foreign public officials under Article 5, of officials of international organisations under Article 9 or of judges and officials of international courts under Article 11, only to the extent that the public official or judge acts or refrains from acting in breach of his duties.

Article 37

Reservations

1   Any State may, at the time of signature or when depositing its instrument of ratification, acceptance, approval or accession, reserve its right not to establish as a criminal offence under its domestic law, in part or in whole, the

conduct referred to in Articles 4, 6 to 8, 10 and 12 or the passive bribery offences defined in Article 5.

2   Any State may, at the time of signature or when depositing its instrument of ratification, acceptance, approval or accession declare that it avails itself of the reservation provided for in Article 17, paragraph 2.

3   Any State may, at the time of signature or when depositing its instrument of ratification, acceptance, approval or accession declare that it may refuse mutual legal assistance under Article 26, paragraph 1, if the request concerns an offence which the requested Party considers a political offence.

4   No State may, by application of paragraphs 1, 2 and 3 of this article, enter reservations to more than five of the provisions mentioned thereon. No other reservation may be made. Reservations of the same nature with respect to Articles 4, 6 and 10 shall be considered as one reservation.

Article 38

Validity and review of declarations and reservations

1   Declarations referred to in Article 36 and reservations referred to in Article 37 shall be valid for a period of three years from the day of the entry into force of this Convention in respect of the State concerned. However, such declarations and reservations may be renewed for periods of the same duration.

2   Twelve months before the date of expiry of the declaration or reservation, the Secretariat General of the Council of Europe shall give notice of that expiry to the State concerned. No later than three months before the expiry, the State shall notify the Secretary General that it is upholding, amending or withdrawing its declaration or reservation. In the absence of a notification by the State concerned, the Secretariat General shall inform that State that its declaration or reservation is considered to have been extended automatically for a period of six months. Failure by the State concerned to notify its intention to uphold or modify its declaration or reservation before the expiry of that period shall cause the declaration or reservation to lapse.

3   If a Party makes a declaration or a reservation in conformity with Articles 36 and 37, it shall provide, before its renewal or upon request, an explanation to GRECO, on the grounds justifying its continuance.

Article 39

Amendments

1   Amendments to this Convention may be proposed by any Party, and shall be communicated by the Secretary General of the Council of Europe to the member States of the Council of Europe and to every non-member State which has acceded to, or has been invited to accede to, this Convention in accordance with the provisions of Article 33.

2 Any amendment proposed by a Party shall be communicated to the European Committee on Crime Problems (CDPC), which shall submit to the Committee of Ministers its opinion on that proposed amendment.

3 The Committee of Ministers shall consider the proposed amendment and the opinion submitted by the CDPC and, following consultation of the non-member States Parties to this Convention, may adopt the amendment.

4 The text of any amendment adopted by the Committee of Ministers in accordance with paragraph 3 of this article shall be forwarded to the Parties for acceptance.

5 Any amendment adopted in accordance with paragraph 3 of this article shall come into force on the thirtieth day after all Parties have informed the Secretary General of their acceptance thereof.

Article 40

Settlement of disputes

1 The European Committee on Crime Problems of the Council of Europe shall be kept informed regarding the interpretation and application of this Convention.

2 In case of a dispute between Parties as to the interpretation or application of this Convention, they shall seek a settlement of the dispute through negotiation or any other peaceful means of their choice, including submission of the dispute to the European Committee on Crime Problems, to an arbitral tribunal whose decisions shall be binding upon the Parties, or to the International Court of Justice, as agreed upon by the Parties concerned.

Article 41

Denunciation

1 Any Party may, at any time, denounce this Convention by means of a notification addressed to the Secretary General of the Council of Europe.

2 Such denunciation shall become effective on the first day of the month following the expiration of a period of three months after the date of receipt of the notification by the Secretary General.

Article 42

Notification

The Secretary General of the Council of Europe shall notify the member States of the Council of Europe and any State which has acceded to this Convention of:

a any signature;

b the deposit of any instrument of ratification, acceptance, approval or accession;

c   any date of entry into force of this Convention in accordance with Articles 32 and 33;

d   any declaration or reservation made under Article 36 or Article 37;

e   any other act, notification or communication relating to this Convention.

In witness whereof the undersigned, being duly authorised thereto, have signed this Convention.

Done at Strasbourg, this 27th day of January 1999, in English and in French, both texts being equally authentic, in a single copy which shall be deposited in the archives of the Council of Europe. The Secretary General of the Council of Europe shall transmit certified copies to each member State of the Council of Europe, to the non-member States which have participated in the elaboration of this Convention, and to any State invited to accede to it.

EXPLANATORY REPORT ON
THE CRIMINAL LAW CONVENTION
ON CORRUPTION*

I. INTRODUCTION

1. Corruption has existed ever since antiquity as one of the worst and, at the same time, most widespread forms of behaviour, which is inimical to the administration of public affairs. Naturally, over time, customs as well as historical and geographical circumstances have greatly changed public sensitivity to such behaviour, in terms of the significance and attention attached to it. As a result, its treatment in laws and regulations has likewise changed substantially. In some periods of history, certain "corrupt" practices were actually regarded as permissible, or else the penalties for them were either fairly light, or generally not applied. In Europe, the French Napoleonic Code of 1810 may be regarded as a landmark at which tough penalties were introduced to combat corruption in public life, comprising both acts which did not conflict with one's official duties and acts which did. Thus, the arrival of the modern State-administration in the 19th century made public officials' misuse of their offices a serious offence against public confidence in the administration's probity and impartiality.

2. Notwithstanding the long history and the apparent spread of the phenomenon of corruption in today's society, it seemed difficult to arrive at a common definition and it was rightly said "no definition of corruption will be equally accepted in every nation". Possible definitions have been discussed for a number of years in different fora but it has not been possible for the international community to agree to on a common definition. Instead international fora have preferred to concentrate on the definition of certain forms

---

* ETS No. 173 (1999).

of corruption, e.g. "illicit payments" (UN), "bribery of foreign public officials in international business transactions" (OECD), "corruption involving officials of the European Communities or officials of Member States of the European Union" (EU).

3. Even if no common definition has yet been found by the international community to describe corruption as such, everyone seems at least to agree that certain political, social or commercial practices are corrupt. The qualification of some practices as "corrupt" and their eventual moral reprobation by public opinion vary however from country to country and do not necessarily imply that they are criminal offences under national criminal law.

4. More recently, the deepening interest and concern shown in such matters everywhere have produced national and international reactions. From the beginning of the 90s corruption has always been in the headlines of the press. Although it had always been present in the history of humanity, it does appear to have virtually exploded across the newspaper columns and law reports of a number of States from all corners of the world, irrespective of their economic or political regime. Countries of Western, Central and Eastern Europe have been literally shaken by huge corruption scandals and some consider that corruption now represents one of the most serious threats to the stability of democratic institutions and the functioning of the market economy.

5. This illustrates that corruption needs to be taken seriously by Governments and Parliaments. The fact that corruption is widely talked of in some States and not at all in others, is in no way indicative that corruption is not present in the latter because no system of government and administration is immune to corruption. In such countries corruption may be either non-existent (which seems in most cases rather improbable), or so efficiently organised as not to give rise to suspicion. In some cases silence over corrupt activities is merely the result of citizen's resignation in face of widespread corruption. In such situations corruption is seen no longer not as unacceptable criminal behaviour, liable to severe sanctions, but as a normal or at least necessary or tolerated practice. The survival of the State is at stake in such extreme cases of endemic corruption.

II. THE PREPARATORY WORK

6. At their 19th Conference held in Valletta in 1994, the European Ministers of Justice considered that corruption was a serious threat to democracy, to the rule of law and to human rights. The Council of Europe, being the pre-eminent European institution defending these fundamental values, was called upon to respond to that threat. The Ministers were convinced that the fight against corruption should take a multidisciplinary approach and that it was necessary to adopt appropriate legislation in this area as soon as possible. They expressed the belief that an effective fight against corruption required increased cross-border co-operation between States, as well as between States

and international institutions, through the promotion of co-ordinated measures at European level and beyond, which in turn implied involving States which were not members of the Council of Europe. The Ministers of Justice recommended to the Committee of Ministers the setting up of a Multidisciplinary Group on Corruption, under the responsibility of the European Committee on Crime Problems (CDPC) and the European Committee on Legal Co-operation (CDC), with the task of examining what measures might be suitable to be included in a programme of action at the international level as well as examining the possibility of drafting model laws or codes of conduct, including international conventions, on this subject. The Ministers expressly referred to the importance of elaborating a follow-up mechanism to implement the undertakings contained in such instruments.

7. In the light of these recommendations, the Committee of Ministers set up, in September 1994, the Multidisciplinary Group on Corruption (GMC) and gave it terms of reference to examine what measures might be suitable to be included in an international programme of action against corruption. The GMC was also invited to make proposals to the Committee of Ministers before the end of 1995 as to appropriate priorities and working structures, taking due account of the work of other international organisations. It was furthermore invited to examine the possibility of drafting model laws or codes of conduct in selected areas, including the elaboration of an international convention on this subject, as well as the possibility of elaborating a follow-up mechanism to implement undertakings contained in such instruments.

8. The GMC started work in March 1995 and prepared a draft Programme of Action against Corruption, an ambitious document covering all aspects of the international fight against this phenomenon. This draft Programme was submitted to the Committee of Ministers, which, in January 1996, took note of it, invited the European Committee on Crime Problems (CDPC) and the European Committee on Legal Co-operation (CDC) to express their opinions thereon and, in the meantime, gave interim terms of reference to the GMC, authorising it to start some of the actions contained in the said Programme, such as work on one or several international instruments.

9. The Committee of Ministers finally adopted the Programme of Action in November 1996 and instructed the GMC to implement it before 31 December 2000. The Committee of Ministers welcomed in particular the GMC's intention to elaborate, as a matter of priority, one or more international Conventions to combat corruption and a follow-up mechanism to implement undertakings contained in such instruments or any other legal instrument in this area. According to the terms of reference given to the GMC, the CDPC and CDC were to be consulted on any draft legal text relating to corruption and their views taken into account.

10. The GMC's terms of reference are as follows:

"Under the responsibility of the European Committee on Crime Problems (CDPC) and the European Committee on Legal Co-operation (CDCJ),

- to elaborate as a matter of priority one or more international conventions to combat corruption, and a follow-up mechanism to implement undertakings contained in such instruments, or any other legal instrument in this area;
- to elaborate as a matter of priority a draft European Code of Conduct for Public Officials;
- after consultation of the appropriate Steering Committee(s) to initiate, organise or promote research projects, training programmes and the exchange at national and international level of practical experiences of corruption and the fight against it;
- to implement the other parts of the Programme of Action against Corruption, taking into account the priorities set out therein;
- to take into account the work of other international organisations and bodies with a view to ensuring a coherent and co-ordinated approach;
- to consult the CDCJ and/or CDPC on any draft legal text relating to corruption and take into account its/their views."

11. The Ministers participating in the 21st Conference of European Ministers of Justice, held in Prague in June 1997, expressed their concern about the new trends in modern criminality and, in particular, by the organised, sophisticated and transnational character of certain criminal activities. They declared themselves persuaded that the fight against organised crime necessarily implies an adequate response to corruption and emphasised that corruption represents a major threat to the rule of law, democracy, human rights, fairness and social justice, that it hinders economic development and endangers the stability of democratic institutions and the moral foundations of society. Therefore, the Ministers recommended to speed up the implementation of the Programme of Action against Corruption and, with this in mind, to intensify the efforts with a view to an early adoption of, inter alia, a criminal law Convention providing for the co-ordinated criminalisation of corruption offences and for enhanced co-operation in the prosecution of such offences. They further recommended the Committee of Ministers to ensure that the relevant international instruments would provide for an effective follow-up mechanism open to member States and non-member States of the Council of Europe on an equal footing.

12. At their Second Summit, held in Strasbourg on 10–11 October 1997, the Heads of State and Government of the member States of the Council of Europe decided to seek common responses to the challenges posed by the growth in corruption and organised crime. The Heads of State and Government adopted an Action Plan in which, with a view to promoting co-operation in the fight against corruption, including its links with organised crime and money laundering, they instructed the Committee of Ministers, inter alia, to adopt guiding principles to be applied in the development of domestic legislation and practice, to secure the rapid completion of international legal instruments pursuant to the Programme of Action against Corruption and to establish without delay an appropriate and efficient mechanism, for

monitoring observance of the guiding principles and the implementation of the said international instruments.

13. At its 101st Session on 6 November 1997 the Committee of Ministers of the Council of Europe adopted the 20 Guiding Principles for the Fight against Corruption. Firmly resolved to fight corruption by joining their countries' efforts, the Ministers agreed, inter alia, to ensure co-ordinated criminalisation of national and international corruption (Principle 2), to ensure that those in charge of prevention, investigation, prosecution and adjudication of corruption offences enjoy the independence and autonomy appropriate to their functions, are free from improper influence and have effective means for gathering evidence, protecting the persons who help the authorities in combating corruption and preserving the confidentiality of investigations (Principle 3), to provide appropriate measures for the seizure and deprivation of the proceeds of corruption offences (Principle 4), to prevent legal persons being used to shield corruption offences (Principle 5), to promote the specialisation of persons or bodies in charge of fighting corruption and to provide them with appropriate means and training to perform their tasks (Principle 7) and to develop to the widest extent possible international co-operation in all areas of the fight against corruption (Principle 20).

14. Moreover, the Committee of Ministers instructed the GMC rapidly to complete the elaboration of international legal instrument pursuant to the Programme of Action against Corruption and to submit without delay a draft text proposing the establishment of an appropriate and efficient mechanism for monitoring the observance of the Guiding Principles and the implementation of the international legal instruments to be adopted.

15. At its 102nd Session (5 May 1998), the Committee of Ministers adopted Resolution (98) 7 authorising the establishment of the "Group of States against Corruption—GRECO" in the form of a partial and enlarged agreement. In this Resolution the Committee of Ministers invited member States and non-member States of the Council of Europe having participated in the elaboration of the Agreement to notify to the Secretary General their intention to join the GRECO, the agreement setting up the GRECO being considered as adopted as soon as fourteen member States of the Council of Europe made such a notification.

16. The agreement establishing the GRECO and containing its Statute was adopted on 5 May 1998. GRECO is a body called to monitor, through a process of mutual evaluation and peer pressure, the observance of the Guiding Principles in the Fight against Corruption and the implementation of international legal instruments adopted in pursuance of the Programme of Action against Corruption. Full membership of the GRECO is reserved to those who participate fully in the mutual evaluation process and accept to be evaluated.

17. The GRECO has been conceived as a flexible and efficient follow-up mechanism, which will contribute to the development of an effective and dynamic process for preventing and combating corruption. The agreement provides

for the participation in the GRECO, on an equal footing, of member States, of those non-member States which have participated in the elaboration of the agreement, and of other non-member States that are invited to join.

18. In accordance with the objectives set by the Programme of Action and on the basis of the interim terms of reference referred in paragraph 8 above, the Criminal Law Working Group of the GMC (GMCP) started work on a draft criminal law convention in February 1996. Between February 1996 and November 1997, the GMCP held 10 meetings and completed two full readings of the draft Convention. In November 1997 it transmitted the text to the GMC for consideration.

19. The GMC started the examination of the draft submitted by the GMCP at its 11th (November 1997) plenary meeting. It pursued its work at its 12th (January 1998), 13th (March 1998) and 14th meetings (September 1998). In February 1998, the GMC consulted the CDPC on the first reading version of the draft Convention. The Bureau of the CDPC, having consulted in writing the heads of delegation to the CDPC, formulated an opinion on the draft in March 1998 (see Appendix II, document CDPC-BU (98) 3). The GMC took account of the views expressed by the CDPC at its 13th meeting (March 1998) and finalised the second reading on that occasion. In view of the wish expressed by the CDPC to be consulted again on the final version, the GMC agreed to transmit the second reading version of the draft Convention to the CDPC. Moreover, in view of the request made by the President of the Parliamentary Assembly on 11 February 1998 to the Chairman-in-office of the Minister's Deputies, the GMC transmitted the second reading text to the Committee of Ministers with a view to enabling it to accede to that request. At the 628th meeting of the Ministers' Deputies (April 1998), the Committee of Ministers agreed to consult the Parliamentary Assembly on the draft Convention and instructed the GMC to examine the opinions formulated by the Assembly and by the CDPC.

20. At its 47th Plenary Session, the CDPC formulated a formal opinion on the draft Convention. The Parliamentary Assembly, for its part, adopted its opinion in the third part of its 1998 Session in June 1998. In conformity with its terms of reference the GMC considered both opinions at its 14th plenary meeting in September 1998. On that occasion it approved the final draft and submitted it to the Committee of Ministers. At its 103rd Session at ministerial level (November 1998) the Committee of Ministers adopted the Convention, decided to open it for signature on 27 January 1999 and authorised the publication of the present explanatory report.

III. THE CONVENTION

21. The Convention aims principally at developing common standards concerning certain corruption offences, though it does not provide a uniform definition of corruption. In addition, it deals with substantive and procedural law matters, which closely relate to these corruption offences and seeks to improve

international co-operation. Recent practice shows that international co-operation meets two kinds of difficulties in the prosecution of transnational corruption cases, particularly that of bribery of foreign public officials: one
relates to the definition of corruption offences, often diverging because of
the meaning of "public official" in domestic laws; the other relates to means
and channels of international co-operation, where procedural and sometimes political obstacles delay or prevent the prosecution of the offenders.
By harmonising the definition of corruption offences, the requirement of
dual criminality will be met by the Parties to the Convention, while the provisions on international co-operation are designed to facilitate direct and
swift communication between the relevant national authorities.

22. The European Union Convention on the fight against corruption involving officials of the European Communities or officials of Member States of the European Union (Council Act of 26 May 1997) defines active corruption as "the
deliberate action of whosoever promises or gives, directly or through an
intermediary, an advantage of any kind whatsoever to an official for himself
or for a third party for him to act or refrain from acting in accordance with
his duty or in the exercise of his functions in breach of his official duties"
(Article 3). Passive corruption is defined along the same lines.

23. The Convention on Combating Bribery of Foreign Public Officials in International Business Transactions (adopted within the OECD on 17 December
1997) defines, for its part, active corruption, as the act by any person of
"intentionally to offer, promise or give any undue pecuniary or other advantage, whether directly or through intermediaries, to a foreign public official,
for that official or for a third party, in order that the official act or refrain
from acting in relation to the performance of official duties, in order to
obtain or retain business or other improper advantage in the conduct of
international business".

24. The GMC started its work on the basis of the following provisional definition: "Corruption as dealt with by the Council of Europe's GMC is bribery
and any other behaviour in relation to persons entrusted with responsibilities
in the public or private sector, which violates their duties that follow from
their status as a public official, private employee, independent agent or other
relationship of that kind and is aimed at obtaining undue advantages of any
kind for themselves or for others".

25. The purpose of this definition was to ensure that no matter would be
excluded from its work. While such a definition would not necessarily match
the legal definition of corruption in most member States, in particular not
the definition given by the criminal law, its advantage was that it would not
restrict the discussion to excessively narrow confines. As the drafting of the
Convention's text progressed, that general definition translated into several
common operational definitions of corruption which could be transposed
into national laws, albeit, in certain cases, with some amendment to those
laws. It is worth underlining, in this respect, that the present Convention not
only contains a commonly agreed definition of bribery, both from the passive

and active side, which serves as the basis of various forms of criminalisation but also defines other forms of corrupt behaviour, such as private sector corruption and trading in influence, closely linked to bribery and commonly understood as specific forms of corruption. Thus, the present Convention has, as one of its main characteristics, its wide scope, which reflects the Council of Europe's comprehensive approach to the fight against corruption as a threat to democratic values, the rule of law, human rights and social and economic progress.

IV. COMMENTARY

CHAPTER I—USE OF TERMS

Article 1—Use of terms

26. Only three terms are defined under Article 1, as all other notions are addressed at the appropriate place in the Explanatory Report.

27. The drafters of this Convention wanted to cover all possible categories of public officials in order to avoid, as much as possible, loopholes in the criminalisation of public sector bribery. This, however, does not necessarily mean that States have to redefine their concept of "public official" in general. In reference to the "national law" it should be noted that it was the intention of the drafters of the Convention that Contracting Parties assume obligations under this Convention only to the extent consistent with their Constitution and the fundamental principles of their legal system, including, where appropriate, the principles of federalism.

28. The term "public official" is used in Articles 2 and 3 as well as in Article 5. Littera a. of Article 1 defines the concept of "public official" in terms of an official or public officer, a mayor, a minister or judge as defined in the national law of the State, for the purposes of its own criminal law. The criminal law definition is therefore given priority. Where a public official of the prosecuting State is involved, this means that its national definition is applicable. However, the term "public official" should include "mayor" and "minister". In many countries mayors and ministers are assimilated to public officials for the purpose of criminal offences committed in the exercise of their powers. In order to avoid any loopholes that could have left such important public figures outside the scope of the present Convention, express reference is made to them in Article 1 littera a.

29. Also, the term "public official" encompasses, for the purpose of this Convention, "judges", who are included in point (b) as holders of judicial office, whether elected or appointed. This notion is to be interpreted to the widest extent possible: the decisive element being the functions performed by the person, which should be of a judicial nature, rather than his or her official title. Prosecutors are specifically mentioned as falling under this definition, although in some States they are not considered as members of the "judiciary". Members of the judiciary—judges and, in some countries, prosecutors

are an independent and impartial authority separated from the executive branch of Government. It is obvious that the definition found in Article 1, littera a is solely for the purpose of the present Convention and only requires Contracting Parties to consider or treat judges or prosecutors as public officials for the purposes of the application of this Convention.

30. Where any of the offences under the Convention involves a public official of another State, Article 1 littera (c) applies. It means that the definition in the law of the latter State is not necessarily conclusive where the person concerned would not have had the status of public official under the law of the prosecuting State. This follows from point (c) of Article 1, according to which a State may determine that corruption offences involving public officials of another State refer only to such officials whose status is compatible with that of national public officials under the national law of the prosecuting State. This reference to the law of the public official's State means that due account can be taken of specific national situations regarding the status of persons exercising public functions.

31. The term "legal person" appears in Article 18 (Corporate liability). Again, the Convention does not provide an autonomous definition, but refers back to national laws. Littera d. of Article 1 thus permits States to use their own definition of "legal person", whether such definition is contained in company law or in criminal law. For the purpose of active corruption offences however, it expressly excludes from the scope of the definition the State or other public bodies exercising State authority, such as ministries or local government bodies as well as public international organisations such as the Council of Europe. The exception refers to the different levels of government: State, Regional or Local entities exercising public powers. The reason is that the responsibilities of public entities are subject to specific regulations or agreements/treaties, and in the case of public international organisations, are usually embodied in administrative law. It is not aimed at excluding the responsibility of public enterprises. A contracting State may, however, go further as to allow the imposition of criminal law or administrative law sanctions on public bodies as well. It goes without saying that this provision does not restrict, in any manner, the responsibility of individuals employed by the different State organs for passive corruption offences under Articles 3 to 6 and 9 to 12 of the present Convention.

CHAPTER II—MEASURES TO BE TAKEN AT NATIONAL LEVEL

Article 2—Active bribery of domestic public officials

32. Article 2 defines the elements of the active bribery of domestic public officials. It is intended to ensure in particular that public administration functions properly, i.e. in a transparent, fair and impartial manner and in pursuance of public interests, and to protect the confidence of citizens in their Administration and the officials themselves from possible manoeuvres against them.

The definition of active bribery in Article 2 draws its inspiration from national and international definitions of bribery/corruption, e.g. the one contained in the Protocol to the European Union Convention on the protection of the European Communities' financial interests (Article 3). This offence, in current criminal law theory and practice and in the view of the drafters of the Convention, is mirrored by passive bribery, though they are considered to be separate offences for which prosecutions can be brought independently. It emerges that the two types of bribery are, in general, two sides of the same phenomenon, one perpetrator offering, promising or giving the advantage and the other perpetrator accepting the offer, promise or gift. Usually, however, the two perpetrators are not punished for complicity in the other one's offence.

33. The definition provided in Article 2 is referred to in subsequent provisions of the Convention, e.g., in Articles 4, 5, 6, 9 and, through a double reference, in Article 10. These provisions do not repeat the substantive elements but extend the criminalisation of the active bribery to further categories of persons.

34. The offence of active bribery can only be committed intentionally under Article 2 and the intent has to cover all other substantive elements of the offence. Intent must relate to a future result: the public official acting or refraining from acting as the briber intends. It is, however, immaterial whether the public official actually acted or refrained from acting as intended.

35. The briber can be anyone, whatever his capacity (businessman, public official, private individual etc). If, however, the briber acts for the account or on behalf of a company, corporate liability may also apply in respect of the company in question (Article 18). Nevertheless, the liability of the company does not exclude in any manner criminal proceedings against the natural person (paragraph 3 of Article 18). The bribed person must be a public official, as defined under Article 1, irrespective of whether the undue advantage is actually for himself or for someone else.

36. The material components of the offence are promising, offering or giving an undue advantage, directly or indirectly for the official himself or for a third party. The three actions of the briber are slightly different. "Promising" may, for example, cover situations where the briber commits himself to give an undue advantage later (in most cases only once the public official has performed the act requested by the briber) or where there is an agreement between the briber and the bribee that the briber will give the undue advantage later. "Offering" may cover situations where the briber shows his readiness to give the undue advantage at any moment. Finally, "giving" may cover situations where the briber transfers the undue advantage. The undue advantage need not necessarily be given to the public official himself: it can be given also to a third party, such as a relative, an organisation to which the official belongs, the political party of which he is a member. When the offer, promise or gift is addressed to a third party, the public official must at least

have knowledge thereof at some point. Irrespective of whether the recipient or the beneficiary of the undue advantage is the public official himself or a third party, the transaction may be performed through intermediaries.

37. The undue advantages given are usually of an economic nature but may also be of a non-material nature. What is important is that the offender (or any other person, for instance a relative) is placed in a better position than he was before the commission of the offence and that he is not entitled to the benefit. Such advantages may consist in, for instance, money, holidays, loans, food and drink, a case handled within a swifter time, better career prospects, etc.

38. What constitutes "undue" advantage will be of central importance in the transposition of the Convention into national law. "Undue" for the purposes of the Convention should be interpreted as something that the recipient is not lawfully entitled to accept or receive. For the drafters of the Convention, the adjective "undue" aims at excluding advantages permitted by the law or by administrative rules as well as minimum gifts, gifts of very low value or socially acceptable gifts.

39. Bribery provisions of certain member States of the Council of Europe make some distinctions, as to whether the act, which is solicited, is a part of the official's duty or whether he is going beyond his duties. In this connection, attention should be drawn to the work currently carried out by the GMC to draft a European model code of conduct for public officials specifying professional duties and standards for public officials in order to prevent corruption. As far as criminal law is concerned, if an official receives a benefit in return for acting in accordance with his duties, this would already constitute a criminal offence. Should the official act in a manner, which is prohibited or arbitrary, he would be liable for a more serious offence. If he should not have handled the case at all, for instance a licence should not have been given, the official would be liable to having committed a more serious form of bribery which usually carries a heavier penalty. Such an extra-element of "breach of duty" was, however, not considered to be necessary for the purposes of this Convention. The drafters of the Convention considered that the decisive element of the offence was not whether the official had any discretion to act as requested by the briber, but whether he had been offered, given or promised a bribe in order to obtain something from him. The briber may not even have known whether the official had discretion or not, this element being, for the purpose of this provision, irrelevant. Thus, the Convention aims at safeguarding the confidence of citizens in the fairness of Public Administration which would be severely undermined, even if the official would have acted in the same way without the bribe. In a democratic State public servants are, as a general rule, remunerated from public budgets and not directly by the citizens or by private companies. In addition, the notion of "breach of duty" adds an element of ambiguity that makes more difficult the prosecution of this offence, by requiring to prove that the public official was expected to act against his duties or was expected to exercise his discretion for the benefit of the briber. States that require such an extra-element for bribery would therefore have to ensure that they could

implement the definition of bribery under Article 2 of this Convention without hindering its objective.

Article 3 — Passive bribery of domestic public officials

40. Article 3 defines passive bribery of public officials. As this offence is closely
linked with active bribery, some comments made thereon, e.g. in respect of the
mental element and the undue advantage apply accordingly here as well. The
"perpetrator" in Article 3 can only be a public official, in the meaning of Article 1. The material elements of his act include requesting or receiving an
undue advantage or accepting the offer or the promise thereof.

41. "Requesting" may for example refer to a unilateral act whereby the public
official lets another person know, explicitly or implicitly, that he will have to
"pay" to have some official act done or abstained from. It is immaterial
whether the request was actually acted upon, the request itself being the
core of the offence. Likewise, it does not matter whether the public official
requested the undue advantage for himself or for anyone else.

42. "Receiving" may for example mean the actual taking the benefit, whether by
the public official himself or by someone else (spouse, colleague, organisation, political party, etc) for himself or for someone else. The latter case supposes at least some kind of acceptance by the public official. Again, intermediaries can be involved: the fact that an intermediary is involved, which
would extend the scope of passive bribery to include indirect action by the
official, necessarily entails identifying the criminal nature of the official's conduct, irrespective of the good or bad faith of the intermediary involved.

43. If there is a unilateral request or a corrupt pact, it is essential that the act or
the omission of acting by the public official takes place after the request or
the pact, whereas it is immaterial in such a case at what point in time the
undue advantage is actually received. Thus, it is not a criminal offence under
the Convention to receive a benefit after the act has been performed by the
public official, without prior offer, request or acceptance. Moreover, the word
"receipt" means keeping the advantage or gift at least for some time so that
the official who, having not requested it, immediately returns the gift to
the sender would not be committing an offence under Article 3. This provision is not applicable either to benefits unrelated to a specific subsequent
act in the exercise of the public official's duties.

Article 4 — Bribery of members of domestic public assemblies

44. This Article extends the scope of the active and passive bribery offences
defined in Articles 2 and 3 to members of domestic public assemblies, at local,
regional and national level, whether elected or appointed. This category of
persons is also vulnerable to bribery and recent corruption scandals, sometimes combined with illegal financing of political parties, showed that it was
important to make it also criminally liable for bribery. Concerning the active

bribery-side, the protected legal interest is the same as that protected by Article 2. However, it is different as regards the passive bribery-side, i.e. when a member of a domestic public assembly is bribed: here this provision protects the transparency, the fairness and impartiality of the decision-making process of domestic public assemblies and their members from corrupt manoeuvres. Obviously, the financial support granted to political parties in accordance with national law falls outside the scope of this provision.

45. Since the definition of "public official" refers to the applicable national definition, it is understood that Contracting Parties would apply, in a similar manner, their own definition of "members of domestic public assemblies". This category of persons should primarily cover members of Parliament (where applicable, in both houses), members of local and regional assemblies and members of any other public body whose members are elected or appointed and which "exercise legislative or administrative powers" (Article 4, paragraph 1, in fine). As indicated in paragraph 21 above, this broad notion could cover, in some countries, also mayors, as members of local councils, or ministers, as members of Parliament. The expression "administrative powers" is aimed at bringing into the scope of this provision members of public assemblies which do not have legislative powers, as it could be the case with regional or provincial assemblies or local councils. Such public assemblies, although not competent to enact legislation, may have considerable powers, for instance in the planning, licensing or regulatory areas.

46. Apart from the persons who are bribed, i.e. members of domestic public assemblies, the substance of this bribery offence is identical to the one defined under Articles 2 and 3.

Article 5 — Bribery of foreign public officials

47. Corruption not only undermines good governance and destroys public trust in the fairness and impartiality of public administrations but it may also seriously distort competition and endanger economic development when foreign public officials are bribed, e.g. by corporations to obtain businesses. With the globalisation of economic and financial structures and the integration of domestic markets into the world-market, decisions taken on capital movements or investments in one country may and do exert effects in others. Multinational corporations and international investors play a determining role in nowadays economy and know of no borders. It is both in their interest and the interest of the global economy in general to keep competition rules fair and transparent.

48. The international community has for long been considering the introduction of a specific criminal offence of bribery of foreign public officials, e.g. to ensure respect of competition rules in international business transactions. The protected legal interest is twofold in the case of this offence: transparency and fairness of the decision-making process of foreign public administrations-this was traditionally considered a domestic affair but the globalisa-

tion has made this consideration obsolete-and the protection of fair competition for businesses. The criminalisation of corrupt behaviour occurring outside national territories finds its justification in the common interest of States to protect these interests. The European Union was the first European organisation which succeeded in adopting an international treaty criminalising, inter alia, the corruption of foreign public officials: the Convention on the fight against corruption involving officials of the European Communities or officials of the member States of the EU (adopted on 26 May 1997). After several years, the OECD has also concluded, in November 1997 a landmark agreement on criminalising, in a co-ordinated manner, the bribery of foreign public officials, i.e. to bribe such an official in order to obtain or retain business or other improper advantage.

49. This Article goes beyond the EU Convention in that it provides for the criminalisation of bribery of foreign public officials of any foreign country. It also goes beyond the OECD provision in two respects. Firstly it deals with both the active and passive sides. Of course, the latter, for Contracting Parties to this Convention, will be already covered by Article 3. However, the inclusion of passive corruption of foreign officials in Article 5 seeks to demonstrate the solidarity of the community of States against corruption, wherever it occurs. The message is clear: corruption is a serious criminal offence that could be prosecuted by all Contracting Parties and not only by the corrupt official's own State. Secondly Article 5 contains no restriction as to the context in which the bribery of the foreign official occurs. Again, the aim is not only to protect free competition but the confidence of citizens in democratic institutions and the rule of law. As regards the definition of "foreign public official", reference is made to paragraph 30 above concerning Article 1.

50. Apart from the persons who are bribed, i.e. foreign public officials, the substance of this bribery offence is identical to the one defined under Articles 2 and 3.

Article 6 — Bribery of members of foreign public assemblies

51. This Article criminalises the active and passive bribery of members of foreign public assemblies. The reasons and the protected legal interests are identical to those described under Article 4, but in a foreign context, "in any other State". It is part of the common effort undertaken by States Parties to ensure respect for democratic institutions, independently of whether they are national or foreign in character. Apart from the persons who are bribed, i.e. members of foreign public assemblies, the substance of this bribery offence is identical to the one defined under Articles 2 and 3. The notion of "member of a public assembly" is to be interpreted in the light of the domestic law of the foreign State.

Article 7 — Active bribery in the private sector

52. This Article extends criminal responsibility for bribery to the private sector. Corruption in the private sector has, over the last century, been dealt with by

civil (e.g. competition), or labour laws or general criminal law provisions. Criminalising private corruption appeared as a pioneering but necessary effort to avoid gaps in a comprehensive strategy to combat corruption. The reasons for introducing criminal law sanctions for corruption in the private sphere are manifold. First of all, because corruption in the private sphere undermines values like trust, confidence or loyalty, which are necessary for the maintenance and development of social and economic relations. Even in the absence of a specific pecuniary damage to the victim, private corruption causes damage to society as a whole. In general, it can be said that there is an increasing tendency towards limiting the differences between the rules applicable to the public and private sectors. This requires redesigning the rules that protect the interests of the private sector and govern its relations with its employees and the public at large. Secondly, criminalisation of private sector corruption was necessary to ensure respect for fair competition. Thirdly, it also has to do with the privatisation process. Over the years important public functions have been privatised (education, health, transport, telecommunication etc). The transfer of such public functions to the private sector, often related to a massive privatisation process, entails transfers of substantial budgetary allocations and of regulatory powers. It is therefore logical to protect the public from the damaging effects of corruption in businesses as well, particularly since the financial or other powers concentrated in the private sector, necessary for their new functions, are of great social importance.

53.   In general, the comments made on active bribery of public officials (Article 2) apply mutatis mutandis here as well, in particular as regards the corrupt acts performed, the mental element and the briber. There are, nevertheless, several important differences between the provisions on public and private sector bribery. First of all, Article 7 restricts the scope of private bribery to the domain of "business activity", thus deliberately excluding any non-profit oriented activities carried out by persons or organisations, e.g. by associations or other NGOs. This choice was made to focus on the most vulnerable sector, i.e. the business sector. Of course, this may leave some gaps, which Governments may wish to fill: nothing would prevent a signatory State from implementing this provision without the restriction to "in the course of business activities". "Business activity" is to be interpreted in a broad sense: it means any kind of commercial activity, in particular trading in goods and delivering services, including services to the public (transport, telecommunication etc).

54.   The second important difference concerns the scope of recipient persons in Article 7. This provision prohibits bribing any persons who "direct or work for, in any capacity, private sector entities". Again, this a sweeping notion to be interpreted broadly as it covers the employer-employee relationship but also other types of relationships such as partners, lawyer and client and others in which there is no contract of employment. Within private enterprises it should cover not only employees but also the management from the top to the bottom, including members of the board, but not the shareholders. It would also include persons who do not have the status of employee or do

not work permanently for the company—for example, consultants, commercial agents etc.—but can engage the responsibility of the company. "Private sector entities" refer to companies, enterprises, trusts and other entities, which are entirely or to a determining extent owned by private persons. This of course covers a whole range of entities, notably those engaged "in business activities". They can be corporations but also entities with no legal personality. For the purpose of this provision, the word "entity" should be understood as meaning also, in this context, an individual. Public entities fall therefore outside the scope of this provision.

55. The third important difference relates to the behaviour of the bribed person in the private sector. If, in the case of public officials, it was immaterial whether there had been a breach of his duties, given the general expectation of transparency, impartiality and loyalty in this regard, a breach of duty is required for private sector persons. Criminalisation of bribery in the private sector seeks to protect the trust, the confidence and the loyalty that are indispensable for private relationships to exist. Rights and obligations related to those relationships are governed by private law and, to a great extent, determined by contracts. The employee, the agent, the lawyer is expected to perform his functions in accordance with his contract, which will include, expressly or implicitly, a general obligation of loyalty towards his principal, a general obligation not to act to the detriment of his interests. Such an obligation can be laid down, for example, in codes of conduct that private companies are increasingly developing. The expression, "in breach of their duties" does not aim only at ensuring respect for specific contractual obligations but rather to guarantee that there will be no breach of the general duty of loyalty in relation to the principal's affairs or business. The employee, partner, or managing director who accepts a bribe to act or refrain from acting in a manner that is contrary to his principal's interest, will be betraying the trust placed upon him, the loyalty owed to his principal. This justifies the inclusion of private sector corruption as a criminal offence. The Convention, in Article 7, retained this philosophy and requires the additional element of "breach of duty" in order to criminalise private sector corruption. The notion of "breach of duty" can also be linked to that of "secrecy", that is, the acceptance of the gift to the detriment of the employer or principal and without obtaining his authorisation or approval. It is the secrecy of the benefit rather than the benefit itself that is the essence of the offence. Such a secret behaviour threatens the interests of the private sector entity and makes it dangerous.

Article 8—Passive bribery in the private sector

56. The comments made on passive bribery of domestic public officials (Article 3) apply accordingly here as far as the corrupt acts and the mental element are concerned. So do the comments on active bribery in the private sector (Article 7), as far as the specific context, the persons involved and the extra-condition of "breach of duty" are concerned. The mirror-principle, already referred to in the context of public sector bribery, is also applicable here.

Article 9 — Bribery of officials of international organisations

57. The necessity of extending the criminalisation of acts of bribery to the international sphere was already highlighted under Article 5 (Bribery of foreign public officials). Recent initiatives in the framework of the EU, which led to the adoption on 27 September 1996 (Official Journal of the European Communities No. C 313 of 23. 10. 96) of the Protocol (on corruption) to the EU Convention on the protection of the European Communities' financial interests and that of the Convention on the fight against corruption involving officials of the European Communities or officials of the member States of the EU (26 May 1997), are evidence that criminal law protection is needed against the corruption of officials of international institutions, which must have the same consequences as the one of national public officials. The need to criminalise bribery is even greater in the case of officials of public international organisations than in the case of foreign public officials, since, as already pointed out above, passive bribery of a foreign public official is already an offence under the officials' own domestic legislation, whereas the laws on bribery only exceptionally cover acts committed by their nationals abroad, in particular when they are permanently employed by public international organisations. The protected legal interest in general is the transparency and impartiality of the decision-making process of public international organisations which, according to their specific mandate, carry out activities on behalf or in the interest of their member States. Some of these organisations do handle large quantities of goods and services. Fair competition in their public procurement procedures is also worth protecting by criminal law.

58. Since this Article refers back to Articles 2 and 3 for the description of the bribery offences, the comments made thereon apply accordingly. The persons involved as recipients of the bribes are, however, different. It covers the corruption of "any official or other contracted employee within the meaning of the staff regulations, of any public international or supranational organisation or body of which the Party is a member, and any person, whether seconded or not, carrying out functions corresponding to those performed by such officials or agents."

59. Two main categories are therefore involved: firstly, officials and other contracted employees who, under the staff regulations, can be either permanent or temporary members of the staff, but irrespective of the duration of their employment by the organisation, have identical duties and responsibilities, governed by contract. Secondly, staff members who are seconded (put at the disposal of the organisation by a government or any public or private body), to carry out functions equivalent to those performed by officials or contracted employees.

60. Article 9 restricts the obligation of signatories to criminalise only those cases of bribery involving the above-mentioned persons employed by international organisations of which they are members. This restriction is necessary for various practical reasons, for example to avoid problems related to immunity.

61. Article 9 mentions "public international or supranational organisations", which means that they are set up by governments and not individuals or private organisations. It also means that international non-governmental organisations (NGOs) fall outside its scope, although in some cases members of NGOs may be covered by other provisions like Articles 7 and 8. There are many regional or global public international organisations, for example the Council of Europe, whereas there's only one supranational, i.e. the European Union.

Article 10 — Bribery of members of international parliamentary assemblies

62. The comments made on the bribery of members of domestic public assemblies (Article 4) apply here as well, as far as the corrupt acts and the mental element are concerned. These assemblies perform legislative, administrative or advisory functions on the basis of the statute of the international organisation which created them. As far as the specific international context and the restriction of membership of the organisation are concerned, the comments on the bribery of officials of international organisations (Article 9) apply here as well. The persons involved on the passive side are, however, different: members of parliamentary assemblies of international (e.g., the Parliamentary Assembly of the Council of Europe) or supranational organisations (the European Parliament).

Article 11 — Bribery of judges and officials of international courts

63. The comments made on the bribery of domestic public official (Articles 2 and 3), whose definition, according to Article 1.a, includes "judges", apply here as well, as far as the corrupt acts and the mental element are concerned. Similarly, the above comments on the bribery of officials of international organisations (Article 9) should be extended to this provision as far as the specific international context and the restriction of membership of the organisation are concerned. The persons involved are, however, different: "any holders of judicial office or officials of any international court". These persons include not only "judges" in international courts (e.g. at the European Court of Human Rights) but also other officials for example the Prosecutors of the UN Tribunal on the former Yugoslavia) or members of the clerk's office. Arbitration courts are in principle not included in the notion of "international courts" because they do not perform judicial functions in respect of States. It will be for each Contracting Party to determine whether or not it accepts the jurisdiction of the court.

Article 12 — Trading in influence

64. This offence is somewhat different from the other—bribery-based—offences defined by the Convention, though the protected legal interests are the same: transparency and impartiality in the decision-making process of public

administrations. Its inclusion in the present Convention illustrates the comprehensive approach of the Programme of Action against Corruption, which views corruption, in its various forms, as a threat to the rule of law and the stability of democratic institutions. Criminalising trading in influence seeks to reach the close circle of the official or the political party to which he belongs and to tackle the corrupt behaviour of those persons who are in the neighbourhood of power and try to obtain advantages from their situation, contributing to the atmosphere of corruption. It permits Contracting Parties to tackle the so-called "background corruption", which undermines the trust placed by citizens on the fairness of public administration. The purpose of the present Convention being to improve the battery of criminal law measures against corruption it appeared essential to introduce this offence of trading in influence, which would be relatively new to some States.

65. This provision criminalises a corrupt trilateral relationship where a person having real or supposed influence on persons referred to in Articles 2, 4, 5, and 9-11, trades this influence in exchange for an undue advantage from someone seeking this influence. The difference, therefore, between this offence and bribery is that the influence peddler is not required to "act or refrain from acting" as would a public official. The recipient of the undue advantage assists the person providing the undue advantage by exerting or proposing to exert an improper influence over the third person who may perform (or abstain from performing) the requested act. "Improper" influence must contain a corrupt intent by the influence peddler: acknowledged forms of lobbying do not fall under this notion. Article 12 describes both forms of this corrupt relationship: active and passive trading in influence. As has been explained (see document GMC (95) 46), "passive" trading in influence presupposes that a person, taking advantage of real or pretended influence with third persons, requests, receives or accepts the undue advantage, with a view to assisting the person who supplied the undue advantage by exerting the improper influence. "Active" trading in influence presupposes that a person promises, gives or offers an undue advantage to someone who asserts or confirms that he is able to exert an improper over third persons.

66. States might wish to break down the offence into two different parts: the active and the passive trading in influence. The offence on the active side is quite similar to active bribery, as described in Article 2, with some differences: a person gives an undue advantage to a another person (the "influence peddler") who claims, by virtue of his professional position or social status, to be able to exert an improper influence over the decision making of domestic or foreign public officials (Articles 2 and 5), members of domestic public assemblies (Article 4), officials of international organisations, members of international parliamentary assemblies or judges and officials of international courts (Articles 9-11). The passive trading in influence side resembles passive bribery, as described in Article 3, but, again the influence peddler is the one who receives the undue advantage, not the public official. What is important to note is the outsider position of the influence peddler: he cannot [make] decisions himself, but misuses his real or alleged influence on other persons. It is

immaterial whether the influence peddler actually exerted his influence on the above persons or not as is whether the influence leads to the intended result.

67. The comments made on active and passive bribery apply therefore here as well, with the above additions, in particular as regards the corrupt acts and the mental element.

Article 13—Money laundering of proceeds from corruption offences

68. This Article provides for the criminalisation of the laundering of proceeds deriving from corruption offences defined under Articles 2-12, i.e. all bribery offences and trading in influence. The technique used by this Article is to make a cross-reference to another Council of Europe Convention (ETS No. 141), which is the Convention on laundering, search, seizure and confiscation of the proceeds from crime (November 1990). The offence of laundering is defined in Article 6, paragraph 1 of the latter convention, whereas certain conditions of application are set out in paragraph 2. The laundering offence, whose objective is to disguise the illicit origin of proceeds, always requires a predicate offence from which the said proceeds originate. For a number of years anti-laundering efforts focused on drug proceeds, but recent international instruments, including above all the Council of Europe Convention No. 141 but also the revised 40 Recommendations of the Financial Action Task Force (FATF), recognise that virtually any offence can generate proceeds which may need to be laundered for subsequent recycling in legitimate businesses (e.g. fraud, terrorism, trafficking in stolen goods, arms, etc). In principle, therefore, Convention No. 141 already applies to the proceeds of any kind of criminal activity, including corruption, unless a Party has entered a reservation to Article 6 whereby restricting its scope to proceeds form particular offences or categories of offences.

69. The authors of this Convention felt that given the close links that are proved to exist between corruption and money laundering, it was of primary importance that this Convention also criminalises the laundering of corruption proceeds. Another reason to include this offence was the possibly different circles of States ratifying the two instruments: some non-member States which have participated in the elaboration of this Convention could only ratify Convention No. 141 with the authorisation of the Committee of Ministers of the Council of Europe, while they can do so with the present Convention automatically by virtue of its Article 32, paragraph 1.

70. This provision lays down the principle that Contracting Parties are obliged to consider corruption offences as predicate offences for the purpose of anti-money laundering legislation. Exceptions to this principle are only allowed to the extent that the Party has made a reservation in relation to the relevant Articles of this Convention. Moreover, if a country does not consider some of these corruption offences as "serious" ones under its money laundering legislation, it will not be obliged to modify its definition of laundering.

Article 14 — Account offences

71. Account offences may have a twofold relationship to corruption offences: these offences are either preparatory acts to the latter or acts disguising the "predicate" corruption or other corruption-related offences. Article 16 covers both forms of this relationship and, in principle, all corruption offences defined in Articles 2–12. These account offences do not apply to money laundering of corruption proceeds (Article 13), since the main feature of laundering is precisely to disguise the origin of illicit funds. Disguising money laundering would, therefore, be redundant.

72. Given that these acts aim at committing, concealing or disguising corruption offences, either by act or by omission, they can also be qualified as preparatory-stage acts. Such acts are usually treated as administrative offences in certain domestic laws. Article 14 allows therefore the Contracting Parties to choose between criminal law or administrative law sanctions. Though the choice offered might facilitate the implementation of the Convention for certain countries it could hamper international co-operation in respect of the present offence.

73. Account offences can only be committed intentionally. Concerning the material elements of the offence, it is described in two different forms: one relates to a positive action, i.e. the creation or use of invoices or other kinds of accounting documents or records which contain false or incomplete information. This fraud-type behaviour clearly aims at deceiving a person (e.g. an auditor) as to the genuine and reliable nature of the information contained therein, with a view to concealing a corruption offence. The second indent contains an omission act, i.e. someone fails to record a payment, coupled with a specific qualifying element, i.e. "unlawfully". The latter indicates that only where a legal duty is placed upon the relevant persons (e.g. company accountants) to record payments, the omission thereof should become a punishable act.

74. If a Party has made a reservation in respect of any of the corruption offences defined in Articles 2–12, it is not obliged to extend the application of the account offence to such corruption offence(s). The obligation arising out of this Article to establish certain acts as offences is to be implemented in the framework of the Party's laws and regulations regarding the maintenance of books and records, financial statement disclosures, and accounting and auditing standards. Moreover, this provision does not aim at the establishment of specific accounting offences related to corruption, since general accounting offences would be quite sufficient in this field. It should be further specified that Article 14 does not require a particular branch of the law (fiscal, administrative or criminal) to deal with this matter.

75. This provision requires Contracting Parties to establish offences "liable to criminal or other sanctions". The expression "other sanctions" means "non-criminal sanctions" imposed by the courts.

Article 15 — Participatory acts

76. The purpose of this provision is not the establishment of an additional offence but to criminalise participatory acts in the offences defined in Articles 2 to 14. It therefore provides for the liability of participants in intentional offences established in accordance with the Convention. Though it is not indicated specifically, it flows from the general principles of criminal law that any form of participation (aiding and abetting) needs to be committed intentionally.

Article 16 — Immunity

77. Article 16 provides that the Convention is without prejudice to provisions laid down in treaties, protocols or statutes governing the withdrawal of immunity. The acknowledgement of customary international law is not excluded in this field. Such provisions may, in particular, concern members of staff in public international or supranational organisations (Article 9), members of international parliamentary assemblies (Article 10) as well as judges and officials of international courts (Article 11). Withdrawal of immunity is thus a prior condition for exercising jurisdiction, according to the particular rules applying to each of the above-mentioned categories of persons. The Convention recognises the obligation of each of the institutions concerned to give effect to the provisions governing privileges and immunities.

Article 17 — Jurisdiction

78. This Article establishes a series of criteria under which Contracting Parties have to establish their jurisdiction over the criminal offences enumerated in Articles 2–14 of the Convention.

79. Paragraph 1, littera a. lays down the principle of territoriality. It does not require that a corruption offence as a whole be committed exclusively on the territory of a State to enable it establishing jurisdiction. If only parts of the offence, e.g. the acceptance or the offer of a bribe, were committed on its territory, a State may still do so: the principle of territoriality should thus be interpreted broadly. In many member States, albeit not in all, for the purpose of allowing the exercise of jurisdiction in accordance with the principle of territoriality, the place of commission is determined on the basis of what is known as the doctrine of ubiquity: it means that an offence as a whole may be considered to have been committed in the place where a part of it has been committed. According to one form of the doctrine of ubiquity, an offence may be considered to have been also committed in the place where the consequences or effects of the offence become manifest. The doctrine of effects is accepted in several member states of the Council of Europe (Council of Europe Report on extraterritorial criminal jurisdiction, op. cit. pages 8–9).* It means that wherever a constituent element of an offence is committed or an

---

* The cited provisions are not included among the documents contained in these appendices.

effect occurs, that is usually considered as the place of perpetration. In this context, it may be noted that the intention of the offender is irrelevant and does not affect the jurisdiction based on the territorial principle. Likewise, it is immaterial which is the nationality of the briber or of the person who is bribed.

80. Paragraph 1, littera b. sets out the principle of nationality. The nationality theory is also based upon the State sovereignty: it provides that nationals of a State are obliged to comply with the domestic law even when they are outside its territory. Consequently, if a national commits an offence abroad, the Party has, in principle, to take jurisdiction, particularly if it does not extradite its nationals. The paragraph further specifies that jurisdiction has to be established not only if nationals commit one of the offences defined by the Convention but also when public officials and members of domestic assemblies of the Party commit such an offence. Naturally, in most cases the latter two categories are, at the same time, nationals as well (in some countries nationality is a pre-condition for qualifying for these positions), but exceptions do exist.

81. Paragraph 1, littera c. is also based on both the principle of protection (of national interests) and of nationality. The difference with the previous paragraph is that here jurisdiction is based on the bribed person's status: either he is a public official or a member of a domestic public assembly of the Party (therefore not necessarily a national) or he is a national who is at the same time an official of an international organisation, a member of an international parliamentary assembly or a judge or an official of an international court.

82. Paragraph 2 allows States to enter a reservation to the jurisdiction grounds laid down in paragraph 1, litterae b and c. In such cases, however, it stems from the principle of *aut dedere aut iudicare,* "extradite or punish," laid down in paragraph 3 that there is an obligation for the contracting party to establish jurisdiction over cases where extradition of the alleged offender was refused on the basis of his nationality and the offender is present on its territory.

83. Jurisdiction is traditionally based on territoriality or nationality. In the field of corruption these principles may, however, not always suffice to exercise jurisdiction, for example over cases occurring outside the territory of a Party, not involving its nationals, but still affecting its interests (e.g. national security). Paragraph 4 of this Article allows the Parties to establish, in conformity with their national law, other types of jurisdiction as well. Among them, the universality principle would permit States to establish jurisdiction over serious offences, regardless where and by whom they are committed, because they may be seen as threatening universal values and the interest of mankind. So far, this principle has not yet gained a general international recognition, although some international documents make reference to it.

Article 18 — Corporate liability

84. Article 18 deals with the liability of legal persons. It is a fact that legal persons are often involved in corruption offences, especially in business transactions, while practice reveals serious difficulties in prosecuting natural persons acting on behalf of these legal persons. For example, in view of the largeness

of corporations and the complexity of structures of the organisation, it becomes more and more difficult to identify a natural person who may be held responsible (in a criminal sense) for a bribery offence. Legal persons thus usually escape their liability due to their collective decision-making process. On the other hand, corrupt practices often continue after the arrest of individual members of management, because the company as such is not deterred by individual sanctions.

85. The international trend at present seems to support the general recognition of corporate liability, even in countries, which only a few years ago, were still applying the principle according to which corporations cannot commit criminal offences. Therefore, the present provision of the Convention is in harmony with these recent tendencies, e.g. in the area of international anti-corruption instruments, such as the OECD Convention on Combating Bribery of Foreign Public Officials in International Business Transactions (Article 2).

86. Article 18, paragraph 1 does not stipulate the type of liability it requires for legal persons. Therefore this provision does not impose an obligation to establish that legal persons will be held criminally liable for the offences mentioned therein. On the other hand it should be made clear that by virtue of this provision Contracting Parties undertake to establish some form of liability for legal persons engaging in corrupt practices, liability that could be criminal, administrative or civil in nature. Thus, criminal and non-criminal administrative, civil sanctions are suitable, provided that they are "effective, proportionate and dissuasive" as specified by paragraph 2 of Article 19. Legal persons shall be held liable if three conditions are met. The first condition is that an active bribery offence, an offence of trading in influence or a money laundering offence must have been committed, as defined in Articles 2, 4, 5, 6, 7, 9, 10, 11, 12 and 13. The second condition is that the offence must have been committed for the benefit or on behalf of the legal person. The third condition, which serves to limit the scope of this form of liability, requires the involvement of "any person who has a leading position". The leading position can be assumed to exist in the three situations described—a power of representation or an authority to take decisions or to exercise control-which demonstrate that such a physical person is legally or in practice able to engage the liability of the legal person.

87. Paragraph 2 expressly mentions Parties' obligation to extend corporate liability to cases where the lack of supervision within the legal person makes it possible to commit the corruption offences. It aims at holding legal persons liable for the omission by persons in a leading position to exercise supervision over the acts committed by subordinate persons acting on behalf of the legal person. A similar provision also exists in the Second Protocol to the European Union Convention on the Protection of the financial interest of the European Communities. As paragraph 1, it does not impose an obligation to establish criminal liability in such cases but some form of liability to be decided by the Contracting Party itself.

88. Paragraph 3 clarifies that corporate liability does not exclude individual liability. In a concrete case, different spheres of liability may be established at

the same time, for example the responsibility of an organ etc. separately from the liability of the legal person as a whole. Individual liability may be combined with any of these categories of liability.

Article 19 — Sanctions and measures

89. This Article is closely related to Articles 2–14, which define various corruption offences that should be made, according to this convention, punishable under criminal law. In accordance with the obligations imposed by those articles, this paragraph obliges explicitly the Contracting Parties to draw the consequence from the serious nature of these offences by providing for criminal sanctions that are "effective, proportionate and dissuasive", expression that can also be found in Article 5 of the European Union Convention of 26 May 1997 and in Article 3, paragraph 1 of the OECD Convention of 20 November 1997. This provision involves the obligation to attach to the commission of these offences by natural persons penalties of imprisonment of a certain duration ("which can give rise to extradition"). This provision does not mean that a prison sentence must be imposed every time that a person is found guilty of having committed a corruption offence established in accordance with this Convention but that the Criminal Code should provide for the possibility of imposing prison sentences of a certain level in such cases.

90. Because the offences referred to in Article 14 shall be made punishable under either criminal or administrative law, this article is only applicable to those offences in so far as these offences have been established as criminal offences.

91. Legal persons, whose liability is to be established in accordance with Article 18 shall also be subject to sanctions that are "effective, proportionate and dissuasive", which can be penal, administrative or civil in nature. Paragraph 2 compels Contracting Parties to provide for the possibility of imposing monetary sanctions of a certain level to legal persons held liable of a corruption offence.

92. It is obvious that the obligation to make corruption offences punishable under criminal law would lose much of its effect if it was not supplemented by an obligation to provide for adequately severe sanctions. While prescribing that imprisonment and pecuniary sanctions should be the sanctions that can be imposed for the relevant offences, the Article leaves open the possibility that other sanctions reflecting the seriousness of the offences are provided for. It cannot, of course, be the aim of this Convention to give detailed provisions regarding the criminal sanctions to be linked to the different offences mentioned in Articles 2–14. On this point the Parties inevitably need the discretionary power to create a system of criminal offences and sanctions that is in coherence with their existing national legal systems.

93. Paragraph 3 of this Article prescribes a general obligation for Contracting Parties to provide for adequate legal instruments to ensure that confiscation, or other forms of legal deprivation (such as civil forfeiture) of instrumentalities and proceeds of corruption, related to the value of offences mentioned in Articles 2–14, is possible thereof. This paragraph must be examined in view of

the background of the Council of Europe Convention on Laundering, Search, Seizure and Confiscation of the Proceeds from Crime (Strasbourg, 8 November 1990). The Convention is based on the idea that confiscation of the proceeds is one of the effective methods in combating crime. Taking into account that the undue advantage promised, given, received or accepted in most corruption offence is of material nature, it is clear that measures resulting in the deprivation of property related to or gained by the offence should, in principle, be available in this field too.

94. Article 1 of the Laundering Convention is instrumental in the interpretation of the terms "confiscate", "instrumentalities", "proceeds" and "property", used in this Article. By the word "confiscate" reference is made to any criminal sanction or measure ordered by a court following proceedings in relation to a criminal offence resulting in the final deprivation of property. "Instrumentalities" cover the broad range of objects that are used or intended to be used, in any way, wholly or in part, to commit the relevant criminal offences established in accordance with Articles 2–14. The term "proceeds" means any economic advantage as well as any savings by means of reduced expenditure derived from such an offence. It may consist of any "property" in the interpretation that the term is being given below. In the wording of this paragraph, it is taken into account that the national legal systems may show differences as to what property can be confiscated in relation to an offence. Confiscation may be possible of objects that (directly) form the proceeds of the offence or of other property belonging to the offender that—although not (directly) gained by the offence—equals the value of the directly gained illegal proceeds, the so called "substitute assets". "Property" therefore has to be interpreted, in this context, as including property of any description, whether corporal or incorporeal, movable or immovable, and legal documents or instruments evidencing title to or interest in such property. It is to be noted that Contracting Parties are under no obligation to provide for the criminal confiscation of substitute assets as the words "otherwise deprive" allow for their civil forfeiture also.

Article 20—Specialised authorities

95. This Article requires States Parties to adopt the necessary measures to ensure that persons or entities be appropriately specialised in the fight against corruption. This provision is inspired, inter alia, by the need of improving both the specialisation and independence of persons or entities in charge of the fight against corruption, which was stated in numerous Council of Europe documents. The requirement of specialisation is not meant to apply to all levels of law enforcement. It does not require in particular that in each prosecutor's office or in each police station there is a special unit or expert for corruption offences. At the same time, this provision implies that wherever it is necessary for combating effectively corruption there are sufficiently trained law-enforcement units or personnel.

96. In this context, reference should firstly be made to the Conclusions and Recommendations of the 1st Conference for law-enforcement officers specialised in the fight against corruption, which took place in Strasbourg in April 1996.

In the Recommendations, participants agreed, inter alia, that "corruption is a phenomenon the prevention, investigation and prosecution of which need to be approached on numerous levels, using specific knowledge and skills from a variety of fields (law, finance, economics, accounting, civil engineers, etc.). Each State should therefore have experts specialised in the fight against corruption. They should be of a sufficient number and be given appropriate material resources. Specialisa-tion may take different forms: the specialisation of a number of police officers, judges, prosecutors and administrators or of the bodies or units specially entrusted with (several aspects of) the fight against corruption. The power available to the specialised units or individuals must be relatively broad and include right of access to all information and files which could be of values to the fight against corruption."

97. Secondly, it should be noted that the Conclusions and Recommendations of the 2nd European Conference of specialised services in the fight against corruption, which took place in Tallinn in October 1997, also recommended that "judges and prosecutors enjoy independence and impartiality in the exercise of their functions, are properly trained in combating this type of criminal behaviour and have sufficient means and resources to achieve the objective".

98. Thirdly, Resolution (97)24 on the 20 Guiding Principles for the fight against corruption, in its Principle n° 3, provides that States should "ensure that those in charge of the prevention, investigation, prosecution and adjudication of corruption offences, enjoy the independence and autonomy appropriate to their functions, are free from improper influence and have effective means for gathering evidence, protecting the persons who help the authorities in combating corruption and preserving the confidentiality of investigations".

99. It should be noted that the independence of specialised authorities for the fight against corruption, referred to in this Article, should not be an absolute one. Indeed, their activities should be, as far as possible, integrated and co-ordinated with the work carried out by the police, the administration or the public prosecutor's office. The level of independence required for these specialised services is the one that is necessary to perform properly their functions.

100. Moreover, the entities referred to in Article 20 can either be special bodies created for the purposes of combating corruption, or specialised entities within existing bodies. These entities should have the adequate know-how and legal and material means at least to receive and centralise all information necessary for the prevention of corruption and for the revealing of corruption. In addition, and without prejudice to the role of other national bodies dealing with international co-operation, one of the tasks of such specialised authorities could also be to serve as counterparts for foreign entities in charge of fighting corruption.

Article 21—Co-operation between authorities

101. The responsibility for fighting corruption does not lie exclusively with law-enforcement authorities. The 20 Guiding Principles on the fight against corruption already recognised the role that tax authorities can perform in this

field (see Principle 8). The drafters of this Convention considered that co-operation with the authorities in charge of investigating and prosecuting criminal offences was an important aspect of a coherent an efficient action against those committing the corruption offences defined therein. This provision introduces a general obligation to ensure co-operation of all public authorities with those investigating and prosecuting criminal offences. Obviously the purpose of this provision cannot be to guarantee that a sufficient level of co-operation will be achieved in all cases but to impose on Contracting Parties the adoption of the steps that are necessary to try and ensure an adequate level of co-operation between the national authorities. The authorities responsible for reporting corruption offences are not defined, but national legislatures should adopt a broad approach. It could be tax authorities, administrative authorities, public auditors, labour inspectors . . . whoever in the exercise of his functions comes across information regarding potential corruption offences. Such information, necessary for the law enforcement authorities, is likely to be available, primarily, from those authorities that have a supervisory and controlling competence over the functioning of different aspects of public administration.

102. This Article provides that the general duty to co-operate with law-enforcement authorities in the investigation and prosecution of corruption offences is to be carried out "in accordance with national law". The reference to national law means that the extent of the duty to co-operate with law enforcement is to be defined by the provisions of national law applicable to the official or authority concerned (e.g. an authorisation procedure). This provision does not carry an obligation to modify those legal systems, in existence in some Contracting Parties, which do not provide for a general obligation of public officials to report crimes or have established specific procedures for so doing.

103. This is confirmed by the fact that the means of co-operation, specified in litteras a) and b) are not cumulative but alternative. As a result, the obligation to co-operate with the authorities responsible for investigating and prosecuting criminal offences can be fulfilled either by informing them, on the authority's own initiative, of the existence of reasonable grounds to believe that an offence has been committed or by providing them with the information they request. Contracting Parties will be entitled to choose between the available options.

Littera a)

104. The first option is to allow or even compel the authority or official in question to inform law-enforcement authorities whenever it comes across a possible corruption offence. The terms "reasonable grounds" mean that the obligation to inform has to be observed as soon as the authority considers that there is a likelihood that a corruption offence has been committed. The level of likelihood should be the same as the one that is required for starting a police investigation or a prosecutorial investigation.

Littera b)

105. This paragraph concerns the obligation to inform on request. It lays down that the fundamental principle that authorities must provide the investigating and prosecuting authorities with all necessary information, in accordance with safeguards and procedures established by national law. What is considered as "necessary information" will also be decided in accordance with national law.

106. Of course, national law might provide for some exceptions to the general principle of providing information, for instance, where the information touches upon secrets relating to the protection of national or other essential interests.

Article 22 – Protection of collaborators of justice and witnesses

107. Article 22 of the Convention requires States to take the necessary measures to provide for an effective and appropriate protection of collaborators of justice and witnesses.

108. In this context, it should be noted that already in the Conclusions and Recommendations of the 2nd European Conference of specialised services in the fight against corruption (Tallinn, October 1997), participants agreed that, in order to fight corruption effectively, "an appropriate system of protection for witnesses and other persons co-operating with the judicial authorities should be introduced, including not only an appropriate legal framework, but also the financial resources needed to achieve the result." Moreover, "provisions should be made for the granting of immunity or the adequate reduction of penalties in respect of persons charged with corruption offences who contribute to the investigation, disclosure or prevention of crime".

109. However, it is in Recommendation N° R(97)13 on the intimidation of witnesses and the rights of the defence, which has been adopted by the Committee of Ministers of the Council of Europe on 10 September 1997, that the question of the protection of collaborators of justice and witnesses has been addressed in a comprehensive way in the framework of the Council of Europe. This Recommendation establishes a set of principles which could guide national legislation when addressing the problems of witness intimidation, either in the framework of criminal procedure law or when designing out-of-court protection measures. The Recommendation suggests to Member States a list of measures which may contribute to ensuring efficiently the protection of both the interests of witnesses and that of the criminal justice system, while maintaining appropriate opportunities for the defence to exercise its right in criminal proceedings.

110. The drafters of this Convention, inspired, inter alia, by the above-mentioned Recommendation, considered that the words "collaborators of justice" refer to persons who face criminal charges, or are convicted, of having taken part in corruption offences, as contained in Articles 2–14 of the Convention, but agree to co-operate with criminal justice authorities, particularly by giving information concerning those corruption offences in which they were

involved, in order for the competent law-enforcement authorities to investigate and prosecute them.

111. Moreover, the word "witnesses" refers to persons who possess information relevant to criminal proceedings concerning corruption offences as contained in Articles 2–14 of the Convention and includes whistleblowers.

112. Intimidation of witnesses, which may be carried out either directly or indirectly, may occur in a number of ways, but its purpose is the same, i.e. to eliminate evidence against defendants with a view to their acquittal for lack of sufficient evidence, or exceptionally, to provide evidence against defendants with a view to have them convicted.

113. The terms "effective and appropriate" protection in Article 20, refer to the need to adapt the level of protection granted to the risks that exist for collaborators of justice, witnesses or whistleblowers. In some cases it could be sufficient, for instance, to maintain their name undisclosed during the proceedings; in other cases they would need bodyguards; in extreme cases more far-reaching witnesses' protection measures such as change of identity, work, domicile, etc. might be necessary.

Article 23—Measures to facilitate the gathering of evidence and the confiscation of proceeds

114. This provision acknowledges the difficulties that exist to obtain evidence that may lead to the prosecution and punishment of persons having committed those corruption offences defined in accordance with the present Convention. Behind almost every corruption offence lies a pact of silence between the person who pays the bribe and the person who receives it. In normal circumstances, none of them will have any interest in disclosing the existence or the modalities of the corrupt agreement concluded between them. In conformity with paragraph 1, States Parties are therefore required to adopt measures, which will facilitate the gathering of evidence in cases related to the commission of one of the offences defined in Articles 2–14. In view of the already mentioned difficulties to obtain evidence, this provision includes an obligation for the Parties to permit the use of "special investigative techniques". No list of these techniques is included, but the drafters of the Convention were referring in particular to the use of undercover agents, wire-tapping, bugging, interception of telecommunications, access to computer systems and so on. Reference to these special investigative techniques can also be found in previous instruments such as the United Nations Convention of 1988, the Council of Europe Convention on the Laundering, Search, Seizure and Confiscation of the Proceeds from Crime (ITS No. 141, Article 4) or the Forty Recommendations adopted by the Financial Action Task Force (FATF). Most of these techniques are highly intrusive and may give rise to constitutional difficulties as regards their compatibility with fundamental rights and freedoms. Therefore, the Parties are free to decide that some of these techniques will not be admitted in their domestic legal system. Also the reference made by paragraph 1 to "national law" should enable Parties to surround the use of these

special investigative techniques with as many safeguards and guarantees as may be required by the imperative of protecting human rights and fundamental freedoms.

115. The second part of paragraph 1 of this Article is closely related to paragraph 3 of Article 19. It requires, for the implementation of the latter Article, the adoption of legal instruments allowing the Contracting Parties to take the necessary provisional steps, before measures leading to confiscation can be imposed. The effectiveness of confiscation measures depends in practice on the possibilities to carry out the necessary investigations as to the quantity of the proceeds gained or the expenses saved and the way in which profits (openly or not) are deposited. In combination with these investigations, it is necessary to ensure that the investigating authorities have the power to freeze located tangible and intangible property in order to prevent that it disappears before a decision on confiscation has been taken or executed (cf. Articles 3 and 4 in the Money Laundering Convention).

CHAPTER III—MONITORING OF IMPLEMENTATION

Article 24 — Monitoring

116. The implementation of the Convention will be monitored by the "Group of States against Corruption—GRECO". The establishment of an efficient and appropriate mechanism to monitor the implementation of international legal instruments against corruption was considered, from the outset, as an essential element for the effectiveness and credibility of the Council of Europe initiative in this field (see, inter alia, the Resolutions adopted at the 19th and 21st Conferences of the European Ministers of Justice, the terms of reference of the Multidisciplinary Group on Corruption, the Programme of Action against Corruption, the Final Declaration and Action Plan of the Second Summit of Heads of State and Government). In Resolution (98) 7 adopted at its 102nd Session (5 May 1998), the Committee of Ministers authorised the establishment of a monitoring body, the GRECO, in the form of a partial and enlarged Agreement under Statutory Resolution (93) 28 (as completed by Resolution (96) 36). Member States and non-member States having participated in the elaboration of the Agreement were invited to notify their intention to participate in GRECO, which would start functioning on the first day of the month following the date on which the 14th notification by a member State would reach the Secretary General of the Council of Europe. Consequently, on . . . 1998, . . . [member States], joined in by [nonmember States included in the constituent Resolution] adopted Resolution (98) . . . establishing the GRECO and containing its Statute.

117. The GRECO will monitor the implementation of this Convention in accordance with its Statute, appended to Resolution (98) . . . . The aim of GRECO is to improve the capacity of its members to fight corruption by following up, through a dynamic process of mutual evaluation and peer pressure, compliance with their undertakings in this field (Article 1 of the Statute).

The functions, composition, operation and procedures of GRECO are described in its Statute.

118. If a State is already a member of GRECO at the time the present Convention enters into force or, subsequently, at the time of ratifying it, the consequence will be that the scope of the monitoring carried out by GRECO will be extended to cover the implementation of the present Convention. If a State is not a member of GRECO at the time of entry into force or subsequent ratification of this Convention, this provision combined with Article 32, paragraphs 3 and 4 or with Article 33, paragraph 2 imposes a compulsory and automatic membership of GRECO. It consequently implies, in particular, an obligation to accept to be monitored in accordance with the procedures detailed in its Statute, as from the date in which the Convention enters into force in respect of that State.

CHAPTER IV—INTERNATIONAL CO-OPERATION

Article 25—General principles and measures for international co-operation

119. The Guiding Principles for the fight against corruption (Principle 20) contain an undertaking to develop to the widest extent possible international co-operation in all areas of the fight against corruption. The present Chapter IV on measures to be taken at international level was the subject of lengthy and thorough discussions within the Group, which drafted the Convention. These deliberations concentrated upon the question of whether or not the Convention should include a free-standing, substantial and rather detailed section covering several topics in the field of international co-operation in criminal matters, or, whether it should simply make a cross-reference to existing multilateral or bilateral treaties in that field. Some arguments militated in favour of this latter option, such as the risk of confusing practitioners with the multiplication of co-operation rules in conventions dealing with specific offences or a possible reduction in the willingness to accede to general conventions. The usefulness of inserting a chapter that could serve as the legal basis for co-operating in the area of corruption was justified by the particular difficulties encountered to obtain the co-operation required for the prosecution of corruption offences—a problem widely recognised and eloquently stated, inter alia, by the «Appel de Geneve»-. Also by the fact that this Convention is an open Convention, and some of the Contracting Parties to it would not be—in some cases could not be—Parties to Council of Europe treaties on international co-operation in criminal matters or would not be parties to bilateral treaties in this field with many of the other Contracting Parties. In the absence of treaty provisions, some Parties non-members of the Council of Europe would experience difficulties in co-operating with the other Parties. Thus, non-member countries, which could potentially become Parties to this Convention, underlined that co-operation would be facilitated if the present Convention was self-contained and included provisions on inter-

national co-operation that could serve as a legal basis for affording the co-operation demanded by other Contracting Parties. The drafters of the Convention finally agreed to insert this Chapter in the Convention, as a set of subsidiary rules that would be applied in the absence of multilateral or bilateral treaties containing more favourable provisions.

120. Article 25 has been conceived, therefore, as an introductory provision to the whole Chapter IV. It aims at conciliating the respect for treaties or arrangements on international co-operation in criminal matters with the need to establish a specific legal basis for co-operating under the present Convention. According to paragraph 1, the Parties undertake to grant to each other the widest possible co-operation on the basis of existing international instruments, arrangements agreed on the basis of uniform or reciprocal legislation and their national law for the purpose of investigations and proceedings related to criminal offences established in accordance with the present Convention. The reference made to instruments on international co-operation in criminal matters is formulated in a general way. It includes, of course, the Council of Europe Conventions on Extradition (ITS 24) and its additional Protocols (ITS No. 86 and 98), on Mutual Assistance in Criminal Matters (ITS No. 30) and its Protocol (ITS No. 99), on the Supervision of Conditionally Sentenced or Conditionally Released offenders (ITS No. 51), on the International Validity of Criminal Judgements (ITS No. 70), on the Transfer of Proceedings in Criminal Matters (ITS No. 73), on the Transfer of Sentenced Persons (ITS No. 112), on the Laundering, Search, Seizure and Confiscation of the Proceeds of Crime (ITS No. 141). It also covers multilateral agreements concluded within other supranational or international organisations as well as bilateral agreements entered upon by the Parties. The reference to international instruments on international co-operation in criminal matters is not limited to those instruments in force at the time of entry into force of the present Convention but also covers instruments that may be adopted in the future.

121. According to paragraph 1 the co-operation can also be based on "arrangements agreed on the basis of uniform or reciprocal legislation". This refers, inter alia, to the system of co-operation developed among the Nordic countries, which is also admitted by the European Convention on Extradition (ITS No. 24, Article 28, paragraph 3) and by the European Convention on Mutual Assistance in Criminal Matters (ITS No. 30, Article 26, paragraph 4). Of course, co-operation can also be granted on the basis of the Parties' own national law.

122. The second paragraph enshrines the subsidiary nature of Chapter IV by providing that Articles 26–31 shall apply in the absence of the international instruments or arrangements referred to in the previous paragraph. Obviously no reference is made here to national law, since the Parties can always apply their own law in the absence of international instruments. The purpose of this provision is to provide a legal basis for granting the co-operation required to those Parties which are prevented from so doing in the absence of an international treaty.

123. Paragraph 3 embodies a derogation to the subsidiary nature of Chapter IV, by providing that in spite of the existence of international instruments or arrangements in force, Articles 26–31 shall also apply when they are more favourable. "More favourable" refers to international co-operation. It means that these provisions must be applied if thanks to their application it will be possible to afford a form of co-operation that it would not have been possible to afford otherwise. This will be the case, for instance, with the provisions contained in Article 26, paragraph 3, Article 27, paragraphs 1 and 3 or with Article 28. It also means that the granting of the co-operation required will be simplified, facilitated or speeded up through the application of Articles 26–31.

Article 26 — Mutual assistance

124. This provision translates into the specific area of mutual legal assistance the obligation to co-operate to the widest possible extent that is contained in Article 25, paragraph 1. Requests for mutual legal assistance need not be restricted to the gathering of evidence in corruption cases, as they could cover other aspects, such as notifications, restitution of proceeds, transmission of files. This provision incorporates an additional requirement: that the request be processed "promptly". Experience shows that very often acts that need to be performed outside the territory of the State where the investigation is being conducted require lengthy delays, which become an obstacle to the good course of the investigation and may even jeopardise it.

125. Paragraph 2 provides for the possibility of refusing requests of mutual legal assistance made on the basis of the present Convention. Refusal of such requests may be based on grounds of prejudice to the sovereignty of the State, security, ordre public and other essential interests of the requested country. The expression "fundamental interests of the country" may be interpreted as allowing the requested state to refuse mutual legal assistance in cases where the fundamental principles of its legal system are at stake, where human rights' consideration should prevail and, more generally, in cases where the requested State has reasonable grounds to believe that the criminal proceedings instituted in the requesting State have been distorted or misused for purposes other than combating corruption.

126. Paragraph 3 of this provision is drafted along the lines of that of Article 18, paragraph 7 of the Convention on the Laundering, Search, Seizure and Confiscation of the Proceeds of Crime (ITS No. 141). A similar provision is also to be found in the OECD Convention on Combating Bribery of Foreign Public Officials (Article 9, paragraph 3). Before affording the assistance required involving the lifting of bank secrecy, the requested Party may, if its domestic law so provides, require the authorisation of a judicial authority competent in relation to criminal offences.

Article 27 — Extradition

127. Drawing all the consequences from their serious nature, paragraphs 1 and 3 provide that corruption offences falling within the scope of the present Con-

vention shall be deemed as extraditable offences. Such an obligation also stems from Article 19, paragraph 1, according to which these offences should have attached a penalty of deprivation of liberty, which can give rise to extradition. This does not mean that extradition must be granted on every occasion that a request is made but rather that the possibility must be available of granting the extradition of persons having committed one of the offences established in accordance with the present Convention. Pursuant to paragraph 1, there is an obligation to include corruption offences in the list of those that can give rise to extradition both in existing or in future extradition treaties. Pursuant to paragraph 3 the extraditable nature of these offences must be recognised among Parties which do not make extradition conditional upon the existence of a treaty.

128. In accordance with paragraph 2, the Convention can serve as a legal basis for extradition for those Parties that make extradition conditional upon the existence of a treaty. A Party that would not grant the extradition either because it has no extradition treaty with the requesting Party or because the existing treaties would not cover a request made in respect of a corruption offence established in accordance with this Convention, may use the Convention itself as basis for surrendering the person requested.

129. Paragraph 4 provides for the possibility of refusing an extradition request, because the conditions set up in applicable treaties are not fulfilled. The requested Party can also refuse on the grounds allowed by those treaties. It should be noted in particular that the Convention does not deprive Contracting Parties from the right of refusing extradition if the offence in respect of which it is requested is regarded as a political offence.

130. Paragraph 5 contains the principle of *aut dedere aut iudicare*, "extradite or punish". It is inspired by Article 6, paragraph 2 of the European Convention on Extradition (ITS No. 24). The purpose of this provision is to avoid impunity of corruption offenders. The Party that refuses extradition and institutes proceedings against the offender is under the specific obligations to institute criminal proceedings against him and to inform the requesting Party of the result of such proceedings.

Article 28 — Spontaneous information

131. It happens more and more frequently, in view of the transnational character of many corruption offences, that an authority investigating a corruption offence in their own territory comes across information showing that an offence might have been committed in the territory of another State. This provision, drafted along the lines of Article 10 of the Convention on the Laundering, Search, Seizure and Confiscation of the Proceeds from Crime (ITS No. 141), eliminates the need of a prior request for the transmission of information that may assist the receiving Party to investigate or institute proceedings concerning criminal offences established in accordance with this Convention. However, the spontaneous disclosure of such an information

does not prevent the disclosing Party, if it has jurisdiction, from investigating or instituting proceedings in relation to the facts disclosed.

Article 29 — Central authority

132. The institution of Central authorities responsible for sending and answering requests is a common feature of modern instruments dealing with international co-operation in criminal matters. It is a means to ensure that such requests are properly and swiftly channelled. In the case of federal or confederal States, the competent authorities of the States, Cantons or entities forming the Federation are sometimes in a better position to deal more swiftly with co-operation requests emanating from other Parties. The reference to the possibility of designating "several central authorities" addresses such particular issue. The Contracting Parties are not obliged, under this provision, to designate a specific central authority for the purpose of international co-operation against offences established in accordance with this Convention. They could designate already existing authorities that are generally competent for dealing with international co-operation.

133. Each Party is called to provide the Secretary General of the Council of Europe with relevant details on the Central authority or authorities designated under paragraph 1. In accordance with Article 40, the Secretary General will put that information at the disposal of the other Contracting Parties.

Article 30 — Direct communication

134. Central authorities designated in accordance with the previous Article shall communicate directly with one another. However, if there is urgency, requests for mutual legal assistance may be sent directly by judges and prosecutors of the Requesting State to the judges and prosecutors of the Requested State. The urgency is to be appreciated by the judge or prosecutor sending the request. The judge or prosecutor following this procedure must address a copy of the request made to his own central authority with a view to its transmission to the central authority of the Requested State. According to paragraph 3 of this Article requests may be channelled through Interpol. In accordance with paragraph 5, they may also be transmitted directly—that is, without channelling them through central authorities—even if there is no urgency, when the authority of the Requested State is able to comply with the request without making use of coercive action. The authorities of the Requested State, which receive a request falling outside their field of competence, are, according to paragraph 4, under a two-fold obligation. Firstly they must transfer the request to the competent authority of the requested State. Secondly they must inform the authorities of the Requesting State of the transfer made. Paragraph 6 of this Article enables a Party to inform the others, through the Secretary General of the Council of Europe, that, for reasons of efficiency, direct communications are to be addressed to the central authority. Indeed, in some countries

direct communications between judicial authorities could be the source of longer delays and greater difficulties for providing the co-operation required.

Article 31—Information

135. This provision embodies an obligation for the Requested Party to inform the Requesting Party of the result of actions undertaken in pursuance of the request of international co-operation. There is a further requirement that the information be addressed promptly if there are circumstances that make it impossible to carry out the request made or are likely to delay it significantly.

CHAPTER V—FINAL PROVISIONS

136. With some exceptions, the provisions contained in this Section are, for the most part, based on the "Model final clauses for conventions and agreements concluded within the Council of Europe" which were approved by the Committee of Ministers of the Council of Europe at the 315th meeting of their Deputies in February 1980. Most of these articles do not therefore call for specific comments, but the following points require some explanation.

137. Article 32, paragraph 1 has been drafted on several precedents established in other Conventions elaborated within the framework of the Council of Europe, for instance the Convention on the Transfer of Sentenced Persons (ITS No. 112) and the Convention on Laundering, Search, Seizure and Confiscation of the Proceeds from Crime (ITS No. 141), which allow for signature, before the Convention's entry into force, not only by member States of the Council of Europe, but also by non-member States which have participated in the elaboration of the Convention. These States are Belarus, Bosnia and Herzegovina, Canada, Georgia, Holy See, Japan, Mexico and the United States of America. Once the Convention enters into force, in accordance with paragraph 3 of this Article, other non-member States not covered by this provision may be invited to accede to the Convention in conformity with Article 33, paragraph 1.

138. Article 32, paragraph 3, requires 14 ratifications for the entry into force of the Convention. This is an unusually high number of ratifications for a criminal law Convention drafted within the Council of Europe. The reason is that criminalisation of corruption, particularly of international corruption, can only be effective if a high number of States undertake to take the necessary measures at the same time. It is widely recognised that corrupt practices bear an impact on international trade because they hinder the application of competition rules and modify the proper functioning of the market economy. Some countries considered that they would penalise their national companies if they entered into international commitments to criminalise corruption without other countries having assumed similar obligations. In order to avoid becoming a handicap for the national companies of a few Contracting Parties,

the present Convention requires that a large number of States undertake to implement it at the same time.

139. The second sentence of paragraphs 3 and 4 of Article 32 as well as of Article 33, paragraph 2, combined with Article 24, entail an automatic and compulsory membership of GRECO for Contracting Parties, which were not already members of this monitoring body at the time of ratification.

140. Article 33 has also been drafted on several precedents established in other conventions elaborated within the framework of the Council of Europe. The Committee of Ministers may, on its own initiative or upon request, and after consulting the Parties, invite any non-member State to accede to the Convention. This provision refers only to non-member States not having participated in the elaboration of the Convention. In conformity with the 1969 Vienna Convention on the law of treaties, Article 35 is intended to ensure the co-existence of the Convention with other treaties—multilateral or bilateral—dealing with matters which are also dealt with in the present Convention. Such matters are characterised in paragraph 1 of Article 35 as "special matters". Paragraph 2 of Article 35 expresses in a positive way that Parties may, for certain purposes, conclude bilateral or multilateral agreements relating to matters dealt with in the Convention. The drafting permits to deduct, a contrail, that Parties may not conclude agreements which derogate from the Convention. Paragraph 3 of Article 35 safeguards the continued application of agreements, treaties or relations relating to subjects which are dealt with in the present Convention, for instance in the Nordic co-operation.

141. Article 36 provides Parties with the possibility of declaring that they shall criminalise active bribery of foreign public officials, of officials of international organisations or of judges and officials of international courts only to the extent that the undue advantage offered, promised or given to the bribee induces him or is intended to induce him to act or refrain from acting in breach of his duties as an official or judge. For the drafters of the Convention the notion of "breach of duties" is to be understood in a broad sense and therefore also implies that the public official had a duty to exercise judgement or discretion impartially. In particular this notion does not require a proof of the law allegedly violated by the official.

142. Article 37 contains, in its paragraphs 1 and 2, for a large number of reservation possibilities. This stems from the fact the present Convention is an ambitious document, which provides for the criminalisation of a broad range of corruption offences, including some which are relatively new to many States. In addition, it provides for far reaching rules on grounds of jurisdiction. It seemed, therefore, appropriate to the drafters of the Convention to include reservation possibilities that may allow future Contracting Parties to bring their anti-corruption legislation progressively in line with the requirements of the Convention. Furthermore, these reservations aim at enabling the largest possible ratification of the Convention, whilst permitting Contracting Parties to preserve some of their fundamental legal concepts. Of course, it appeared

necessary to strike a balance between, on the one hand, the interest of Contracting Parties to enjoy as much flexibility as possible in the process of adapting to conventional obligations with the need, on the other hand, to ensure the progressive implementation of this instrument.

143.   Of course, the drafters endeavoured to restrict the possibilities of making reservations in order to secure to the largest possible extent a uniform application of the Convention by the Contracting Parties. Thus, Article 37 contains a number of restrictions to the making of reservations. It indicates, first of all, that reservations or declarations can only be made at the time of ratification in respect of the provisions mentioned in paragraphs 1 and 2, which contain, therefore, a numerus clausus. More importantly paragraph 4 of this provision limits the number of reservations that each Contracting Party may enter.

144.   In addition, in accordance with Article 38, paragraph 1 reservations and declarations have a limited validity of 3 years. After this deadline, they will lapse unless they are expressly renewed. Paragraph 2 of Article 38 contains a procedure for the automatic lapsing of non-renewed reservations or declarations. Finally, pursuant to Article 38, paragraph 3, Contracting Parties will be obliged to justify before the GRECO the continuation of a reservation or reservation. The Parties will have to provide to GRECO, at its request, an explanation on the grounds justifying the continuation of a reservation or declaration made. The GRECO may require such an explanation during the initial or during the subsequent periods of validity of reservations or declarations. In cases of renewal of a reservation or declaration, there shall be no need of a prior request by GRECO, Contracting Parties being under an automatic obligation to provide explanations before the renewal is made. In all cases GRECO will have the possibility of examining the explanations provided by the Party to justify the continuance of its reservations or declarations. The drafters of the Convention expected that the peer-pressure system followed by GRECO would have an influence on decisions by Contracting Parties to maintain or withdraw reservations or declarations.

145.   The amendment procedure provided for by Article 39 is mostly thought to be for minor changes of a procedural character. Indeed, major changes to the Convention could be made in the form of additional protocols. Moreover, in accordance with paragraph 5 of Article 37, any amendment adopted would come into force only when all Parties had informed the Secretary General of their acceptance. The procedure for amending the present Convention involves the consultation of non-member States Parties to it, who are not members of the Committee of Ministers or the CDPC.

146.   Article 40, paragraph 1, provides that the CDPC should be kept informed about the interpretation and application of the provisions of the Convention. Paragraph 2 of this Article imposes an obligation on the Parties to seek a peaceful settlement of any dispute concerning the interpretation or the application of the Convention. Any procedure for solving disputes should be agreed upon by the Parties concerned.

APPEAL BY THE COMMITTEE OF MINISTERS TO STATES

TO LIMIT AS FAR AS POSSIBLE THEIR RESERVATIONS TO THE CRIMINAL LAW CONVENTION ON CORRUPTION

At this, its 103rd Ministerial Session (4 November 1998), the Committee of Ministers has adopted the Criminal Law Convention on Corruption. In the Committee's view, this is an ambitious text with a broad legal scope which will have a considerable impact on the fight against this phenomenon in Europe.

The text of the Convention provides for a certain number of possible reservations. It has transpired that this is necessary so that Parties can make a progressive adaptation to the undertakings enshrined in this instrument. The Committee of Ministers is convinced that regular examination of reservations by the "Group of States against Corruption—GRECO" will make it possible to bring about a rapid reduction of reservations made upon ratification or accession to the Convention.

Nonetheless, in order to maintain the greatest possible uniformity with regard to the undertakings enshrined in the Convention, and to allow full advantage to be taken of this text from the moment it enters into force, the Committee of Ministers appeals to all States wishing to become party to the Convention to reduce as far as possible the number of reservations that they declare, when expressing their consent to be bound by this treaty, and to States which nevertheless find themselves obliged to declare reservations, to use their best endeavours to withdraw them as soon as possible.

ADDITIONAL PROTOCOL TO THE COUNCIL OF EUROPE CRIMINAL LAW CONVENTION ON CORRUPTION*

STRASBOURG, 15.V.2003

The member States of the Council of Europe and the other States signatory hereto,

Considering that it is desirable to supplement the Criminal Law Convention on Corruption (ETS No. 173, hereafter "the Convention") in order to prevent and fight against corruption;

Considering also that the present Protocol will allow the broader implementation of the 1996 Programme of Action against Corruption,

Have agreed as follows:

CHAPTER I—USE OF TERMS

Article 1—Use of terms

For the purpose of this Protocol:

1 The term *"arbitrator"* shall be understood by reference to the national law of the States Parties to this Protocol, but shall in any case include a person who by virtue of an arbitration agreement is called upon to render a legally binding decision in a dispute submitted to him/her by the parties to the agreement.

2 The term *"arbitration agreement"* means an agreement recognised by the national law whereby the parties agree to submit a dispute for a decision by an arbitrator.

3 The term *"juror"* shall be understood by reference to the national law of the States Parties to this Protocol but shall in any case include a lay person acting

---

* ETS No. 191 (2003).

as a member of a collegial body which has the responsibility of deciding on the guilt of an accused person in the framework of a trial.

4   In the case of proceedings involving a foreign arbitrator or juror, the prosecuting State may apply the definition of arbitrator or juror only in so far as that definition is compatible with its national law.

CHAPTER II—MEASURES TO BE TAKEN AT NATIONAL LEVEL

Article 2—Active bribery of domestic arbitrators

Each Party shall adopt such legislative and other measures as may be necessary to establish as criminal offences under its domestic law, when committed intentionally, the promising, offering or giving by any person, directly or indirectly, of any undue advantage to an arbitrator exercising his/her functions under the national law on arbitration of the Party, for himself or herself or for anyone else, for him or for her to act or refrain from acting in the exercise of his or her functions.

Article 3—Passive bribery of domestic arbitrators

Each Party shall adopt such legislative and other measures as may be necessary to establish as criminal offences under its domestic law, when committed intentionally, the request or receipt by an arbitrator exercising his/her functions under the national law on arbitration of the Party, directly or indirectly, of any undue advantage for himself or herself or for anyone else, or the acceptance of an offer or promise of such an advantage, to act or refrain from acting in the exercise of his or her functions.

Article 4—Bribery of foreign arbitrators

Each Party shall adopt such legislative and other measures as may be necessary to establish as criminal offences under its domestic law the conduct referred to in Articles 2 and 3, when involving an arbitrator exercising his/her functions under the national law on arbitration of any other State.

Article 5—Bribery of domestic jurors

Each Party shall adopt such legislative and other measures as may be necessary to establish as criminal offences under its domestic law the conduct referred to in Articles 2 and 3, when involving any person acting as a juror within its judicial system.

Article 6—Bribery of foreign jurors

Each Party shall adopt such legislative and other measures as may be necessary to establish as criminal offences under its domestic law the conduct referred to in Articles 2 and 3, when involving any person acting as a juror within the judicial system of any other State.

CHAPTER III—MONITORING OF IMPLEMENTATION AND FINAL PROVISIONS

Article 7—Monitoring of implementation

The Group of States against Corruption (GRECO) shall monitor the implementation of this Protocol by the Parties.

Article 8—Relationship to the Convention

1   As between the States Parties the provisions of Articles 2 to 6 of this Protocol shall be regarded as additional articles to the Convention.

2   The provisions of the Convention shall apply to the extent that they are compatible with the provisions of this Protocol.

Article 9—Declarations and reservations

1   If a Party has made a declaration in accordance with Article 36 of the Convention, it may make a similar declaration relating to Articles 4 and 6 of this Protocol at the time of signature or when depositing its instrument of ratification, acceptance, approval or accession.

2   If a Party has made a reservation in accordance with Article 37, paragraph 1, of the Convention restricting the application of the passive bribery offences defined in Article 5 of the Convention, it may make a similar reservation concerning Articles 4 and 6 of this Protocol at the time of signature or when depositing its instrument of ratification, acceptance, approval or accession. Any other reservation made by a Party, in accordance with Article 37 of the Convention shall be applicable also to this Protocol, unless that Party otherwise declares at the time of signature or when depositing its instrument of ratification, acceptance, approval or accession.

3   No other reservation may be made.

Article 10—Signature and entry into force

1   This Protocol shall be open for signature by States which have signed the Convention. These States may express their consent to be bound by:

a   signature without reservation as to ratification, acceptance or approval; or

b   signature subject to ratification, acceptance or approval, followed by ratification, acceptance or approval.

2   Instruments of ratification, acceptance or approval shall be deposited with the Secretary General of the Council of Europe.

3   This Protocol shall enter into force on the first day of the month following the expiry of a period of three months after the date on which five States have expressed their consent to be bound by the Protocol in accordance with the provisions of paragraphs 1 and 2, and only after the Convention itself has entered into force.

4   In respect of any signatory State which subsequently expresses its consent to be bound by it, the Protocol shall enter into force on the first day of the month following the expiry of a period of three months after the date of the expression of its consent to be bound by the Protocol in accordance with the provisions of paragraphs 1 and 2.

5   A signatory State may not ratify, accept or approve this Protocol without having, simultaneously or previously, expressed its consent to be bound by the Convention.

Article 11 — Accession to the Protocol

1   Any State or the European Community having acceded to the Convention may accede to this Protocol after it has entered into force.

2   In respect of any State or the European Community acceding to the Protocol, it shall enter into force on the first day of the month following the expiry of a period of three months after the date of the deposit of an instrument of accession with the Secretary General of the Council of Europe.

Article 12 — Territorial application

1   Any State or the European Community may, at the time of signature or when depositing its instrument of ratification, acceptance, approval or accession, specify the territory or territories to which this Protocol shall apply.

2   Any Party may, at any later date, by declaration addressed to the Secretary General of the Council of Europe, extend the application of this Protocol to any other territory or territories specified in the declaration and for whose international relations it is responsible or on whose behalf it is authorised to give undertakings. In respect of such territory the Protocol shall enter into force on the first day of the month following the expiry of a period of three months after the date of receipt of such declaration by the Secretary General.

3   Any declaration made in pursuance of the two preceding paragraphs may, in respect of any territory mentioned in such declaration, be withdrawn by means of a notification addressed to the Secretary General of the Council of Europe. Such withdrawal shall become effective on the first day of the month following the expiry of a period of three months after the date of receipt of the notification by the Secretary General.

Article 13 — Denunciation

1   Any Party may, at any time, denounce this Protocol by means of a notification addressed to the Secretary General of the Council of Europe.

2   Such denunciation shall become effective on the first day of the month following the expiry of a period of three months after the date of receipt of the notification by the Secretary General.

3   Denunciation of the Convention automatically entails denunciation of this Protocol.

Article 14—Notification

The Secretary General of the Council of Europe shall notify the member States of the Council of Europe and any State, or the European Community, having acceded to this Protocol of:

a   any signature of this Protocol;

b   the deposit of any instrument of ratification, acceptance, approval or accession;

c   any date of entry into force of this Protocol in accordance with Articles 10, 11 and 12;

d   any declaration or reservation made under Articles 9 and 12;

e   any other act, notification or communication relating to this Protocol.

In witness whereof the undersigned, being duly authorised thereto, have signed this Protocol.

Done at Strasbourg, this 15th day of May 2003, in English and in French, both texts being equally authentic, in a single copy which shall be deposited in the archives of the Council of Europe. The Secretary General of the Council of Europe shall transmit certified copies to each of the signatory and acceding Parties.

EXPLANATORY REPORT ON THE ADDITIONAL PROTOCOL TO THE COUNCIL OF EUROPE CRIMINAL LAW CONVENTION ON CORRUPTION*

(ETS NO. 191)

EXPLANATORY REPORT

The text of this Explanatory Report does not constitute an instrument providing an authoritative interpretation of the Protocol, although it might be of such a nature as to facilitate the application of the provisions contained therein. This Protocol has been opened for signature in Strasbourg, on 15 May 2003, on the occasion of the 112th Session of the Committee of Ministers of the Council of Europe.

INTRODUCTION

1. At its 103rd Session (November 1998), the Committee of Ministers adopted the Criminal Law Convention on Corruption, decided to open it for signature on 27 January 1999 and authorised the publication of the Explanatory Report thereto. This Convention aims at harmonising national legislation regarding the criminalisation of corruption offences, promoting the adoption of complementary criminal law measures and improving international co-operation in the investigation and prosecution of these offences. According to the text of the Convention, the Contracting Parties undertake to criminalise active and passive bribery of national, foreign and international public officials, of members of national, international and supranational parliaments and assemblies, of national, foreign and international judges. It also provides for the criminalisation of active and passive corruption in the private sector, trading in influence, laundering of corruption proceeds. In addition, the Convention deals with accounting offences and other substantial or procedural issues, such as

---

* ETS No. 191 (2003).

jurisdiction, sanctions and measures, liability of legal persons, setting up of specialised authorities, co-operation among national authorities, witness protection. Besides, the Convention introduced a set of rules in order to conciliate the respect for existing treaties or arrangements on international co-operation in criminal matters with the need to establish a specific legal basis for co-operating in the fight against corruption, in particular in cases where other treaties or arrangements do not apply. The Convention is a complex and ambitious document, which provides for the criminalisation of a broad range of corruption offences.

2. The Group of States against Corruption (GRECO) is responsible for monitoring the implementation of the Convention.

3. Following the adoption by the Committee of Ministers of the Criminal Law Convention on Corruption, a significant part of the objectives defined by the Council of Europe's Programme of Action against Corruption (PAC) in the criminal law field were reached. However, the Convention did not deal with all criminal law matters covered by the PAC. It should also be underlined that during the elaboration of this Convention, the GMC agreed to postpone consideration of the criminalisation at international level of some other offences related to corruption.

4. Therefore the working group on criminal law (GMCP) discussed during several meetings about the necessity of criminalising at international level other forms of corrupt behaviour or behaviour that could be assimilated to corruption, namely:
    *   illegal acquisitions of interest
    *   insider trading
    *   "la concussion" (extortion by a public official)
    *   illicit enrichment
    *   corruption of members of non-governmental organisations
    *   corruption of sport referees
    *   buying and selling of votes

5. The GMCP also discussed certain aspects of criminal procedure and international co-operation, which could possibly be the subject of new international standards, such as:
    *   confiscation of proceeds of crime, possibly entailing shifting the burden of proof;
    *   extension of the material scope of the offence dealt with in article 13 of the Criminal law Convention criminalising the laundering of money originating from corruption offences;
    *   enforcement of foreign legal decisions of confiscation of proceeds of crime;
    *   measures of ensuring the integrity of investigation;
    *   the duration of limitation periods for offences covered by the Convention.

6. While recognising the importance of most of these issues for the fight against corruption, the discussion showed that some of them were of a general nature and that some others could be covered by already existing provisions in

the Convention or by national law. The GMCP felt that it would be preferable to postpone consideration of additional standards in this area, work which could be undertaken in the future in the light of the GRECO evaluations. The GMCP decided, therefore, to interrupt for the time being the work on the above listed issues.

7. On the other hand, the GMCP agreed, as a result of the debate to draft an additional Protocol to the Criminal law Convention on corruption providing for the criminalisation of corruption in the field of arbitration. For reasons spelled out later, the GMCP further decided to extend the scope of the draft Protocol to cover corruption committed by or against jurors as well.

COMMENTARY

CHAPTER I—USE OF TERMS

Article 1—Use of terms

8. Only three terms are defined under Article 1, as all other notions are addressed at the appropriate place in the Explanatory report or have been already used in the Criminal Law Convention on Corruption.

9. The term "arbitrator" is used in Articles 2 to 4. Paragraph 1 of Article 1 defines the concept of "arbitrator" in two ways: on the one hand it refers to the respective national laws—as does the Criminal Law Convention on Corruption concerning the term "public official" (cf. Article 1 littera a of the Convention: "... *shall be understood by reference to the definition ... in the national law of the State ...*"); on the other hand—and contrary to the Convention—it establishes an autonomous definition insofar as it sets a commonly binding minimum standard. In reference to the "national law" it should be noted—as has been done with respect to the Criminal Law Convention on Corruption— that it was the intention of the drafters of the Protocol, too, that Contracting Parties assume obligations under this Protocol only to the extent consistent with their Constitution and the fundamental principles of their legal system. This means in particular that no provision of this Protocol should be understood in a way that Parties to this Protocol should feel obliged to establish a system of arbitration (or lay justice) along the lines of the given definition (or any such system; notwithstanding the fact that during the negotiations better protection against corrupt behaviour by means of this Protocol has been mentioned as a supportive factor forpromoting plans to introduce such a system) or even to change an already existing system by adjusting it to the Protocol's scope.

10. However, States Parties to this Protocol will be obliged to provide for criminal responsibility in the field of arbitration for offences as foreseen under Articles 2 to 4 committed—at least—by persons who by virtue of an arbitration agreement are called upon to render a legally binding decision in a dispute submitted to them by the parties to the agreement.

11. What is meant by "arbitration agreement" is defined in paragraph 2 of Article 1 (for the purpose of giving further explanation to the notion of arbitrator in paragraph 1 since the term "arbitration agreement" is not used elsewhere in the Protocol). Like the definition of arbitrator the definition of arbitration agreement also uses a very broad concept: for the purposes of this Protocol arbitration agreement means any agreement recognised by the national law whereby the parties agree to submit a dispute for a decision by an arbitrator.

12. This broad concept, in fact, could turn what might look like a "minimum standard" in the sense of a small common denominator into something like a general clause. Speaking in terms of criminalisation, this would mean that the obligation stemming from this Protocol would also be a broad one. There is, for example, no restriction to the field of legal relationships to which the definition may be applied. In particular it should be pointed out, that the scope of this Protocol is not limited to commercial arbitration. Consequently, the concept of "arbitration agreement" should be understood in a broad way in order to reflect the reality and variety of civil, commercial and other relations, and not be limited to the formal expression of commitments based on reciprocal obligations.

13. Although the drafters of this Protocol intended to keep the text as flexible as possible, they considered it to be helpful to give some indications in the Explanatory report about typical aspects of arbitration and insofar focussing on commercial arbitration: in the view of the drafters commercial arbitration is an extra judiciary form of solving disputes which could arise during the implementation of a commercial agreement; the arbitrators are appointed on the basis of a common decision by the parties to a transaction and the parties being bound by the arbitration decision; an arbitration agreement (preliminary or subsequent to the dispute) should exist between the parties; the arbitrators could be chosen by the parties or be part of an arbitration tribunal; according to the agreement or applicable rules, the decision could be definitive or could be subject of appeal; the arbitrators apply the substantive applicable law to the dispute and are subject to procedural rules defined beforehand; the arbitrators should be independent while exercising their functions.

14. Some of these elements have gone into the text of the Protocol, while others have been deemed sufficiently highlighted by mentioning them in the Explanatory report. Summing up in this respect it can be pointed out that the arbitration agreement could be concluded preliminary or subsequent to the dispute, that the arbitrators can be acting individually or in the framework of an arbitration tribunal and that the fact that arbitrators are called upon to render a legally binding decision would not mean that there must not be any judicial remedy against it at all.

15. This potentially broad concept, however, again is subject to compatibility with national law (on arbitration), since the arbitration agreements must be "recognised by the national law". Therefore, a Party to this Protocol that, for example, knows only commercial arbitration in its national law (i.e. its national law would only recognise arbitration agreements in commercial rela-

tionships) would not be obliged to criminalise corruption in other (possible) fields of arbitration.

16. As concerns the definition of "juror", paragraph 3 of Article 1 also refers to the national law of the Parties to this Protocol. Therefore, the same principles apply as mentioned above with respect to arbitrators. Concerning the term juror, however, there is a fixed, really autonomous minimum standard (contrary to the Convention) by simply stating which kind of persons it shall include "in any case" without any further dependence on national law. This means that the criminalisation of the bribery of "lay persons acting as members of a collegial body which has the responsibility of deciding on the guilt of an accused person in the framework of a trial" is obligatory, no matter what national law says about jurors in general. Therefore, Parties to this Protocol, whose national law knows a broader concept of juror than that (by including, for example, civil law matters) would be obliged to criminalise corruption of jurors in this broader sense. On the other hand, Parties, whose national law would not include lay persons in the sense of paragraph 3 of Article 1 or would not know the concept of jurors at all, would have to adjust their criminal law accordingly in order to fulfil the obligations stemming from this Protocol. (Further adjustments of the legal system concerning the use of jurors etc. as such would, of course, not be necessary.)

17. With respect to foreign arbitrators or jurors paragraph 4 of Article 1 makes use of the same technique as the Criminal Law Convention on Corruption does with respect to foreign public officials (cf. Article 1 littera c of the Convention). It means that the definition of arbitrator or juror in the law of the other (foreign) State is not necessarily conclusive where the person concerned would not have had the status of arbitrator or juror under the law of the prosecuting State. This follows from paragraph 4 of Article 1, according to which a State may determine that corruption offences involving a foreign arbitrator or juror refer only to such officials whose status is compatible with that of arbitrator or juror under the national law of the prosecuting State.

CHAPTER II—MEASURES TO BE TAKEN AT NATIONAL LEVEL

Article 2 — Active bribery of domestic arbitrators

18. During the final stages of the negotiations of the Convention the question was raised, how to deal with possible corruption of arbitrators. There was agreement that arbitrators should be covered—on the one hand because of the importance of their tasks, not seldom involving decisions with considerable pecuniary or other economic consequences, but not to a lesser degree also because of the similarity of their tasks with those of judges and, generally speaking, for matters of completeness. The opinion, however, about whether or not arbitrators were already covered by the Convention (and if, by which Article) was split: whereas some delegations found it compatible with their

national law to treat them as judges (what would make them fall under Articles 2, 3, 5 and 11 of the Convention) and others referred to Articles 7 and 8 of the Convention (private sector corruption), there was also the opinion that they might not be covered by any of the Convention's provisions. After all it was decided to postpone the discussions on this issue until after the finalisation of the Convention; the results of those discussions are reflected in the present Protocol.

19. Article 2 defines the elements of the active bribery of domestic arbitrators following the text of Article 2 of the Criminal Law Convention on Corruption ("Active Bribery of domestic public officials"). Therefore, the corresponding explanatory remarks are applicable here, too. The offence of active bribery, in current criminal law theory and practice and in the view of the drafters of this Protocol, too, is mirrored by passive bribery, though they are considered to be separate offences for which prosecutions can be brought independently. It emerges that the two types of bribery are, in general, two sides of the same phenomenon, one perpetrator offering, promising or giving the advantage and the other perpetrator accepting the offer, promise or gift. Usually, however, the two perpetrators are not punished for complicity in the other one's offence.

20. The definition provided in Article 2 is, through a double reference, referred to in Articles 4, 5 and 6 of this Protocol. These provisions do not repeat the substantive elements but extend the criminalisation of the active bribery to further categories of persons.

21. The offence of active bribery can only be committed intentionally under Article 2 and the intent has to cover all other substantive elements of the offence. Intent must relate to a future result: the arbitrator (or juror) acting or refraining from acting as the briber intends. It is, however, immaterial whether the arbitrator (or juror) actually acted or refrained from acting as intended.

22. The briber can be anyone, whatever his capacity (businessman, public official, private individual etc). If, however, the briber acts for the account or on behalf of a company, corporate liability may also apply in respect of the company in question (cf. Article 8 of this Protocol and Article 18 of the Convention). Nevertheless, the liability of the company does not exclude in any manner criminal proceedings against the natural person (paragraph 3 of Article 18 of the Convention). The bribed person must be an arbitrator (or juror), as defined under Article 1, irrespective of whether the undue advantage is actually for himself or for someone else.

23. The material components of the offence are promising, offering or giving an undue advantage, directly or indirectly for the arbitrator (or juror) himself or for a third party. The three actions of the briber are slightly different. "Promising" may, for example, cover situations where the briber commits himself to give an undue advantage later (in most cases only once the arbitrator (or juror) has performed the act requested by the briber) or where there is an agreement between the briber and the bribe that the briber will give the undue advantage later. "Offering" may cover situations where the briber shows his readiness to give the undue advantage at any moment. Finally, "giving" may cover situations where the briber transfers the undue

advantage. The undue advantage need not necessarily be given to the arbitrator (or juror) himself: it can be given also to a third party, such as a relative, an organisation to which the arbitrator (or juror) belongs, the political party of which he or she is a member. When the offer, promise or gift is addressed to a third party, the arbitrator (or juror) must at least have knowledge thereof at some point. Irrespective of whether the recipient or the beneficiary of the undue advantage is the arbitrator (or juror) himself or a third party, the transaction may be performed through intermediaries.

24. The undue advantages given are usually of an economic nature but may also be of a non-material nature. What is important is that the offender (or any other person, for instance a relative) is placed in a better position than he was before the commission of the offence and that he is not entitled to the benefit. Such advantages may consist in, for instance, money, holidays, loans, food and drink, a case handled within a swifter time, better career prospects, etc.

25. What constitutes "undue" advantage will be of central importance in the transposition of the Protocol into national law. "Undue" for the purposes of the protocol—as well as of the Convention—should be interpreted as something that the recipient is not lawfully entitled to accept or receive. For the drafters of the Protocol, too, the adjective "undue" aims at excluding advantages permitted by the law or by administrative rules as well as minimum gifts, gifts of very low value or socially acceptable gifts.

26. Bribery provisions of certain member States of the Council of Europe make some distinctions, as to whether the act, which is solicited, is a part of the arbitrator's (or juror's) duty or whether he or she is going beyond his or her duties. Such an extra-element of "breach of duty" was, however, not considered to be necessary for the purposes of this Protocol. The drafters of the Protocol considered that the decisive element of the offence was not whether the arbitrator (or juror) had any discretion to act as requested by the briber, but whether he or she had been offered, given or promised a bribe in order to obtain something from him or her in the exercise of his or her duties. The briber may not even have known whether the arbitrator (or juror) had discretion or not, this element being, for the purpose of this provision, irrelevant. The notion of "breach of duty" adds an element of ambiguity that makes more difficult the prosecution of this offence, by requiring to prove that the arbitrator (or juror) was expected to act against his duties or was expected to exercise his discretion for the benefit of the briber. States that require such an extra-element for bribery would therefore have to ensure that they could implement the definition of bribery under Article 2 of this Protocol (as well as the Convention) without hindering its objective.

Article 3—Passive bribery of domestic arbitrators

27. Article 3 defines passive bribery of arbitrators, again following the text of the Criminal Law Convention on Corruption (cf. Article 3 therein, "Passive bribery of domestic public officials"). Because of that here, too, the corresponding deliberations of the Explanatory Report to the Convention should

apply. As the offence of passive bribery is closely linked with active bribery, some comments made thereon, e.g. in respect of the mental element and the undue advantage apply accordingly here as well. The material elements of the perpetrator's act include requesting or receiving an undue advantage or accepting the offer or the promise thereof.

28. "Requesting" may for example refer to a unilateral act whereby the arbitrator lets another person know, explicitly or implicitly, that he will have to "pay" to have some task-related act done or abstained from. It is immaterial whether the request was actually acted upon, the request itself being the core of the offence. Likewise, it does not matter whether the arbitrator requested the undue advantage for himself or for anyone else.

29. "Receiving" may, for example, mean the actual taking the benefit, whether by the arbitrator himself or by someone else (spouse, colleague, organisation, political party, etc) for himself or for someone else. The latter case supposes at least some kind of acceptance by the arbitrator. Again, intermediaries can be involved: the fact that an intermediary is involved, which would extend the scope of passive bribery to include indirect action by the arbitrator, necessarily entails identifying the criminal nature of the arbitrator's conduct, irrespective of the good or bad faith of the intermediary involved.

30. If there is a unilateral request or a corrupt pact, it is essential that the act or the omission of acting by the arbitrator takes place after the request or the pact, whereas it is immaterial in such a case at what point in time the undue advantage is actually received. Thus, it is not a criminal offence under this Protocol to receive a benefit after the act has been performed by the arbitrator, without prior offer, request or acceptance. Moreover, the word "receipt" means keeping the advantage or gift at least for some time so that the arbitrator who, having not requested it, immediately returns the gift to the sender or turns it over to the competent authorities would not be committing an offence under Article 3. This provision is not applicable either to benefits unrelated to a specific subsequent act in the exercise of the arbitrator's functions.

Article 4 — Bribery of foreign arbitrators

31. This article obliges Parties to the Protocol to criminalise active and passive bribery of foreign arbitrators. Apart from the persons who are bribed, i.e. foreign arbitrators, the substance of this bribery offence is identical to the ones defined under Articles 2 and 3. Again it can only be repeated what has been explained in the commentary to the Convention as the motivation for expanding the scope of the core bribery offences as laid down in the Convention to acts involving foreign public officials:

32. "Corruption not only undermines good governance and destroys public trust in the fairness and impartiality of public administrations but it may also seriously distort competition and endanger economic development [...]. With the globalisation of economic and financial structures and the integration of domestic markets into the world market, decisions taken on capital move-

ments or investments in one country may and do exert effects in others. Multinational corporations and international investors play a determining role in nowadays economy and know of no borders. It is both in their interest and the interest of the global economy in general to keep competition rules fair and transparent."[1]

33. The decisive element for qualifying an offence as a case of bribery of a foreign arbitrator is not the nationality of the arbitrator or the parties involved, but that the arbitrator exercises his or her functions under the national law on arbitration of a State other than the prosecuting State. There is no specific definition for the term "foreign arbitrator" in this Protocol. Therefore, the general definition given in paragraphs 1 and 2 of Article 1 applies also to foreign arbitrators. In addition, paragraph 4 of Article 1 may be applied in cases where the definition of arbitrator under the law of the prosecuting State differs from the definition provided by the law under which the arbitrator exercises his or her functions.

34. After having discussed the issue of international arbitration the drafters of this Protocol have decided not to include a separate Article on the bribery of international arbitrators (that—according to some preliminary drafts of this Protocol—would have covered cases involving any person acting as arbitrator "under the competence of an international organisation to which the Party is member"). Therefore, a case of bribery in international arbitration where the arbitrator's exercising of his or her functions cannot be attributed to any national law (be it—from the point of view of the prosecuting State—domestic or foreign) would not fall under the scope of this Protocol. This would concern mainly public international arbitration. Insofar as there may be any practical relevance at all, the potential for loopholes in this field, however, has been deemed justifiable, in particular since the Criminal Law Convention on Corruption itself might be considered applicable in some cases. (If, for example, an arbitrator acts in his capacity as official of an international organisation, Article 9 of the Convention could apply.)

Article 5 — Bribery of domestic jurors

35. This article extends the scope of the active and passive bribery offences defined in Articles 2 and 3 (thereby following Articles 2 and 3 of the Criminal Law Convention on Corruption) to jurors. The definition of the term juror is given in paragraph 3 of Article 1, using the technique of referring to national law while setting up an autonomous minimum-standard at the same time. Aside from the common understanding of the term juror this minimum-standard (i.e. the inclusion of lay persons acting as members of a collegial body which has the responsibility of deciding on the guilt of an accused person in the framework of a trial) clearly indicates that jurors are fulfilling tasks in the judiciary. The question raised during the negotiations of this Protocol whether this task would not qualify jurors to be covered by the notion of judge/holder of judicial office in the sense of Article 1 littera a and b of the

Criminal Law Convention on Corruption—which would mean that bribery of such persons (then being considered public officials) was already covered by Articles 2 and 3 of the Convention—has not been answered in the affirmative by all delegations. Although the Explanatory report to the Convention is of the opinion that the notion of judge in the sense of holder of judicial office should be interpreted to the widest extent possible (the decisive element being the functions performed by the person, which should be of a judicial nature, rather than his or her official title), it seemed useful in the end to address jurors explicitly in this Protocol. Given the importance of their task on the one hand and the fact that it is honorary (unpaid) on the other hand could make jurors targets for corruption which they should be prevented from to the same extent as professional judges.

36. Apart from the persons who are bribed, i.e. domestic jurors, the substance of this bribery offence is identical to the one defined under Articles 2 and 3.

Article 6—Bribery of foreign jurors

37. This article criminalises the active and passive bribery of foreign jurors. The reasons and the protected legal interests are the same as those described under Article 5, but in a foreign context, "in any other State". It is part of the common effort undertaken by States Parties to ensure respect for judicial and democratic institutions, independently whether they are national or foreign in character. Apart from the persons who are bribed, i.e. foreign jurors, the substance of this bribery offence is identical to the one defined under Articles 2 and 3. There is no specific definition for the term "foreign juror" in this Protocol. Therefore, the general definition given in paragraph 3 of Article 1 applies also to foreign jurors. In addition, paragraph 4 of Article 1 may be applied in cases where the definition of juror under the law of the prosecuting State differs from the definition provided by the law of the State the juror exercises his or her functions for.

CHAPTER III—MONITORING OF IMPLEMENTATION AND FINAL PROVISIONS

Article 7—Monitoring of implementation

38. As the implementation of the Criminal Law Convention on Corruption itself (cf. Article 24 of the Convention) the implementation of this Protocol will also be monitored by the Group of States against Corruption (GRECO).

39. GRECO was established on the basis of the Council of Europe Resolutions (98) 7 and (99) 5. This monitoring mechanism aims to improve the capacity of its members to fight corruption by following up, through a dynamic process of mutual evaluation and peer pressure (including on-site visits), States' respect of the twenty Guiding Principles for the Fight against Corruption, the Criminal Law Convention on Corruption, the Civil Law Convention on

Corruption, as well as other international instruments adopted by the Council of Europe in application of the Programme of Action against Corruption (such as the present Protocol).

Article 8 — Relationship to the Convention

40. Article 8 defines the relationship between this Protocol and the Criminal Law Convention on Corruption as follows: As between the States Parties (of both the Convention and the Protocol) the substantive part of this Protocol (Articles 2 to 6) shall be regarded as additional articles to the Convention (paragraph 1). Paragraph 2 further declares explicitly that the provisions of the Convention shall apply to this Protocol (to the extent that they are compatible with the latter's provisions). Paragraph 2 should be understood as making Articles 12 to 23 of the Convention applicable to this Protocol, as well as Chapter IV and those elements of Chapter V not provided for in the Protocol. This is why it was not necessary to include provisions dealing with issues such as jurisdiction (cf. Article 17 of the Convention), corporate liability (cf. Article 18 of the Convention), sanctions and measures (cf. Article 19 of the Convention) or international co-operation (cf. Chapter IV of the Convention) in this Protocol, too.

Article 9 — Declarations and reservations

41. During the negotiations of this Protocol it has been discussed, whether—in particular with respect to the very specific and therefore rather narrow scope of this Protocol—there was room for possible declarations or reservations at all. The drafters of this Protocol came to the conclusion, that it would be desirable not to provide for additional (new) declaration or reservation possibilities, but to allow only such declarations and reservations that are a consequence of declarations or reservations already made in respect of the Convention. Consequently, paragraph 1 provides for the possibility of a declaration similar to one based on Article 36 of the Convention relating to Articles 4 and 6 of this Protocol (i.e. the bribery of foreign arbitrators and jurors) only if the respective Contracting State has already made such a declaration with respect to the Convention (i.e. a declaration that foreign or international corruption in the sense of Articles 5, 9 or 11 of the Convention would be criminalised only to the extent that the public official or judge acts or refrains from acting in breach of his or her duties). Likewise, sentence 1 of paragraph 2 allows a reservation similar to a reservation based on Article 37 paragraph 1 restricting the application of the passive bribery offences concerning foreign arbitrators (cf. Article 4 of this Protocol) or jurors (cf. Article 6 of this Protocol) only if a Party has already made such a reservation with relation to the passive bribery of foreign public officials according to Article 5 of the Convention. In such a case, and considering that both reservations are similar, the reservation made to the Protocol would not be counted under

Article 37 paragraph 4 of the Convention (which limits to five the maximum number of reservations to the Convention). According to sentence 2 of paragraph 2 other reservations based on Article 37 (concerning Articles 12 [trading in influence], 17 [jurisdiction—cf. Art. 37 par. 2] and 26 [refusal of mutual assistance on the grounds of political offence—cf. Art. 37 par. 3]) of the Convention apply accordingly to this Protocol. According to paragraph 3 no other reservation may be made.

Articles 10 to 14 — (Signature and entry into force — Accession to the Protocol — Territorial application — Denunciation — Notification)

42. The final clauses have been drafted along the lines of already existing provisions, notably in the Convention itself as well as in other Council of Europe additional Protocols such as the Additional Protocols to the European Conventions on Extradition (ETS 86 and 98), on Mutual Assistance in Criminal Matters (ETS 99) and on the Transfer of Sentenced Persons (ETS 167).

43. Since the Protocol may not enter into force before the Convention has done so, and since a signatory State may not ratify this Protocol without having, simultaneously or previously ratified the Convention, it was possible to fix the number of ratifications necessary for the entry into force of this Protocol (5) considerably lower than that of the Convention itself (14) (Article 10 of this Protocol).

NOTES

1. Cf. paragraph 47 of the *Explanatory Report to the Criminal Law Convention on Corruption.*

PART 1

COUNCIL OF EUROPE CIVIL LAW CONVENTION ON CORRUPTION*

STRASBOURG, 4.XI.1999

PREAMBLE

The member States of the Council of Europe, the other States and the European Community, signatories hereto,

Considering that the aim of the Council of Europe is to achieve a greater unity between its members;

Conscious of the importance of strengthening international co-operation in the fight against corruption;

Emphasising that corruption represents a major threat to the rule of law, democracy and human rights, fairness and social justice, hinders economic development and endangers the proper and fair functioning of market economies;

Recognising the adverse financial consequences of corruption to individuals, companies and States, as well as international institutions;

Convinced of the importance for civil law to contribute to the fight against corruption, in particular by enabling persons who have suffered damage to receive fair compensation;

Recalling the conclusions and resolutions of the 19th (Malta, 1994), 21st (Czech Republic, 1997) and 22nd (Moldova, 1999) Conferences of the European Ministers of Justice;

Taking into account the Programme of Action against Corruption adopted by the Committee of Ministers in November 1996;

Taking also into account the feasibility study on the drawing up of a convention on civil remedies for compensation for damage resulting from acts of corruption, approved by the Committee of Ministers in February 1997;

---

* ETS No. 174 (1999).

Having regard to Resolution (97) 24 on the 20 Guiding Principles for the Fight against Corruption, adopted by the Committee of Ministers in November 1997, at its 101st Session, to Resolution (98) 7 authorising the adoption of the Partial and Enlarged Agreement establishing the "Group of States against Corruption (GRECO)," adopted by the Committee of Ministers in May 1998, at its 102nd Session, and to Resolution (99) 5 establishing the GRECO, adopted on 1 May 1999;

Recalling the Final Declaration and the Action Plan adopted by the Heads of State and Government of the member States of the Council of Europe at their 2nd summit in Strasbourg, in October 1997,

Have agreed as follows:

CHAPTER I—MEASURES TO BE TAKEN AT NATIONAL LEVEL

Article 1—Purpose

Each Party shall provide in its internal law for effective remedies for persons who have suffered damage as a result of acts of corruption, to enable them to defend their rights and interests, including the possibility of obtaining compensation for damage.

Article 2—Definition of corruption

For the purpose of this Convention, *"corruption"* means requesting, offering, giving or accepting, directly or indirectly, a bribe or any other undue advantage or prospect thereof, which distorts the proper performance of any duty or behaviour required of the recipient of the bribe, the undue advantage or the prospect thereof.

Article 3—Compensation for damage

1   Each Party shall provide in its internal law for persons who have suffered damage as a result of corruption to have the right to initiate an action in order to obtain full compensation for such damage.

2   Such compensation may cover material damage, loss of profits and non-pecuniary loss.

Article 4—Liability

1   Each Party shall provide in its internal law for the following conditions to be fulfilled in order for the damage to be compensated:

   i the defendant has committed or authorised the act of corruption, or failed to take reasonable steps to prevent the act of corruption;

   ii the plaintiff has suffered damage; and

   iii there is a causal link between the act of corruption and the damage.

2   Each Party shall provide in its internal law that, if several defendants are liable for damage for the same corrupt activity, they shall be jointly and severally liable.

Article 5 — State responsibility

Each Party shall provide in its internal law for appropriate procedures for persons who have suffered damage as a result of an act of corruption by its public officials in the exercise of their functions to claim for compensation from the State or, in the case of a non-state Party, from that Party's appropriate authorities.

Article 6 — Contributory negligence

Each Party shall provide in its internal law for the compensation to be reduced or disallowed having regard to all the circumstances, if the plaintiff has by his or her own fault contributed to the damage or to its aggravation.

Article 7 — Limitation periods

1   Each Party shall provide in its internal law for proceedings for the recovery of damages to be subject to a limitation period of not less than three years from the day the person who has suffered damage became aware or should reasonably have been aware, that damage has occurred or that an act of corruption has taken place, and of the identity of the responsible person. However, such proceedings shall not be commenced after the end of a limitation period of not less than ten years from the date of the act of corruption.

2   The laws of the Parties regulating suspension or interruption of limitation periods shall, if appropriate, apply to the periods prescribed in paragraph 1.

Article 8 — Validity of contracts

1   Each Party shall provide in its internal law for any contract or clause of a contract providing for corruption to be null and void.

2   Each Party shall provide in its internal law for the possibility for all parties to a contract whose consent has been undermined by an act of corruption to be able to apply to the court for the contract to be declared void, notwithstanding their right to claim for damages.

Article 9 — Protection of employees

Each Party shall provide in its internal law for appropriate protection against any unjustified sanction for employees who have reasonable grounds to suspect corruption and who report in good faith their suspicion to responsible persons or authorities.

Article 10—Accounts and audits

1   Each Party shall, in its internal law, take any necessary measures for the annual accounts of companies to be drawn up clearly and give a true and fair view of the company's financial position.

2   With a view to preventing acts of corruption, each Party shall provide in its internal law for auditors to confirm that the annual accounts present a true and fair view of the company's financial position.

Article 11—Acquisition of evidence

Each Party shall provide in its internal law for effective procedures for the acquisition of evidence in civil proceedings arising from an act of corruption.

Article 12—Interim measures

Each Party shall provide in its internal law for such court orders as are necessary to preserve the rights and interests of the parties during civil proceedings arising from an act of corruption.

CHAPTER II—INTERNATIONAL CO-OPERATION AND MONITORING OF IMPLEMENTATION

Article 13—International co-operation

The Parties shall co-operate effectively in matters relating to civil proceedings in cases of corruption, especially concerning the service of documents, obtaining evidence abroad, jurisdiction, recognition and enforcement of foreign judgements and litigation costs, in accordance with the provisions of relevant international instruments on international co-operation in civil and commercial matters to which they are Party, as well as with their internal law.

Article 14—Monitoring

The Group of States against Corruption (GRECO) shall monitor the implementation of this Convention by the Parties.

CHAPTER III—FINAL CLAUSES

Article 15—Signature and entry into force

1   This Convention shall be open for signature by the member States of the Council of Europe, by non-member States that have participated in its elaboration and by the European Community.

2   This Convention is subject to ratification, acceptance or approval. Instruments of ratification, acceptance or approval shall be deposited with the Secretary General of the Council of Europe.

3   This Convention shall enter into force on the first day of the month following the expiration of a period of three months after the date on which fourteen signatories have expressed their consent to be bound by the Convention in accordance with the provisions of paragraph 1. Any such signatory, which is not a member of the Group of States against Corruption (GRECO) at the time of ratification, acceptance or approval, shall automatically become a member on the date the Convention enters into force.

4   In respect of any signatory which subsequently expresses its consent to be bound by it, the Convention shall enter into force on the first day of the month following the expiration of a period of three months after the date of the expression of their consent to be bound by the Convention in accordance with the provisions of paragraph 1. Any signatory, which is not a member of the Group of States against Corruption (GRECO) at the time of ratification, acceptance or approval, shall automatically become a member on the date the Convention enters into force in its respect.

5   Any particular modalities for the participation of the European Community in the Group of States against Corruption (GRECO) shall be determined as far as necessary by a common agreement with the European Community.

Article 16—Accession to the Convention

1   After the entry into force of this Convention, the Committee of Ministers of the Council of Europe, after consulting the Parties to the Convention, may invite any State not a member of the Council and not having participated in its elaboration to accede to this Convention, by a decision taken by the majority provided for in Article 20.d. of the Statute of the Council of Europe and by the unanimous vote of the representatives of the Parties entitled to sit on the Committee.

2   In respect of any State acceding to it, the Convention shall enter into force on the first day of the month following the expiration of a period of three months after the date of deposit of the instrument of accession with the Secretary General of the Council of Europe. Any State acceding to this Convention shall automatically become a member of the GRECO, if it is not already a member at the time of accession, on the date the Convention enters into force in its respect.

Article 17—Reservations

No reservation may be made in respect of any provision of this Convention.

Article 18—Territorial application

1   Any State or the European Community may, at the time of signature or when depositing its instrument of ratification, acceptance, approval or accession, specify the territory or territories to which this Convention shall apply.

2   Any Party may, at any later date, by a declaration addressed to the Secretary General of the Council of Europe, extend the application of this Convention to any other territory specified in the declaration. In respect of such territory the Convention shall enter into force on the first day of the month following the expiration of a period of three months after the date of receipt of such declaration by the Secretary General.

3   Any declaration made under the two preceding paragraphs may, in respect of any territory specified in such declaration, be withdrawn by a notification addressed to the Secretary General. The withdrawal shall become effective on the first day of the month following the expiration of a period of three months after the date of receipt of such notification by the Secretary General.

Article 19 — Relationship to other instruments and agreements

1   This Convention does not affect the rights and undertakings derived from international multilateral instruments concerning special matters.

2   The Parties to the Convention may conclude bilateral or multilateral agreements with one another on the matters dealt with in this Convention, for purposes of supplementing or strengthening its provisions or facilitating the application of the principles embodied in it or, without prejudice to the objectives and principles of this Convention, submit themselves to rules on this matter within the framework of a special system which is binding at the moment of the opening for signature of this Convention.

3   If two or more Parties have already concluded an agreement or treaty in respect of a subject which is dealt with in this Convention or otherwise have established their relations in respect of that subject, they shall be entitled to apply that agreement or treaty or to regulate these relations accordingly, in lieu of the present Convention.

Article 20 — Amendments

1   Amendments to this Convention may be proposed by any Party, and shall be communicated by the Secretary General of the Council of Europe to the member States of the Council of Europe, to the non member States which have participated in the elaboration of this Convention, to the European Community, as well as to any State which has acceded to or has been invited to accede to this Convention in accordance with the provisions of Article 16.

2   Any amendment proposed by a Party shall be communicated to the European Committee on Legal Co-operation (CDCJ) which shall submit to the Committee of Ministers its opinion on that proposed amendment.

3   The Committee of Ministers shall consider the proposed amendment and the opinion submitted by the European Committee on Legal Co-operation (CDCJ) and, following consultation of the Parties to the Convention which are not members of the Council of Europe, may adopt the amendment.

4   The text of any amendment adopted by the Committee of Ministers in accordance with paragraph 3 of this article shall be forwarded to the Parties for acceptance.

5   Any amendment adopted in accordance with paragraph 3 of this article shall come into force on the thirtieth day after all Parties have informed the Secretary General of their acceptance thereof.

Article 21 — Settlement of disputes

1   The European Committee on Legal Co-operation (CDCJ) of the Council of Europe shall be kept informed regarding the interpretation and application of this Convention.

2   In case of a dispute between Parties as to the interpretation or application of this Convention, they shall seek a settlement of the dispute through negotiation or any other peaceful means of their choice, including submission of the dispute to the European Committee on Legal Co-operation (CDCJ), to an arbitral tribunal whose decisions shall be binding upon the Parties, or to the International Court of Justice, as agreed upon by the Parties concerned.

Article 22 — Denunciation

1   Any Party may, at any time, denounce this Convention by means of a notification addressed to the Secretary General of the Council of Europe.

2   Such denunciation shall become effective on the first day of the month following the expiration of a period of three months after the date of receipt of the notification by the Secretary General.

Article 23 — Notification

The Secretary General of the Council of Europe shall notify the member States of the Council and any other signatories and Parties to this Convention of:

a any signature;

b the deposit of any instrument of ratification, acceptance, approval or accession;

c any date of entry into force of this Convention, in accordance with Articles 15 and 16;

d any other act, notification or communication relating to this Convention.

In witness whereof the undersigned, being duly authorised thereto, have signed this Convention.

Done at Strasbourg, the 4th day of November 1999, in English and in French, both texts being equally authentic, in a single copy which shall be deposited in the archives of the Council of Europe. The Secretary General of the Council of Europe shall transmit certified copies to each member State of the Council of Europe, to the non-member States which have participated in the elaboration of this Convention, to the European Community, as well as to any State invited to accede to it.

EXPLANATORY REPORT
ON THE COUNCIL OF EUROPE
CIVIL LAW CONVENTION
ON CORRUPTION*

(ETS NO. 174)

EXPLANATORY REPORT

I.   INTRODUCTION

a) General considerations

1.   The Council of Europe became strongly interested in the international fight against corruption because of the obvious threat corruption poses to the basic principles this Organisation stands for: the rule of law, the stability of democratic institutions, human rights and social and economic progress. Also because corruption is a subject well-suited for international co-operation: it is a problem shared by most, if not all, member States and it often contains transnational elements. However, the specificity of the Council of Europe lies its multidisciplinary approach, meaning that it deals with corruption from a criminal, civil and administrative law point of view.

2.   At the 1994 Malta Conference of the European Ministers of Justice, the Council of Europe launched its initiative against corruption. The Ministers considered that corruption was a serious threat to democracy, the rule of law and human rights and that the Council of Europe, being the pre-eminent European institution defending these fundamental values, should respond to that threat.

3.   The Resolution adopted at this Conference endorsed the need for a multidisciplinary approach, and recommended the setting up of a Multidisciplinary Group on Corruption with the task to examine what measures could be included in a programme of action at international level, and the possibility of drafting model laws or codes of conduct, including international conventions, on this subject.

---

* ETS No. 174 (1999).

The importance of elaborating a follow-up mechanism to implement the under-takings contained in such instruments was also underlined.

4. In the light of these recommendations, the Committee of Ministers agreed, in September 1994, to set up the Multidisciplinary Group on Corruption (GMC) under the joint responsibility of the European Committee on Crime Problems (CDPC) and the European Committee on Legal Co-operation (CDCJ) and invited it to examine what measures would be suitable for a programme of action at international level against corruption, to make proposals on priorities and working structures, taking due account of the work of other international organisations and to examine the possibility of drafting model laws or codes of conduct in selected areas, including the elaboration of an international con-vention on this subject and a follow-up mechanism to implement undertakings contained in such instruments. The GMC started operating in March 1995.

5. The Programme of Action against Corruption (PAC), prepared by the GMC in the course of 1995 and adopted by the Committee of Ministers at the end of 1996, is an ambitious document, which attempts to cover all aspects of the international fight against this phenomenon. It defines the areas in which action is necessary and provides for a number of measures, to be followed in order to realise a global, multidisciplinary and comprehensive approach to tackling corruption. The Committee of Ministers instructed the GMC to implement this programme before the end of the year 2000.

6. At their 21st Conference (Prague 1997), the European Ministers of Justice adopted Resolution No. 1 on the links between corruption and organised crime. The Ministers emphasised that corruption represents a major threat to the rule of law, democracy and human rights, fairness and social justice, hinders eco-nomic development and endangers the stability of democratic institutions and the moral foundations of society. They further underlined that a successful strat-egy to combat corruption and organised crime requires a firm commitment by States to join their efforts, share their experience and take common actions. The European Ministers of Justice specifically recommended speeding up the imple-mentation of the Programme of Action against corruption and to pursue the work concerning the preparation of an international civil law instrument, deal-ing, *inter alia*, with compensation for damage resulting from corruption.

7. On 10 and 11 October 1997, the 2nd Summit of the Heads of State and Gov-ernment of the member States of the Council of Europe took place in Stras-bourg. The Heads of State and Government, in order to seek common responses to the challenges posed by corruption throughout Europe and to promote co-operation among Council of Europe member States in the fight against corruption, instructed, *inter alia*, the Committee of Ministers to secure the rapid completion of international legal instruments pursuant to the Council of Europe's Programme of Action against Corruption.

8. The Committee of Ministers, at its 101st Session on 6 November 1997, adopted Resolution (97) 24 on the 20 Guiding Principles for the fight against Corruption. Principle 17 specifically indicates that States should "ensure that civil law takes

into account the need to fight corruption and in particular provides for effective remedies for those whose rights and interests are affected by corruption."

9. At their 22nd Conference (Chisinau, June 1999), the European Ministers of Justice adopted Resolution No. 3 on the fight against corruption, urging the Committee of Ministers to adopt the draft Convention on civil aspects of corruption and open it for signature before the end of 1999.

10. Consequently, following the adoption of the Criminal Law Convention on Corruption (European Treaty Series No. 173), and of Resolutions (98) 7 and (99) 5, authorising and establishing, respectively, the "Group of States against Corruption (GRECO)", the Council of Europe finalised an international legal instrument aiming at fighting corruption through civil law remedies. Indeed, the possibility to tackle corruption phenomena through civil law measures is an outstanding feature of the Council of Europe approach to the fight against corruption.

11. Therefore, one of the characteristics of the Council of Europe approach in the fight against corruption is the possibility to tackle corruption phenomena from a civil law point of view.

12. The Programme of Action against corruption indicates that when fighting against corruption, "civil law is directly linked to criminal law and administrative law. If an offence such as corruption is prohibited under criminal law, a claim for damages can be made which is based on the commission of the criminal act. Victims might find it easier to safeguard their interests under civil law than to use criminal law. Similarly, if an administration does not exercise sufficiently its supervisory responsibilities, a claim for damages may be made."

b) Terms of reference and feasibility study

13. On 15 February 1996, the Committee of Ministers at the 558th meeting of the Ministers' Deputies decided to ask to the GMC, *inter alia*, "to start a feasibility study on the drawing up of a convention on civil remedies for compensation for damage resulting from acts of corruption."

14. A questionnaire on corruption was circulated to the States to provide a basis for this feasibility study. After having received replies from most Council of Europe member States, the GMC finalised the feasibility study which was submitted to the Committee of Ministers in March 1997.

15. The study gives as complete a picture as possible of the civil law aspects related to cases of corruption, underlining in particular the reasons for or against drafting one or several international instruments on this issue.

16. The study shows that it is possible to conceive a number of scenarios where the use of civil law remedies might be useful against any form of corruption. The text deals with, *inter alia*, the following questions:
    • the accessibility and effectiveness of civil law remedies in general,
    • the determination of the main potential victims of corrupt behaviours,

- the problems of evidence and of proof of the causal link between acts and damage,
- the fiscal aspects of illicit payments and their relation to the distortion of competition,
- validity of contracts,
- the role of auditors,
- protection of employees,
- procedures (including litigation costs) and international co-operation.

17. The feasibility study indicates that from the analysis of the replies to the questionnaire, it is clear that States have different laws against corrupt practices. However, common ground can be found and it would seem useful to continue to analyse and clarify the similarities and the differences. After all, all the laws are based on one common denominator, namely that corrupt practices should not be encouraged or tolerated.

18. Therefore, the study underlines that, notwithstanding different national legislation, an international approximation of civil law remedies in the fight against corruption is both possible and necessary.

19. The feasibility study concludes with a number of recommended items to be considered when drafting a future international instrument on the matter, such as compensation for damage, liability (including State responsibility), contributory negligence, limitation periods, the validity of contracts, the protection of employees, accounts and audits, the acquisition of evidence, interim measures and international co-operation.

c) The Civil Law Convention on Corruption

20. The GMC's Working Group on Civil Law met twice in 1997 and twice in 1998 to discuss and finalise the draft Civil Law Convention on Corruption, which was then forwarded to the GMC Plenary. The GMC examined this text at its 15th (December 1998) and 16th (February 1999) Plenary meetings. The draft Convention was then transmitted to the European Committee on Legal Co-operation (CDCJ) for its opinion, and to the Committee of Ministers with a view to enabling it to consult the Parliamentary Assembly. At their 662nd meeting (March 1999), the Ministers' Deputies invited the Parliamentary Assembly to give an opinion on this text. The GMC also consulted Transparency International (TI), the International Chamber of Commerce (ICC), the International Commission of Jurists (ICJ) and the International Bar Association (IBA) on this draft Convention. After having examined at its 17th meeting (June 1999) the opinions of the CDCJ (CDCJ (99) 48 Appendix III) and of the Parliamentary Assembly (Opinion 213(1999)), as well as those of Transparency International (TI) and the International Chamber of Commerce (ICC), the GMC approved, on 24 June 1999, the draft Civil Law Convention on Corruption and decided to transmit it to the Committee of Ministers for adoption.

21. At its . . . meeting, the Committee of Ministers adopted the Civil Law Convention on Corruption, decided to open it to signature on [4 November 1999], and authorised the publication of this Explanatory Report.

22. The Civil Law Convention aims at requiring each Party to provide in its internal law for effective remedies for persons who have suffered damage as a result of corruption, in order to enable them to defend their rights and interests, including the possibility of obtaining compensation for damage.

23. The Convention, which is divided in three Chapters (measures to be taken at a national level, international co-operation and monitoring, and final clauses), is a non-self-executing Convention. This means that States Parties will have to transpose the principles and rules contained in the Convention in their internal law, by taking into account their own particular circumstances.

24. Therefore, States Parties which already comply with the provisions of the Convention or have more favourable provisions, are not required to take further actions. It will be for the Group of States against Corruption (GRECO), in its monitoring activity in accordance with Article 14 of the Convention, to ensure that States Parties comply with their undertakings under the Civil Law Convention.

25. This Convention, which is the first attempt to define common principles and rules at an international level in the field of civil law and corruption, deals with the definition of corruption, compensation for damage, liability, contributory negligence, limitation periods, the validity of contracts, the protection of employees, accounts and audits, the acquisition of evidence, interim measures, international co-operation and monitoring.

II. COMMENTARY ON THE ARTICLES OF THE CONVENTION

Article 1—Purpose

26. Article 1 deals with the purpose of the Convention, which contains principles and rules which Parties are required to implement in their internal law in order to enable persons who have suffered damage as a result of corruption to defend their rights and interests, including the possibility of obtaining damages.

27. The word "persons" contained in the Convention and in this Explanatory Report refers to both natural and legal persons, and to other bodies existing in certain legal systems, which are able to engage in litigation.

Article 2—Definition

28. At the beginning of its work, the GMC adopted the following provisional definition of corruption:

> *"Corruption as dealt with by the Council of Europe's GMC is bribery and any other behaviour in relation to persons entrusted with responsibilities in the public or private sector, which violates the duties that follow from their status as a public official, private employee, independent agent or other relationship of that kind and is aimed at obtaining undue advantages of any kind for themselves or for others".*

29. The purpose of this definition was to ensure that no matter would be excluded from its work. Obviously, such a definition would not necessarily match the legal definition of corruption in most member States, in particular not the definition given by the criminal law, but its advantage was not to restrict prejudiciously the discussion within excessively narrow confines.

30. The Criminal Law Convention on Corruption contains several common operational definitions of corruption which could be transposed into national laws, even if some amendments may prove necessary in certain national definitions to match them.

31. The Civil Law Convention follows a traditional approach to questions relating to definitions and contains a definition of corruption for the purpose of this Convention. This does not mean that Parties necessarily have to adopt this definition of corruption in their internal law, although they could do so, if they so wished. Indeed, the main aims of this definition are to clarify the meaning of the term "corruption" in the context of this Convention and to provide a proper legal framework within which the other obligations arising out from this Convention operate.

32. Therefore, the word "corruption" in this Convention means "requesting, offering, giving or accepting directly or indirectly a bribe or any other undue advantage or the prospect thereof, which distorts the proper performance of any duty or behaviour required of the recipient of the bribe, the undue advantage or the prospect thereof".

33. It is worth underlining, with respect to this definition, that the present Convention has, as one of its main characteristics, a relatively wide scope, which reflects the Council of Europe comprehensive approach to the fight against corruption as a threat not only to international business or to the financial interests but to the democratic values, the rule of law, human rights and social and economic progress.

34. The term "recipient" refers to the person whose behaviour is distorted by the act of corruption, regardless of whether or not the bribe or the undue advantage was for himself or herself or for anyone else.

Article 3 — Compensation for damage

35. Article 3, paragraph 1, embodies the main purpose of the Convention which is to provide the right to compensation for damage resulting from an act of corruption. This paragraph requires each Party to provide in its internal law for the right to bring a civil action in corruption cases. The judge, in the individual case, will decide whether or not the conditions for compensation are fulfilled.

36. It should be noted that, under the Convention, damages must not be limited to any standard payment but must be determined according to the loss sustained in the particular case. Also, full compensation according to this Convention excludes punitive damages. However, Parties whose domestic law provides for punitive damages are not required to exclude their application in addition to full compensation.

37. It is clear that the compensation for damage suffered may vary according to the nature of the damage. Material damage is normally compensated financially, whereas non-pecuniary loss may also be compensated by other means, such as the publication of a judgement.

38. Paragraph 2 specifies the extent of the compensation to be granted by the Court. The "material damage" (*damnum emergens*) represents the actual reduction in the economic situation of the person who has suffered damage. The "loss of profits" (*lucrum cessans*), represents the profit which could reasonably have been expected but that was not gained as a result of corruption. Finally, "non-pecuniary loss" refers to those losses which cannot immediately be calculated, as they do not amount to a tangible or material economic loss. The most frequent example of non-pecuniary loss is the loss of reputation of the competitor which may be compensated financially or by the publication of a judgement at the costs of the defendant.

39. Finally, it will be up to the Parties to decide, in their domestic law, the nature of non-pecuniary losses which will be covered, as well as the nature of the compensation which will be given. If, for instance, the law of a Party provides, in the framework of compensation for non-pecuniary loss, for compensation of loss of reputation only, this Party shall be deemed to have fulfilled its obligations under this provision.

Article 4 — Liability

Paragraph 1

40. Paragraph 1 of Article 4 contains the prerequisites of a claim for damages. In order to obtain compensation, the plaintiff has to prove the occurrence of the damage, whether the defendant acted with intent or negligently, and the causal link between the corrupt behaviour and the damage. This provision does not give a right to compensation to any person who merely claims that any act of corruption has affected, in one way or another, his rights or interests or might do so in the future.

41. As far as the individual elements of claims for damages are concerned, the following should be indicated:

(a) Unlawful and culpable behaviour on the part of the defendant

42. Those who directly and knowingly participate in the corruption are primarily liable for the damage and, above all, the giver and the recipient of the bribe, as well as those who incited or aided the corruption. Moreover, those who failed to take the appropriate steps, in the light of the responsibilities which lie on them, to prevent corruption would also be liable for damage. This means that employers are responsible for the corrupt behaviour of their employees if, for example, they neglect to organise their company adequately or fail to exert appropriate control over their employees.

(b) Damages

43. The damage referred to in paragraph 1 (ii) of Article 4 must fulfil certain conditions in order to give the right to compensation. Damage, which is capable of

justifying a claim for compensation, must be sufficiently characterised, particularly as regards the connection with the victim himself or herself.

44. Since the Convention lays down minimum standards, paragraph 1.ii of Article 4 does not prevent Parties from allowing a person other than the one who suffered damage to bring a claim for its compensation.

(c) Causal link

45. An adequate causal link must exist between the act and the damage, in order for the latter to be compensated. The damage should be an ordinary and not an extraordinary consequence of corruption. Thus, for instance, "loss of profits" by an unsuccessful competitor, who would have obtained the contract if an act of corruption had not been committed, is an ordinary consequence of corruption and should normally be compensated. On the other hand, there would be no adequate connection if, for example, an unsuccessful competitor, in his or her anger and disappointment over the loss of business, fell down the stairs and broke a leg. Moreover, it should be noted that Parties are free to apply in their domestic law and practice a wider concept of causal link.

Paragraph 2

46. Paragraph 2 of Article 4 provides for joint and several liabilities of several joint offenders, regardless of whether they knowingly co-operated or whether one of them is simply liable as a result of his or her negligent behaviour.

47. In the context of this Convention, "jointly and severally liable" means that persons who have suffered damage as a result of an act of corruption, for which several offenders are liable, may seek full compensation from any one or more of them.

Article 5 — State responsibility

48. Article 5 requires each Party to provide in its internal law for appropriate procedures for persons who have suffered damage as a result of an act of corruption by its public officials in the exercise of their function, to claim for compensation from the State or, in case of a non-State Party, from that Party's appropriate authorities. Indeed such a procedure exists already in a number of European States.

49. Article 5 does not indicate the conditions for the liability of the Party. The Convention leaves each Party free to determine in its internal law the conditions in which the Party would be liable. Therefore, the conditions and procedures for filing claims against the State for damage caused by acts of corruption committed by public officials in the exercise of their functions, will be governed by the domestic law of the Party concerned. However, Article 5 requires Parties to provide "appropriate procedures" to enable victims of acts of corruption by public officials to have effective procedures and reasonable time to seek compensation from the State (or, in the case of a non-State party, from that party's appropriate authorities).

50. The provision contained in Article 5 does not prevent Parties from providing in their internal law for the possibility for persons who have suffered damage as a result of an act of corruption to sue public officials, as well as the possibility for such Parties to sue their public officials for the reimbursement of any loss (including, for instance, the costs of defending the claim), for which they are adjudged to be responsible. In any event, most European legal systems already provide for this possibility.

Article 6 — Contributory negligence

51. Article 6 of the Convention indicates that the behaviour of the plaintiff may have a bearing on his or her right to compensation. It is clear that, when the plaintiff is not the victim of the damage, it is the latter's behaviour which has to be taken into account.

52. Therefore, this Article provides for an exception to the principle of the right to full compensation of the damage suffered contained in Article 3, if the negligent behaviour of the victim may lead to a reduction or a disallowance of compensation, in accordance with domestic law.

53. It should be noted however that this must be a culpable behaviour and that the non-culpable behaviour of the victim will not affect his or her right to compensation.

54. Judges should therefore evaluate the behaviour of the victim in order to ascertain whether or not it constituted a culpable behaviour.

55. Moreover, the degree of culpable behaviour of the victim should be taken into account, as regards his or her contribution to the damage and to its aggravation.

56. It will be up to the judge to establish, in the light of the circumstances which surrounded the act of corruption, the amount of the reduction of the compensation. The judge may even decide that, in the light of the culpable behaviour of the victim, no compensation is to be awarded.

57. For example, employers who leave complete responsibility for dealing with large sums of money to employees, who are also in charge of negotiating certain contracts, without exercising, or having somebody else exercise, proper control over the conditions for the awarding of contracts or whether the contract is awarded to a suitable company may be accused of culpable behaviour which has contributed to the damage.

58. If, after having discovered that an employee had already paid a bribe, the employer did not take the necessary measures to avoid a repetition of the events, his or her claim for compensation might be reduced or even rejected owing to the employer's contribution to the aggravation of the financial damage suffered by the company.

Article 7 — Limitation periods

59. It is widely accepted in most jurisdictions that the ability to take civil proceedings for compensation should be subject to some time limitation, so as

to provide a degree of certainty for plaintiffs and defendants about the risks of litigation. The details vary from country to country, but in general limitation rules require plaintiffs to commence proceedings within a fixed period of becoming aware of the act which gives rise to the claim or of the damage. Most countries also prescribe a longer time period beyond which proceedings may not be commenced, regardless of the plaintiff's date of knowledge.

60. Article 7 of the Convention applies these general principles to corruption claims. Recognising that different countries fix different limitation periods, sometimes varying between different types of cases, the Article does not prescribe a fixed period that must apply to corruption cases. Once the plaintiff has become aware or should have become aware that damage occurred or that an act of corruption has taken place, and of the identity of the responsible person, it is necessary to give the plaintiff at least 3 years to bring an action, owing to the nature of corruption, the difficulty of detection and investigations in order to obtain the information to support the claim. This provision allows Parties either to provide in their internal law that the limitation period starts from the moment when the plaintiff becomes aware of the act of corruption or of the damage. Parties may also provide that the limitation period starts from the moment in which the plaintiff has become aware of both the damage and the act of corruption. In any event, the knowledge of the identity of the responsible person is a requirement which derives from general principles of civil law. Questions of balance and fairness (e.g. the defendant may not have access to the evidence after a great number of years) lead to the conclusion that the absolute bar on commencing proceedings should not come into effect before the expiry of 10 years of the corrupt act. Paragraph 1 of Article 7 makes these provisions.

61. Arrangements for suspending or interrupting limitation periods are also different from country to country, and are closely bound up with other aspects of domestic procedures for the administration of civil justice. It is not necessary or desirable to require a common approach for corruption cases, and paragraph 2 of Article 7 so provides. The expression "if appropriate" is necessary to recognise that different States have different rules about which periods may be suspended or interrupted.

62. Furthermore, it should be noted that, in cases of several acts of corruption, Parties are free to determine the date in which the act of corruption occurred which is relevant for counting the limitation period.

Article 8—Validity of contracts

63. Paragraph 1 of this article provides that any contract or clause of a contract providing for corruption shall be null and void. Indeed, in most European countries, the contract the cause of which is illegal is null and void.

64. Paragraph 2 of this article strengthens the civil law application to the fight against corruption by providing for an additional remedy to be available to

those who have suffered damage as a result of an act of corruption. Notwith-standing the right to sue for compensation for damage, any party whose consent to enter into a contract has been undermined by an act of corruption, shall have the right to apply to Court for the contract to be declared void. It remains open to the parties concerned to continue with the contract if they so decide. The drafting clearly provides that the applicant for such a declaration must be one of the parties to the contract. It remains for the court to decide on the status of the contract, having regard to all the circumstances of the case

65. It should be noted that, as it is clear from the text of this provision, Parties are not obliged to provide in their internal law for the possibility for third parties to ask for the contract to be declared null and void. It is clear that nothing prevent Parties from going further than the content of this provision, if they so wish, by recognising the right of interested persons to request the contract to be declared null and void. In any event, persons who have a legitimate interest may, under other provisions of this Convention (e.g. Articles 3 and 4) bring an action for compensation for damage resulting from an act of corruption.

Article 9—Protection of employees

66. This Article deals with the need for each Party to take the necessary measures to protect employees, who report in good faith and on the basis of reasonable grounds their suspicions on corrupt practices or behaviours, from being victimised in any way.

67. As regards the necessary measures to protect employees provided for by Article 9 of the Convention, the legislation of Parties could, for instance, provide that employers be required to pay compensation to employees who are victims of unjustified sanctions.

68. In practice corruption cases are difficult to detect and investigate and employees or colleagues (whether public or private) of the persons involved are often the first persons who find out or suspect that something is wrong.

69. The "appropriate protection against any unjustified sanction" implies that, on the basis of this Convention, any sanction against employees based on the ground that they had reported an act of corruption to persons or authorities responsible for receiving such reports, will not be justified. Reporting should not be considered as a breach of the duty of confidentiality. Examples of unjustified sanctions may be a dismissal or demotion of these persons or otherwise acting in a way which limits progress in their career.

70. It should be made clear that, although no one could prevent employers from taking any necessary action against their employees in accordance with the relevant provisions (e.g. in the field of labour law) applicable to the circumstances of the case, employers should not inflict unjustified sanctions against employees solely on the ground that the latter had reported their suspicion to the responsible person or authority.

71. Therefore the appropriate protection which Parties are required to take should encourage employees to report their suspicions to the responsible person or authority. Indeed, in many cases, persons who have information of corruption activities do not report them mainly because of fear of the possible negative consequences.

72. As far as employees are concerned, this protection provided covers only the cases where they have reasonable ground to report their suspicion and report them in good faith. In other words, it applies only to genuine cases and not to malicious ones.

Article 10—Accounts and audits

73. Article 10 recognises that national laws on accounts and audits are important tools for identifying and combating corruption. Stringent regulations on accounts and audits may help prevent and discover accounting irregularities such as inadequately identified transactions and liabilities, recording of non-existent expenditure, false documents and off-the-book accounts.

74. Article 10 is inspired by the Fourth Council Directive on the annual accounts of certain types of companies (78/660/EEC, Article 2, paragraph 3), the Seventh Council Directive on consolidated accounts (83/349/EEC, Article 16, paragraph 3) and the Eighth Council Directive on the approval of persons responsible for carrying out the statutory audits of accounting documents (84/253/EEC, Article 1, paragraph 1, letter a). This Article aims to ensure effective procedures without specifying any legal requirements.

75. Paragraph 1 relates to the annual accounts of companies which comprise the balance sheet and other financial statements, the profit and loss account and its appendices. In order to make the fight against corruption more effective, annual accounts should give a true and fair view of all aspects of companies' financial situation.

76. Paragraph 2 underlines the central role of auditors in the fight against corruption. As part of the annual account, the balance sheet is a survey of assets and liabilities at a particular point of time. The provision refers to independent external audits, as well as internal company controls.

Article 11—Acquisition of evidence

77. Corruption is, by its nature, secretive and plaintiffs may encounter great difficulty in obtaining the evidence required to substantiate their claim. There are various methods of meeting this difficulty. For example, certain legal systems provide for an application to court for an order for discovery, while in other legal systems a judge can appoint a specific person to obtain the information required.

78. This Article does not require Parties to adopt a specific procedure for the acquisition of evidence in corruption cases. In particular, it does not provide for any obligation for Parties to introduce the reversing of the burden of proof in civil procedures relating to corruption cases. This Article aims at

encouraging those Parties which do not have any effective procedures for the acquisition of evidence, to adopt such procedures, in particular in order to deal with corruption cases.

79. It should also be noted that the aim of the procedure referred to in Article 11 of the Convention should mainly be the acquisition of documentary evidence during civil proceedings relating to corruption. In particular, by the use of the documents referred to in Article 10, victims of corruption may be in a better position to prove that an act of corruption has taken place.

Article 12 — Interim measures

80. It is a common experience of plaintiffs in most European (and non-European) countries that their attempts to secure recovery through civil proceedings may be frustrated by unscrupulous debtors who conceal or dissipate their assets away before the judgement is rendered. This problem is particularly serious when proceedings are necessary in other countries.

81. This article therefore requires Parties to enable persons to apply to the court for such interim orders as are necessary to preserve their rights and interests (e.g. for the preservation or the custody of property during the course of civil proceedings). This provision aims at preserving the position of both parties (the plaintiff and the defendant) while justice is rendered in the dispute. It is left to the Parties to decide how this aim is to be achieved. They could provide for the possibility of adopting interim measures before the proceedings have formally started, at the beginning or during the proceedings or a combination of these.

82. In fact, in civil law cases (including corruption cases), very often it is necessary to preserve the property which is the object of the civil action (or any other property which belongs to defendants), until the final judgement on the case is given.

83. The measures referred to in this Article aim mainly at:

    (i) providing preliminary means of securing assets out of which an ultimate judgement may be satisfied; or

    (ii) maintaining the status quo pending determination of the issues at stake.

84. In both cases, the object of such measures is to provide a ready means of ensuring that the aims of the civil justice system are not defeated.

Article 13 — International co-operation

85. The Guiding Principles for the fight against corruption (Principle 20) contain an undertaking to develop to the widest extent possible international co-operation in all areas of the fight against corruption.

86. When dealing with cases of corruption involving international elements, several problems could arise, such as the uncertainty on the applicable law, the problems related to evidence, as well as the difficulties in recognising and enforcing foreign judgements.

87. In particular, corruption in international business transactions has become an increasingly common phenomenon. For example, it is possible that a company in country A may find that it has lost a contract in country B on the basis of a bribe which was paid to a company in country C, or to a public official in that country. In such a situation, the company in country A may experience difficulties in trying to seek redress. Such difficulties may relate, for instance, to the transmission of judicial and extra-judicial acts, to the choice of jurisdiction to seek redress, the uncertainties of the applicable law in a situation where several different alternatives may be possible, the obligation for the company to advance security for legal costs if the law suit is filed with the courts of another country and difficulties in having the judgement recognised and executed in a foreign country.

88. However, the Convention deliberately does not address these questions. Indeed, Article 13 of the Convention requires Parties to co-operate, whenever possible, in accordance with existing and relevant international legal instruments in these fields, such as the Brussels and Lugano Conventions on Jurisdiction and Enforcement of Judgements in Civil and Commercial Matters of 1968 and 1988 respectively, the 1965 Hague Convention on the Service Abroad of Judicial and Extra-Judicial Documents in Civil or Commercial Matters, the 1970 Hague Convention on the Taking of Evidence Abroad in Civil or Commercial Matters, the Hague Conventions on Civil Procedures of 1954 and 1980.

89. These Conventions, as well as those which are being negotiated in various international *fora* (such as the Hague Conference on Private International Law), constitute a sufficiently relevant *corpus iuris* which could and should be applicable also in corruption cases involving an international element. Those Parties to this Convention which are not yet Parties to these international instruments are invited to consider doing so whenever possible, in order to be able to comply with the provisions of Article 13 of this Convention.

90. However, although the drafters did not find it necessary to include any provision concerning specific questions of international co-operation relating to corruption cases, the co-operation required by Article 13 of the Convention has to be an effective one. It will be up to the GRECO to monitor the proper and effective implementation by Parties of this provision.

91. Moreover, the drafters of the Convention believed that Parties to this Convention, which have neither signed nor ratified the Conventions dealing with the subjects referred to in this provision, should endeavour to grant each other an equivalent level of mutual legal assistance in judicial matters in the fields covered by this Convention, even if it does not contain a specific legal obligation to that effect.

Article 14—Monitoring

92. The implementation of the Convention will be monitored by the "Group of States against Corruption—GRECO". From the outset, the establishment

of an efficient and appropriate mechanism to monitor the implementation of international legal instruments against corruption was considered as an essential element for the effectiveness and credibility of the Council of Europe initiative in this field (see, *inter alia*, the Resolutions adopted at the 19th and 21st Conferences of the European Ministers of Justice, the terms of reference of the Multidisciplinary Group on Corruption, the Programme of Action against Corruption, the Final Declaration and Action Plan of the Second Summit of Heads of State and Government). In Resolution (98) 7 adopted at its 102nd Session (5 May 1998), the Committee of Ministers authorised the establishment of a monitoring body, the GRECO, in the form of a partial and enlarged Agreement under Statutory Resolution (93) 28 (as completed by Resolution (96) 36). Member States and non-member States having participated in the elaboration of the Agreement were invited to notify their intention to participate in GRECO, which would start functioning on the first day of the month following the date on which the 14th notification by a member State would reach the Secretary General of the Council of Europe. Consequently, on 1 May 1999, Belgium, Bulgaria, Cyprus, Estonia, Finland, France, Germany, Greece, Iceland, Ireland, Lithuania, Luxembourg, Romania, Slovakia, Slovenia, Spain and Sweden, joined by Poland on 19 May 1999, adopted Resolution (99) 5 establishing the GRECO and containing its Statute.

93. The GRECO will monitor the implementation of this Convention in accordance with its Statute, appended to Resolution (99) 5. The aim of GRECO is to improve the capacity of its members to fight corruption by following up, through a dynamic process of mutual evaluation and peer pressure, compliance with their undertakings in this field (Article 1 of the Statute). The functions, composition, operation and procedures of GRECO are described in its Statute.

94. If a Signatory is already a member of GRECO at the time of ratifying the present Convention, the consequence will be that the scope of the monitoring carried out by GRECO will be extended to cover the implementation of the present Convention. If a Signatory or acceding State is not a member of GRECO at the time of ratification, acceptance or approval, this provision combined with Articles 15, paragraphs 3 and 4 or with Article 16, paragraph 2 imposes a compulsory and automatic membership of GRECO. It consequently implies an obligation to accept to be monitored in accordance with the procedures detailed in its Statute, as from the date in which the Convention enters into force in respect of that State or the European Community.

III. FINAL CLAUSES

95. With some exceptions, the provisions contained in this Section are, for the most part, based on the "Model final clauses for conventions and agreements concluded within the Council of Europe" which were approved by the Committee of Ministers of the Council of Europe at the 315th meeting of their

Deputies in February 1980. Most of these Articles do not therefore call for specific comments, but the following points require some explanation.

96. Article 15, paragraph 1 has been drafted on several precedents established in other Conventions elaborated within the framework of the Council of Europe, which allow for signature, before the Convention's entry into force, not only by member States of the Council of Europe, but also by non-member States which have participated in the elaboration of the Convention. These States are Belarus, Bosnia and Herzegovina, Canada, Georgia, the Holy See, Japan, Mexico and the United States of America. Once the Convention enters into force, in accordance with paragraph 3 of this Article, other non-member States not covered by this provision may be invited to accede to the Convention in conformity with Article 16, paragraph 1.

97. Article 15, paragraph 3, requires 14 ratifications for the entry into force of the Convention. This is an unusually high number of ratifications for a civil law Convention drafted within the Council of Europe. The reason is that measures against corruption, particularly of international corruption, can only be effective if a high number of States undertake to take the necessary measures at the same time. It is widely recognised that corrupt practices bear an impact on international trade because they hinder the application of competition rules and undermine the proper functioning of the market economy. Some countries considered that they would penalise their national companies if they entered into international commitments against corruption without other countries having assumed similar obligations. In order to avoid becoming a handicap for the national companies of a few States Parties, the present Convention requires that a large number of States undertake to implement it at the same time. In addition, the number of ratifications required for the entry into force of this Convention is consistent with that provided in other Council of Europe instruments against corruption, such as the Partial and Enlarged Agreement establishing the "Group of States against Corruption— GRECO" and the Criminal law Convention on corruption (ETS No 173).

98. The second sentence of paragraphs 3 and 4 of Article 15 as well as of Article 16, paragraph 2, combined with Article 14, entail an automatic and compulsory membership of GRECO for States and the European Community, which are not already members of this monitoring body at the time of ratification, acceptance or approval. Therefore, it will not be possible to be a Party to this Convention without being a member of GRECO and without being submitted to its monitoring procedures. However, owing to the special nature of the European Community, the modalities of its participation in GRECO will be determined by a common agreement.

99. Article 16 has also been drafted on several precedents established in other conventions elaborated within the framework of the Council of Europe. The Committee of Ministers may, on its own initiative or upon request, and after consulting the Parties, which are not represented in the Committee of Ministers, invite any non-member State to accede to the Convention. This provision refers only to non-member States not having participated in the elaboration of the Convention.

100. In conformity with the 1969 Vienna Convention on the law of treaties, Article 19 is intended to regulate the relationship of the Convention with other treaties—multilateral or bilateral—or instruments dealing with matters which are also dealt with in the present Convention. Paragraph 2 of Article 19 expresses in a positive way that Parties may, for certain purposes, conclude bilateral or multilateral agreements, or any other international instrument, relating to matters dealt with in the Convention. The drafting makes clear, however, that Parties may not conclude agreements which derogate from the Convention. It is possible that the Parties submit themselves, without prejudice to the objectives and principles of this Convention, to rules on this matter within the framework of a special system which is binding at the moment of the adoption of this Convention. This special regime applies to the European Community and to its member States, as well as to future member States from the date of their accession to the European Union. Paragraph 3 of Article 19 safeguards the continued application of agreements, treaties or relations relating to subjects which are dealt with in the present Convention, for instance in the European Community or in the Nordic co-operation.

101. The amendment procedure provided for by Article 20 does not prevent the Parties from introducing major changes into the Convention by means of protocols. Moreover, in accordance with paragraph 5 of Article 20, any amendment adopted after the adoption of this Convention, would come into force only when all Parties had informed the Secretary General of their acceptance. The procedure for amending the present Convention involves the consultation of non-member States Parties to it, which are not represented in the Committee of Ministers or the CDCJ.

102. Article 21, paragraph 1, provides that the CDCJ should be kept informed about the interpretation and application of the provisions of the Convention. Paragraph 2 of this Article imposes an obligation on the Parties to seek a peaceful settlement of any dispute concerning the interpretation or the application of the Convention. Any procedure for solving disputes should be agreed upon by the Parties concerned.

UNITED NATIONS CONVENTION AGAINST CORRUPTION*

PREAMBLE

The States Parties to this Convention,

Concerned about the seriousness of problems and threats posed by corruption to the stability and security of societies, undermining the institutions and values of democracy, ethical values and justice and jeopardizing sustainable development and the rule of law,

Concerned also about the links between corruption and other forms of crime, in particular organized crime and economic crime, including money-laundering,

Concerned further about cases of corruption that involve vast quantities of assets, which may constitute a substantial proportion of the resources of States, and that threaten the political stability and sustainable development of those States,

Convinced that corruption is no longer a local matter but a transnational phenomenon that affects all societies and economies, making international cooperation to prevent and control it essential,

Convinced also that a comprehensive and multidisciplinary approach is required to prevent and combat corruption effectively,

Convinced further that the availability of technical assistance can play an important role in enhancing the ability of States, including by strengthening capacity and by institution-building, to prevent and combat corruption effectively,

Convinced that the illicit acquisition of personal wealth can be particularly damaging to democratic institutions, national economies and the rule of law,

Determined to prevent, detect and deter in a more effective manner international transfers of illicitly acquired assets and to strengthen international cooperation in asset recovery,

---

* G.A. Res. 58/4, U.N. GAOR, 58th Sess., U.N. Doc. A/RES/58/4 (2003), *reprinted in* 43 I.L.M. 37 (2004).

Acknowledging the fundamental principles of due process of law in criminal proceedings and in civil or administrative proceedings to adjudicate property rights,

Bearing in mind that the prevention and eradication of corruption is a responsibility of all States and that they must cooperate with one another, with the support and involvement of individuals and groups outside the public sector, such as civil society, non-governmental organizations and community-based organizations, if their efforts in this area are to be effective,

Bearing also in mind the principles of proper management of public affairs and public property, fairness, responsibility and equality before the law and the need to safeguard integrity and to foster a culture of rejection of corruption,

Commending the work of the Commission on Crime Prevention and Criminal Justice and the United Nations Office on Drugs and Crime in preventing and combating corruption,

Recalling the work carried out by other international and regional organizations in this field, including the activities of the African Union, the Council of Europe, the Customs Cooperation Council (also known as the World Customs Organization), the European Union, the League of Arab States, the Organisation for Economic Cooperation and Development and the Organization of American States,

Taking note with appreciation of multilateral instruments to prevent and combat corruption, including, inter alia, the Inter-American Convention against Corruption, adopted by the Organization of American States on 29 March 1996,[1] the Convention on the Fight against Corruption involving Officials of the European Communities or Officials of Member States of the European Union, adopted by the Council of the European Union on 26 May 1997,[2] the Convention on Combating Bribery of Foreign Public Officials in International Business Transactions, adopted by the Organisation for Economic Cooperation and Development on 21 November 1997,[3] the Criminal Law Convention on Corruption, adopted by the Committee of Ministers of the Council of Europe on 27 January 1999,[4] the Civil Law Convention on Corruption, adopted by the Committee of Ministers of the Council of Europe on 4 November 1999,[5] and the African Union Convention on Preventing and Combating Corruption, adopted by the Heads of State and Government of the African Union on 12 July 2003,

Welcoming the entry into force on 29 September 2003 of the United Nations Convention against Transnational Organized Crime,[6]

Have agreed as follows:

CHAPTER I

GENERAL PROVISIONS

Article 1

Statement of purpose

The purposes of this Convention are:

   a. To promote and strengthen measures to prevent and combat corruption more efficiently and effectively;

b. To promote, facilitate and support international cooperation and technical assistance in the prevention of and fight against corruption, including in asset recovery;

c. To promote integrity, accountability and proper management of public affairs and public property.

Article 2

Use of terms

For the purposes of this Convention:

a. "Public official" shall mean: (i) any person holding a legislative, executive, administrative or judicial office of a State Party, whether appointed or elected, whether permanent or temporary, whether paid or unpaid, irrespective of that person's seniority; (ii) any other person who performs a public function, including for a public agency or public enterprise, or provides a public service, as defined in the domestic law of the State Party and as applied in the pertinent area of law of that State Party; (iii) any other person defined as a "public official" in the domestic law of a State Party. However, for the purpose of some specific measures contained in chapter II of this Convention, "public official" may mean any person who performs a public function or provides a public service as defined in the domestic law of the State Party and as applied in the pertinent area of law of that State Party;

b. "Foreign public official" shall mean any person holding a legislative, executive, administrative or judicial office of a foreign country, whether appointed or elected; and any person exercising a public function for a foreign country, including for a public agency or public enterprise;

c. "Official of a public international organization" shall mean an international civil servant or any person who is authorized by such an organization to act on behalf of that organization;

d. "Property" shall mean assets of every kind, whether corporeal or incorporeal, movable or immovable, tangible or intangible, and legal documents or instruments evidencing title to or interest in such assets;

e. "Proceeds of crime" shall mean any property derived from or obtained, directly or indirectly, through the commission of an offence;

f. "Freezing" or "seizure" shall mean temporarily prohibiting the transfer, conversion, disposition or movement of property or temporarily assuming custody or control of property on the basis of an order issued by a court or other competent authority;

g. "Confiscation", which includes forfeiture where applicable, shall mean the permanent deprivation of property by order of a court or other competent authority;

h. "Predicate offence" shall mean any offence as a result of which proceeds have been generated that may become the subject of an offence as defined in article 23 of this Convention;

i.   "Controlled delivery" shall mean the technique of allowing illicit or suspect consignments to pass out of, through or into the territory of one or more States, with the knowledge and under the supervision of their competent authorities, with a view to the investigation of an offence and the identification of persons involved in the commission of the offence.

Article 3

Scope of application

1.   This Convention shall apply, in accordance with its terms, to the prevention, investigation and prosecution of corruption and to the freezing, seizure, confiscation and return of the proceeds of offences established in accordance with this Convention.

2.   For the purposes of implementing this Convention, it shall not be necessary, except as otherwise stated herein, for the offences set forth in it to result in damage or harm to state property.

Article 4

Protection of sovereignty

1.   States Parties shall carry out their obligations under this Convention in a manner consistent with the principles of sovereign equality and territorial integrity of States and that of non-intervention in the domestic affairs of other States.

2.   Nothing in this Convention shall entitle a State Party to undertake in the territory of another State the exercise of jurisdiction and performance of functions that are reserved exclusively for the authorities of that other State by its domestic law.

CHAPTER II

PREVENTIVE MEASURES

Article 5

Preventive anti-corruption policies and practices

1.   Each State Party shall, in accordance with the fundamental principles of its legal system, develop and implement or maintain effective, coordinated anti-corruption policies that promote the participation of society and reflect the principles of the rule of law, proper management of public affairs and public property, integrity, transparency and accountability.

2.   Each State Party shall endeavour to establish and promote effective practices aimed at the prevention of corruption.

3. Each State Party shall endeavour to periodically evaluate relevant legal instruments and administrative measures with a view to determining their adequacy to prevent and fight corruption.

4. States Parties shall, as appropriate and in accordance with the fundamental principles of their legal system, collaborate with each other and with relevant international and regional organizations in promoting and developing the measures referred to in this article. That collaboration may include participation in international programmes and projects aimed at the prevention of corruption.

Article 6

Preventive anti-corruption body or bodies

1. Each State Party shall, in accordance with the fundamental principles of its legal system, ensure the existence of a body or bodies, as appropriate, that prevent corruption by such means as:

    (a) Implementing the policies referred to in article 5 of this Convention and, where appropriate, overseeing and coordinating the implementation of those policies;

    (b) Increasing and disseminating knowledge about the prevention of corruption.

2. Each State Party shall grant the body or bodies referred to in paragraph 1 of this article the necessary independence, in accordance with the fundamental principles of its legal system, to enable the body or bodies to carry out its or their functions effectively and free from any undue influence. The necessary material resources and specialized staff, as well as the training that such staff may require to carry out their functions, should be provided.

3. Each State Party shall inform the Secretary-General of the United Nations of the name and address of the authority or authorities that may assist other States Parties in developing and implementing specific measures for the prevention of corruption.

Article 7

Public sector

1. Each State Party shall, where appropriate and in accordance with the fundamental principles of its legal system, endeavour to adopt, maintain and strengthen systems for the recruitment, hiring, retention, promotion and retirement of civil servants and, where appropriate, other non-elected public officials:

    (a) That are based on principles of efficiency, transparency and objective criteria such as merit, equity and aptitude;

    (b) That include adequate procedures for the selection and training of individuals for public positions considered especially vulnerable to corruption and the rotation, where appropriate, of such individuals to other positions;

    (c) That promote adequate remuneration and equitable pay scales, taking into account the level of economic development of the State Party;

(d) That promote education and training programmes to enable them to meet the requirements for the correct, honourable and proper performance of public functions and that provide them with specialized and appropriate training to enhance their awareness of the risks of corruption inherent in the performance of their functions. Such programmes may make reference to codes or standards of conduct in applicable areas.

2. Each State Party shall also consider adopting appropriate legislative and administrative measures, consistent with the objectives of this Convention and in accordance with the fundamental principles of its domestic law, to prescribe criteria concerning candidature for and election to public office.

3. Each State Party shall also consider taking appropriate legislative and administrative measures, consistent with the objectives of this Convention and in accordance with the fundamental principles of its domestic law, to enhance transparency in the funding of candidatures for elected public office and, where applicable, the funding of political parties.

4. Each State Party shall, in accordance with the fundamental principles of its domestic law, endeavour to adopt, maintain and strengthen systems that promote transparency and prevent conflicts of interest.

Article 8

Codes of conduct for public officials

1. In order to fight corruption, each State Party shall promote, inter alia, integrity, honesty and responsibility among its public officials, in accordance with the fundamental principles of its legal system.

2. In particular, each State Party shall endeavour to apply, within its own institutional and legal systems, codes or standards of conduct for the correct, honourable and proper performance of public functions.

3. For the purposes of implementing the provisions of this article, each State Party shall, where appropriate and in accordance with the fundamental principles of its legal system, take note of the relevant initiatives of regional, interregional and multilateral organizations, such as the International Code of Conduct for Public Officials contained in the annex to General Assembly resolution 51/59 of 12 December 1996.

4. Each State Party shall also consider, in accordance with the fundamental principles of its domestic law, establishing measures and systems to facilitate the reporting by public officials of acts of corruption to appropriate authorities, when such acts come to their notice in the performance of their functions.

5. Each State Party shall endeavour, where appropriate and in accordance with the fundamental principles of its domestic law, to establish measures and systems requiring public officials to make declarations to appropriate authorities regarding, inter alia, their outside activities, employment, investments, assets

and substantial gifts or benefits from which a conflict of interest may result with respect to their functions as public officials.

6. Each State Party shall consider taking, in accordance with the fundamental principles of its domestic law, disciplinary or other measures against public officials who violate the codes or standards established in accordance with this article.

Article 9

Public procurement and management of public finances

1. Each State Party shall, in accordance with the fundamental principles of its legal system, take the necessary steps to establish appropriate systems of procurement, based on transparency, competition and objective criteria in decision-making, that are effective, inter alia, in preventing corruption. Such systems, which may take into account appropriate threshold values in their application, shall address, inter alia:

    (a) The public distribution of information relating to procurement procedures and contracts, including information on invitations to tender and relevant or pertinent information on the award of contracts, allowing potential tenderers sufficient time to prepare and submit their tenders;

    (b) The establishment, in advance, of conditions for participation, including selection and award criteria and tendering rules, and their publication;

    (c) The use of objective and predetermined criteria for public procurement decisions, in order to facilitate the subsequent verification of the correct application of the rules or procedures;

    (d) An effective system of domestic review, including an effective system of appeal, to ensure legal recourse and remedies in the event that the rules or procedures established pursuant to this paragraph are not followed;

    (e) Where appropriate, measures to regulate matters regarding personnel responsible for procurement, such as declaration of interest in particular public procurements, screening procedures and training requirements.

2. Each State Party shall, in accordance with the fundamental principles of its legal system, take appropriate measures to promote transparency and accountability in the management of public finances. Such measures shall encompass, inter alia:

    (a) Procedures for the adoption of the national budget;

    (b) Timely reporting on revenue and expenditure;

    (c) A system of accounting and auditing standards and related oversight;

    (d) Effective and efficient systems of risk management and internal control; and

    (e) Where appropriate, corrective action in the case of failure to comply with the requirements established in this paragraph.

3. Each State Party shall take such civil and administrative measures as may be necessary, in accordance with the fundamental principles of its domestic law, to preserve the integrity of accounting books, records, financial statements or other documents related to public expenditure and revenue and to prevent the falsification of such documents.

Article 10

Public reporting

Taking into account the need to combat corruption, each State Party shall, in accordance with the fundamental principles of its domestic law, take such measures as may be necessary to enhance transparency in its public administration, including with regard to its organization, functioning and decision-making processes, where appropriate. Such measures may include, inter alia:

    (a) Adopting procedures or regulations allowing members of the general public to obtain, where appropriate, information on the organization, functioning and decision-making processes of its public administration and, with due regard for the protection of privacy and personal data, on decisions and legal acts that concern members of the public;

    (b) Simplifying administrative procedures, where appropriate, in order to facilitate public access to the competent decision-making authorities; and

    (c) Publishing information, which may include periodic reports on the risks of corruption in its public administration.

Article 11

Measures relating to the judiciary and prosecution services

1. Bearing in mind the independence of the judiciary and its crucial role in combating corruption, each State Party shall, in accordance with the fundamental principles of its legal system and without prejudice to judicial independence, take measures to strengthen integrity and to prevent opportunities for corruption among members of the judiciary. Such measures may include rules with respect to the conduct of members of the judiciary.

2. Measures to the same effect as those taken pursuant to paragraph 1 of this article may be introduced and applied within the prosecution service in those States Parties where it does not form part of the judiciary but enjoys independence similar to that of the judicial service.

Article 12

Private sector

1. Each State Party shall take measures, in accordance with the fundamental principles of its domestic law, to prevent corruption involving the private sector, enhance accounting and auditing standards in the private sector and, where appropriate, provide effective, proportionate and dissuasive civil, administrative or criminal penalties for failure to comply with such measures.

2. Measures to achieve these ends may include, inter alia:

    (a) Promoting cooperation between law enforcement agencies and relevant private entities;

    (b) Promoting the development of standards and procedures designed to safeguard the integrity of relevant private entities, including codes of conduct for the correct, honourable and proper performance of the activities of business and all relevant professions and the prevention of conflicts of interest, and for the promotion of the use of good commercial practices among businesses and in the contractual relations of businesses with the State;

  (c) Promoting transparency among private entities, including, where appropriate, measures regarding the identity of legal and natural persons involved in the establishment and management of corporate entities;

  (d) Preventing the misuse of procedures regulating private entities, including procedures regarding subsidies and licences granted by public authorities for commercial activities;

  (e) Preventing conflicts of interest by imposing restrictions, as appropriate and for a reasonable period of time, on the professional activities of former public officials or on the employment of public officials by the private sector after their resignation or retirement, where such activities or employment relate directly to the functions held or supervised by those public officials during their tenure;

  (f) Ensuring that private enterprises, taking into account their structure and size, have sufficient internal auditing controls to assist in preventing and detecting acts of corruption and that the accounts and required financial statements of such private enterprises are subject to appropriate auditing and certification procedures.

3. In order to prevent corruption, each State Party shall take such measures as may be necessary, in accordance with its domestic laws and regulations regarding the maintenance of books and records, financial statement disclosures and accounting and auditing standards, to prohibit the following acts carried out for the purpose of committing any of the offences established in accordance with this Convention:

  (a) The establishment of off-the-books accounts;

  (b) The making of off-the-books or inadequately identified transactions;

  (c) The recording of non-existent expenditure;

  (d) The entry of liabilities with incorrect identification of their objects;

  (e) The use of false documents; and

  (f) The intentional destruction of bookkeeping documents earlier than foreseen by the law.

4. Each State Party shall disallow the tax deductibility of expenses that constitute bribes, the latter being one of the constituent elements of the offences established in accordance with articles 15 and 16 of this Convention and, where appropriate, other expenses incurred in furtherance of corrupt conduct.

Article 13

Participation of society

1. Each State Party shall take appropriate measures, within its means and in accordance with fundamental principles of its domestic law, to promote the active participation of individuals and groups outside the public sector, such as civil society, non-governmental organizations and community-based

organizations, in the prevention of and the fight against corruption and to raise public awareness regarding the existence, causes and gravity of and the threat posed by corruption. This participation should be strengthened by such measures as:

(a) Enhancing the transparency of and promoting the contribution of the public to decision-making processes;

(b) Ensuring that the public has effective access to information;

(c) Undertaking public information activities that contribute to non-tolerance of corruption, as well as public education programmes, including school and university curricula;

(d) Respecting, promoting and protecting the freedom to seek, receive, publish and disseminate information concerning corruption. That freedom may be subject to certain restrictions, but these shall only be such as are provided for by law and are necessary:

(i) For respect of the rights or reputations of others;

(ii) For the protection of national security or *ordre public* or of public health or morals.

2. Each State Party shall take appropriate measures to ensure that the relevant anti-corruption bodies referred to in this Convention are known to the public and shall provide access to such bodies, where appropriate, for the reporting, including anonymously, of any incidents that may be considered to constitute an offence established in accordance with this Convention.

Article 14

Measures to prevent money-laundering

1. Each State Party shall:

(a) Institute a comprehensive domestic regulatory and supervisory regime for banks and non-bank financial institutions, including natural or legal persons that provide formal or informal services for the transmission of money or value and, where appropriate, other bodies particularly susceptible to money-laundering, within its competence, in order to deter and detect all forms of money-laundering, which regime shall emphasize requirements for customer and, where appropriate, beneficial owner identification, record-keeping and the reporting of suspicious transactions;

(b) Without prejudice to article 46 of this Convention, ensure that administrative, regulatory, law enforcement and other authorities dedicated to combating money-laundering (including, where appropriate under domestic law, judicial authorities) have the ability to cooperate and exchange information at the national and international levels within the conditions prescribed by its domestic law and, to that end, shall consider the establishment of a financial intelligence unit to serve as a national centre for the collection, analysis and dissemination of information regarding potential money-laundering.

2. States Parties shall consider implementing feasible measures to detect and monitor the movement of cash and appropriate negotiable instruments across

their borders, subject to safeguards to ensure proper use of information and without impeding in any way the movement of legitimate capital. Such measures may include a requirement that individuals and businesses report the cross-border transfer of substantial quantities of cash and appropriate negotiable instruments.

3. States Parties shall consider implementing appropriate and feasible measures to require financial institutions, including money remitters:

   (a) To include on forms for the electronic transfer of funds and related messages accurate and meaningful information on the originator;

   (b) To maintain such information throughout the payment chain; and

   (c) To apply enhanced scrutiny to transfers of funds that do not contain complete information on the originator.

4. In establishing a domestic regulatory and supervisory regime under the terms of this article, and without prejudice to any other article of this Convention, States Parties are called upon to use as a guideline the relevant initiatives of regional, interregional and multilateral organizations against money-laundering.

5. States Parties shall endeavour to develop and promote global, regional, sub-regional and bilateral cooperation among judicial, law enforcement and financial regulatory authorities in order to combat money-laundering.

CHAPTER III

CRIMINALIZATION AND LAW ENFORCEMENT

Article 15

Bribery of national public officials

Each State Party shall adopt such legislative and other measures as may be necessary to establish as criminal offences, when committed intentionally:

   (a) The promise, offering or giving, to a public official, directly or indirectly, of an undue advantage, for the official himself or herself or another person or entity, in order that the official act or refrain from acting in the exercise of his or her official duties;

   (b) The solicitation or acceptance by a public official, directly or indirectly, of an undue advantage, for the official himself or herself or another person or entity, in order that the official act or refrain from acting in the exercise of his or her official duties.

Article 16

Bribery of foreign public officials and officials of public international organizations

1. Each State Party shall adopt such legislative and other measures as may be necessary to establish as a criminal offence, when committed intentionally,

the promise, offering or giving to a foreign public official or an official of a public international organization, directly or indirectly, of an undue advantage, for the official himself or herself or another person or entity, in order that the official act or refrain from acting in the exercise of his or her official duties, in order to obtain or retain business or other undue advantage in relation to the conduct of international business.

2. Each State Party shall consider adopting such legislative and other measures as may be necessary to establish as a criminal offence, when committed intentionally, the solicitation or acceptance by a foreign public official or an official of a public international organization, directly or indirectly, of an undue advantage, for the official himself or herself or another person or entity, in order that the official act or refrain from acting in the exercise of his or her official duties.

Article 17

Embezzlement, misappropriation or other diversion of property by a public official

Each State Party shall adopt such legislative and other measures as may be necessary to establish as criminal offences, when committed intentionally, the embezzlement, misappropriation or other diversion by a public official for his or her benefit or for the benefit of another person or entity, of any property, public or private funds or securities or any other thing of value entrusted to the public official by virtue of his or her position.

Article 18

Trading in influence

Each State Party shall consider adopting such legislative and other measures as may be necessary to establish as criminal offences, when committed intentionally:

(a) The promise, offering or giving to a public official or any other person, directly or indirectly, of an undue advantage in order that the public official or the person abuse his or her real or supposed influence with a view to obtaining from an administration or public authority of the State Party an undue advantage for the original instigator of the act or for any other person;

(b) The solicitation or acceptance by a public official or any other person, directly or indirectly, of an undue advantage for himself or herself or for another person in order that the public official or the person abuse his or her real or supposed influence with a view to obtaining from an administration or public authority of the State Party an undue advantage.

Article 19

Abuse of functions

Each State Party shall consider adopting such legislative and other measures as may be necessary to establish as a criminal offence, when committed intentionally,

the abuse of functions or position, that is, the performance of or failure to perform an act, in violation of laws, by a public official in the discharge of his or her
functions, for the purpose of obtaining an undue advantage for himself or herself
or for another person or entity.

Article 20

Illicit enrichment

Subject to its constitution and the fundamental principles of its legal system, each
State Party shall consider adopting such legislative and other measures as may be
necessary to establish as a criminal offence, when committed intentionally, illicit
enrichment, that is, a significant increase in the assets of a public official that he
or she cannot reasonably explain in relation to his or her lawful income.

Article 21

Bribery in the private sector

Each State Party shall consider adopting such legislative and other measures as
may be necessary to establish as criminal offences, when committed intentionally
in the course of economic, financial or commercial activities:

(a) The promise, offering or giving, directly or indirectly, of an undue
advantage to any person who directs or works, in any capacity, for a private sector entity, for the person himself or herself or for another person, in order that he or she, in breach of his or her duties, act or refrain
from acting;

(b) The solicitation or acceptance, directly or indirectly, of an undue advantage by any person who directs or works, in any capacity, for a private sector entity, for the person himself or herself or for another person, in order
that he or she, in breach of his or her duties, act or refrain from acting.

Article 22

Embezzlement of property
in the private sector

Each State Party shall consider adopting such legislative and other measures as
may be necessary to establish as a criminal offence, when committed intentionally in the course of economic, financial or commercial activities, embezzlement
by a person who directs or works, in any capacity, in a private sector entity of any
property, private funds or securities or any other thing of value entrusted to him
or her by virtue of his or her position.

Article 23

Laundering of proceeds of crime

1. Each State Party shall adopt, in accordance with fundamental principles of its
domestic law, such legislative and other measures as may be necessary to

establish as criminal offences, when committed intentionally:

(a) (i) The conversion or transfer of property, knowing that such property is the proceeds of crime, for the purpose of concealing or disguising the illicit origin of the property or of helping any person who is involved in the commission of the predicate offence to evade the legal consequences of his or her action;

(ii) The concealment or disguise of the true nature, source, location, disposition, movement or ownership of or rights with respect to property, knowing that such property is the proceeds of crime;

(b) Subject to the basic concepts of its legal system:

(i) The acquisition, possession or use of property, knowing, at the time of receipt, that such property is the proceeds of crime;

(ii) Participation in, association with or conspiracy to commit, attempts to commit and aiding, abetting, facilitating and counselling the commission of any of the offences established in accordance with this article.

2. For purposes of implementing or applying paragraph 1 of this article:

(a) Each State Party shall seek to apply paragraph 1 of this article to the widest range of predicate offences;

(b) Each State Party shall include as predicate offences at a minimum a comprehensive range of criminal offences established in accordance with this Convention;

(c) For the purposes of subparagraph (b) above, predicate offences shall include offences committed both within and outside the jurisdiction of the State Party in question. However, offences committed outside the jurisdiction of a State Party shall constitute predicate offences only when the relevant conduct is a criminal offence under the domestic law of the State where it is committed and would be a criminal offence under the domestic law of the State Party implementing or applying this article had it been committed there;

(d) Each State Party shall furnish copies of its laws that give effect to this article and of any subsequent changes to such laws or a description thereof to the Secretary-General of the United Nations;

(e) If required by fundamental principles of the domestic law of a State Party, it may be provided that the offences set forth in paragraph 1 of this article do not apply to the persons who committed the predicate offence.

Article 24

Concealment

Without prejudice to the provisions of article 23 of this Convention, each State Party shall consider adopting such legislative and other measures as may be necessary to establish as a criminal offence, when committed intentionally after the commission of any of the offences established in accordance with this Convention without having participated in such offences, the concealment or continued retention of property when the person involved knows that such property is the result of any of the offences established in accordance with this Convention.

Article 25

Obstruction of justice

Each State Party shall adopt such legislative and other measures as may be necessary to establish as criminal offences, when committed intentionally:

(a) The use of physical force, threats or intimidation or the promise, offering or giving of an undue advantage to induce false testimony or to interfere in the giving of testimony or the production of evidence in a proceeding in relation to the commission of offences established in accordance with this Convention;

(b) The use of physical force, threats or intimidation to interfere with the exercise of official duties by a justice or law enforcement official in relation to the commission of offences established in accordance with this Convention. Nothing in this subparagraph shall prejudice the right of States Parties to have legislation that protects other categories of public official.

Article 26

Liability of legal persons

1. Each State Party shall adopt such measures as may be necessary, consistent with its legal principles, to establish the liability of legal persons for participation in the offences established in accordance with this Convention.

2. Subject to the legal principles of the State Party, the liability of legal persons may be criminal, civil or administrative.

3. Such liability shall be without prejudice to the criminal liability of the natural persons who have committed the offences.

4. Each State Party shall, in particular, ensure that legal persons held liable in accordance with this article are subject to effective, proportionate and dissuasive criminal or non-criminal sanctions, including monetary sanctions.

Article 27

Participation and attempt

1. Each State Party shall adopt such legislative and other measures as may be necessary to establish as a criminal offence, in accordance with its domestic law, participation in any capacity such as an accomplice, assistant or instigator in an offence established in accordance with this Convention.

2. Each State Party may adopt such legislative and other measures as may be necessary to establish as a criminal offence, in accordance with its domestic law, any attempt to commit an offence established in accordance with this Convention.

3. Each State Party may adopt such legislative and other measures as may be necessary to establish as a criminal offence, in accordance with its domestic law, the preparation for an offence established in accordance with this Convention.

Article 28

Knowledge, intent and purpose as elements of an offence

Knowledge, intent or purpose required as an element of an offence established in accordance with this Convention may be inferred from objective factual circumstances.

Article 29

Statute of limitations

Each State Party shall, where appropriate, establish under its domestic law a long statute of limitations period in which to commence proceedings for any offence established in accordance with this Convention and establish a longer statute of limitations period or provide for the suspension of the statute of limitations where the alleged offender has evaded the administration of justice.

Article 30

Prosecution, adjudication and sanctions

1. Each State Party shall make the commission of an offence established in accordance with this Convention liable to sanctions that take into account the gravity of that offence.
2. Each State Party shall take such measures as may be necessary to establish or maintain, in accordance with its legal system and constitutional principles, an appropriate balance between any immunities or jurisdictional privileges accorded to its public officials for the performance of their functions and the possibility, when necessary, of effectively investigating, prosecuting and adjudicating offences established in accordance with this Convention.
3. Each State Party shall endeavour to ensure that any discretionary legal powers under its domestic law relating to the prosecution of persons for offences established in accordance with this Convention are exercised to maximize the effectiveness of law enforcement measures in respect of those offences and with due regard to the need to deter the commission of such offences.
4. In the case of offences established in accordance with this Convention, each State Party shall take appropriate measures, in accordance with its domestic law and with due regard to the rights of the defence, to seek to ensure that conditions imposed in connection with decisions on release pending trial or appeal take into consideration the need to ensure the presence of the defendant at subsequent criminal proceedings.
5. Each State Party shall take into account the gravity of the offences concerned when considering the eventuality of early release or parole of persons convicted of such offences.
6. Each State Party, to the extent consistent with the fundamental principles of its legal system, shall consider establishing procedures through which a public official accused of an offence established in accordance with this Convention may, where appropriate, be removed, suspended or reassigned by the appro-

priate authority, bearing in mind respect for the principle of the presumption of innocence.

7. Where warranted by the gravity of the offence, each State Party, to the extent consistent with the fundamental principles of its legal system, shall consider establishing procedures for the disqualification, by court order or any other appropriate means, for a period of time determined by its domestic law, of persons convicted of offences established in accordance with this Convention from:

    (a) Holding public office; and

    (b) Holding office in an enterprise owned in whole or in part by the State.

8. Paragraph 1 of this article shall be without prejudice to the exercise of disciplinary powers by the competent authorities against civil servants.

9. Nothing contained in this Convention shall affect the principle that the description of the offences established in accordance with this Convention and of the applicable legal defences or other legal principles controlling the lawfulness of conduct is reserved to the domestic law of a State Party and that such offences shall be prosecuted and punished in accordance with that law.

10. States Parties shall endeavour to promote the reintegration into society of persons convicted of offences established in accordance with this Convention.

Article 31

Freezing, seizure and confiscation

1. Each State Party shall take, to the greatest extent possible within its domestic legal system, such measures as may be necessary to enable confiscation of:

    (a) Proceeds of crime derived from offences established in accordance with this Convention or property the value of which corresponds to that of such proceeds;

    (b) Property, equipment or other instrumentalities used in or destined for use in offences established in accordance with this Convention.

2. Each State Party shall take such measures as may be necessary to enable the identification, tracing, freezing or seizure of any item referred to in paragraph 1 of this article for the purpose of eventual confiscation.

3. Each State Party shall adopt, in accordance with its domestic law, such legislative and other measures as may be necessary to regulate the administration by the competent authorities of frozen, seized or confiscated property covered in paragraphs 1 and 2 of this article.

4. If such proceeds of crime have been transformed or converted, in part or in full, into other property, such property shall be liable to the measures referred to in this article instead of the proceeds.

5. If such proceeds of crime have been intermingled with property acquired from legitimate sources, such property shall, without prejudice to any powers relating to freezing or seizure, be liable to confiscation up to the assessed value of the intermingled proceeds.

6. Income or other benefits derived from such proceeds of crime, from property into which such proceeds of crime have been transformed or converted

or from property with which such proceeds of crime have been intermingled shall also be liable to the measures referred to in this article, in the same manner and to the same extent as proceeds of crime.

7. For the purpose of this article and article 55 of this Convention, each State Party shall empower its courts or other competent authorities to order that bank, financial or commercial records be made available or seized. A State Party shall not decline to act under the provisions of this paragraph on the ground of bank secrecy.

8. States Parties may consider the possibility of requiring that an offender demonstrate the lawful origin of such alleged proceeds of crime or other property liable to confiscation, to the extent that such a requirement is consistent with the fundamental principles of their domestic law and with the nature of judicial and other proceedings.

9. The provisions of this article shall not be so construed as to prejudice the rights of bona fide third parties.

10. Nothing contained in this article shall affect the principle that the measures to which it refers shall be defined and implemented in accordance with and subject to the provisions of the domestic law of a State Party.

Article 32

Protection of witnesses, experts and victims

1. Each State Party shall take appropriate measures in accordance with its domestic legal system and within its means to provide effective protection from potential retaliation or intimidation for witnesses and experts who give testimony concerning offences established in accordance with this Convention and, as appropriate, for their relatives and other persons close to them.

2. The measures envisaged in paragraph 1 of this article may include, inter alia, without prejudice to the rights of the defendant, including the right to due process:

   (a) Establishing procedures for the physical protection of such persons, such as, to the extent necessary and feasible, relocating them and permitting, where appropriate, non-disclosure or limitations on the disclosure of information concerning the identity and whereabouts of such persons;

   (b) Providing evidentiary rules to permit witnesses and experts to give testimony in a manner that ensures the safety of such persons, such as permitting testimony to be given through the use of communications technology such as video or other adequate means.

3. States Parties shall consider entering into agreements or arrangements with other States for the relocation of persons referred to in paragraph 1 of this article.

4. The provisions of this article shall also apply to victims insofar as they are witnesses.

5. Each State Party shall, subject to its domestic law, enable the views and concerns of victims to be presented and considered at appropriate stages of

criminal proceedings against offenders in a manner not prejudicial to the rights of the defence.

Article 33

Protection of reporting persons

Each State Party shall consider incorporating into its domestic legal system appropriate measures to provide protection against any unjustified treatment for any person who reports in good faith and on reasonable grounds to the competent authorities any facts concerning offences established in accordance with this Convention.

Article 34

Consequences of acts of corruption

With due regard to the rights of third parties acquired in good faith, each State Party shall take measures, in accordance with the fundamental principles of its domestic law, to address consequences of corruption. In this context, States Parties may consider corruption a relevant factor in legal proceedings to annul or rescind a contract, withdraw a concession or other similar instrument or take any other remedial action.

Article 35

Compensation for damage

Each State Party shall take such measures as may be necessary, in accordance with principles of its domestic law, to ensure that entities or persons who have suffered damage as a result of an act of corruption have the right to initiate legal proceedings against those responsible for that damage in order to obtain compensation.

Article 36

Specialized authorities

Each State Party shall, in accordance with the fundamental principles of its legal system, ensure the existence of a body or bodies or persons specialized in combating corruption through law enforcement. Such body or bodies or persons shall be granted the necessary independence, in accordance with the fundamental principles of the legal system of the State Party, to be able to carry out their functions effectively and without any undue influence. Such persons or staff of such body or bodies should have the appropriate training and resources to carry out their tasks.

Article 37

Cooperation with law enforcement authorities

1. Each State Party shall take appropriate measures to encourage persons who participate or who have participated in the commission of an offence

established in accordance with this Convention to supply information useful to competent authorities for investigative and evidentiary purposes and to provide factual, specific help to competent authorities that may contribute to depriving offenders of the proceeds of crime and to recovering such proceeds.

2. Each State Party shall consider providing for the possibility, in appropriate cases, of mitigating punishment of an accused person who provides substantial cooperation in the investigation or prosecution of an offence established in accordance with this Convention.

3. Each State Party shall consider providing for the possibility, in accordance with fundamental principles of its domestic law, of granting immunity from prosecution to a person who provides substantial cooperation in the investigation or prosecution of an offence established in accordance with this Convention.

4. Protection of such persons shall be, mutatis mutandis, as provided for in article 32 of this Convention.

5. Where a person referred to in paragraph 1 of this article located in one State Party can provide substantial cooperation to the competent authorities of another State Party, the States Parties concerned may consider entering into agreements or arrangements, in accordance with their domestic law, concerning the potential provision by the other State Party of the treatment set forth in paragraphs 2 and 3 of this article.

Article 38

Cooperation between national authorities

Each State Party shall take such measures as may be necessary to encourage, in accordance with its domestic law, cooperation between, on the one hand, its public authorities, as well as its public officials, and, on the other hand, its authorities responsible for investigating and prosecuting criminal offences. Such cooperation may include:

(a) Informing the latter authorities, on their own initiative, where there are reasonable grounds to believe that any of the offences established in accordance with articles 15, 21 and 23 of this Convention has been committed; or

(b) Providing, upon request, to the latter authorities all necessary information.

Article 39

Cooperation between national authorities and the private sector

1. Each State Party shall take such measures as may be necessary to encourage, in accordance with its domestic law, cooperation between national investigating and prosecuting authorities and entities of the private sector, in particular financial institutions, relating to matters involving the commission of offences established in accordance with this Convention.

2. Each State Party shall consider encouraging its nationals and other persons with a habitual residence in its territory to report to the national investigating and prosecuting authorities the commission of an offence established in accordance with this Convention.

Article 40

Bank secrecy

Each State Party shall ensure that, in the case of domestic criminal investigations of offences established in accordance with this Convention, there are appropriate mechanisms available within its domestic legal system to overcome obstacles that may arise out of the application of bank secrecy laws.

Article 41

Criminal record

Each State Party may adopt such legislative or other measures as may be necessary to take into consideration, under such terms as and for the purpose that it deems appropriate, any previous conviction in another State of an alleged offender for the purpose of using such information in criminal proceedings relating to an offence established in accordance with this Convention.

Article 42

Jurisdiction

1. Each State Party shall adopt such measures as may be necessary to establish its jurisdiction over the offences established in accordance with this Convention when:
    (a) The offence is committed in the territory of that State Party; or
    (b) The offence is committed on board a vessel that is flying the flag of that State Party or an aircraft that is registered under the laws of that State Party at the time that the offence is committed.
2. Subject to article 4 of this Convention, a State Party may also establish its jurisdiction over any such offence when:
    (a) The offence is committed against a national of that State Party; or
    (b) The offence is committed by a national of that State Party or a stateless person who has his or her habitual residence in its territory; or
    (c) The offence is one of those established in accordance with article 23, paragraph 1 (b) (ii), of this Convention and is committed outside its territory with a view to the commission of an offence established in accordance with article 23, paragraph 1 (a) (i) or (ii) or (b) (i), of this Convention within its territory; or
    (d) The offence is committed against the State Party.
3. For the purposes of article 44 of this Convention, each State Party shall take such measures as may be necessary to establish its jurisdiction over the offences established in accordance with this Convention when the alleged

offender is present in its territory and it does not extradite such person solely on the ground that he or she is one of its nationals.

4. Each State Party may also take such measures as may be necessary to establish its jurisdiction over the offences established in accordance with this Convention when the alleged offender is present in its territory and it does not extradite him or her.

5. If a State Party exercising its jurisdiction under paragraph 1 or 2 of this article has been notified, or has otherwise learned, that any other States Parties are conducting an investigation, prosecution or judicial proceeding in respect of the same conduct, the competent authorities of those States Parties shall, as appropriate, consult one another with a view to coordinating their actions.

6. Without prejudice to norms of general international law, this Convention shall not exclude the exercise of any criminal jurisdiction established by a State Party in accordance with its domestic law.

CHAPTER IV

INTERNATIONAL COOPERATION

Article 43

International cooperation

1. States Parties shall cooperate in criminal matters in accordance with articles 44 to 50 of this Convention. Where appropriate and consistent with their domestic legal system, States Parties shall consider assisting each other in investigations of and proceedings in civil and administrative matters relating to corruption.

2. In matters of international cooperation, whenever dual criminality is considered a requirement, it shall be deemed fulfilled irrespective of whether the laws of the requested State Party place the offence within the same category of offence or denominate the offence by the same terminology as the requesting State Party, if the conduct underlying the offence for which assistance is sought is a criminal offence under the laws of both States Parties.

Article 44

Extradition

1. This article shall apply to the offences established in accordance with this Convention where the person who is the subject of the request for extradition is present in the territory of the requested State Party, provided that the offence for which extradition is sought is punishable under the domestic law of both the requesting State Party and the requested State Party.

2. Notwithstanding the provisions of paragraph 1 of this article, a State Party whose law so permits may grant the extradition of a person for any of the offences covered by this Convention that are not punishable under its own domestic law.

3. If the request for extradition includes several separate offences, at least one of which is extraditable under this article and some of which are not extra-

ditable by reason of their period of imprisonment but are related to offences established in accordance with this Convention, the requested State Party may apply this article also in respect of those offences.

4. Each of the offences to which this article applies shall be deemed to be included as an extraditable offence in any extradition treaty existing between States Parties. States Parties undertake to include such offences as extraditable offences in every extradition treaty to be concluded between them. A State Party whose law so permits, in case it uses this Convention as the basis for extradition, shall not consider any of the offences established in accordance with this Convention to be a political offence.

5. If a State Party that makes extradition conditional on the existence of a treaty receives a request for extradition from another State Party with which it has no extradition treaty, it may consider this Convention the legal basis for extradition in respect of any offence to which this article applies.

6. A State Party that makes extradition conditional on the existence of a treaty shall:

   (a) At the time of deposit of its instrument of ratification, acceptance or approval of or accession to this Convention, inform the Secretary-General of the United Nations whether it will take this Convention as the legal basis for cooperation on extradition with other States Parties to this Convention; and

   (b) If it does not take this Convention as the legal basis for cooperation on extradition, seek, where appropriate, to conclude treaties on extradition with other States Parties to this Convention in order to implement this article.

7. States Parties that do not make extradition conditional on the existence of a treaty shall recognize offences to which this article applies as extraditable offences between themselves.

8. Extradition shall be subject to the conditions provided for by the domestic law of the requested State Party or by applicable extradition treaties, including, inter alia, conditions in relation to the minimum penalty requirement for extradition and the grounds upon which the requested State Party may refuse extradition.

9. States Parties shall, subject to their domestic law, endeavour to expedite extradition procedures and to simplify evidentiary requirements relating thereto in respect of any offence to which this article applies.

10. Subject to the provisions of its domestic law and its extradition treaties, the requested State Party may, upon being satisfied that the circumstances so warrant and are urgent and at the request of the requesting State Party, take a person whose extradition is sought and who is present in its territory into custody or take other appropriate measures to ensure his or her presence at extradition proceedings.

11. A State Party in whose territory an alleged offender is found, if it does not extradite such person in respect of an offence to which this article applies solely on the ground that he or she is one of its nationals, shall, at the request of the State Party seeking extradition, be obliged to submit the case without undue delay to its competent authorities for the purpose of prosecution. Those authorities shall take their decision and conduct their proceedings in

the same manner as in the case of any other offence of a grave nature under the domestic law of that State Party. The States Parties concerned shall cooperate with each other, in particular on procedural and evidentiary aspects, to ensure the efficiency of such prosecution.

12. Whenever a State Party is permitted under its domestic law to extradite or otherwise surrender one of its nationals only upon the condition that the person will be returned to that State Party to serve the sentence imposed as a result of the trial or proceedings for which the extradition or surrender of the person was sought and that State Party and the State Party seeking the extradition of the person agree with this option and other terms that they may deem appropriate, such conditional extradition or surrender shall be sufficient to discharge the obligation set forth in paragraph 11 of this article.

13. If extradition, sought for purposes of enforcing a sentence, is refused because the person sought is a national of the requested State Party, the requested State Party shall, if its domestic law so permits and in conformity with the requirements of such law, upon application of the requesting State Party, consider the enforcement of the sentence imposed under the domestic law of the requesting State Party or the remainder thereof.

14. Any person regarding whom proceedings are being carried out in connection with any of the offences to which this article applies shall be guaranteed fair treatment at all stages of the proceedings, including enjoyment of all the rights and guarantees provided by the domestic law of the State Party in the territory of which that person is present.

15. Nothing in this Convention shall be interpreted as imposing an obligation to extradite if the requested State Party has substantial grounds for believing that the request has been made for the purpose of prosecuting or punishing a person on account of that person's sex, race, religion, nationality, ethnic origin or political opinions or that compliance with the request would cause prejudice to that person's position for any one of these reasons.

16. States Parties may not refuse a request for extradition on the sole ground that the offence is also considered to involve fiscal matters.

17. Before refusing extradition, the requested State Party shall, where appropriate, consult with the requesting State Party to provide it with ample opportunity to present its opinions and to provide information relevant to its allegation.

18. States Parties shall seek to conclude bilateral and multilateral agreements or arrangements to carry out or to enhance the effectiveness of extradition.

Article 45

Transfer of sentenced persons

States Parties may consider entering into bilateral or multilateral agreements or arrangements on the transfer to their territory of persons sentenced to imprisonment or other forms of deprivation of liberty for offences established in accordance with this Convention in order that they may complete their sentences there.

Article 46

Mutual legal assistance

1. States Parties shall afford one another the widest measure of mutual legal assistance in investigations, prosecutions and judicial proceedings in relation to the offences covered by this Convention.

2. Mutual legal assistance shall be afforded to the fullest extent possible under relevant laws, treaties, agreements and arrangements of the requested State Party with respect to investigations, prosecutions and judicial proceedings in relation to the offences for which a legal person may be held liable in accordance with article 26 of this Convention in the requesting State Party.

3. Mutual legal assistance to be afforded in accordance with this article may be requested for any of the following purposes:

   (a) Taking evidence or statements from persons;

   (b) Effecting service of judicial documents;

   (c) Executing searches and seizures, and freezing;

   (d) Examining objects and sites;

   (e) Providing information, evidentiary items and expert evaluations;

   (f) Providing originals or certified copies of relevant documents and records, including government, bank, financial, corporate or business records;

   (g) Identifying or tracing proceeds of crime, property, instrumentalities or other things for evidentiary purposes;

   (h) Facilitating the voluntary appearance of persons in the requesting State Party;

   (i) Any other type of assistance that is not contrary to the domestic law of the requested State Party;

   (j) Identifying, freezing and tracing proceeds of crime in accordance with the provisions of chapter V of this Convention;

   (k) The recovery of assets, in accordance with the provisions of chapter V of this Convention.

4. Without prejudice to domestic law, the competent authorities of a State Party may, without prior request, transmit information relating to criminal matters to a competent authority in another State Party where they believe that such information could assist the authority in undertaking or successfully concluding inquiries and criminal proceedings or could result in a request formulated by the latter State Party pursuant to this Convention.

5. The transmission of information pursuant to paragraph 4 of this article shall be without prejudice to inquiries and criminal proceedings in the State of the competent authorities providing the information. The competent authorities receiving the information shall comply with a request that said information remain confidential, even temporarily, or with restrictions on its use. However, this shall not prevent the receiving State Party from disclosing in its proceedings information that is exculpatory to an accused person. In such a case, the receiving State Party shall notify the transmitting State Party prior to the disclosure and, if so requested, consult with the transmitting State Party. If, in

an exceptional case, advance notice is not possible, the receiving State Party shall inform the transmitting State Party of the disclosure without delay.

6. The provisions of this article shall not affect the obligations under any other treaty, bilateral or multilateral, that governs or will govern, in whole or in part, mutual legal assistance.

7. Paragraphs 9 to 29 of this article shall apply to requests made pursuant to this article if the States Parties in question are not bound by a treaty of mutual legal assistance. If those States Parties are bound by such a treaty, the corresponding provisions of that treaty shall apply unless the States Parties agree to apply paragraphs 9 to 29 of this article in lieu thereof. States Parties are strongly encouraged to apply those paragraphs if they facilitate cooperation.

8. States Parties shall not decline to render mutual legal assistance pursuant to this article on the ground of bank secrecy.

9. (a) A requested State Party, in responding to a request for assistance pursuant to this article in the absence of dual criminality, shall take into account the purposes of this Convention, as set forth in article 1;

   (b) States Parties may decline to render assistance pursuant to this article on the ground of absence of dual criminality. However, a requested State Party shall, where consistent with the basic concepts of its legal system, render assistance that does not involve coercive action. Such assistance may be refused when requests involve matters of a de minimis nature or matters for which the cooperation or assistance sought is available under other provisions of this Convention;

   (c) Each State Party may consider adopting such measures as may be necessary to enable it to provide a wider scope of assistance pursuant to this article in the absence of dual criminality.

10. A person who is being detained or is serving a sentence in the territory of one State Party whose presence in another State Party is requested for purposes of identification, testimony or otherwise providing assistance in obtaining evidence for investigations, prosecutions or judicial proceedings in relation to offences covered by this Convention may be transferred if the following conditions are met:

    (a) The person freely gives his or her informed consent;

    (b) The competent authorities of both States Parties agree, subject to such conditions as those States Parties may deem appropriate.

11. For the purposes of paragraph 10 of this article:

    (a) The State Party to which the person is transferred shall have the authority and obligation to keep the person transferred in custody, unless otherwise requested or authorized by the State Party from which the person was transferred;

    (b) The State Party to which the person is transferred shall without delay implement its obligation to return the person to the custody of the State Party from which the person was transferred as agreed beforehand, or as otherwise agreed, by the competent authorities of both States Parties;

(c) The State Party to which the person is transferred shall not require the State Party from which the person was transferred to initiate extradition proceedings for the return of the person;

(d) The person transferred shall receive credit for service of the sentence being served in the State from which he or she was transferred for time spent in the custody of the State Party to which he or she was transferred.

12. Unless the State Party from which a person is to be transferred in accordance with paragraphs 10 and 11 of this article so agrees, that person, whatever his or her nationality, shall not be prosecuted, detained, punished or subjected to any other restriction of his or her personal liberty in the territory of the State to which that person is transferred in respect of acts, omissions or convictions prior to his or her departure from the territory of the State from which he or she was transferred.

13. Each State Party shall designate a central authority that shall have the responsibility and power to receive requests for mutual legal assistance and either to execute them or to transmit them to the competent authorities for execution. Where a State Party has a special region or territory with a separate system of mutual legal assistance, it may designate a distinct central authority that shall have the same function for that region or territory. Central authorities shall ensure the speedy and proper execution or transmission of the requests received. Where the central authority transmits the request to a competent authority for execution, it shall encourage the speedy and proper execution of the request by the competent authority. The Secretary-General of the United Nations shall be notified of the central authority designated for this purpose at the time each State Party deposits its instrument of ratification, acceptance or approval of or accession to this Convention. Requests for mutual legal assistance and any communication related thereto shall be transmitted to the central authorities designated by the States Parties. This requirement shall be without prejudice to the right of a State Party to require that such requests and communications be addressed to it through diplomatic channels and, in urgent circumstances, where the States Parties agree, through the International Criminal Police Organization, if possible.

14. Requests shall be made in writing or, where possible, by any means capable of producing a written record, in a language acceptable to the requested State Party, under conditions allowing that State Party to establish authenticity. The Secretary-General of the United Nations shall be notified of the language or languages acceptable to each State Party at the time it deposits its instrument of ratification, acceptance or approval of or accession to this Convention. In urgent circumstances and where agreed by the States Parties, requests may be made orally but shall be confirmed in writing forthwith.

15. A request for mutual legal assistance shall contain:

(a) The identity of the authority making the request;

(b) The subject matter and nature of the investigation, prosecution or judicial proceeding to which the request relates and the name and functions of the authority conducting the investigation, prosecution or judicial proceeding;

(c) A summary of the relevant facts, except in relation to requests for the purpose of service of judicial documents;

(d) A description of the assistance sought and details of any particular procedure that the requesting State Party wishes to be followed;

(e) Where possible, the identity, location and nationality of any person concerned; and

(f) The purpose for which the evidence, information or action is sought.

16. The requested State Party may request additional information when it appears necessary for the execution of the request in accordance with its domestic law or when it can facilitate such execution.

17. A request shall be executed in accordance with the domestic law of the requested State Party and, to the extent not contrary to the domestic law of the requested State Party and where possible, in accordance with the procedures specified in the request.

18. Wherever possible and consistent with fundamental principles of domestic law, when an individual is in the territory of a State Party and has to be heard as a witness or expert by the judicial authorities of another State Party, the first State Party may, at the request of the other, permit the hearing to take place by video conference if it is not possible or desirable for the individual in question to appear in person in the territory of the requesting State Party. States Parties may agree that the hearing shall be conducted by a judicial authority of the requesting State Party and attended by a judicial authority of the requested State Party.

19. The requesting State Party shall not transmit or use information or evidence furnished by the requested State Party for investigations, prosecutions or judicial proceedings other than those stated in the request without the prior consent of the requested State Party. Nothing in this paragraph shall prevent the requesting State Party from disclosing in its proceedings information or evidence that is exculpatory to an accused person. In the latter case, the requesting State Party shall notify the requested State Party prior to the disclosure and, if so requested, consult with the requested State Party. If, in an exceptional case, advance notice is not possible, the requesting State Party shall inform the requested State Party of the disclosure without delay.

20. The requesting State Party may require that the requested State Party keep confidential the fact and substance of the request, except to the extent necessary to execute the request. If the requested State Party cannot comply with the requirement of confidentiality, it shall promptly inform the requesting State Party.

21. Mutual legal assistance may be refused:

(a) If the request is not made in conformity with the provisions of this article;

(b) If the requested State Party considers that execution of the request is likely to prejudice its sovereignty, security, *ordre public* or other essential interests;

(c) If the authorities of the requested State Party would be prohibited by its domestic law from carrying out the action requested with regard to any similar offence, had it been subject to investigation, prosecution or judicial proceedings under their own jurisdiction;

(d) If it would be contrary to the legal system of the requested State Party relating to mutual legal assistance for the request to be granted.

22. States Parties may not refuse a request for mutual legal assistance on the sole ground that the offence is also considered to involve fiscal matters.

23. Reasons shall be given for any refusal of mutual legal assistance.

24. The requested State Party shall execute the request for mutual legal assistance as soon as possible and shall take as full account as possible of any deadlines suggested by the requesting State Party and for which reasons are given, preferably in the request. The requesting State Party may make reasonable requests for information on the status and progress of measures taken by the requested State Party to satisfy its request. The requested State Party shall respond to reasonable requests by the requesting State Party on the status, and progress in its handling, of the request. The requesting State Party shall promptly inform the requested State Party when the assistance sought is no longer required.

25. Mutual legal assistance may be postponed by the requested State Party on the ground that it interferes with an ongoing investigation, prosecution or judicial proceeding.

26. Before refusing a request pursuant to paragraph 21 of this article or postponing its execution pursuant to paragraph 25 of this article, the requested State Party shall consult with the requesting State Party to consider whether assistance may be granted subject to such terms and conditions as it deems necessary. If the requesting State Party accepts assistance subject to those conditions, it shall comply with the conditions.

27. Without prejudice to the application of paragraph 12 of this article, a witness, expert or other person who, at the request of the requesting State Party, consents to give evidence in a proceeding or to assist in an investigation, prosecution or judicial proceeding in the territory of the requesting State Party shall not be prosecuted, detained, punished or subjected to any other restriction of his or her personal liberty in that territory in respect of acts, omissions or convictions prior to his or her departure from the territory of the requested State Party. Such safe conduct shall cease when the witness, expert or other person having had, for a period of fifteen consecutive days or for any period agreed upon by the States Parties from the date on which he or she has been officially informed that his or her presence is no longer required by the judicial authorities, an opportunity of leaving, has nevertheless remained voluntarily in the territory of the requesting State Party or, having left it, has returned of his or her own free will.

28. The ordinary costs of executing a request shall be borne by the requested State Party, unless otherwise agreed by the States Parties concerned. If expenses of a substantial or extraordinary nature are or will be required to fulfil the request, the States Parties shall consult to determine the terms and

conditions under which the request will be executed, as well as the manner in which the costs shall be borne.

29. The requested State Party:
    (a) Shall provide to the requesting State Party copies of government records, documents or information in its possession that under its domestic law are available to the general public;
    (b) May, at its discretion, provide to the requesting State Party in whole, in part or subject to such conditions as it deems appropriate, copies of any government records, documents or information in its possession that under its domestic law are not available to the general public.

30. States Parties shall consider, as may be necessary, the possibility of concluding bilateral or multilateral agreements or arrangements that would serve the purposes of, give practical effect to or enhance the provisions of this article.

Article 47

Transfer of criminal proceedings

States Parties shall consider the possibility of transferring to one another proceedings for the prosecution of an offence established in accordance with this Convention in cases where such transfer is considered to be in the interests of the proper administration of justice, in particular in cases where several jurisdictions are involved, with a view to concentrating the prosecution.

Article 48

Law enforcement cooperation

1. States Parties shall cooperate closely with one another, consistent with their respective domestic legal and administrative systems, to enhance the effectiveness of law enforcement action to combat the offences covered by this Convention. States Parties shall, in particular, take effective measures:
    (a) To enhance and, where necessary, to establish channels of communication between their competent authorities, agencies and services in order to facilitate the secure and rapid exchange of information concerning all aspects of the offences covered by this Convention, including, if the States Parties concerned deem it appropriate, links with other criminal activities;
    (b) To cooperate with other States Parties in conducting inquiries with respect to offences covered by this Convention concerning:
        (i) The identity, whereabouts and activities of persons suspected of involvement in such offences or the location of other persons concerned;
        (ii) The movement of proceeds of crime or property derived from the commission of such offences;
        (iii) The movement of property, equipment or other instrumentalities used or intended for use in the commission of such offences;
    (c) To provide, where appropriate, necessary items or quantities of substances for analytical or investigative purposes;

    (d) To exchange, where appropriate, information with other States Parties concerning specific means and methods used to commit offences covered by this Convention, including the use of false identities, forged, altered or false documents and other means of concealing activities;

    (e) To facilitate effective coordination between their competent authorities, agencies and services and to promote the exchange of personnel and other experts, including, subject to bilateral agreements or arrangements between the States Parties concerned, the posting of liaison officers;

    (f) To exchange information and coordinate administrative and other measures taken as appropriate for the purpose of early identification of the offences covered by this Convention.

2. With a view to giving effect to this Convention, States Parties shall consider entering into bilateral or multilateral agreements or arrangements on direct cooperation between their law enforcement agencies and, where such agreements or arrangements already exist, amending them. In the absence of such agreements or arrangements between the States Parties concerned, the States Parties may consider this Convention to be the basis for mutual law enforcement cooperation in respect of the offences covered by this Convention. Whenever appropriate, States Parties shall make full use of agreements or arrangements, including international or regional organizations, to enhance the cooperation between their law enforcement agencies.

3. States Parties shall endeavour to cooperate within their means to respond to offences covered by this Convention committed through the use of modern technology.

Article 49

Joint investigations

States Parties shall consider concluding bilateral or multilateral agreements or arrangements whereby, in relation to matters that are the subject of investigations, prosecutions or judicial proceedings in one or more States, the competent authorities concerned may establish joint investigative bodies. In the absence of such agreements or arrangements, joint investigations may be undertaken by agreement on a case-by-case basis. The States Parties involved shall ensure that the sovereignty of the State Party in whose territory such investigation is to take place is fully respected.

Article 50

Special investigative techniques

1. In order to combat corruption effectively, each State Party shall, to the extent permitted by the basic principles of its domestic legal system and in accordance with the conditions prescribed by its domestic law, take such measures as may be necessary, within its means, to allow for the appropriate use by its competent authorities of controlled delivery and, where it deems appropriate, other special investigative techniques, such as electronic or other forms of

surveillance and undercover operations, within its territory, and to allow for the admissibility in court of evidence derived therefrom.

2. For the purpose of investigating the offences covered by this Convention, States Parties are encouraged to conclude, when necessary, appropriate bilateral or multilateral agreements or arrangements for using such special investigative techniques in the context of cooperation at the international level. Such agreements or arrangements shall be concluded and implemented in full compliance with the principle of sovereign equality of States and shall be carried out strictly in accordance with the terms of those agreements or arrangements.

3. In the absence of an agreement or arrangement as set forth in paragraph 2 of this article, decisions to use such special investigative techniques at the international level shall be made on a case-by-case basis and may, when necessary, take into consideration financial arrangements and understandings with respect to the exercise of jurisdiction by the States Parties concerned.

4. Decisions to use controlled delivery at the international level may, with the consent of the States Parties concerned, include methods such as intercepting and allowing the goods or funds to continue intact or be removed or replaced in whole or in part.

CHAPTER V

ASSET RECOVERY

Article 51

General provision

The return of assets pursuant to this chapter is a fundamental principle of this Convention, and States Parties shall afford one another the widest measure of cooperation and assistance in this regard.

Article 52

Prevention and detection of transfers of proceeds of crime

1. Without prejudice to article 14 of this Convention, each State Party shall take such measures as may be necessary, in accordance with its domestic law, to require financial institutions within its jurisdiction to verify the identity of customers, to take reasonable steps to determine the identity of beneficial owners of funds deposited into high-value accounts and to conduct enhanced scrutiny of accounts sought or maintained by or on behalf of individuals who are, or have been, entrusted with prominent public functions and their family members and close associates. Such enhanced scrutiny shall be reasonably designed to detect suspicious transactions for the purpose of reporting to competent authorities and should not be so construed as to discourage

or prohibit financial institutions from doing business with any legitimate customer.

2. In order to facilitate implementation of the measures provided for in paragraph 1 of this article, each State Party, in accordance with its domestic law and inspired by relevant initiatives of regional, interregional and multilateral organizations against money-laundering, shall:

    (a) Issue advisories regarding the types of natural or legal person to whose accounts financial institutions within its jurisdiction will be expected to apply enhanced scrutiny, the types of accounts and transactions to which to pay particular attention and appropriate account-opening, maintenance and record-keeping measures to take concerning such accounts; and

    (b) Where appropriate, notify financial institutions within its jurisdiction, at the request of another State Party or on its own initiative, of the identity of particular natural or legal persons to whose accounts such institutions will be expected to apply enhanced scrutiny, in addition to those whom the financial institutions may otherwise identify.

3. In the context of paragraph 2(a) of this article, each State Party shall implement measures to ensure that its financial institutions maintain adequate records, over an appropriate period of time, of accounts and transactions involving the persons mentioned in paragraph 1 of this article, which should, as a minimum, contain information relating to the identity of the customer as well as, as far as possible, of the beneficial owner.

4. With the aim of preventing and detecting transfers of proceeds of offences established in accordance with this Convention, each State Party shall implement appropriate and effective measures to prevent, with the help of its regulatory and oversight bodies, the establishment of banks that have no physical presence and that are not affiliated with a regulated financial group. Moreover, States Parties may consider requiring their financial institutions to refuse to enter into or continue a correspondent banking relationship with such institutions and to guard against establishing relations with foreign financial institutions that permit their accounts to be used by banks that have no physical presence and that are not affiliated with a regulated financial group.

5. Each State Party shall consider establishing, in accordance with its domestic law, effective financial disclosure systems for appropriate public officials and shall provide for appropriate sanctions for non-compliance. Each State Party shall also consider taking such measures as may be necessary to permit its competent authorities to share that information with the competent authorities in other States Parties when necessary to investigate, claim and recover proceeds of offences established in accordance with this Convention.

6. Each State Party shall consider taking such measures as may be necessary, in accordance with its domestic law, to require appropriate public officials having an interest in or signature or other authority over a financial account in a foreign country to report that relationship to appropriate authorities and to maintain appropriate records related to such accounts. Such measures shall also provide for appropriate sanctions for non-compliance.

Article 53

Measures for direct recovery of property

Each State Party shall, in accordance with its domestic law:

(a) Take such measures as may be necessary to permit another State Party to initiate civil action in its courts to establish title to or ownership of property acquired through the commission of an offence established in accordance with this Convention;

(b) Take such measures as may be necessary to permit its courts to order those who have committed offences established in accordance with this Convention to pay compensation or damages to another State Party that has been harmed by such offences; and

(c) Take such measures as may be necessary to permit its courts or competent authorities, when having to decide on confiscation, to recognize another State Party's claim as a legitimate owner of property acquired through the commission of an offence established in accordance with this Convention.

Article 54

Mechanisms for recovery of property through international cooperation in confiscation

1. Each State Party, in order to provide mutual legal assistance pursuant to article 55 of this Convention with respect to property acquired through or involved in the commission of an offence established in accordance with this Convention, shall, in accordance with its domestic law:

   (a) Take such measures as may be necessary to permit its competent authorities to give effect to an order of confiscation issued by a court of another State Party;

   (b) Take such measures as may be necessary to permit its competent authorities, where they have jurisdiction, to order the confiscation of such property of foreign origin by adjudication of an offence of money-laundering or such other offence as may be within its jurisdiction or by other procedures authorized under its domestic law; and

   (c) Consider taking such measures as may be necessary to allow confiscation of such property without a criminal conviction in cases in which the offender cannot be prosecuted by reason of death, flight or absence or in other appropriate cases.

2. Each State Party, in order to provide mutual legal assistance upon a request made pursuant to paragraph 2 of article 55 of this Convention, shall, in accordance with its domestic law:

   (a) Take such measures as may be necessary to permit its competent authorities to freeze or seize property upon a freezing or seizure order issued by a court or competent authority of a requesting State Party that provides a reasonable basis for the requested State Party to believe that there are sufficient grounds for taking such actions and that the property would eventually be subject to an order of confiscation for purposes of paragraph 1(a) of this article;

(b) Take such measures as may be necessary to permit its competent authorities to freeze or seize property upon a request that provides a reasonable basis for the requested State Party to believe that there are sufficient grounds for taking such actions and that the property would eventually be subject to an order of confiscation for purposes of paragraph 1(a) of this article; and

(c) Consider taking additional measures to permit its competent authorities to preserve property for confiscation, such as on the basis of a foreign arrest or criminal charge related to the acquisition of such property.

Article 55

International cooperation for purposes of confiscation

1. A State Party that has received a request from another State Party having jurisdiction over an offence established in accordance with this Convention for confiscation of proceeds of crime, property, equipment or other instrumentalities referred to in article 31, paragraph 1, of this Convention situated in its territory shall, to the greatest extent possible within its domestic legal system:

   (a) Submit the request to its competent authorities for the purpose of obtaining an order of confiscation and, if such an order is granted, give effect to it; or

   (b) Submit to its competent authorities, with a view to giving effect to it to the extent requested, an order of confiscation issued by a court in the territory of the requesting State Party in accordance with articles 31, paragraph 1, and 54, paragraph 1(a), of this Convention insofar as it relates to proceeds of crime, property, equipment or other instrumentalities referred to in article 31, paragraph 1, situated in the territory of the requested State Party.

2. Following a request made by another State Party having jurisdiction over an offence established in accordance with this Convention, the requested State Party shall take measures to identify, trace and freeze or seize proceeds of crime, property, equipment or other instrumentalities referred to in article 31, paragraph 1, of this Convention for the purpose of eventual confiscation to be ordered either by the requesting State Party or, pursuant to a request under paragraph 1 of this article, by the requested State Party.

3. The provisions of article 46 of this Convention are applicable, mutatis mutandis, to this article. In addition to the information specified in article 46, paragraph 15, requests made pursuant to this article shall contain:

   (a) In the case of a request pertaining to paragraph 1(a) of this article, a description of the property to be confiscated, including, to the extent possible, the location and, where relevant, the estimated value of the property and a statement of the facts relied upon by the requesting State

Party sufficient to enable the requested State Party to seek the order under its domestic law;

(b) In the case of a request pertaining to paragraph 1(b) of this article, a legally admissible copy of an order of confiscation upon which the request is based issued by the requesting State Party, a statement of the facts and information as to the extent to which execution of the order is requested, a statement specifying the measures taken by the requesting State Party to provide adequate notification to bona fide third parties and to ensure due process and a statement that the confiscation order is final;

(c) In the case of a request pertaining to paragraph 2 of this article, a statement of the facts relied upon by the requesting State Party and a description of the actions requested and, where available, a legally admissible copy of an order on which the request is based.

4. The decisions or actions provided for in paragraphs 1 and 2 of this article shall be taken by the requested State Party in accordance with and subject to the provisions of its domestic law and its procedural rules or any bilateral or multilateral agreement or arrangement to which it may be bound in relation to the requesting State Party.

5. Each State Party shall furnish copies of its laws and regulations that give effect to this article and of any subsequent changes to such laws and regulations or a description thereof to the Secretary-General of the United Nations.

6. If a State Party elects to make the taking of the measures referred to in paragraphs 1 and 2 of this article conditional on the existence of a relevant treaty, that State Party shall consider this Convention the necessary and sufficient treaty basis.

7. Cooperation under this article may also be refused or provisional measures lifted if the requested State Party does not receive sufficient and timely evidence or if the property is of a *de minimis* value.

8. Before lifting any provisional measure taken pursuant to this article, the requested State Party shall, wherever possible, give the requesting State Party an opportunity to present its reasons in favour of continuing the measure.

9. The provisions of this article shall not be construed as prejudicing the rights of bona fide third parties.

Article 56

Special cooperation

Without prejudice to its domestic law, each State Party shall endeavour to take measures to permit it to forward, without prejudice to its own investigations, prosecutions or judicial proceedings, information on proceeds of offences established in accordance with this Convention to another State Party without prior request, when it considers that the disclosure of such information might assist the receiving State Party in initiating or carrying out investigations, prosecutions or judicial proceedings or might lead to a request by that State Party under this chapter of the Convention.

Article 57

Return and disposal of assets

1. Property confiscated by a State Party pursuant to article 31 or 55 of this Convention shall be disposed of, including by return to its prior legitimate owners, pursuant to paragraph 3 of this article, by that State Party in accordance with the provisions of this Convention and its domestic law.

2. Each State Party shall adopt such legislative and other measures, in accordance with the fundamental principles of its domestic law, as may be necessary to enable its competent authorities to return confiscated property, when acting on the request made by another State Party, in accordance with this Convention, taking into account the rights of bona fide third parties.

3. In accordance with articles 46 and 55 of this Convention and paragraphs 1 and 2 of this article, the requested State Party shall:

   (a) In the case of embezzlement of public funds or of laundering of embezzled public funds as referred to in articles 17 and 23 of this Convention, when confiscation was executed in accordance with article 55 and on the basis of a final judgement in the requesting State Party, a requirement that can be waived by the requested State Party, return the confiscated property to the requesting State Party;

   (b) In the case of proceeds of any other offence covered by this Convention, when the confiscation was executed in accordance with article 55 of this Convention and on the basis of a final judgement in the requesting State Party, a requirement that can be waived by the requested State Party, return the confiscated property to the requesting State Party, when the requesting State Party reasonably establishes its prior ownership of such confiscated property to the requested State Party or when the requested State Party recognizes damage to the requesting State Party as a basis for returning the confiscated property;

   (c) In all other cases, give priority consideration to returning confiscated property to the requesting State Party, returning such property to its prior legitimate owners or compensating the victims of the crime.

4. Where appropriate, unless States Parties decide otherwise, the requested State Party may deduct reasonable expenses incurred in investigations, prosecutions or judicial proceedings leading to the return or disposition of confiscated property pursuant to this article.

5. Where appropriate, States Parties may also give special consideration to concluding agreements or mutually acceptable arrangements, on a case-by-case basis, for the final disposal of confiscated property.

Article 58

Financial intelligence unit

States Parties shall cooperate with one another for the purpose of preventing and combating the transfer of proceeds of offences established in accordance with this Convention and of promoting ways and means of recovering such proceeds and, to that end, shall consider establishing a financial intelligence unit to be responsible for receiving, analysing and disseminating to the competent authorities reports of suspicious financial transactions.

Article 59

Bilateral and multilateral agreements and arrangements

States Parties shall consider concluding bilateral or multilateral agreements or arrangements to enhance the effectiveness of international cooperation undertaken pursuant to this chapter of the Convention.

CHAPTER VI

TECHNICAL ASSISTANCE AND INFORMATION EXCHANGE

Article 60

Training and technical assistance

1. Each State Party shall, to the extent necessary, initiate, develop or improve specific training programmes for its personnel responsible for preventing and combating corruption. Such training programmes could deal, inter alia, with the following areas:
   (a) Effective measures to prevent, detect, investigate, punish and control corruption, including the use of evidence-gathering and investigative methods;
   (b) Building capacity in the development and planning of strategic anti-corruption policy;
   (c) Training competent authorities in the preparation of requests for mutual legal assistance that meet the requirements of this Convention;
   (d) Evaluation and strengthening of institutions, public service management and the management of public finances, including public procurement, and the private sector;
   (e) Preventing and combating the transfer of proceeds of offences established in accordance with this Convention and recovering such proceeds;
   (f) Detecting and freezing of the transfer of proceeds of offences established in accordance with this Convention;
   (g) Surveillance of the movement of proceeds of offences established in accordance with this Convention and of the methods used to transfer, conceal or disguise such proceeds;
   (h) Appropriate and efficient legal and administrative mechanisms and methods for facilitating the return of proceeds of offences established in accordance with this Convention;
   (i) Methods used in protecting victims and witnesses who cooperate with judicial authorities; and
   (j) Training in national and international regulations and in languages.

2. States Parties shall, according to their capacity, consider affording one another the widest measure of technical assistance, especially for the benefit of developing countries, in their respective plans and programmes to combat corruption, including material support and training in the areas referred to in paragraph 1 of this article, and training and assistance and the mutual exchange of relevant experience and specialized knowledge, which will facilitate international cooperation between States Parties in the areas of extradition and mutual legal assistance.

3. States Parties shall strengthen, to the extent necessary, efforts to maximize operational and training activities in international and regional organizations and in the framework of relevant bilateral and multilateral agreements or arrangements.

4. States Parties shall consider assisting one another, upon request, in conducting evaluations, studies and research relating to the types, causes, effects and costs of corruption in their respective countries, with a view to developing, with the participation of competent authorities and society, strategies and action plans to combat corruption.

5. In order to facilitate the recovery of proceeds of offences established in accordance with this Convention, States Parties may cooperate in providing each other with the names of experts who could assist in achieving that objective.

6. States Parties shall consider using subregional, regional and international conferences and seminars to promote cooperation and technical assistance and to stimulate discussion on problems of mutual concern, including the special problems and needs of developing countries and countries with economies in transition.

7. States Parties shall consider establishing voluntary mechanisms with a view to contributing financially to the efforts of developing countries and countries with economies in transition to apply this Convention through technical assistance programmes and projects.

8. Each State Party shall consider making voluntary contributions to the United Nations Office on Drugs and Crime for the purpose of fostering, through the Office, programmes and projects in developing countries with a view to implementing this Convention.

Article 61

Collection, exchange and analysis of information on corruption

1. Each State Party shall consider analysing, in consultation with experts, trends in corruption in its territory, as well as the circumstances in which corruption offences are committed.

2. States Parties shall consider developing and sharing with each other and through international and regional organizations statistics, analytical expertise concerning corruption and information with a view to developing, insofar

as possible, common definitions, standards and methodologies, as well as information on best practices to prevent and combat corruption.

3. Each State Party shall consider monitoring its policies and actual measures to combat corruption and making assessments of their effectiveness and efficiency.

Article 62

Other measures: implementation of the Convention through economic development and technical assistance

1. States Parties shall take measures conducive to the optimal implementation of this Convention to the extent possible, through international cooperation, taking into account the negative effects of corruption on society in general, in particular on sustainable development.

2. States Parties shall make concrete efforts to the extent possible and in coordination with each other, as well as with international and regional organizations:

    (a) To enhance their cooperation at various levels with developing countries, with a view to strengthening the capacity of the latter to prevent and combat corruption;

    (b) To enhance financial and material assistance to support the efforts of developing countries to prevent and fight corruption effectively and to help them implement this Convention successfully;

    (c) To provide technical assistance to developing countries and countries with economies in transition to assist them in meeting their needs for the implementation of this Convention. To that end, States Parties shall endeavour to make adequate and regular voluntary contributions to an account specifically designated for that purpose in a United Nations funding mechanism. States Parties may also give special consideration, in accordance with their domestic law and the provisions of this Convention, to contributing to that account a percentage of the money or of the corresponding value of proceeds of crime or property confiscated in accordance with the provisions of this Convention;

    (d) To encourage and persuade other States and financial institutions as appropriate to join them in efforts in accordance with this article, in particular by providing more training programmes and modern equipment to developing countries in order to assist them in achieving the objectives of this Convention.

3. To the extent possible, these measures shall be without prejudice to existing foreign assistance commitments or to other financial cooperation arrangements at the bilateral, regional or international level.

4. States Parties may conclude bilateral or multilateral agreements or arrangements on material and logistical assistance, taking into consideration the financial arrangements necessary for the means of international cooperation provided for by this Convention to be effective and for the prevention, detection and control of corruption.

CHAPTER VII

MECHANISMS FOR IMPLEMENTATION

Article 63

Conference of the States Parties to the Convention

1. A Conference of the States Parties to the Convention is hereby established to improve the capacity of and cooperation between States Parties to achieve the objectives set forth in this Convention and to promote and review its implementation.

2. The Secretary-General of the United Nations shall convene the Conference of the States Parties not later than one year following the entry into force of this Convention. Thereafter, regular meetings of the Conference of the States Parties shall be held in accordance with the rules of procedure adopted by the Conference.

3. The Conference of the States Parties shall adopt rules of procedure and rules governing the functioning of the activities set forth in this article, including rules concerning the admission and participation of observers, and the payment of expenses incurred in carrying out those activities.

4. The Conference of the States Parties shall agree upon activities, procedures and methods of work to achieve the objectives set forth in paragraph 1 of this article, including:

   (a) Facilitating activities by States Parties under articles 60 and 62 and chapters II to V of this Convention, including by encouraging the mobilization of voluntary contributions;

   (b) Facilitating the exchange of information among States Parties on patterns and trends in corruption and on successful practices for preventing and combating it and for the return of proceeds of crime, through, inter alia, the publication of relevant information as mentioned in this article;

   (c) Cooperating with relevant international and regional organizations and mechanisms and non-governmental organizations;

   (d) Making appropriate use of relevant information produced by other international and regional mechanisms for combating and preventing corruption in order to avoid unnecessary duplication of work;

   (e) Reviewing periodically the implementation of this Convention by its States Parties;

   (f) Making recommendations to improve this Convention and its implementation;

   (g) Taking note of the technical assistance requirements of States Parties with regard to the implementation of this Convention and recommending any action it may deem necessary in that respect.

5. For the purpose of paragraph 4 of this article, the Conference of the States Parties shall acquire the necessary knowledge of the measures taken by States Parties in implementing this Convention and the difficulties encountered by them in doing so through information provided by them and

through such supplemental review mechanisms as may be established by the Conference of the States Parties.

6. Each State Party shall provide the Conference of the States Parties with information on its programmes, plans and practices, as well as on legislative and administrative measures to implement this Convention, as required by the Conference of the States Parties. The Conference of the States Parties shall examine the most effective way of receiving and acting upon information, including, inter alia, information received from States Parties and from competent international organizations. Inputs received from relevant non-governmental organizations duly accredited in accordance with procedures to be decided upon by the Conference of the States Parties may also be considered.

7. Pursuant to paragraphs 4 to 6 of this article, the Conference of the States Parties shall establish, if it deems it necessary, any appropriate mechanism or body to assist in the effective implementation of the Convention.

Article 64

Secretariat

1. The Secretary-General of the United Nations shall provide the necessary secretariat services to the Conference of the States Parties to the Convention.

2. The secretariat shall:
   (a) Assist the Conference of the States Parties in carrying out the activities set forth in article 63 of this Convention and make arrangements and provide the necessary services for the sessions of the Conference of the States Parties;
   (b) Upon request, assist States Parties in providing information to the Conference of the States Parties as envisaged in article 63, paragraphs 5 and 6, of this Convention; and
   (c) Ensure the necessary coordination with the secretariats of relevant international and regional organizations.

CHAPTER VIII

FINAL PROVISIONS

Article 65

Implementation of the Convention

1. Each State Party shall take the necessary measures, including legislative and administrative measures, in accordance with fundamental principles of its domestic law, to ensure the implementation of its obligations under this Convention.

2. Each State Party may adopt more strict or severe measures than those provided for by this Convention for preventing and combating corruption.

Article 66

Settlement of disputes

1. States Parties shall endeavour to settle disputes concerning the interpretation or application of this Convention through negotiation.

2. Any dispute between two or more States Parties concerning the interpretation or application of this Convention that cannot be settled through negotiation within a reasonable time shall, at the request of one of those States Parties, be submitted to arbitration. If, six months after the date of the request for arbitration, those States Parties are unable to agree on the organization of the arbitration, any one of those States Parties may refer the dispute to the International Court of Justice by request in accordance with the Statute of the Court.

3. Each State Party may, at the time of signature, ratification, acceptance or approval of or accession to this Convention, declare that it does not consider itself bound by paragraph 2 of this article. The other States Parties shall not be bound by paragraph 2 of this article with respect to any State Party that has made such a reservation.

4. Any State Party that has made a reservation in accordance with paragraph 3 of this article may at any time withdraw that reservation by notification to the Secretary-General of the United Nations.

Article 67

Signature, ratification, acceptance, approval and accession

1. This Convention shall be open to all States for signature from 9 to 11 December 2003 in Merida, Mexico, and thereafter at United Nations Headquarters in New York until 9 December 2005.

2. This Convention shall also be open for signature by regional economic integration organizations provided that at least one member State of such organization has signed this Convention in accordance with paragraph 1 of this article.

3. This Convention is subject to ratification, acceptance or approval. Instruments of ratification, acceptance or approval shall be deposited with the Secretary-General of the United Nations. A regional economic integration organization may deposit its instrument of ratification, acceptance or approval if at least one of its member States has done likewise. In that instrument of ratification, acceptance or approval, such organization shall declare the extent of its competence with respect to the matters governed by this Convention. Such organization shall also inform the depositary of any relevant modification in the extent of its competence.

4. This Convention is open for accession by any State or any regional economic integration organization of which at least one member State is a Party to this Convention. Instruments of accession shall be deposited with the Secretary-

General of the United Nations. At the time of its accession, a regional economic integration organization shall declare the extent of its competence with respect to matters governed by this Convention. Such organization shall also inform the depositary of any relevant modification in the extent of its competence.

Article 68

Entry into force

1. This Convention shall enter into force on the ninetieth day after the date of deposit of the thirtieth instrument of ratification, acceptance, approval or accession. For the purpose of this paragraph, any instrument deposited by a regional economic integration organization shall not be counted as additional to those deposited by member States of such organization.

2. For each State or regional economic integration organization ratifying, accepting, approving or acceding to this Convention after the deposit of the thirtieth instrument of such action, this Convention shall enter into force on the thirtieth day after the date of deposit by such State or organization of the relevant instrument or on the date this Convention enters into force pursuant to paragraph 1 of this article, whichever is later.

Article 69

Amendment

1. After the expiry of five years from the entry into force of this Convention, a State Party may propose an amendment and transmit it to the Secretary-General of the United Nations, who shall thereupon communicate the proposed amendment to the States Parties and to the Conference of the States Parties to the Convention for the purpose of considering and deciding on the proposal. The Conference of the States Parties shall make every effort to achieve consensus on each amendment. If all efforts at consensus have been exhausted and no agreement has been reached, the amendment shall, as a last resort, require for its adoption a two-thirds majority vote of the States Parties present and voting at the meeting of the Conference of the States Parties.

2. Regional economic integration organizations, in matters within their competence, shall exercise their right to vote under this article with a number of votes equal to the number of their member States that are Parties to this Convention. Such organizations shall not exercise their right to vote if their member States exercise theirs and vice versa.

3. An amendment adopted in accordance with paragraph 1 of this article is subject to ratification, acceptance or approval by States Parties.

4. An amendment adopted in accordance with paragraph 1 of this article shall enter into force in respect of a State Party ninety days after the date of the

deposit with the Secretary-General of the United Nations of an instrument of ratification, acceptance or approval of such amendment.

5. When an amendment enters into force, it shall be binding on those States Parties which have expressed their consent to be bound by it. Other States Parties shall still be bound by the provisions of this Convention and any earlier amendments that they have ratified, accepted or approved.

Article 70

Denunciation

1. A State Party may denounce this Convention by written notification to the Secretary-General of the United Nations. Such denunciation shall become effective one year after the date of receipt of the notification by the Secretary-General.

2. A regional economic integration organization shall cease to be a Party to this Convention when all of its member States have denounced it.

Article 71

Depositary and languages

1. The Secretary-General of the United Nations is designated depositary of this Convention.

2. The original of this Convention, of which the Arabic, Chinese, English, French, Russian and Spanish texts are equally authentic, shall be deposited with the Secretary-General of the United Nations.

3. IN WITNESS WHEREOF, the undersigned plenipotentiaries, being duly authorized thereto by their respective Governments, have signed this Convention.

NOTES

1. *See* E/1996/99.
2. Official Journal of the European Communities, C 195, 25 June 1997.
3. *See* Corruption and Integrity Improvement Initiatives in Developing Countries (United Nations publication, Sales No. E.98.III.B.18).
4. Council of Europe, European Treaty Series, No. 173.
5. *Id.*, No. 174.
6. General Assembly resolution 55/25, annex I.

INTERPRETATIVE NOTES FOR THE OFFICIAL RECORDS (TRAVAUX PRÉPARATOIRES) OF THE NEGOTIATION OF THE UNITED NATIONS CONVENTION AGAINST CORRUPTION*

FIFTY-EIGHTH SESSION
AGENDA ITEM 110

Crime prevention and criminal justice Report of the Ad Hoc Committee for the Negotiation of a Convention against Corruption on the work of its first to seventh sessions

Addendum

I.   INTRODUCTION

1. The present document contains interpretative notes that were discussed by the Ad Hoc Committee for the Negotiation of a Convention against Corruption throughout the process of negotiation of the draft convention. These notes will be included in the official records of the negotiation process, which the Secretariat will prepare in accordance with standard practice. The present document is submitted to the General Assembly for information purposes only; the Ad Hoc Committee took no formal action on these notes and none is expected of the Assembly at its fifty-eighth session.

---

* U.N. Doc. A/58/422/Add.1 (2003).

II.   INTERPRETIVE NOTES

Chapter I

Article 2

Subparagraph (a)

2. The *travaux préparatoires* will indicate that the word "executive" is understood to encompass the military branch, where appropriate.

3. The *travaux préparatoires* will indicate that the term "office" is understood to encompass offices at all levels and subdivisions of government from national to local. In States where subnational governmental units (for example, provincial, municipal and local) of a self-governing nature exist, including States where such bodies are not deemed to form a part of the State, "office" may be understood by the States concerned to encompass those levels also.

4. The *travaux préparatoires* will indicate that, for the purpose of defining "public official", each State Party shall determine who is a member of the categories mentioned in subparagraph (a) (i) of article 2 and how each of those categories is applied.

Subparagraph (b)

5. The *travaux préparatoires* will indicate that the term "foreign country" includes all levels and subdivisions of government, from national to local.

Subparagraph (d)

6. The *travaux préparatoires* will indicate that the phrase "assets of every kind" is understood to include funds and legal rights to assets.

Subparagraph (f)

7. The *travaux préparatoires* will indicate that the word "temporarily" is understood to encompass the concept of renewability.

Article 3

Paragraph 1

8. The *travaux préparatoires* will indicate that the phrase "in accordance with its terms" is not intended to limit the application of mutual legal assistance.

9. The *travaux préparatoires* will indicate that offences established in accordance with the Convention should not be understood to require the adoption of new domestic legislation for the inclusion of an offence under domestic law where a corresponding offence already exists under such law.

Article 4

Paragraph 1

10. The *travaux préparatoires* will indicate that the principle of non-intervention is to be understood in the light of Article 2 of the Charter of the United Nations.

Chapter II

Article 6

11. The *travaux préparatoires* will indicate that the body or bodies referred to in this article may be the same as those referred to in article 36.

Article 7

Paragraph 1

12. The *travaux préparatoires* will indicate that the existence of the systems referred to in paragraph 1 of article 7 shall not prevent States Parties from maintaining or adopting specific measures for disadvantaged groups.

Article 9

Paragraph 1

13. The *travaux préparatoires* will indicate that nothing in paragraph 1 shall be construed as preventing any State Party from taking any action or not disclosing any information that it considers necessary for the protection of its essential interests related to national security.

Article 10

Subparagraph (a)

14. The *travaux préparatoires* will indicate that, regarding the protection of personal information, the use of which is addressed in the Convention, States Parties may be inspired by principles laid down in the guidelines for the regulation of computerized personal data files adopted by the General Assembly in its resolution 45/95 of 14 December 1990.

Article 11

Paragraph 2

15. The *travaux préparatoires* will indicate that reference to similar independence should be understood to include cases where such independence is identical.

Article 13

Paragraph 1

16. The *travaux préparatoires* will indicate that reference to non-governmental organizations and community-based organizations relates to such organizations established or located in the country. This note is intended as an explanation and not as an amendment to paragraph 1.

Subparagraph (d)

17. The *travaux préparatoires* will indicate that the intention behind paragraph 1 (d) is to stress those obligations which States Parties have already undertaken in

various international instruments concerning human rights to which they are parties and should not in any way be taken as modifying their obligations.

Article 14

Paragraph 1

Subparagraph (a)

18. The *travaux préparatoires* will indicate that the words "other bodies" may be understood to include intermediaries, which in some jurisdictions may include stockbroking firms, other securities dealers, currency exchange bureaux or currency brokers.

19. The *travaux préparatoires* will indicate that the words "suspicious transactions" may be understood to include unusual transactions that, by reason of their amount, characteristics and frequency, are inconsistent with the customer's business activity, exceed the normally accepted parameters of the market or have no clear legal basis and could constitute or be connected with unlawful activities in general.

Subparagraph (b)

20. The *travaux préparatoires* will indicate that the establishment of a financial intelligence unit called for by this subparagraph is intended for cases where such a mechanism does not yet exist.

Paragraph 4

21. The *travaux préparatoires* will indicate that, during the negotiations, the words "relevant initiatives of regional, interregional and multilateral organizations" were understood to refer in particular to the Forty Recommendations and the Eight Special Recommendations of the Financial Action Task Force on Money Laundering, as revised in 2003 and 2001, respectively, and, in addition, to other existing initiatives of regional, interregional and multilateral organizations against money-laundering, such as the Caribbean Financial Action Task Force, the Commonwealth, the Council of Europe, the Eastern and Southern African Anti-Money-Laundering Group, the European Union, the Financial Action Task Force of South America against Money Laundering and the Organization of American States.

Chapter III

22. The *travaux préparatoires* will indicate that it is recognized that States may criminalize or have already criminalized conduct other than the offences listed in this chapter as corrupt conduct.

Article 16

23. The *travaux préparatoires* will indicate that this article is not intended to affect any immunities that foreign public officials or officials of public international organizations may enjoy in accordance with international law. The States Parties noted the relevance of immunities in this context and encourage public international organizations to waive such immunities in appropriate cases.

Paragraph 1

24. The *travaux préparatoires* will indicate that a statute that defined the offence in terms of payments "to induce a breach of the official's duty" could meet the standard set forth in each of these paragraphs, provided that it was understood that every public official had a duty to exercise judgement or discretion impartially and that this was an "autonomous" definition not requiring proof of the law or regulations of the particular official's country or international organization.

25. The *travaux préparatoires* will indicate that the phrase "the conduct of international business" is intended to include the provision of international aid.

Paragraph 2

26. The *travaux préparatoires* will indicate that negotiating delegations considered it quite important that any State Party that had not established this offence should, insofar as its laws permitted, provide assistance and cooperation with respect to the investigation and prosecution of this offence by a State Party that had established it in accordance with the Convention and avoid, if at all possible, allowing technical obstacles such as lack of dual criminality to prevent the exchange of information needed to bring corrupt officials to justice.

27. The *travaux préparatoires* will indicate that the word "intentionally" was included in this paragraph primarily for consistency with paragraph 1 and other provisions of the Convention and is not intended to imply any weakening of the commitment contained in paragraph 2, as it is recognized that a foreign public official cannot "unintentionally" solicit or accept a bribe.

28. The *travaux préparatoires* will indicate that paragraph 1 requires that States Parties criminalize active bribery of foreign public officials and paragraph 2 requires only that States Parties "consider" criminalizing solicitation or acceptance of bribes by foreign officials in such circumstances. This is not because any delegation condoned or was prepared to tolerate the solicitation or acceptance of such bribes. Rather, the difference in degree of obligation between the two paragraphs is due to the fact that the core conduct addressed by paragraph 2 is already covered by article 15, which requires that

States Parties criminalize the solicitation and acceptance of bribes by their own officials.

Article 17

29. The *travaux préparatoires* will indicate that this article is not intended to require the prosecution of *de minimis* offences.

30. The *travaux préparatoires* will indicate that the term "diversion" is understood in some countries as separate from "embezzlement" and "misappropriation", while in others "diversion" is intended to be covered by or is synonymous with those terms.

Article 19

31. The *travaux préparatoires* will indicate that this article may encompass various types of conduct such as improper disclosure by a public official of classified or privileged information.

Article 23

32. The *travaux préparatoires* will indicate that money-laundering offences established in accordance with this article are understood to be independent and autonomous offences and that a prior conviction for the predicate offence is not necessary to establish the illicit nature or origin of the assets laundered. The illicit nature or origin of the assets and, in accordance with article 28, any knowledge, intent or purpose may be established during the course of the money-laundering prosecution and may be inferred from objective factual circumstances.

Article 27

Paragraph 1

33. The *travaux préparatoires* will indicate that the formulation of paragraph 1 was intended to capture different degrees of participation, but was not intended to create an obligation for States Parties to include all of those degrees in their domestic legislation.

Article 30

Paragraph 2

34. The *travaux préparatoires* will indicate the understanding that the appropriate balance referred to in this paragraph would be established or maintained in law and in practice.

Paragraph 4

35. The *travaux préparatoires* will indicate the understanding that the expression "pending trial" is considered to include the investigation phase.

Article 31

Paragraph 5

36. The *travaux préparatoires* will indicate that this provision is intended as a minimum threshold and that States Parties would be free to go beyond it in their domestic legislation.

Article 35

37. The *travaux préparatoires* will indicate that the expression "entities or persons" is deemed to include States, as well as legal and natural persons.

38. The *travaux préparatoires* will indicate that this article is intended to establish the principle that States Parties should ensure that they have mechanisms permitting persons or entities suffering damage to initiate legal proceedings, in appropriate circumstances, against those who commit acts of corruption (for example, where the acts have a legitimate relationship to the State Party where the proceedings are to be brought). While article 35 does not restrict the right of each State Party to determine the circumstances under which it will make its courts available in such cases, it is also not intended to require or endorse the particular choice made by a State Party in doing so.

Article 36

39. The *travaux préparatoires* will indicate that the body or bodies referred to in this article may be the same as those referred to in article 6.

Article 41

40. The *travaux préparatoires* will indicate that the term "conviction" should be understood to refer to a conviction no longer subject to appeal.

Article 42

Paragraph 1

Subparagraph (a)

41. The *travaux préparatoires* will reflect the understanding that the offence might be committed in whole or in part in the territory of the State Party.

Chapter IV

Article 46

Paragraph 9

Subparagraph (b)

42. The *travaux préparatoires* will indicate that the requested State Party would define "coercive action", taking into account the purposes of the Convention.

Paragraph 19

43. The *travaux préparatoires* will reflect the understanding that the requesting State Party would be under an obligation not to use any information received that was protected by bank secrecy for any purpose other than the proceedings for which that information was requested, unless authorized to do so by the requested State Party.

Paragraph 28

44. The *travaux préparatoires* will indicate that many of the costs arising in connection with compliance with requests made pursuant to article 46, paragraphs 10, 11 and 18, would generally be considered extraordinary in nature. Further, the *travaux préparatoires* will also indicate the understanding that developing countries might encounter difficulties in meeting even some ordinary costs and should be provided with appropriate assistance to enable them to meet the requirements of this article.

Article 48

Paragraph 1

Subparagraph (b) (i)

45. The *travaux préparatoires* will indicate that the term "identity" should be understood to include such features or other pertinent information as might be necessary to establish a person's identity.

Subparagraph (d)

46. The *travaux préparatoires* will indicate that this subparagraph does not imply that the type of cooperation described therein would not be available under the United Nations Convention against Transnational Organized Crime (General Assembly resolution 55/25, annex I).

Paragraph 3

47. The *travaux préparatoires* will indicate that, in considering a proposal made by Chile for a provision on jurisdiction and cooperation with regard to offences

committed through the use of computer technology (A/AC.261/L.157 and Corr.1), there was general understanding that article 42, paragraph 1 (a), already covered the exercise of jurisdiction over offences established in accordance with the Convention that were committed using computers if all other elements of the offence were met, even if the effects of the offence occurred outside the territory of a State Party. In that regard, States Parties should also keep in mind the provisions of article 4 of the Convention. The second part of the proposal of Chile suggested that States Parties should note the possible advantage of using electronic communications in exchanges arising under article 46. That proposal noted that States Parties might wish to consider the use of electronic communications, when feasible, to expedite mutual legal assistance. However, the proposal also noted that such use might raise certain risks regarding interception by third parties, which should be avoided.

Chapter V

Article 51

48. The *travaux préparatoires* will indicate that the expression "fundamental principle" would not have legal consequences on the other provisions of this chapter.

Article 52

Paragraph 1

49. The *travaux préparatoires* will indicate that paragraphs 1 and 2 should be read together and that the obligations imposed on financial institutions may be applied and implemented with due regard to particular risks of money-laundering. In that regard, States Parties may guide financial institutions on appropriate procedures to apply and whether relevant risks require application and implementation of these provisions to accounts of a particular value or nature, to its own citizens as well as to citizens of other States and to officials with a particular function or seniority. The relevant initiatives of regional, interregional and multilateral organizations against money-laundering shall be those referred to in the note to article 14 in the travaux préparatoires.

50. The *travaux préparatoires* will indicate that the term "close associates" is deemed to encompass persons or companies clearly related to individuals entrusted with prominent public functions.

51. The *travaux préparatoires* will indicate that the words "discourage or prohibit financial institutions from doing business with any legitimate customer" are understood to include the notion of not endangering the ability of financial institutions to do business with legitimate customers.

Paragraph 2

Subparagraph (a)

52. The *travaux préparatoires* will indicate that the obligation to issue advisories may be fulfilled by the State Party or by its financial oversight bodies.

Paragraph 3

53. The *travaux préparatoires* will indicate that this paragraph is not intended to expand the scope of paragraphs 1 and 2 of this article.

Paragraph 4

54. The *travaux préparatoires* will indicate that the term "physical presence" is understood to mean "meaningful mind and management" located within the jurisdiction. The simple existence of a local agent or low-level staff would not constitute physical presence. Management is understood to include administration, that is, books and records.

55. The *travaux préparatoires* will indicate that banks that have no physical presence and are not affiliated with a regulated financial group are generally known as "shell banks".

Article 53

Subparagraph (c)

56. The *travaux préparatoires* will indicate that, during the consideration of this paragraph, the representative of the Office of Legal Affairs of the Secretariat drew the attention of the Ad Hoc Committee to the proposal submitted by his Office, together with the Office of Internal Oversight Services and the United Nations Office on Drugs and Crime (see A/AC.261/L.212) to include in this paragraph a reference to the recognition of the claim of a public international organization in addition to the recognition of the claim of another State Party. Following discussion of the proposal, the Ad Hoc Committee decided not to include such a reference, based upon the understanding that States Parties could, in practice, recognize the claim of a public international organization of which they were members as the legitimate owner of property acquired through conduct established as an offence in accordance with the Convention.

Article 54

Paragraph 1

Subparagraph (a)

57. The *travaux préparatoires* will indicate that the reference to an order of confiscation in paragraph 1 (a) of this article may be interpreted broadly, as including monetary confiscation judgements, but should not be read as requiring enforcement of an order issued by a court that does not have criminal jurisdiction.

Subparagraph (b)

58. The *travaux préparatoires* will indicate that paragraph 1 (b) of this article shall be interpreted as meaning that the obligation contained in this provision

would be fulfilled by a criminal proceeding that could lead to confiscation orders.

Subparagraph (c)

59. The *travaux préparatoires* will indicate that, in the context of paragraph 1 (c) of this article, the term "offender" might in appropriate cases be understood to include persons who may be title holders for the purpose of concealing the identity of the true owners of the property in question.

Paragraph 2

Subparagraph (a)

60. The *travaux préparatoires* will indicate that the term "sufficient grounds" used in paragraph 2 (a) of this article should be construed as a reference to a prima facie case in countries whose legal systems employ this term.

61. The *travaux préparatoires* will indicate in relation to paragraph 2 (a) of this article that a State Party may choose to establish procedures either for recognizing and enforcing a foreign freezing or seizure order or for using a foreign freezing or seizure order as the basis for seeking the issuance of its own freezing or seizure order. Reference to a freezing or seizure order in paragraph 2 (a) of this article should not be construed as requiring enforcement or recognition of a freezing or seizure order issued by an authority that does not have criminal jurisdiction.

Article 55

62. The *travaux préparatoires* will indicate that references in this article to article 31, paragraph 1, should be understood to include reference to article 31, paragraphs 5-7.

Paragraph 1

63. The *travaux préparatoires* will indicate that the term "instrumentalities" should not be interpreted in an overly broad manner.

Paragraph 3

Subparagraph (a)

64. The *travaux préparatoires* will indicate that the statement of facts may include a description of the illicit activity and its relationship to the assets to be confiscated.

Paragraph 7

65. The *travaux préparatoires* will reflect the understanding that the requested State Party will consult with the requesting State Party on whether the property is

of *de minimis* value or on ways and means of respecting any deadline for the provision of additional evidence.

Article 57

Paragraph 1

66. The *travaux préparatoires* will indicate that prior legitimate ownership will mean ownership at the time of the offence.

Paragraph 2

67. The *travaux préparatoires* will indicate that return of confiscated property may in some cases mean return of title or value.

68. The *travaux préparatoires* will indicate that the domestic law referred to in paragraph 1 and the legislative and other measures referred to in paragraph 2 would mean the national legislation or regulations that enable the implementation of this article by States Parties.

Paragraph 3

Subparagraphs (a) and (b)

69. The *travaux préparatoires* will indicate that subparagraphs (a) and (b) of paragraph 3 of this article apply only to the procedures for the return of assets and not to the procedures for confiscation, which are covered in other articles of the Convention. The requested State Party should consider the waiver of the requirement for final judgement in cases where final judgement cannot be obtained because the offender cannot be prosecuted by reason of death, flight or absence or in other appropriate cases.

Paragraph 4

70. The *travaux préparatoires* will indicate that "reasonable expenses" are to be interpreted as costs and expenses incurred and not as finders' fees or other unspecified charges. Requested and requesting States Parties are encouraged to consult on likely expenses.

Article 58

71. The *travaux préparatoires* will indicate that each State Party may consider creating a new financial intelligence unit, establishing a specialized branch of an existing financial intelligence unit or simply using its existing financial intelligence unit. Further, the *travaux préparatoires* will indicate that this article should be interpreted in a manner consistent with paragraph 1 (b) of article 14 of the Convention.

Chapter VI

Article 62

Paragraph 2

Subparagraph (c)

72. The *travaux préparatoires* will indicate that this subparagraph is not intended to prejudice the application of article 57.

Chapter VII

Article 63

Paragraph 3

73. The *travaux préparatoires* will indicate that financing should not be linked to the recovery of assets.

Paragraph 7

74. The *travaux préparatoires* will indicate that nothing in this paragraph is intended to limit the discretion of the Conference of the States Parties as the only forum competent to consider whether the mechanism or body to assist in the effective implementation of the Convention is necessary.

Chapter VIII

Article 67

Paragraph 2

75. The *travaux préparatoires* will indicate that "regional economic integration organization" shall mean an organization constituted by sovereign States of a given region, to which its member States have transferred competence in respect of matters governed by the Convention and which has been duly authorized, in accordance with its internal procedures, to sign, ratify, accept, approve or accede to it; references to "States Parties" under the Convention shall apply to such organizations within the limits of their competence.

WORLD BANK PROCUREMENT GUIDELINES

Procurement Guidelines under International Bank for Reconstruction and Development Loans and International Development Association Credits for Fraud and Corruption★

★ ★ ★ ★ ★

1.15. It is the Bank's policy to require that Borrowers (including beneficiaries of Bank loans), as well as bidders/Suppliers/Contractors under Bank-financed contracts, observe the highest standard of ethics during the procurement and execution of such contracts. In pursuance of this policy, the Bank:

a. defines, for the purposes of this provision, the terms set forth below as follows:

(i) "corrupt practice" means the offering, giving, receiving, or soliciting of anything of value to influence the action of a public official in the procurement process or in contract execution; and

(ii) "fraudulent practice" means a misrepresentation of facts in order to influence a procurement process or the execution of a contract to the detriment of the Borrower, and includes collusive practices among bidders (prior to or after bid submission) designed to establish bid prices at artificial, non-competitive levels and to deprive the Borrower of the benefits of free and open competition;

b. will reject a proposal for award if it determines that the bidder recommended for award has engaged in corrupt or fraudulent practices in competing for the contract in question;

★ The entire text is available at **http://www.worldbank.org/html/opr/procure/guidelin.html.**

  c. will cancel the portion of the loan allocated to a contract for goods or works if it at any time determines that corrupt or fraudulent practices were engaged in by representatives of the Borrower or of a beneficiary of the loan during the procurement or the execution of that contract, without the Borrower having taken timely and appropriate action satisfactory to the Bank to remedy the situation;

  d. will declare a firm ineligible, either indefinitely or for a stated period of time, to be awarded a Bank-financed contract if it at any time determines that the firm has engaged in corrupt or fraudulent practices in competing for, or in executing, a Bank-financed contract; and

  e. will have the right to require that, in contracts financed by a Bank loan, a provision be included requiring Suppliers and Contractors to permit the Bank to inspect their accounts and records relating to the performance of the contract and to have them audited by auditors appointed by the Bank.

★ ★ ★ ★ ★

CONSULTANT GUIDELINES FOR FRAUD AND CORRUPTION[†]

★ ★ ★ ★ ★

1.22. It is the Bank's policy to require that Borrowers (including beneficiaries of Bank loans), as well as consultants under Bank-financed contracts, observe the highest standard of ethics during the selection and execution of such contracts. In pursuance of this policy, the Bank:

  a. defines, for the purposes of this provision, the terms set forth below as follows:

   (i) "corrupt practice" means the offering, giving, receiving, or soliciting of any thing of value to influence the action of a public official in the selection process or in contract execution; and

   (ii) "fraudulent practice" means a misrepresentation of facts in order to influence a selection process or the execution of a contract to the detriment of the Borrower, and includes collusive practices among consultants (prior to or after submission of proposals) designed to establish prices at artificial, non-competitive levels and to deprive the Borrower of the benefits of free and open competition;

  b. will reject a proposal for award if it determines that the Consultant recommended for award has engaged in corrupt or fraudulent activities in competing for the contract in question;

  c. will cancel the portion of the loan allocated to the Consultant's contract if it at any time determines that corrupt or fraudulent practices were engaged in by representatives of the Borrower or of a beneficiary of the loan during the selection process or the execution of that contract, without the Borrower having taken timely and appropriate action satisfactory to the Bank to remedy the situation;

[†] The entire text is available at **http://www.worldbank.org/html/opr/consult/contents.html.**

d. will declare a Consultant ineligible, either indefinitely or for a stated period of time, to be awarded a Bank-financed contract if it at any time determines that the Consultant has engaged in corrupt or fraudulent practices in competing for, or in executing, a Bank-financed contract; and

e. will have the right to require that, in contracts financed by a Bank loan, a provision be included requiring consultants to permit the Bank to inspect their accounts and records relating to the performance of the contract and to have them audited by auditors appointed by the Bank.

★ ★ ★ ★ ★

APPENDIX II-G

WORLD BANK SANCTIONS COMMITTEE PROCEDURES*

I. INTRODUCTION

(a) It is the duty of the World Bank, under its Articles of Agreement, to ensure that the proceeds of any loan are used only for the purposes for which the loan was granted.

(b) Fraud and corruption divert resources from Bank-financed projects and undermine public confidence in the Bank and its processes. A central part of the Bank's mission to reduce poverty and improve the quality of people's lives depends on the elimination of fraud and corruption from all Bank-related activities.

(c) The Bank has announced a series of procedures for handling allegations of corrupt and fraudulent practices. The procedures have evolved and been refined as a result of the Bank's ongoing effort to establish an approach that enables the Bank to fulfill its responsibilities in an effective and fair manner.

(d) The Bank is issuing the Procedures set forth in this document to inform Bank officials, parties accused of wrongdoing, and other interested parties of the procedures currently to be followed in sanctioning corrupt and fraudulent practices in connection with a Bank-financed or Bank-executed project. These Procedures are intended to assist in facilitating the reasonable exercise of discretion by Bank officials in responding to allegations of corrupt and fraudulent practices, and do not in themselves confer any rights or privileges.

---

* The World Bank Sanctions Committee Procedures are reproduced here in their entirety. The Sanctions Committee Procedures can be found on the Web site for the World Bank at **http://www .worldbank.org;** go to "Projects and Programs", then go to "Procurement/Tender"; then go to "List of Debarred Firms" in "Shortcuts".

323

(e) The Bank reserves its right to amend, supplement, or revise any of the procedures set forth in this document at any time, with or without notice. In particular, the Bank retains all options afforded to it under its Articles of Agreement for pursuing entities and individuals engaged in corrupt and fraudulent practices, and the Bank is not obligated to retain or follow any particular procedures, in any future revision, simply by virtue of their inclusion in this document.

(f) Nothing in these Procedures, and nothing revealed during proceedings under these Procedures, shall be considered to alter, abrogate, or waive the Bank's Status, Immunities and Privileges as set forth in the Bank's Articles of Agreement or other provisions of national or international law.

II. OPERATIONAL RESPONSIBILITIES

Section 1. Sanctions Committee

(a) *Jurisdiction and Purpose:*

(1) **Composition:** The President of the Bank shall appoint the members of the Sanctions Committee (the "Committee"), which shall consist of at least five members, including two Managing Directors (one of whom shall be appointed by the President to serve as Chairman of the Committee), the General Counsel, and two other senior members of the Bank staff. Each member shall serve a two-year appointment (with the possibility of reappointment), or until the member's earlier resignation or removal.

(2) **Scope of Responsibilities:** The Committee shall determine whether contractors, bidders, suppliers, consultants, and individuals have engaged in fraudulent or corrupt practices in connection with Bank-financed or Bank-executed activities ("Bank Projects"). If the Committee finds that fraud or corruption has occurred, it shall recommend an appropriate sanction to the President of the Bank.

(3) **Definitions of "fraud" and "corruption":** For purposes of these Procedures, the terms "fraudulent practice," "fraud," "corrupt practice" and "corruption" shall have the meanings assigned to them in the Bank's Procurement Guidelines and Consultant Guidelines. As of the date of the issuance of these Procedures, these terms have the following meanings:

(A) "fraudulent practice" or "fraud" means a misrepresentation of facts in order to influence a procurement or selection process or the execution of a contract to the detriment of the borrower, and includes collusive practices among bidders or consultants (prior to or after submission of bids or proposals) designed to establish prices at artificial, noncompetitive levels and to deprive the borrower of the benefits of free and open competition; and

(B) "corrupt practice" or "corruption" means the offering, giving, receiving, or soliciting of any thing of value to influence the action of a public official in the procurement or selection process or in contract execution.

(b) *Proceedings:*

(1) **Notice:** Notice of a meeting or hearing of the Committee, together with the agenda, shall be given to Committee members at least two days prior to the meeting or hearing, unless there is an emergency. Lack of notice to members of the Committee shall not invalidate any meeting or hearing where a quorum is present.

(2) **Quorum:** At all meetings or hearings conducted by the Committee, the attendance of a majority of the members of the Committee shall constitute a quorum.

(3) **Attendance:** One or more members of the Committee may attend a meeting or hearing of the Committee by means of conference telephone or similar communications media by means of which all persons participating in the meeting or hearing can hear one another.

(4) **Decision Making:** The decisions or acts of a majority of the members of the Committee attending and voting at a meeting or hearing at which a quorum is present shall be the decisions or acts of the Committee.

(5) **Language:** Committee proceedings shall be conducted in English.

Section 2. Secretary to the Committee

(a) *Role of the Secretary:* The Committee shall appoint a Bank Staff member to serve as the Secretary to the Committee and as a confidential, impartial adviser to the Committee (the "Secretary"). Specifically, the Secretary shall:

(1) schedule all Committee meetings and hearings relating to debarment proceedings;

(2) brief the Committee members on all aspects of a matter;

(3) assist the Committee during its deliberations;

(4) draft the Committee's written decision pertaining to each matter brought before the Committee, as directed by the Committee;

(5) perform other duties assigned to the Secretary in these Procedures; and

(6) assist the Committee in other ways not inconsistent with these Procedures.

(b) *Recusal; Appointment of Acting Secretary:* The Secretary shall be recused from involvement in any matter before the Committee in which the Secretary had prior substantive involvement, and an Acting Secretary who has not had such prior substantive involvement shall be appointed by the Committee to perform the duties of the Secretary for the matter.

Section 3. Department of Institutional Integrity

(a) *Responsibilities:* Allegations of fraud or corruption within the Bank or in connection with a Bank Project shall be referred to the Department of Institutional Integrity ("INT"). The Director of the INT shall be responsible for the overall investigation of such allegations to determine if fraud or corruption was committed.

(b) *Investigations:* The Director may, in the exercise of professional discretion and in the interest of the most effective usage of Bank resources and of the promotion and protection of the Bank's mission and effectiveness, decide whether to commence, suspend, or terminate an investigation, and the manner in which an investigation is to be conducted. In particular, the Director may decide not to pursue the investigation of an allegation pertaining to an incident that occurred more than three years earlier. The Director shall, semi-annually, file a report with the President summarizing the reasons for all decisions not to pursue an investigation of fraud or corruption allegations, and shall provide copies of such report to the Sanctions Committee and the Corporate Committee on Fraud and Corruption Policy.

(c) *Referrals to Sanctions Committee:* If, upon such investigation, the Director of the INT believes that there is reasonably sufficient evidence to support a finding that fraud or corruption was committed, the INT shall present to the Secretary a proposed Notice of Debarment Proceedings, as described in Section 4(b).

(d) *Disclosures of Exculpatory or Mitigating Evidence:* In transmitting to the Secretary of the Sanctions Committee a proposed Notice of Debarment Proceedings, and in transmitting to the Sanctions Committee any other written submissions pursuant to Section 5, the INT shall present all relevant evidence in INT's possession or known to the INT that would reasonably tend to exculpate the Respondent, or that would mitigate the Respondent's culpability, subject to Section 7(c).

III. COMMENCEMENT OF PROCEEDINGS

Section 4. Notice of Debarment Proceedings

(a) *Issuance of Proposed Notice of Debarment Proceedings:*
  (1) **Review of Notice:** The Secretary shall review the proposed Notice of Debarment Proceedings and, within 15 days from its receipt from the INT, shall submit the proposed Notice, together with the Secretary's comments, if any, to a subcommittee of the Committee composed of the Chairman of the Committee and the General Counsel.
  (2) **Issuance of Notice:** Unless the subcommittee objects within 10 days of its receipt of the proposed Notice, the Secretary shall issue the Notice to each organization or individual who may be subject to sanctions thereunder ("Respondent") and the Secretary shall notify the Committee and the Director of the INT accordingly.
  (3) **Referral Back to the INT:** If the subcommittee objects to the issuance of the proposed Notice, the Secretary shall not issue the Notice and shall notify the Director of the INT of the basis for the objection.

(b) *Contents of Notice of Debarment Proceedings:* The Notice of Debarment Proceedings shall:

  (1) state the specific allegation of fraud or corruption;

  (2) summarize the facts constituting the fraudulent or corrupt practice;

  (3) attach or identify all evidence that the INT intends to present to the Committee in support of any proposed sanction;

  (4) state the sanction recommended by the INT, if any, and the maximum sanction that may be imposed by the Committee;

  (5) explain the opportunity for the Respondent to respond as described in Sections 5 and 6; and

  (6) append a copy of these Procedures, as then in effect.

IV. SUBMISSIONS TO THE COMMITTEE

Section 5. Written Submissions

(a) *Respondent's Response to Notice of Debarment Proceedings:* Within 60 days after issuance of the Notice of Debarment Proceedings, the Respondent may submit written materials presenting arguments and evidence in response to the Notice. Upon request, the Chairman of the Committee may, as a matter of discretion, grant a reasonable extension of time for the filing of the Response. The Response shall contain a certification, signed by an individual Respondent or an authorized officer of the Respondent's entity, that the information contained therein is truthful to the best of the signer's knowledge after the exercise of due diligence in reviewing the matter.

(b) *Bank's Reply in Support of Notice of Debarment Proceedings:* Within 20 days after the Respondent's filing of its Response, the INT may submit additional written materials presenting arguments and evidence in reply to the arguments and evidence set forth by the Respondent. Upon request, the Chairman of the Committee may, as a matter of discretion, grant an extension of time not to exceed 10 days. Such materials shall be sent to the Respondent by the Secretary.

(c) *Submission of Additional Materials:* In the event additional material evidence becomes available to the INT or to the Respondent after the applicable deadline for the submission of written materials has passed, but prior to the conclusion of the hearing to be held on the matter, the Chairman of the Committee may, as a matter of discretion, authorize such additional evidence to be submitted to the Committee, together with a brief argument predicated upon such evidence. The Chairman also may authorize either the INT (in the case of the submission of additional materials by the Respondent) or the Respondent (in the case of the submission of additional materials by the INT) to submit, within a reasonable timeframe, additional arguments and evidence responding or replying to the evidence and argument presented in such additional materials.

(d) *Language:* All written materials submitted to the Committee shall be in English, except that exhibits shall be in the original language with the pertinent parts translated into English.

Section 6. Admissions of Culpability

A Respondent may admit all or part of any allegation set forth in the Notice of Debarment Proceedings. The Respondent may also present evidence or arguments of mitigating circumstances, the intervening implementation of programs to detect or prevent fraud or corruption, or other facts relevant to the Committee's decision concerning an appropriate sanction. Such evidence or arguments shall be submitted in accordance with the schedule for written submissions set forth in these Procedures.

Section 7. Distribution of Written Materials

(a) *Distribution of Materials to the INT and the Respondent:* The Secretary shall provide to the INT and the Respondent, in a timely manner, in addition to copies of the Notice of Debarment Proceedings, all related written submissions and evidence, records of any related proceedings, and any other materials received or issued by the Committee relating to the proceedings, except as provided in subsection (c) of this section. The Respondent shall have no right to review or obtain any other information or documents in the Bank's possession.

(b) *Distribution of Materials to Others:* The Secretary may at any time, upon approval of the Chairman of the Committee, make available materials submitted to the Committee to other respondents in debarment proceedings involving related allegations, facts, or matters, as well as to relevant governmental authorities. In determining whether to approve the disclosure of such materials, the Chairman of the Committee shall consider, among other things, the standard for withholding sensitive materials set forth in subsection (c).

(c) *Distribution of Sensitive Materials:* Although all evidence presented to the Committee by the INT, including all relevant evidence in the INT's possession or known to the INT that would reasonably tend to exculpate the Respondent or mitigate the Respondent's culpability, shall ordinarily be provided by the Committee to the Respondent, the Committee may, in its discretion and upon request by the INT, withhold particular evidence upon a determination by the Committee that there is a reasonable basis to conclude that revealing the particular evidence might endanger the life, health, safety, or well-being of a person.

Section 8. Contents of Record

The record to be considered by the Committee shall consist of the Notice of Debarment Proceedings, all related written submissions of arguments and evidence, and all arguments presented at any hearing before the Committee.

V. HEARINGS

Section 9. Representation at Hearings

    (a) *The INT:* The Bank shall be represented before the Committee by a representative of the INT.

    (b) *The Respondent:* A Respondent may be self-represented or represented by an attorney or other individual.

Section 10. Conduct of Hearings

    (a) *Attendance:* The representative of the INT, and the Respondent and its representative, may be present throughout the hearing, but shall be dismissed when the Committee begins its deliberations.

    (b) *Presentations:*

        (1) **Order:** The representative of the INT shall present its case first. The Respondent's case shall be presented second. The INT shall be permitted to reply.

        (2) **Length:** The Chairman shall set a reasonable period of time for each presentation.

        (3) **Form:** Presentations shall be informal. They shall be limited to arguments and evidence contained in the written submissions filed with the Committee, and may rely upon or refute individual items of evidence.

        (4) **Live Testimony**: No live witness testimony shall be taken, except that the Committee may choose to call one or more witnesses who may be questioned only by the Committee, and except that a Respondent who appears in person may make a statement to the Committee. There shall be no cross-examination, although rebuttal evidence may be presented.

        (5) **Matters Relating to the Sanction:** The INT or a Respondent may present to the Committee evidence of mitigating or aggravating factors relating to the appropriateness of a particular sanction.

    (c) *Responses to Questions:* The representative of the INT and the individual presenting the Respondent's case shall be subject to questions by the members of the Committee. Refusal to answer, or the failure to answer truthfully, may be construed against that party. The Committee may grant either the INT or the Respondent up to 10 days after the hearing to provide a written supplement to any answers provided during the hearing. The INT or the Respondent shall have 10 days to respond to any such supplemental answers. There shall be no reply to any such response.

VI. EVIDENCE

Section 11. Forms of Evidence

Any kind of evidence may form the basis of arguments presented to the Committee and conclusions reached by the Committee. The Committee shall have discretion to determine the relevance, materiality, weight, and sufficiency of all evidence offered. Hearsay evidence or documentary evidence shall be given the weight deemed appropriate by the Committee. Formal rules of evidence shall not apply.

Section 12. Privileged Materials

Communication between an attorney, or a person acting at the direction of an attorney, and a client for the purpose of providing or receiving legal advice ("attorney-client communications"), and writings reflecting the mental impressions of an attorney in connection with a legal representation ("attorney work product") shall be privileged and exempt from disclosure.

VII. IMPOSITION OF SANCTIONS

Section 13. Committee's Findings and Recommendations

(a) *Basis for Findings:* The Committee's review and deliberation shall be restricted to the record as defined in Section 8 and to other facts contained in the public record.

(b) *Findings:*

   (1) **Insufficient Evidence:** If the Committee finds that the evidence is not reasonably sufficient to support a finding that the Respondent engaged in a fraudulent or corrupt practice in connection with a Bank Project, the Committee shall direct the Secretary to so notify the INT and the Respondent in writing, and the matter shall be closed.

   (2) **Recommendation of Sanctions:** If the Committee finds that the evidence is reasonably sufficient to support a finding that the Respondent engaged in a fraudulent or corrupt practice in connection with a Bank Project, the Committee shall determine an appropriate sanction from the range of possible sanctions, and shall recommend that sanction to the President of the Bank.

(c) *Range of Possible Sanctions:*

   (1) **Reprimand:** The Committee may issue a recommendation that the Respondent be reprimanded in the form of a formal letter of censure of the Respondent's behavior. A reprimand may be imposed in addition to other sanctions.

   (2) **Debarment:** The Committee may issue a recommendation that the Respondent be declared ineligible, either indefinitely or for a stated period of time, to be awarded a Bank-financed contract.

   (3) **Other Sanctions:** The Committee may issue a recommendation that the Respondent be made subject to any other sanctions that the Committee deems appropriate under the circumstances.

(d) *Parties Subject to Sanction:* When the Committee recommends to the President that a sanction be imposed on a particular Respondent, the Committee may also recommend to the President that an appropriate sanction be imposed on any individual or organization that, directly or indirectly, controls or is controlled by the Respondent.

(e) *Factors Affecting Sanction Decision:* The Committee may consider the following factors in determining an appropriate sanction:

(1) egregiousness and severity of the Respondent's actions;

(2) past conduct of the Respondent involving fraudulent or corrupt practices;

(3) magnitude of any losses caused by the Respondent;

(4) damage caused by the Respondent to the credibility of the procurement process;

(5) quality of the evidence against the Respondent;

(6) mitigating circumstances;

(7) savings of Bank resources or facilitation of an investigation being conducted by the INT occasioned by the Respondent's admission of culpability or cooperation in the investigation or hearing process; and

(8) any other factor that the Committee deems relevant.

(f) *Written Recommendation:* Upon a finding that a Respondent engaged in a fraudulent or corrupt practice and a determination of an appropriate recommended sanction, the Committee shall transmit to the President a written recommendation stating its findings of fact and its recommended sanction. At the same time that the Committee's written recommendation is submitted to the President, the Secretary shall provide copies to the Respondent and the INT, and to the Executive Directors representing the borrowing country concerned and the country of the Respondent.

Section 14. Entry of Final Decision

(a) *Decision by the President:* After a period of no less than 10 days from the time the Committee issues its recommendation, the President of the Bank shall issue a final decision concurring with or modifying the Committee's recommendation and proposed sanction. Neither the INT nor the Respondent shall have a right to present additional evidence or arguments to the President.

(b) *Final Nature of Decision:* The President's decision shall be final and shall take effect immediately, without prejudice to any action taken by any government under its applicable law.

(c) *Dissemination of Decision:* The President's decision shall be provided by the Secretary to the Respondent and the INT, and to the Executive Directors representing the borrowing country concerned and the country of the Respondent.

VIII. DISCLOSURE

Section 15. Disclosure of a Sanction to the Public

If a sanction is imposed on a Respondent, or on another organization or individual as provided in Section 13(d), information concerning the identity of each sanctioned party and the sanctions imposed shall be publicly disclosed.

Section 16. Disclosure of Evidence to Law Enforcement Authorities and Other Organizations

(a) *Evidence Pertaining to Illegal Activities:* If the Director of the INT determines that laws of member countries may have been violated by a Respondent, the Director may at any time make available to the law enforcement or administrative authorities of the countries involved any information relating to such a violation.

(b) *Evidence Pertaining to a Project Financed by another Organization:* If the Director of the INT determines that there is evidence of fraud or corruption in connection with a project financed by another international or multinational organization, including another development bank, or by an agency of a member government that promotes international development, the Director may at any time make available to that organization or agency any information relating to such fraud or corruption.

(c) *Sharing of Evidence with other Organizations:* The Secretary may at any time, upon approval of the Chairman of the Committee, make available materials submitted to the Committee to another international or multinational organization, including another development bank, or to an agency of a member government that promotes international development, that has agreed to make similar information available from its own files to the Bank. In determining whether to approve the disclosure of such materials, the Chairman of the Committee shall consider, among other things, the standard for withholding sensitive materials set forth in Section 7(c).

IX. ADDITIONAL PROVISIONS

Section 17. Definitions

Unless stated otherwise, "days" means days on which the World Bank's Headquarters offices in Washington, D.C. are officially open for business.

Section 18. Effective Date

These Procedures shall become effective on the day they are approved by the Chairman of the Sanctions Committee, and shall apply to all pending proceedings in cases then before the Committee as well as to all future cases.

WEB SITES RELEVANT TO ANTI-CORRUPTION ISSUES*

UNITED STATES GOVERNMENT

Department of Commerce

- Commerce Home Page: **http://www.doc.gov**
- Market Access and Compliance/Trade Compliance Center: Annual Reports to Congress on Implementation of the OECD Bribery Convention, Trade Complaint Hotline, Trade and Related Agreements Database (TARA), Exporter's Guides, Market Access Reports, Market Monitor, and "Market Access and Compliance-Rule of Law for Business Initiatives": **http://www.export.gov/tcc**
- Also, Country Commercial reports and guides, trade and export-related information: **http://www.ita.doc.gov/ita_home/itacnreg.html;** trade counseling and other services in other countries (1-800-USA-TRADE); Office of the Chief Counsel for International Commerce, Information on Legal Aspects of International Trade and Investment, The Anti-Corruption Review, the FCPA, and other anti-corruption materials: **http://www.ita doc.gov/ogc/occic**

Department of State

- Information on the OECD Bribery Convention and First Global Forum on Fighting Corruption Materials; documents related to the OECD Bribery Convention: **http://www.state.gov/www/issues/economic/bribery.html**

---

* Primary source: The Fourth Annual Report under Section 6 of the International Anti-Bribery and Fair Competition Act of 1998, U.S. Department of Commerce, International Trade Administration (July 2002), Appendix, at **http://www.tcc.mac.doc.gov/cgi-bin/doit.cgi?204:71:252628624:78**.

- First Global Forum on Fighting Corruption and Safeguarding Integrity, Washington, D.C., February 1999: **http://www.state.gov**
- Second Global Forum, The Hague, The Netherlands, May 28-31, 2001: **http://www.gfcorruption.org**
- Country Reports, Economic Practices and Trade Practices: **http://www.state.gov**

Department of Justice, Fraud Section

- Comprehensive information on the FCPA, legislative history of FCPA, 1998 amendments, opinion procedures, and international agreements: **http://www.usdoj.gov/criminal/fraud/fcpa**

Office of Government Ethics (OGE)

- Information on ethics, latest developments in ethics, ethics programs, and informational and educational materials including OECD Public Service Management (PUMA): **http://www.usoge.gov**

Department of the Treasury

- Information on money laundering, customs, and international financial institutions: **http://www.treas.gov**

Securities and Exchange Commission (SEC)

- Information about SEC enforcement actions, Complaint Center, and further information for accountants and auditors: **http://www.sec.gov**

Agency for International Development (USAID)

- Center for Democracy and Governance, USAID's Anti-corruption Efforts, Handbook on Fighting Corruption: **http://www.usaid.gov/our_work/democracy_and_governance/technical_areas/anti-corruption**

Inter-Governmental Organizations

Organization for Economic Cooperation and Development (OECD)

- Anticorruption-OECD AntiBribery Convention. Country compliance assessment reports: **http://www.oecd.org/document/24/0,2340,en_2649_34855_1933144_1_1_1_37447,00.html**
- ANCORRSEB, OECD Anticorruption Ring Online, materials on effective policies and practices: **http://www.oecd.org/document/43/0,2340,en_2649_34855_2757867_1_1_1_37447,00.html**

Financial Action Task Force on Money Laundering (FATF)

- **http://www.oecd.org/fatf/**

International Criminal Police Organization (INTERPOL)

- **http://www.interpol.int**

Council of Europe (COE)

- COE Anticorruption Convention, related programs, and resources: **http://www.coe.int**

Organization for Security and Cooperation in Europe (OSCE)

- Charter for European Security, Rule of Law and Fight Against Corruption: **http://www.osce.org**

Stability Pact for South Eastern Europe

- Special Coordinator of the Stability Pact for South Eastern Europe, Anti-corruption Initiative and Compact of the Stability Pact: **http://www.stabilitypact.org**

Organization of American States (OAS)

- The Fight Against Corruption in the Americas; Inter-American Convention Against Corruption; resolutions of the General Assembly, studies, and supporting documents: **http://www.oas.org/juridico/english/FightCur.html**

Middle East and North Africa (MENA)

- The World Bank Group: **http://wbln0018.worldbank.org/mna/mena.nsf**
- World Bank Institute, Anticorruption: **http://www.worldbank.org/wbi/governance/links.html**

Asia-Pacific Economic Cooperation (APEC)

- Information on the Transparency Initiative, investment, government procurement, and customs: **http://www.apecsec.org.sg**

Association of Southeast Asian Nations (ASEAN)

- **http://www.aseansec.org**

United Nations—Centre for International Crime Prevention (CICP)

- Global Program Against Corruption: **http://www.UNCJIN.org/CICP/cicp.html**
- UN Development Program (UNDP), Accountability, Transparency and Anti-corruption : **http://www.undp.org/governance/account.htm**

World Trade Organization (WTO)

- Working Group on Transparency in Government Procurement Practices: **http://www.wto.org**

The Global Corporate Governance Forum

- An OECD and World Bank Initiative to help countries improve corporate governance standards and corporate ethics **http://www.worldbank.org/privatesector/map.htm**

- OECD Principles of Corporate Governance: **http://www.oecd.org/ topic/0,2686,en_2649_34813_1_1_1_1_37439,00.html**

World Customs Organization (WCO)

- **http://www.wcoomd.org**

International Financial Institutions

The World Bank

- Public Sector Group, World Bank Anticorruption Strategy, information on preventing corruption in World Bank projects, helping countries reduce corruption, and supporting international efforts: **http://www1.worldbank .org/publicsector/anticorrupt**
- Economic Development Institute (EDI), World Bank Anticorruption Diagnostic Surveys: **http://www.worldbank.org/wbi/governance**

International Monetary Fund (IMF)

- Codes of Good Practices in Monetary and Financial Policies: **http:// www.imf.org/external/np/mae/mft/index.htm**

Inter-American Development Bank (IDB)

- **http://www.iadb.org**

Asian Development Bank (ADB)

- **http://www.adb.org**

African Development Bank (AfDB)

- **http://www.afdb.org**

European Bank for Reconstruction and Development (EBRD)

- **http://www.ebrd.com/index.htm**

Other Organizations

U.S. Chamber of Commerce (USCOC)

- Center for International Private Enterprise (CIPE), an affiliate of the USCOC, information on corporate governance and anti-corruption: **http:// www.cipe.org**

International Chamber of Commerce (ICC)

- Rules of Conduct and Bribery, ICC Commercial Crime Services, and due diligence: **http://www.iccwbo.org**

Transparency International (TI)

- TI Corruption Index and Bribe Propensity Index; TI Source Book on anticorruption strategies and other international initiatives by governments, NGOs, and the private sector: **http://www.transparency.org**

- 10th International Anti-Corruption Conference, Prague 2001: **http://www.10iacc.org**
- 11th International Anti-Corruption Conference, Seoul 2003: **http://www.11iacc.org**

U.S. International Council for Business

- **http://www.uscib.org**

The Conference Board

- Information on corporate ethics: **http://www.conference-board.org**

White Collar Crime Professor Blog

- **http://lawprofessors.typepad.com/whitecollarcrime_blog/fcpa/index.html**

American Bar Association (ABA)

- Taskforce on International Standards on Corrupt Practices: **http://www.abanet.org/intlaw/divisions/public/corrupt.html**
- ABA-Central and East European Law Initiative (CEELI): **http://www.abanet.org/ceeli/**

Ethics Resource Center

- **http://www.ethics.org**

COSO

- The Committee of Sponsoring Organizations of the Treadway Commission: **http://www.coso.org.** COSO is a volunteer private sector organization consisting of five financial professional associations:

  American Accounting Association (AAA): **http://aaahq.org/index.cfm**
  American Institute of Certified Public Accountants (AICPA): **http://www.aicpa.org/index.htm**
  Financial Executives Institute (FEI): **http://www.fei.org**
  Institute of Internal Auditors (IIA): **http://www.theiia.org**
  Institute of Management Accountants (IMA): **http://www.imanet.org**
  Association of Government Accountants (AGA): **http://www.agacgfm.org**
- Sites Directory for U.S. and International Accounting Associations and State CPA Societies: **http://www.taxsites.com/associations2.html**
- International Organization of Supreme Audit Organizations (INTOSAI) **http://www.intosai.org**

Global Coalition for Africa (GCA)

- Principles to Combat Corruption in Africa Countries; Collaborative Frameworks to Address Corruption: **http://www.gca-cma.org/ecorrtion.htm**

South Asian Association for Regional Cooperation

- http://www.saarc.org

Pacific Basin Economic Council (PBEC)

- An association of senior business leaders, which represents more than 1,200 businesses in 20 economies in the Pacific Basin region: **http://www.pbec.org**

Americas' Accountability/Anti-Corruption (AAA) Project

- http://www.respondanet.com/english/index.htm

Anti-Corruption Network for Transition Economies

- http://www.nobribes.org

Inter-Parliamentary Union

- http://www.ipu.org

World Forum on Democracy

- http://www.fordemocracy.net

National Democratic Institute for International Affairs (NDI)

- http://www.ndi.org

The International Republican Institute (IRI)

- http://www.iri.org

International Center for Journalists

- http://www.icfj.org

World Association of Newspapers

- http://www.wan-press.org

The Carter Center

- http://www.cartercenter.org

The Asia Foundation

- http://www.asiafoundation.com

The National Endowment for Democracy (NED)

- http://www.ned.org

WEB SITES WITH COUNTRY-SPECIFIC CONVENTION-RELATED LEGISLATION

- Implementing legislation of many parties to the OECD Convention can be down-loaded directly from the OECD Web site: **http://www.oecd .org/document/30/0,2340,en_2649_34855_2027102_1_1_1_37447,00 .html**. Open the **http://www.oecd.org** home page, and then look for links to the information you want.
- Several countries also have posted legislation on their government Web sites. Legislation and/or other related information of the following countries is available from one or more of these sources.

Argentina

- Ministry of Justice: : **http://www.jus.gov.ar**

Australia

- The government response (tabled in the Senate on March 11, 1999) to the Treaties Committee Report on the OECD Convention and the Draft Implementing Legislation may be found at **http://www.aph.gov.au/ hansard/hanssen.htm** (select March 11, 1999 and go to p.2634).
- The Criminal Code Amendment (Bribery of Foreign Public Officials) Bill 1999 is at **http://www.aph.gov.au/parlinfo/billsnet/main.htm** (select "old bills"). The Bill's Explanatory Memorandum is also on that Web site.

Austria

- The German text of the Austrian implementing legislation (Strafrechtsanderungsgesetz 1998 BGBl No. I 153) is available in pdf format on the OECD Web site, and at the Austrian government Web site: **http://www. ris.bka.gv.at**

Belgium

- Belgian Ministry of Justice: **http://www.just.fgov.be**
- The text of the law passed on February 10, 1999, is available in French at **http://www.194.7.188.126/justice/index_fr.htm** (to find the text, choose the Moniteur published on 23.03.1999). It is also available in French in pdf format on the OECD Web site: **http://www.oecd.org/pdf/M00007000/ M00007659.pdf**

Brazil

- The English text of the relevant legal document is available in pdf format on the OECD Web site: **http://www.oecd.org/dataoecd/43/26/ 33783624.pdf**

Bulgaria

- Council of Ministers: **http://www.government.bg**

Canada

- Access to the legislation can be obtained through the Web site for the Department of Justice/Ministére de la Justice: **http://laws.justice.gc.ca/ en/index.html**
- Alternatively, the Act concerning the Corruption of Foreign Public Officials is located at **http://www.parl.gc.ca/36/1/parlbus/chambus/house/ bills/government/S-21/S-21_3/90062be.html**
- The English text is also available in pdf format on the OECD Web site: **http://www.oecd.org/dataoecd/9/32/2376610.pdf**

Czech Republic

- Ministry of Justice: **http://www.mvcr.cz/english.html**

Denmark

- Implementing legislation can be found on the Department of Justice web site (in Danish only) at: **http://www.folketinget.dk/Samling/19981/ lovforslag_oversigtsformat/L232.htm**

Finland

- Implementing legislation can be found on the government Web site (in Finnish and Swedish) at **http://www.valtioneuvosto.fi/vn/liston/base .lsp?k=en**
- Excerpts showing amendments to the Finnish Penal Code are also available in pdf format on the OECD Web site: **http://www.oecd.org/pdf/ M00007000/M00007668.pdf**

France

- The draft law modifying the penal code and the penal procedure code relating to combating bribery and corruption can be found on the Web site of Legifrance (in French only) at **http://www.legifrance.gouv.fr/ citoyen/index.ow**
- The French text of the legislation is also available in pdf format on the OECD Web site: **http://www.legifrance.gouv.fr/html/codes_traduits/ code_penal_textan.htm**

Germany

The following are available in pdf format on the OECD Web site:

- The English (unofficial translation) text of the implementing legislation dated September 10, 1998: **http://www.oecd.org/dataoecd/62/3/2377209 .pdf**
- The relevant criminal code in unofficial English translation: **http:// www.oecd.org/dataoecd/62/10/2377370.pdf**
- The Administrative Offence Act in German, **http://www.oecd.org/pdf/ M00007000/M00007681.pdf,** and in unofficial English translation, **http:// www.oecd.org/pdf/M00007000/M00007682.pdf**

Greece

The following are both available in pdf format on the OECD Web site:
- The unofficial French translated text of the implementing legislation dated November 11, 1998: **http://www.oecd.org/dataoecd/62/34/2377562.pdf**
- The English text of Greek law No. 2331 on money laundering of August 1995: **http://www.oecd.org/dataoecd/62/40/2377562.pdf**

Hungary

- The English text of the relevant implementing legislation is available in pdf format on the OECD Web site: **http://www.oecd.org/dataoecd/63/18/2377726.pdf**

Iceland

The following are both available in pdf format on the OECD Web site:
- The English text of the Icelandic Prevention of Corruption (Amendment) Act (2001, no. 27 of 2001): **http://www.oecd.org/dataoecd/23/34/2735449.pdf**
- The relevant discussions: **http://www.irlgov.ie/bills28/bills/2000/0100/default.htm**

Ireland

- Legislation pending in the Irish parliament can be viewed or tracked at **http://www.Irlgov.ie/oireachtas**

Italy

- Law number 231, which implements the Convention can be found at **http://www.parlamento.it/parlam/leggi/deleghe/01231dl.htm**. Open the **http://www.parlamento.it** home page, and then look for links to the information you want.
- Legislation to ratify the Convention (Law of 29 September n. 300, published in Ordinary Supplement 176-L to the Official Journal of 25 October 2000 n. 250) is available in English in pdf format: **http://www.oecd.org/pdf/M00007000/M00007688.pdf**
- Other relevant legislation can be downloaded from: **http://www.oecd.org/daf/nocorruptionweb**

Japan

- An unofficial English translation of the Japanese implementing legislation (the amended Unfair Competition Act, adopted on September 18, 1998), is available in pdf format: **http://www.oecd.org/dataoecd/63/6/2377955.pdf** on the OECD Web site.

- 2001 Amendments deleting the provision on the main office exception and modifying the definition of foreign public officials (entered into force on 25 December 2001): **http://www.oecd.org/dataoecd/11/60/33652884.pdf**

- 2004 Amendment introducing nationality jurisdiction (adopted on 26 May 2004, entry into force foreseen on 1 January 2005): **http://www.oecd.org/ dataoecd/11/59/33652892.pdf**

Korea

- An English translation of the Korean implementing legislation (The Act on Preventing Bribery of Foreign Public Officials in International Business Transactions) is available in pdf format on the OECD Web site: **http://www.oecd.org/dataoecd/63/49/2378002.pdf**

Luxembourg

- The implementing legislation of 15 January 2001 is available in pdf format: **http://www.oecd.org/dataoecd/63/30/2378062.pdf.** (Official title: Loi du 15 janvier 2001 portant approbation de la Convention de l OCDE du 21 novembre 1997 sur la lutte contre la corruption d'agents publics étrangers dans les transactions commerciales internationales et relatif aux détournements, aux destructions d'actes et de titres, à la concussion, à la prise illégale d'intérêts, à la corruption et portant modification d'autres dispositions légales.)

Mexico

- The Mexican Penal Code is available on the Government's Web site in Spanish: **http://www.cddhcu.gob.mx/leyinfo/9**
- The Mexican Criminal Code is available in English in pdf format: **http://www.oecd.org/dataoecd/40/60/2739935.pdf**
- Secretariat of Public Evaluation (SECODAM) Web site with general corruption development information: **http://www.secodam.gob.mx.** Open the **http://www.secodam.gob.mx** home page, and then look for links to the information you want.

Netherlands

- The law ratifying the OECD Bribery Convention: **http://www.oecd.org/ dataoecd/41/16/2739897.pdf**
- The law implementing the OECD Bribery Convention are available in Dutch in pdf format: **http://www.oecd.org/dataoecd/40/59/2739921.pdf**

New Zealand

The following are both available in pdf format:

The relevant implementing legislation: **http://www.oecd.org/dataoecd/1/ 31/2379885.pdf**

The Crimes (Bribery of Foreign Public Officials) Amendment Act 2001: **http://www.oecd.org/dataoecd/1/33/2379956.pdf**

Norway

The implementing legislation (Amendments to the Norwegian Penal Code of May 22, 1902, chapter 2, para. 128) is available in pdf format on the following Web sites:

The OECD Web site: **http://www.oecd.org/dataoecd/53/3/33667716.pdf**
The Norwegian government Web site: **http://www.lovdata.no/all/**

Portugal

- Law no. 13/2001 transposing to national law the OECD Bribery Convention is available in English: **http://www.oecd.org/dataoecd/25/13/2736543.pdf**
- Furthermore, the law 108/2001 of 28 November 2001, amending the rules governing the offense of trading in influence and corruption, is available in the following translations:

  Portuguese: **http://www.oecd.org/dataoecd/25/15/2736563.pdf**
  French: **http://www.oecd.org/pdf/M00024000/M00024112.pdf**

Slovak Republic

- The main provisions implementing the OECD Bribery Convention can be found in the Criminal Code of the Slovak Republic of which the relevant extracts are available in pdf format: **http://www.oecd.org/dataoecd/22/63/2734815.pdf**
- Other relevant provisions are available on AnCorR web: **http://www1.oecd.org/daf/nocorruptionweb/Law/oecd.htm#Slovak Republic**

Slovenia

- The following are available in Slovenian:

  The Slovenian Penal Code of 1994: **http://www2.gov.si/zak/Zak_vel.nsf/067cd1764ec38042c12565da002f2781/a1675736157f9c0ec1256628002fa68?OpenDocument**

  The law amending the Penal Code (including on corruption issues) of 1999: **http://www2.gov.si/zak/Zak_vel.nsf/067cd1764ec38042c12565da002f2781/c12563a400338836c125673e002de2df?OpenDocument**

- The translation into English of the relevant excerpts of these laws are available in pdf: **http://www.oecd.org/dataoecd/50/18/34287694.pdf**
- The Liability of Legal Persons for Criminal Offences Act of 1999 is available in Slovenian: **http://www2.gov.si/zak/Zak_vel.nsf/067cd1764ec38042c12565da002f2781/c12563a400338836c12567a8003552bd?OpenDocument**

Spain

- Implementing legislation accessible via the following Web sites:

  Spanish presidency with links to ministries: **http://www.la-moncloa.es**
  Ministry of Justice: **http://www.mju.es**
  Ministry of Economy: **http://www.mineco.es**
  Official state bulletins: **http://www.boe.es**

- The provisions to the Spanish Penal Code, implementing the OECD Convention, is available in pdf format on the OECD Web site: **http://www.oecd.org/dataoecd/2/14/2380099.pdf**

Sweden

- The Swedish implementing legislation is available in pdf format on the OECD Web site: **http://www.oecd.org/dataoecd/1/57/2380179.pdf**

Switzerland

- Swiss laws can be found on R ecueil Systématique du Droit Fédéral (available in French, German and Italian only) at **http://www.admin.ch/ch/f/rs/rs.html.**
- The following legislation is available in French on the OECD Web site:

  Modification of the Swiss Penal Code and the Amendments to the Swiss Penal Code: **http://www.oecd.org/dataoecd/2/0/2380317.pdf**
  The Law of April 19, 1999, authorizing the ratification of the Convention: **http://www.oecd.org/dataoecd/1/59/2380246.pdf**

- The Recueil Systématique du Droit Fédéral is available in pdf-format in French: **http://www.admin.ch/ch/f/rs/rs.html**
  German: **http://www.admin.ch/ch/d/sr/sr.html**
  Italian: **http://www.admin.ch/ch/i/rs/rs.html**

United Kingdom

- The UK Anti-Terrorism, Crime and Security Act 2001 (2001 Chapter 24), Part 12: Bribery and Corruption: **http://www.uk-legislation.hmso.gov.uk/acts/acts2001/20010024.htm**
- The corresponding explanatory notes: **http://www.parliament.the-stationery-office.co.uk/pa/cm200102/cmbills/049/2002049.htm**
- The government's statement on the consolidation and amendment of the Prevention of Corruption Acts 1889-1996 and the UK whitepaper on government proposals for the reform of criminal law of corruption in England and Wales are available on the Web page of the UK home office on public life: **http://www.homeoffice.gov.uk/docs/4759.pdf**

PART **III**

COMPLIANCE

CHAPTER **XIII**

INSTITUTING PROTECTIVE MEASURES

Management of any entity must be sensitive to the prohibitions of the anti-bribery provisions of the FCPA and the new international norms. For an issuer, sensitivity is required as to the affirmative requirements of the accounting and record-keeping provisions of the FCPA. Clear and unambiguous policies should be established. These policies must be supported by practices and procedures that are systemic in nature. This includes an adequate system of internal controls and an effective compliance program.

AVOIDING THE ISSUANCE OF A SUBPOENA

In establishing an entity's policies and instituting measures to address foreign corrupt practice concerns and, for issuers, to also address accounting and record-keeping concerns, a perspective broader than the literal language of the FCPA and the new anti-corruption conventions must be kept carefully in mind. A good working knowledge of their provisions is important. However, technical expertise can never be a substitute for good judgment and an appreciation for what factors are suggestive of potential problems and what factors are apt to prompt an investigation.

Disruptions Associated with Investigations

In terms of enforcement of the FCPA by U.S. enforcement officials, the Justice Department and the SEC cast a broad net in their efforts to obtain evidence. Preventing the issuance of the first subpoena, and all of the attendant problems associated with the onset of an investigation, should be the goal of an entity's compliance policies. Typically, the subpoena will be very broad in scope. Often there will be more than one subpoena. But securing an acquittal, dismissal, or a declination to take enforcement action comes far too late in the process. Even with a good result, few investigations are short-lived.

By the time of trial, the substantial out-of-pocket costs for legal, accounting, and other experts will usually be insignificant compared to the significant opportunity costs associated with the massive disruption to an entity's operations. Enormous amounts of time are expended in determining the source of the problem, responding to requests for records, and interviewing witnesses. Schedules are changed, and meetings are cancelled. Time and resources are reallocated to address the emergency. And then there is the anxiety that permeates an organization and that inevitably undermines productivity.

In many situations, the prospect of fines and the disruption to an entity may be less of a concern than the collateral effects of an investigation. An entity that is found to be in violation of the FCPA may be subject to debarment from contracting with U.S. government agencies and to various forms of governmental assistance. Under some circumstances, an indictment alone can lead to suspension of the right to do business with the U.S. government. And protracted proceedings can cripple individuals or entities dependent upon the U.S. government for substantial portions of their revenue.

Perception

In criminal investigations, there are no special set of criteria that must be met for the issuance of a grand jury subpoena. A preliminary finding of "probable cause" or *"prima facie"* evidence is not required. The basic consideration is whether a federal prosecutor believes that there appear to be circumstances that warrant an investigation and that the use of a grand jury, and its subpoena power, could facilitate the investigation. Although prosecutors are normally careful in how the investigatory arm of a grand jury is used, for all practical purposes, a hunch or a whim can suffice as a basis for grand jury subpoenas to be issued. In a civil context, the threshold for prompting an informal investigation by the SEC is also very low.

For an entity, the overriding consideration must be how the Justice Department and the SEC will view the conduct in question. These agencies have primary responsibility for enforcing the anti-bribery provisions of the FCPA. Within these agencies the critical decision is often the initial decision by an Assistant U.S. Attorney, an FBI special agent, or a staff attorney with the Enforcement Division of the SEC. These "intake" persons typically make the early and the most critical decision to issue subpoenas or to bring the situation to the attention of the Fraud Section of the Justice Department, which oversees FCPA investigations. A similar phenomenon is associated with an SEC investigation.

Only at higher levels are policy considerations apt to play a major role as to whether an investigation will be undertaken. Cases traditionally arise out of leads brought to the attention of Assistant U.S. Attorneys, FBI special agents, and SEC enforcement attorneys. These individuals are usually overworked and plagued with limited resources. For them, it will take something out of the ordinary to turn their attention from seemingly more important and more immediate concerns. This is particularly so with white-collar investigations, which can be painstakingly complex, terribly time-consuming, and a tremendous drain on resources.

How enforcement officials will perceive a particular situation must be constantly borne in mind. The prospect of a case concerning a foreign payment by a major corporation can appeal to enforcement officials. There is the likelihood of foreign travel and visibility. At the same time, these cases can be drawn out and very time-consuming. The more graphic the nature of the violation, the more likely enforcement officials will evince interest. Similarly, the greater the degree to which an entity is complicit and engaged in some form of cover-up, the greater the likelihood of an investigation and enforcement action. As opposed to the underlying conduct itself, often it is the efforts made to conceal a violation that serve as the undoing of many individuals and entities.

IMPACT OF U.S. FEDERAL SENTENCING GUIDELINES

The most practical way for an entity to counter the prospect of an investigation is the establishment of an effective compliance program. An effective compliance program must be more than a document. It must be a program that is actively implemented and enforced. It must have the full attention of all employees at all levels. It must also extend to agents, representatives, and consultants, and to independent contractors acting on behalf of an entity. To be credible, sanctions must be actually and consistently enforced against senior as well as lower-level officials. There must not be even a hint of a double standard. The compliance program must have the full support of senior management.

It should not be necessary to establish a separate FCPA compliance program if an entity has in place an effective compliance program for other regulatory concerns. An FCPA compliance program can serve as an adjunct or a supplement to existing compliance programs. Its effectiveness will be enhanced if the process is not made more cumbersome or confusing by being part of a myriad of unrelated policies or an endless series of admonitions.

With an effective compliance program, an entity will be more likely to deter prohibited conduct and, if necessary, to take timely and corrective action. In so doing, an entity counters the very essence of corrupt intent. Properly implemented compliance practices and documented due diligence can serve as persuasive evidence that an entity did not have the requisite knowledge. They provide a credible response to an inquiry concerning a violation of the anti-bribery provisions of the FCPA and the anti-bribery conventions being implemented by many countries. In essence, it helps demonstrate that an entity did everything reasonable to prevent a violation.

COMPLIANCE PROGRAMS

The advent of the U.S. Federal Sentencing Guidelines for organizations was instrumental in promoting the development of compliance programs aimed at limiting an entity's criminal exposure for actions of its employees, as well as civil and regulatory responsibility, in a wide range of situations. Significant reductions are provided from fines and other sanctions if entities charged with criminal violations have effective compliance programs.[1] To take advantage of the sentencing guidelines, an entity must take reasonable steps "to achieve compliance with its standards, e.g., by utilizing monitoring and auditing systems reasonably designed to detect criminal conduct by its employees and other agents."[2] A convergence of developments now makes compliance programs almost mandatory from a legal standpoint. This is particularly so with issuers.

Caremark *Decision*

One outgrowth of the U.S. Federal Sentencing Guidelines is the heightened obligations of officers and directors of issuers. In a landmark case involving Caremark International, Inc., a Delaware Court of Chancery suggested that, to satisfy their obligations, corporate boards should ensure that reasonably designed systems exist to provide senior management and the board with "timely, accurate information sufficient to allow management and the board, each within its scope, to reach informed judgments concerning both the corporation's compliance with law and its business performance."[3] In other words, officers and directors could be subject to civil liability for failing to make a good faith effort to ensure that their organization has an adequate compliance program.

But even good faith efforts in establishing a compliance program may not be enough. The SEC has found that a compliance program may not suffice. It has taken the position that "if an officer or director knows or should know that his or her company's statements concerning particular issues are inadequate or incomplete, he or she has an obligation to correct that failure."[4] Aside from taking advantage of the sentencing guidelines and meeting the heightened obligations of officers and directors, the key to an effective compliance program is deterring and detecting potential problems in a timely way.

General Considerations

The basic contours of an effective internal compliance program should resemble those set forth in the U.S. Federal Sentencing Guidelines for organizations. There should be a clear policy statement supported by an effective compliance program, a comprehensive system of internal controls, and ongoing training of personnel. An effective compliance program must be more than a document or a series of admonitions. It must be a program that is actively implemented and enforced. It must have the full attention of the entity, extend to all levels of the organization, and apply to its agents, consultants, and representatives. To be credible, sanctions must be enforced against senior as well as lower-level officials.

Avoid Undue Burden

An entity's compliance program should not necessarily be separate from its system of internal accounting controls. An effective system of internal accounting controls includes a range of review and approval guidelines designed to detect and deter questionable conduct. Indeed, the planning, implementation, and monitoring of a compliance program should be closely linked to if not intertwined with an entity's system of internal accounting controls. The challenge is to design a compliance program that effectively addresses areas of concern without becoming unduly bureaucratic, unresponsive, and unable to adjust to ever-changing needs.

Serious consideration should be given to a team approach, preferably with input from a variety of areas of expertise. Lawyers with criminal experience and auditors with an understanding of internal accounting controls should be involved. But officials familiar with the nuances of an entity's business, especially those officials with knowledge or experience relative to where problems are most likely to occur, should also be involved in the process. Parent organizations must give subsidiaries sufficient leeway to develop compliance programs that are effective in their respective settings. And within each entity, the compliance program must be tailored to address relevant issues. For example, a member of the maintenance staff of an entity based in the United States would not need to know about the anti-bribery provisions of the FCPA. Yet that individual may need to know about occupational and safety regulations.

Although employee handbooks and introductory materials can be helpful, written materials cannot address all situations. Procedures should be put in place so that knowledgeable officials can quickly answer questions. The typical situation is one where an entity's employees and agents must make a quick decision. Procedures must not be cumbersome or unresponsive. Nor should they be perceived as being solely punitive. Otherwise, guidance will not be sought and corrective action cannot be taken. The focus should be on sensitizing employees and agents as to what conduct is prohibited and on providing adequate resources to assist them in working through problems that arise. A quick and timely response can play a critical role in helping an entity and its employees and agents extract themselves from difficult situations.

Protecting Those Who Seek Guidance or Make Disclosures

Often overlooked is the degree to which efforts by employees or agents to seek guidance or to make disclosures may be inhibited due to fear of reprisal. Essential to an effective compliance program are the protections afforded to those who bring legitimate concerns to the attention of compliance officials. Genuine efforts need to be made to ensure that anyone seeking in good faith to secure guidance or to make appropriate disclosures is not subject to retaliation. Even the most subtle forms of retaliation must not be tolerated. Consistent and unequivocal support of top management is crucial. Key human resource staff must also be involved to ensure that employees are not subject to adverse employment consequences. Where there is an audit committee, senior compliance officials should have direct access to it.

But allegations known to be baseless must never be tolerated. Hotlines and other means of reporting questionable conduct cannot be allowed to be abused. This can be particularly difficult in view of the need to provide an anonymous means of reporting questionable conduct. Yet even a disclosure made out of spite is not necessarily invalid. Compliance officials must always maintain the delicate balance between serving as an enforcement mechanism and serving as an effective and timely means of solving problems.

The success of a compliance program in addressing these competing considerations will ultimately depend upon the degree to which compliance officials are viewed as being open-minded in their perspective and truly independent of management pressures. An entity's staff must have sufficient trust in the compliance officials to be comfortable to make disclosures to them in sensitive situations and to seek their advice when potential problems arise. To be credible, senior compliance officials must be individuals of the utmost integrity and of sufficient stature within an entity to command the respect of the most senior members of management. They must be individuals who are, and who are perceived as being, prepared to make tough decisions, to challenge management even at considerable risk to their own careers, and to recommend disciplinary action against friends, colleagues, and senior management.

Key Components:

By insisting upon and setting forth minimum components of a compliance and ethics program as part of a settlement in a civil enforcement action for violations of the anti-bribery provisions of the FCPA, the Justice Department has provided guidance as to what it considers an adequate compliance program.[5] The components include

- establishment of a clear ethics policy;
- establishment of compliance standards and procedures that are reasonably capable of reducing the prospect of violations;
- assignment of responsibility for the compliance program to senior managers;
- establishment of procedures to ensure that substantial discretionary authority is not delegated to individuals with a propensity to engage in illegal activities;
- establishment of procedures, including recorded due diligence inquiries, to ensure that the entity forms business relationships with reputable agents, consultants, and representatives;
- implementation of regular training of officers, employees, agents, and consultants;
- implementation of appropriate disciplinary mechanisms for violations or failure to detect violations;
- establishment of a system by which officers, employees, agents, and consultants can report suspected violations without fear of retribution or going through the chain of command, including immediate managers;
- inclusion of warranties as to compliance with the relevant legal or regulatory scheme in all contracts with agents, consultants, joint venture partners, and other representatives;

- inclusion of a warranty in all agreements with agents, consultants, and other representatives that the agent, consultant, or representative shall not retain any subagent or representative without the prior written consent of a senior official; and
- inclusion in all agreements of a provision for termination for breach of any warranty, undertaking, and representation relating to compliance issues.

Affiliates

The measures that an entity should take to prevent prohibited conduct by a foreign affiliate are similar to those that should be taken in dealing with a foreign agent. The foreign affiliate should be required to adopt a compliance program and to secure periodic certifications of compliance by the affiliate's management and relevant employees. Control procedures, such as prohibitions on cash and third-country payments and measures to ensure adequate internal controls and adequate record-keeping, should be sought.

An individual or entity with only a minority interest in another entity may have limited ability to impose adequate internal controls and compliance programs. To avoid being held vicariously liable for improper activities on the part of a noncontrolled affiliate, an entity should take all reasonable steps within its power to cause the affiliate to establish, implement, and maintain appropriate compliance programs. These steps as well as the leverage that is used to prompt the other entity to take corrective action should be carefully documented. Whatever leverage is available should be fully exercised. Otherwise, questions may arise later as to whether there was knowing acquiescence to prohibited conduct.

Foreign Auditors

Without prior experience with a foreign auditor, reliance upon its representations concerning compliance issues should be circumspect. In terms of the FCPA, it is essential that the U.S. auditor or the U.S. component of a multinational accounting firm be directly involved in overseeing the audit work associated with the foreign components of an issuer. The competence of a foreign auditor may be equal to that of a U.S. auditor, but a foreign auditor is not likely to have the same understanding of the nuances of the FCPA that a U.S. auditor may have. The same limitations can also be expected to apply to a U.S. auditor's understanding of the legal regime of a foreign country's equivalent of the anti-bribery and accounting and record-keeping provisions of the FCPA.

⊛ PERFORMING DUE DILIGENCE

The U.S. Congress rejected a due diligence defense to the anti-bribery provisions whereby an entity could escape liability for the unauthorized actions of its employees or agents by establishing a compliance program. Yet, as a practical matter, if an entity has done everything reasonable in terms of implementing and actively enforcing its compliance program, an enforcement official will have difficulty convincing a judge or jury that there was corrupt intent. In essence, when a defense attorney can justifiably argue that an entity did everything reasonable under the circumstances, and enforcement officials cannot rebut such a claim, the chances of an investigation, and a successful prosecution, are greatly reduced.

To reduce the risk of problems with the anti-bribery provisions, an individual or entity contemplating investment in a foreign venture or a business relationship with a foreign partner, representative, or agent should conduct thorough due diligence. Especially where by law or by practical realities there may be great difficulty getting out of an investment or severing a relationship, the inquiry should be even more probing. In each situation, the extent of the inquiry should be governed by the circumstances.

Documentation

All aspects of the due diligence process should be carefully documented. The documentation should summarize the sources consulted and results of the review process. Any questions raised by the results of the initial review should be addressed fully in the report with an explicit statement of how those questions were resolved or an explanation as to why they remain unresolved. Due care must be exercised to ensure that the sources consulted can be depended upon to provide candid assessments.

Favorable reports from unreliable sources are never acceptable. Reports from sources that can be influenced or essentially "bought" should never be used. The validity of the due diligence, and the deference that will be given to it, will ultimately depend on the credibility, the competence, and the reputation of the source of a report or opinion. The identity of the sources should be expected to be subject to disclosure at some point in time.

The due diligence should also serve the important purpose of confirming that a prospective investment or business relationship is prudent and well supported. The factors that went into making the decision should be identified along with the evidence that the investment or business relationship had the requisite qualities to address those factors. If, for example, a consultant is retained, his or her experience, expertise, and resources should all be identified as among the bases for selecting the consultant.

An explanation to the effect that "this is the way business is done there" or "this is what everyone else does" is never a sufficient basis for proceeding in a certain manner. It may well be that the practical aspects of doing business in certain parts of the world may dictate the use of unconventional practices. But the use of unconventional practices and the reasons for using them should be carefully examined and documented. The reasons given must be more than conclusory, and they should be fully annotated for future reference.

Any due diligence documentation should be carefully maintained well past the withdrawal from an investment or the severance of a business relationship. The documentation should also be maintained well past any theoretical statute of limitations. The period of limitations can vary among jurisdictions. Capable enforcement officials can often find a means of effectively extending the period of limitations. Also, it should never be assumed that any privileges or immunities associated with the work of an attorney will preclude production at a later time. Indeed, a range of unanticipated factors may ultimately prompt a waiver or a finding that the due diligence documentation is not protected.

Red Flags

As to the potential of an improper inducement, the particular circumstances will dictate what factors should require special attention. These factors are commonly referred to as red flags. Red flags are not, in and of themselves, conclusive evidence of prohibited conduct. However, they are a basis for concern and suggest the need for additional due diligence and caution.

What constitutes a red flag will depend highly on the circumstances associated with a particular situation. What may be questionable in one set of circumstances may be entirely appropriate in another set of circumstances. But, in general, a red flag is a set of facts that, in a given context, would prompt a reasonable person to have a basis for concern as to whether prohibited conduct is intended or is likely to occur. Some of the more traditional red flags that have been found in various contexts include the following:

Country

Where an agent or entity is located or where the work is to be performed can serve as a basis for concern. The likelihood of corruption is often greater in those parts of the world where the rule of law is not consistently observed or enforced. A specific country and, in some instances, a specific locale within a country can serve as a heightened basis for concern. If one is not familiar with the reputation of a certain country, the corruption surveys performed by organizations like TI and the World Bank Institute can provide insights on countries and regions.[6]

Industry

The nature of the industry involved can serve as a basis for concern. Certain industries like oil, construction, aircraft, and defense have a history of being plagued with various forms of corruption. There may be other industries or subsets of industries that have a history of corruption. But, in general, when large governmental expenditures are involved, the prospect of improper inducements is heightened. Similarly, when access to vital markets or rare resources is subject to governmental approvals, the prospect of improper inducements is also enhanced.

History and Reputation

At the very least, an individual's or entity's history or reputation should serve as a critical early indicator before making an investment or entering into a business relationship. At the very least, it should lead to additional due diligence. As anyone with law enforcement experience can attest, it is highly unusual for someone who engages in questionable activity to limit his or her conduct to an isolated incident. In almost every instance, the questionable activity is likely to be repeated in one form or another.

News accounts of an individual or entity being in some way associated with bribes, payoffs, or kickbacks should prompt attention. So should information that an entity has been subject to a special audit in the recent past. Information that is suggestive of a questionable reputation should be taken into account. Rumor or the experiences of others can serve as a basis for concern. Neither should be treated as conclusive. But they should not be disregarded. They should prompt further inquiry and due diligence. At the same time, evidence of a good reputation and an absence of derogatory information are among the factors, along with the identity of the source of the favorable information, that should be documented as part of the due diligence process.

Misrepresentations and Inconsistencies

As with any relationship, a pattern of misrepresentations or, at the very least, inconsistencies should give rise to serious concerns. They arise directly from a prospective investment or business relationship and are among the most crucial indicators of the prospect of future problems. They are also likely to be symptomatic of an inability to address underlying issues when allegations of questionable practices arise. A satisfactory explanation for misrepresentations or inconsistencies needs to be sought. Without a clear understanding as to the basis of the misrepresentations or inconsistencies, and a well-supported basis as to why they will not continue, proceeding with such a business relationship should be undertaken only with the utmost caution and only with special mechanisms in place to minimize the likelihood of prohibited conduct.

Refusal of Certification or Confirmation

A basis for concern should arise in a situation when an employee or agent refuses to certify that he or she will abide by a prohibition with respect to engaging in prohibited practices. The refusal to execute a certification does not constitute a violation. It is suggestive although not conclusive of a basis for concern. On the other hand, execution of a certification does not absolve an individual or entity of a possible violation. But what a certification provides is a measure of compliance. It also serves to educate employees and agents and reaffirms the importance placed on compliance policies by an entity.

Another indicator is the reaction to language in a proposed agreement relative to compliance with applicable laws and regulations relating to improper inducements and to accounting and record-keeping practices. Resistance or refusal to agree to such language may be indicative of a potential problem. Understanding the basis for resistance or refusal is essential before proceeding. Otherwise, the agreement should not be entered into or, in the alternative, special measures need to be put in place to limit if not preclude the prospect of prohibited conduct.

Ties to Government, a Political Party, or a Political Candidate

Whether those involved with a prospective investment or whether a prospective partner, agent, or representative has ties to a particular government official should give rise to special inquiry. The inquiry should focus on the precise nature of the relationship as well as to what bearing the relationship may have on facilitating prohibited conduct. A similar concern and inquiry should take place if there is a relationship with an official of a political party or a candidate or prospective candidate for public office. In all of these situations, any indirect relationship, through family members or through other intermediaries, should be carefully analyzed to determine what the implications might be.

Anonymity

Any intimation to the effect that the identity of an agent, representative, consultant, or, in some situations, a party to a transaction will or must remain anonymous should be a basis for concern. There may well be unique circumstances that serve as a legitimate basis for anonymity. If so, the basis for anonymity should be credible and well supported. It should also be well documented.

Along these lines, concerns should be raised if a statement is made to the effect that things will be undertaken without anyone having to know the details of how a particular objective is achieved. This is a classic example of willful blindness. It is also representative of a transaction that is not transparent. The more transparent a relationship or transaction, the less the likelihood of questionable conduct. And when a relationship or transaction is transparent, suspicions are also less likely to arise.

Nature and Source of Recommendation

If a public official, political candidate, or party official suggests that a certain agent be retained or used in conjunction with a transaction, an inquiry should be made to determine why. Recommendations of this nature, at least on the surface, may be suggestive of a coordinated effort to facilitate an improper payment. It should never be assumed that the recommendation was coincidental or an act of kindness.

Peculiar Statements or Requests

There continually needs to be sensitivity as to what is actually said or inferred with respect to prospective investments or business relationships. The unexpected need for funds to secure business or to make certain arrangements should give rise to concern. If the individual or entity had the appropriate contacts at the time the business relationship was negotiated, the unexpected need for additional funds should prompt further inquiry. The answer may be obvious. But the precise basis for the need for the additional funds should be well understood and documented.

Any request outside the norm for the industry or for a particular part of the world should give rise to additional due diligence as to the basis for such a request. Among the types of requests that should cause concern are those for unusual or extraordinary payments, including unorthodox or substantial up-front payments; requests for unusually large lines of credit; and requests to disregard invoices or to pay unsubstantiated invoices.

Size of Payment or Commission

Where the size of the payment or commission appears to be disproportionate to the experience, expertise, or resources of the individual or entity providing the service, questions should be raised as to what is really being proposed. A determination needs to be made as to

- how much time will be involved;
- what sort of resources will be needed;
- whether there are any protections to ensure that there is not a pass through to another individual or entity; and
- what has been paid in the past for comparable expertise or assistance.

Among the factors to consider is whether the individual or entity has a record of proven experience in the pertinent field or industry. A determination needs to be made as to whether there is qualified staff or appropriate facilities that lend credence to the validity of the compensation sought. Factors that may bear on the analysis include whether documented expenses are substantial, whether substantial risk is involved, and whether the individual or entity is committing capital or substantial resources to the endeavor.

Method of Payment

Payment through unusual or convoluted means should raise concerns. This would extend to requests that payment be made in cash, that checks be made to "cash" or "bearer," that payments be made in a third country, or that payment be made in otherwise unconventional ways. Requests for false or unusually vague invoices or for no documentation should certainly raise concerns.

Illegal Agency

In many countries there are specific limitations as to who can serve as an agent. A determination should always be made as to whether the proposed individual or entity is prohibited by the written law of a country from serving as an agent, representative, or consultant. When some sort of investment is contemplated, such as a joint venture, a similar determination needs to be made. A proposed investment or business relationship should not proceed if prohibited by the written law of a country or political subdivision or governmental unit of that country. Care must always be exercised to ensure that any legal assessment is provided by competent and respected legal counsel. As is the case with other aspects of the due diligence process, the adequacy of the due diligence may ultimately depend upon the competence and reputation of the legal counsel who renders the opinion.

WRITTEN AGREEMENTS

Written agreements can assist in creating a legal structure to minimize the risk of prohibited conduct. In and of themselves, written agreements can seldom, if ever, serve as a complete defense to an enforcement action. But they may help deter prohibited conduct by educating the parties and by providing a means of impressing upon them as to the importance of the prohibitions on improper inducements to foreign officials, and, similarly, the affirmative duty to maintain adequate internal controls and accurate records. This is particularly important when a failure to abide by compliance obligations serves as a basis for terminating a relationship.

Termination Provisions

The Justice Department has on occasion insisted that a party withdraw from a business relationship. The Justice Department encourages the inclusion of provisions in written agreements that set up a means for termination for the failure to abide by the compliance obligations associated with the anti-bribery provisions of the FCPA. By delineating the serious consequences of a failure to comply, the termination provisions emphasize the importance of compliance. But a party may actually need to terminate a relationship to definitively register its disavowal of questionable conduct.

Cultural Sensitivities

Agreements should include an acknowledgment of a commitment to implement express policies against improper inducements to foreign officials. To minimize cross-cultural sensitivities as well as the perception that U.S. values are being imposed, it is usually preferable to refer to the language in the anti-corruption conventions that are designed to deter improper inducements in the conduct of international business. Since the OECD Convention created an autonomous standard as a point of reference for a number of legal systems, its language is particularly well suited for inclusion in an agreement.

However, for individuals and entities subject to the anti-bribery provisions, the language in the OECD Convention, and the other anti-corruption conventions, must be broadened to take into account the prohibitions of the FCPA with respect to political parties, party officials, and political candidates. In these situations, the definition of "public official" needs to be expanded to include political parties, party officials, and candidates for public office.[7] Otherwise, the language of the OECD Convention should be acceptable.

Facilitating Payments

Particular care needs to be taken in crafting agreements where facilitating payments are not expressly prohibited. Traditionally, most agreements include language requiring compliance with all applicable laws. Seemingly innocuous provisions of this nature present a number of potential problems that must be carefully considered and fully understood. Modifications may be needed to clarify the intentions of the parties and to address the conflicts that are often inherent in the use of this language.

By their very nature, facilitating payments are prohibited in the host country. They may also be prohibited by the laws of the country of incorporation of one of the other parties to the agreement. Unless specific provision is made, a default in a contractual agreement may result from a facilitating payment for a failure to comply with all laws. It may make no difference that the failure to comply in the form of a facilitating payment may be expressly permitted by the laws of the country of the party's incorporation. In addition, depending upon the law governing a contractual relationship, a facilitating payment also has the prospect of precluding the enforceability of a contract.[8]

Structuring Agreements

In situations where the due diligence cannot satisfactorily address concerns and a decision is still made to go forward, how a transaction or relationship is structured can be extremely critical in limiting exposure. No document can preclude or eliminate the possibility of prohibited conduct. But properly structured, and with a system of checks and balances that are carefully monitored and consistently enforced to ensure that there is compliance with terms of an agreement, an agreement can be helpful in providing ways to protect an individual or entity from the concerns that may arise in the course of the due diligence process.

The contours of a how a transaction or relationship is structured will vary depending upon the circumstances. The permutations are almost endless. No one component will necessarily suffice in addressing a particular concern. Some may be impractical or unacceptable for different reasons. The following are among the factors that should be taken into consideration:

- *Controlling expenditures.* By making payments directly to third parties as opposed to delegating that function to, for example, a joint venture partner, the prospect for improper inducements can be reduced. By actually making the payment, steps can be taken to ensure that public officials, or intermediaries acting on their behalf, are not recipients. Vouchers or other forms of documentary evidence can be required as a condition of payment. In addition, payments that may pose a concern can be withheld subject to further inquiry.
- *Excluding outstanding debts.* Agreeing to make payments on debts that were incurred by the other party prior to making an investment or entering into a business relationship should, in most situations, be avoided. It is difficult after the fact to ascertain what really prompted the incurrence of such a debt. If the debt is or was associated with a prohibited payment, the payment of that debt may constitute a form of reimbursement for the prohibited payment.
- *Audit requirement.* Insisting upon a right to audit the records of the other party to an agreement or to audit certain aspects of the other party's busi-

ness or operations can serve as a means of deterrence. To the degree that the audit is actually undertaken on a regular basis, an added and documented means of demonstrating a lack of knowledge is established. At the same time, such a mechanism may detect prohibited conduct at an early stage, when effective remedial action is most likely to be possible.

- *Third-party due diligence.* Whether it be with respect to an audit or due diligence, at times there is great reluctance to permit a party to probe into the internal affairs of another party to a prospective arrangement or to an existing business relationship. For example, as part of an acquisition, a need for due diligence is normally required. One approach that is sometimes employed is the selection of a competent and respected individual or entity, such as a law firm with no connection to either party, to conduct the due diligence. That individual or entity will conduct the specific due diligence sought by the acquiring party and render an opinion without disclosing confidential or proprietary information. Sensitive information is thereby protected and, at the same time, the acquiring party is afforded the level of assurance that it needs in determining whether to proceed with a transaction.

- *Cooperation.* In a large number of situations there is likely to be little or no support for allegations that are made or for concerns that may have been raised. However, difficulties in gaining access to records or information from another party to a business relationship can only make a situation worse and, at times, raise added concerns. Including clear and unambiguous language in an agreement that mandates cooperation and access to information can be an important and useful safeguard. It helps to defuse problems and sets the tone with respect to a business relationship.

- *No link to government approvals.* Where government approvals may be involved, payments—and, in particular, progress payments—should not be linked to government approval. Eliminating such a linkage does not alleviate the prospect of improper inducements. But the absence of any linkage lessens both the incentives for improper inducements and the likelihood that certain actions may be misinterpreted.

- *Limiting contacts with government officials.* Entirely barring any contact with public officials, or barring any contact without representatives of a party being present, may, in certain circumstances, limit the likelihood of the prohibited conduct taking place.

- *Recusals.* Particularly where an individual may be part of an organization that has ties to a government or a political party, it may be prudent in an agreement to include language requiring that individual to be recused from making certain decisions or from having authority to act on certain categories of matters.

The opinions issued by the Justice Department as part of the opinion procedure process are also an excellent source of ideas on how to structure a transaction or relationship to limit the prospect of prohibited conduct.[9] Adopting a procedure suggested by the Justice Department does not furnish a safe harbor for an individual or entity. However, the procedures recommended by the Justice Department reflect the insights of experts with years of experience. There may also be derivations of what has been recommended by the Justice Department in the opinion procedure process that may be of assistance in addressing a particular concern.

WITHDRAWAL

If there is a reluctance to take into account or to accommodate the needs of an individual or entity subject to the anti-bribery provisions of the FCPA or the anti-corruption conventions, the individual or entity should consider whether the reluctance will be perceived as a red flag. Although the need should be rare, the individual or entity may need to consider whether the potential benefits of an investment or a business relationship are sufficient to offset the risk of continued association with an individual or entity that may engage in prohibited conduct. The most prudent decision in many circumstances may ultimately be for an individual or entity to withdraw from or to sever such a business relationship.

NOTES

1. *See supra* 45, n. 7.
2. U.S.S.G. § 8A1.2 Commentary 3(k).
3. *In re* Caremark Int'l Inc. Derivative Litig., 698 A.2d 959, 970 (1996).
4. Securities Exchange Act of 1934 Release No. 39157 (September 30, 1997), Report of Investigation Pursuant to Section 21(a) of the Securities Exchange Act of 1934 Concerning the Conduct of Certain Former Officers and Directors of W.R. Grace & Co., at **http://www.sec.gov/litigation/investreport/ 34-39157.txt.**
5. United States v. Metcalf & Eddy, Inc., No. 99CV12566NG, Consent and Undertaking (D.Mass., Dec. 14, 1999), *reprinted in* Business Laws, Inc. (FCPA) at § 699.749.
6. The pertinent Web page for TI is **http://www.transparency.org/surveys/index.html,** and the pertinent Web page for the World Bank is **http://www.worldbank.org/wbi/governance/data .html#dataset2001.**
7. Sample language that is likely to meet these terms is located in the Sample Compliance Language and Explanatory Note in Appendix III-A, *infra* at 389 and 393.
8. *See infra* at 381. *See also* Sample Compliance Language, Explanatory Note, Appendix III-A, *infra* at 389–392.
9. Department of Justice, FCPA Opinion Procedure Releases, *at* **http://www.usdoj.gov/criminal/ fraud/fcpa/opiindx.htm;** Department of Justice, FCPA Review Procedure Releases, *at* **http:// www.usdoj.gov/criminal/fraud/fcpa/revindx.htm.**

CHAPTER **XIV**

RESPONDING TO
POTENTIAL VIOLATIONS

The massive disruption combined with the collateral consequences of an investigation pose a serious financial threat to any entity. An entity can reduce the disruption, and the prospect of enforcement action, by investigating and properly reporting the offenses before the detection of those offenses by enforcement officials. There are numerous practical advantages to a prompt response. But regardless of what those advantages might be, the current legal framework in the United States essentially mandates a prompt response.

IDENTIFYING POTENTIAL VIOLATIONS

Vicarious liability under the FCPA for the conduct of others, typically in far-off settings, is seldom well-defined. Many times the allegations are unfounded or, at best, cannot be confirmed. But that can never be assumed. Obviously, not every unconfirmed allegation will prompt an internal investigation. Careful analysis and thoughtful planning are required. Inducements to foreign officials do not always equate to violations of the FCPA. Sometimes, even improper inducements do not constitute a violation of either the anti-bribery provisions or the accounting and record-keeping provisions. But no longer can an analysis be limited to the implications of the FCPA. Increasingly, the anti-bribery laws of other counties as well as their legal regimes for accounting and record-keeping practices may be involved.

By law and professional standards, accountants are increasingly required to search for fraud, not just report it. Contingent liabilities stemming from an allegation of an anti-bribery violation can be material and, in turn, mandate disclosure. Even when a material contingent liability is not involved, situations can arise where an allegation of a violation of the anti-bribery provisions could be material in a qualitative sense. The impetus for prompt disclosure under the U.S. Federal Sentencing Guidelines and the U.S. securities laws must be balanced against gaining an understanding of the facts. Resources must be marshaled to ensure reliable and timely answers. Yet an unfocused investigation can waste time and resources and, most importantly, lead to an incorrect result. Accurate disclosure can, in many ways, be almost as important as timely disclosure.

Assessing the Situation

The specter of scandal often breeds chaos when allegations of FCPA violations come to light. Massive costs are incurred. Resources are seemingly sent in almost every direction at once. From a compliance standpoint, an audit committee can do no wrong by bringing on more lawyers and accountants. But from a business standpoint, an internal investigation can be very disruptive. Many audit committees are given few options. Yet a quick, unfocused reaction is not always the best approach. Careless, precipitous action can prompt a chain of counterproductive events. It can unnecessarily disrupt a wide range of activities and, most importantly, it can waste precious time.

A critical factor in any analysis is the existence of an effective compliance program. A determination needs to be made as to whether good faith efforts to install effective compliance programs in an entity's domestic and foreign operations have truly taken place over the years. This would include regular educational programs and strong support from senior management. This would also include a history of disciplinary action being taken against senior executives as well as lower-level officials. If a compliance program is to be relied upon, it must have a history of consistent, balanced, and active enforcement.

Internal Investigations

Internal investigations can serve several purposes. They can enable an entity to gain control of a situation and make informed decisions. An internal investigation may also indicate whether disclosure is required. An internal investigation can avoid the more disruptive aspects of an investigation by government officials. If properly conducted, internal investigations can at times eliminate the need for a governmental investigation. Of course, a fundamental consideration is the adequacy of the internal investigation. As opposed to an internal investigation, a governmental investigation can be much broader in scope, much more drawn out in terms of time and expense, and, in a host of ways, much more disruptive.

In allocating resources and determining the scope and focus of an internal investigation, a number of factors need to be taken into account. At the outset, it is helpful to know whether a formal investigation has been commenced or whether there is even a hint of one. If so, subject to the limitations as to what can be learned about official investigations, it is helpful to know as much as is reasonably possible, and proper, about an official inquiry. But under no set of circumstances should the objective be to alter testimony, to destroy pertinent records, or to take evasive action. The sole purpose should be to enhance an entity's ability to adequately, promptly, and fully respond. By understanding the source of concern, resources and efforts can be more effectively directed to facilitate an appropriate response.

Directed by an Attorney

The lack of an official inquiry does not eliminate the need to move quickly. But it affords an opportunity to focus on the allegations as opposed to reacting to developments. An understanding of how the entity is organized is critical to guiding an internal investigation. The answer can have significant implications. An entity's relationship to, and control over, subsidiaries and affiliates is important. It is also important whether the allegations relate to a foreign subsidiary or a joint venture partner.

The focus of an internal investigation should be to ensure that an entity learns what actually occurred. Typically, it is preferable that an internal investigation be conducted at the direction of an attorney. Accountants, consultants, and other members of the staff can work at the attorney's direction. But without an attorney's direction and control, the protections of the attorney-client privilege as well as the attorney work-product doctrine may not apply. It must be borne in mind that simply conducting an internal investigation under the direction of an attorney does not ensure that the attorney-client privilege or that attorney work-product immunity will apply. For either to apply, the internal investigation must be for the purpose of providing legal advice as opposed to being solely fact-finding in nature.

Another important concern is whether in-house counsel or an outside firm conducts the internal investigation. Several factors must be considered. In addition to an attorney's legal skills, it is important that he or she has a good rapport with and the confidence of officers and employees. It is also preferable for the attorney to have had prior investigative experience, especially as a prosecutor or a defense attorney, and to have some familiarity with an entity's operations.

In-House Counsel

As long as no conflicts are presented, there are distinct advantages in having an entity's attorneys (in-house counsel) join in the process. In-house counsel are already familiar with the entity, and they can often gather and interpret information more quickly and effectively than outside counsel can. They are also more likely to have a good rapport with employees. But in-house counsel should be precluded from an internal investigation when they have been involved in developing and implementing policies or practices that may in any way relate to the internal investigation. In-house counsel should also be precluded when they are likely to be influenced by familiarity with individuals in senior positions or by implications for career advancement.

Use of Outside Firms

Especially when the best interests of its client is used as the sole consideration in rendering advice, an outside law firm is apt to ensure greater impartiality and quicker resolution. But this can lead to substantial additional costs. Often what is reasonable and necessary must be determined on a case-by-case basis.

No overview of this nature can adequately identify all the factors that need to be taken into account in conducting an internal investigation. It can be a daunting process that can have severe and often unforeseen consequences. The utmost care must be exercised. Often the manner in which a concern or allegation is addressed is more important than the source of the concern or allegation. Consultation with experienced attorneys is always wise in these circumstances.

Potential Conflicts

One of the more complex issues that arises is the problem with undertaking to represent an entity and its employees. Multiple representations can greatly assist and expedite the fact-finding process. However, where an actual conflict exists, it is improper for attorneys to proceed with a dual representation. Generally, the best approach at the beginning of an internal investigation is to act solely for an entity. An employee should be advised that the attorney ultimately represents the entity. If an employee feels awkward in speaking with the attorney representing the entity, the attorney should suggest that the individual seek legal advice from a different attorney.

Given the financial implications associated with securing separate representation, the ability to secure their own counsel might not resolve the dilemma for many employees. To hasten and to facilitate the resolution of a matter, at times it is prudent for entities to work out arrangements so that legal costs can be paid for individuals. In many instances, individuals are inclined to be much more forthcoming once they are provided adequate assurances by an attorney who represents their interests as opposed to those of the entity.

Foreign Settings

Consideration must always be given to where the internal investigation is conducted. If it is conducted outside the United States, there may be limitations in who conducts the internal investigation as well as how it is conducted. Increasingly, the implications of a country's privacy laws, especially with respect to personal information, are a critical consideration. In a foreign jurisdiction, seeking input from local counsel is therefore always advisable.

Disclosure Issues

Disclosure to enforcement officials is an important consideration associated with the development of information suggesting the existence of prohibited conduct. A number of considerations may bear upon whether disclosure is made. U.S. law strongly encourages self-reporting or disclosure by individuals and entities. Yet an overriding consideration is whether an individual or an entity is involved. An entity cannot be subject to incarceration. Although substantial fines and other sanctions may be imposed, it is a dramatic difference from the exposure of an individual who may be subject to a substantial prison term in addition to fines, a criminal record, and being barred from an industry. Since the consequences can be severe, any decision with respect to disclosure must be carefully considered.

SEC DISCLOSURE POLICY

The SEC has given great impetus to self-reporting. Making disclosure does not mean that an individual or entity will avoid enforcement action. But by making a timely, candid, and complete disclosure, an individual or entity can take an important step in reducing the severity and, in some instances, the likelihood of sanctions. But it must always be borne in mind that only the Justice Department can make determinations relative to criminal charges. Although the Justice Department may be influenced by the same factors as the SEC, it is not bound by the position that the SEC takes. Especially for individuals, care needs to be exercised to ensure that concerns relative to criminal exposure are adequately addressed before disclosures are made to SEC officials.

Seriousness of Violation

A number of factors bear on how allegations concerning a violation may be perceived by the SEC:

- *The harm inflicted.* The degree of harm inflicted upon investors and others dependent upon the issuer will be taken into account. Consideration may be given to the impact of the harm on share price and other factors relating to the ability of an issuer to continue as a going concern.
- *The nature of the prohibited conduct.* A critical consideration will be what caused the prohibited conduct. Inadvertence, honest mistake, or simple negligence is significantly different from conduct that is intentional, prompted by internal pressures, or the result of a questionable internal culture of an issuer.
- *The systematic nature of the problem.* Whether the prohibited conduct is systematic or an isolated incident will be taken into account. Related considerations are whether the prohibited conduct took place over a lengthy period and why the prohibited conduct was not detected.
- *The involvement of management.* Management's involvement, especially at senior levels, will be evaluated. Consideration may be given to where and at what level in an organization the prohibited conduct occurred and to the degree of knowledge and involvement of management.
- *The timing and the context of the prohibited conduct.* That prohibited conduct was associated with prior management, an earlier iteration of an issuer, or an acquisition may be taken into account. Yet the implications are quite different if the prohibited conduct may have permitted an issuer to go public or to make an acquisition.

Cooperation

The SEC's Disclosure Policy takes into account four broad measures in evaluating an issuer's cooperation.[1]

Self-Policing

Consideration is given to the existence of an effective compliance program genuinely supported by management as opposed to one that exists only in form. This consideration takes into account whether the prohibited conduct was uncovered by the issuer and, if so, whether its compliance program played a role. If a formal compliance program was not in place, an issuer's pattern of preventing significant problems, making disclosures, and taking effective action will be taken into account.

Self-Reporting

Self-reporting includes the manner and the degree to which misconduct is disclosed to the public, to regulators, and to self-regulators. Whether the issuer sought in an expeditious and comprehensive manner to learn what really occurred is part of the evaluation process. The role of the audit committee, the board of directors, and the outside directors may be considered. Another factor is whether an internal review was conducted by an issuer's staff or by an outside individual or entity with no preexisting relationship to the issuer. Constraints or limitations placed on the internal review will affect its credibility.

Remediation

Prompt, complete, and effective disclosure to the public and to relevant regulatory and law enforcement bodies is required. This includes identifying related prohibited conduct that is likely to have occurred. Delay in bringing an end to the misconduct and in implementing an effective response is to be avoided. Disciplinary action must be taken. This may require termination, removal, reassignment, or other measures. Another important consideration is whether, when, and to what degree modifications to existing controls and procedures were instituted to prevent a recurrence. The extent of damage to investors and to other pertinent parties must be identified. The extent of efforts to compensate victims is among the other factors that may be considered.

Level of Disclosure

Full disclosure on the part of an issuer's staff is crucial. All information relevant to the underlying violations and remedial efforts must be furnished. The information must be of sufficient precision to facilitate prompt enforcement action. Providing information that is not requested or that might not otherwise have been uncovered relative to other violations can be an important factor in assessing the adequacy of the disclosure.

The information provided must be sufficient for enforcement officials to evaluate whether the measures taken are adequate to correct the underlying causes and to ensure against recurrence. The results of a thorough and complete report of an issuer's internal review should be promptly produced. However, with some exceptions, U.S. courts generally view such disclosure, even if mandated by law enforcement agencies, as constituting a waiver of the attorney-client privilege and of work-product immunity.

JUSTICE DEPARTMENT DISCLOSURE POLICY

The U.S. Federal Sentencing Guidelines provide a series of incentives designed to encourage the making of self-disclosure to enforcement officials. The timing of a disclosure is important. A prompt disclosure in advance of other individuals or entities who may be involved can be significant in reducing an individual's or entity's criminal exposure. As a general rule, the last to cooperate can expect to suffer the most severe consequences.

Regardless of the circumstances, disclosure must be complete and entirely forthright. Nothing should be held back from enforcement officials. No aspect of what may have occurred should be withheld or characterized in a way that could be misleading. A presentation should not gloss over or understate the seriousness of what occurred. The disclosure must be entirely earnest and forthright in every respect. If there is to be any advantage associated with a disclosure, enforcement officials must be fully informed in a dispassionate manner. There should be no surprises for enforcement officials when information is obtained from other sources.

For entities, it is always prudent and more effective to have a disclosure made by an entity's most senior officials. Simply sending an entity's attorneys, or sending subordinates with an entity's attorneys, is far less likely to be perceived as an act of contrition or an acceptance of responsibility. Enforcement officials must not be given any reason to believe that an individual or entity is simply going through the motions.

DISCLOSURES IN FINANCIAL STATEMENTS

One of the most challenging issues for an issuer is whether to disclose a suspected violation of the anti-bribery or accounting and record-keeping provisions of the FCPA or of the anti-bribery prohibitions of other countries. Frequently misunderstood, or overlooked, is the obligation to make timely disclosures in financial statements or filings with the SEC. These disclosures are required to be made regardless of whether an investigation is launched or any other action is being undertaken by enforcement authorities.

Disclosure in financial statements or filings is dependent upon an issuer's obligations under U.S. securities laws to make timely disclosure of information that may be material to shareholders. A failure to make timely disclosure of material information can also expose an issuer to civil liability to claims brought by its shareholders under U.S. securities laws as well as to the prospect of criminal and civil enforcement action.

Determining whether information suggestive of a violation of the FCPA, or any other prohibition, is material and requires disclosure entails a series of considerations that cannot be adequately addressed in the context of this book. Consultation with experts is strongly urged as to whether a disclosure in financial statements is required. Any determination as to whether disclosure is required is made even more complex when the information is inconclusive as to whether there may have been a violation under the anti-bribery or the accounting and record-keeping provisions. Traditionally, the focus has been on the quantitative materiality of a suspected violation of the FCPA. But qualitative factors may also bear upon materiality.

Qualitative Materiality

Traditionally, considerations of materiality have focused on quantitative materiality. However, through the issuance of Staff Accounting Bulletin (SAB) No. 99, the SEC has emphasized the care that needs to be taken in considering qualitative as well as quantitative materiality. "[E]valuation of materiality requires a registrant and its auditor to consider *all* the relevant circumstances."[2] There are many circumstances where misstatements having a bearing of less than 5 percent on the "bottom line" of an issuer could be material. The Financial Accounting Standards Board (FASB) has also stated that "magnitude by itself, without regard to the nature of the item and circumstances in which the judgment has to be made, will not generally be a sufficient basis for a materiality judgment."[3]

Although not an all-inclusive list, the SEC staff believes that a quantitatively small misstatement of a financial statement may be rendered material by any number of factors:

- Whether the misstatement arises from an item capable of precise measurement or whether it arises from an estimate and, if so, the degree of imprecision inherent in the estimate;
- Whether the misstatement masks a change in earnings or other trends;
- Whether the misstatement hides a failure to meet analysts' consensus expectations for the enterprise;
- Whether the misstatement changes a loss into income or vice versa;
- Whether the misstatement concerns a segment or other portion of the [issuer's] business that has been identified as playing a significant role in the [issuer's] operations or profitability;
- Whether the misstatement affects the [issuer's] compliance with regulatory requirements;
- Whether the misstatement affects the [issuer's] compliance with loan covenants or other contractual requirements;
- Whether the misstatement has the effect of increasing management's compensation—for example, by satisfying requirements for the award of bonuses or other forms of incentive compensation; and
- Whether the misstatement involves concealment of an unlawful transaction.[4]

The demonstrated volatility of the price of an issuer's securities in response to certain types of disclosure may provide guidance as to whether investors regard quantitatively small misstatements as material. "When, however, management or the independent auditor expects (based, for example, on a pattern of market performance) that a known misstatement may result in a significant positive or negative market reaction, that expected reaction should be taken into account when considering whether a misstatement is material."[5] Small intentional misstatements relative to managing earnings can also be material.

Misstatements should be considered separately and in the aggregate. Moreover, in assessing whether a misstatement results in a violation of an issuer's obligation to keep books and records that are accurate and "in reasonable detail," issuers and their auditors should consider the significance of the misstatement; how the misstatement arose; the cost of correcting the misstatement; and the clarity of authoritative accounting guidance with respect to the misstatement. Implicit in this literature is the degree to which the conduct involved may bear upon the integrity of management and an issuer's internal accounting controls.

Contingent Liabilities

Under Statement of Auditing Standards (SAS) No. 47, "an illegal payment of an otherwise immaterial amount could be material if there is a reasonable possibility that it could lead to a material contingent liability or a material loss of income."[6] Contingent monetary effects can include fines, penalties, and damages. Moreover,

> [i]f material revenue or earnings are derived from transactions involving illegal acts, or if illegal acts create significant unusual risks associated with material revenue or earnings (such as loss of significant business relationship), that information should be considered for disclosure.[7]

Loss contingencies that may arise from an illegal act can also include the threat of expropriation of assets, discontinuance of operations in another country, debarment, and litigation.[8]

When illegal acts are involved, sentencing guidelines should be taken into consideration in determining the quantitative materiality of a contingent liability associated with an illegal act. A number of factors come into play in determining the amount of a fine for a violation of the anti-bribery provisions. The amount of the bribe is one factor. But if the amount of the benefit is greater than the bribe, the amount of the benefit will be the starting point for the calculation of the fine. This can make an almost exponential difference since the amount of the benefit is typically much higher than the amount of the bribe.

In addition, under the alternative sentencing provisions,[9] a fine can be twice the gross gain or, if there is a pecuniary loss to a person other than the defendant, the fine can be the greater of twice the gross gain or twice the gross loss. As a result, where a relatively small bribe may have had the effect of securing a large amount of business for an entity, circumstances may exist where materiality can be established on a quantitative basis.

⊕ NOTES

1. *See* Report of Investigation Pursuant to Section 21(a) of the Securities Exchange Act of 1934 and Commission Statement on the Relationship of Cooperation to Agency Enforcement Decisions, Securities Exchange Act of 1934 Release No. 44969 (Oct. 23, 2001), *at* **http://www.sec.gov/litigation/ investreport/34-44969.htm;** Stephen M. Cutler, Director, Division of Enforcement, U.S. Securities and Exchange Commission, remarks before the Investment Company Institute, Securities Law Developments Conference (Dec. 6, 2001), *at* **http://www.sec.gov/news/speech/spch527.htm.**

2. SEC Staff Accounting Bulletin: No. 99—Materiality [hereinafter SAB No. 99], 17 C.F.R. pt. 211, subpt. B, § M, *available at* **http://www.sec.gov/rules/acctreps/sab99.htm,** at 3, *reprinted in* Business Laws, Inc. (FCPA) at § 201.047. Appendix I-D, *supra* at 77.

3. FASB Concepts Statement No. 2 at 123.

4. SAB No. 99, Appendix I-D, *supra* at 80–81.

5. *Id.* However, SAB No. 99 provides that "[i]f management does not expect a significant market reaction, a misstatement still may be material and should be evaluated under the criteria discussed in [SAB No. 99]."

6. *Codification of Statements on Auditing Standards* [hereinafter AU], 1 AICPA PROFESSIONAL STANDARDS, § 312.11 (2005 ed.).

7. *Id.*, § 317.15.

8. *Id.*, § 317.14.

9. 18 U.S.C. § 3571(d).

CHAPTER **XV**

OTHER CONSIDERATIONS

Private parties cannot enforce the FCPA through what are commonly referred to as private rights of action. To date, the courts in the United States have determined that neither the anti-bribery nor the accounting and record-keeping provisions provide an independent basis for a private rights of action.[1] However, conduct that violates the anti-bribery provisions of the FCPA may give rise to a private cause of action for treble damages under the Racketeer Influenced and Corrupt Organizations Act,[2] or to actions under other legal theories. A violation of the anti-bribery and the accounting and record-keeping provisions of the FCPA can have other legal implications far beyond the potential of enforcement actions by authorities in the United States or elsewhere.

NEW DISCLOSURE REQUIREMENTS

In the context of the accounting and record-keeping provisions, the detection of prohibited conduct can have ramifications for an issuer and its accountants. The role of auditors in detecting and disclosing illegal acts has been heightened in recent years. Management also has heightened obligations.

Historically, through two reporting mechanisms—the filing of modified audit reports or the filing of a Form 8-K when an issuer changes its certifying accountant—the accounting profession played a role in alerting the SEC to possible illegal acts or other irregularities. Notice of a change in the registrant's independent public accountant must be filed with the SEC on Form 8-K within five business days of the auditor's resignation or dismissal. The Form 8-K requires disclosure of disagreements and "reportable events" involving the issuer and the auditor.

"Reportable events" include determinations or conclusions that

- Adequate internal controls do not exist;
- Information has come to the accountant's attention making the accountant unable to rely upon management's representations, or making the accountant unwilling to be associated with management's financial statements;
- There was a need to expand significantly the scope of the audit and, due to the accountant's resignation or for any other reason, the scope was not expanded; or
- The reliability of past audit reports or financial statements was put in question, and (1) the issue has not been resolved to the accountant's satisfaction prior to the accountant's resignation or dismissal, or (2) if not satisfactorily resolved, the issue would have caused the auditor to qualify his or her report.[3]

Auditor's Role in Detecting Fraud

Reporting mechanisms for issuers and their auditors were enhanced by legislation adding new disclosure obligations under what is now commonly referred to as Section 10A of the Private Securities Litigation Reform Act of 1995.[4] The adoption of Section 10A emphasized the importance of the independent accountant's role in the detection of financial fraud by codifying the existing auditing standards and practices that bore most directly on the discovery of fraudulent activity. Section 10A requires the audits of financial statements to include:

- procedures designed to provide reasonable assurance of detecting illegal acts that would directly and materially affect financial statements;
- procedures designed to identify related party transactions material to the financial statements; and
- an evaluation of whether there is substantial doubt about the issuer's ability to continue as a going concern over the next fiscal year.[5]

The focus of Section 10A is on illegal acts that directly and materially affect the financial statements. For illegal acts having an indirect effect on financial statements, the auditor is not required to perform specific audit procedures that have as their primary purpose the detection of such illegal acts, except for certain inquiries of management. Nonetheless, if specific information comes to an auditor's attention about possible illegal acts, the auditor is required to perform additional procedures to gain an understanding of the nature of the act and to evaluate the effect on the financial statements, including any related contingent effect of the violation and related disclosure.

Laws and regulations having an indirect effect on an issuer's financial statements may include, among others, those related to occupational safety and health, environmental protections, food and drug safety, and equal employment. These laws generally relate more to the issuer's operations then to its accounting and financial reporting. An auditor ordinarily does not have the expertise or evidence required to recognize potential violations of these laws. Once an auditor becomes aware of a potential violation, however, consideration must be given as to the need to disclose the indirect effect of the potential violation as a contingent liability, or other item, in the financial statements.

Actions upon Discovery

Section 10A requires auditors to take certain actions upon discovery of an "illegal act."[6] The accounting interpretations further provide that the auditor should, if possible, inquire of management at a level above those involved. If management does not provide satisfactory information as to there having been no illegal act, the auditor should consult with the client's attorneys or other specialist about the application of relevant laws and regulations to the circumstances and the possible effects on the financial statements.

Arrangements for consultation with a client's attorneys should be made by the client. Applying additional procedures may be necessary to further understand what may have occurred. If an auditor becomes aware of information indicating that an illegal act has or may have occurred, the auditor must determine "whether it is likely that an illegal act has occurred."[7] If it is determined that it is likely an illegal act occurred, an auditor must "determine and consider the possible effect of the illegal act on the financial statements of the issuer, including any contingent monetary effects such as fines, penalties and damages."[8]

In addition, once there is a determination as to whether an illegal act has or may have occurred, the "independent public accountant" shall,

> as soon as practicable, inform the appropriate level of the management of the issuer and assure that the audit committee of the issuer, or the board of directors of the issuer in the absence of such a committee, is adequately informed with respect to illegal acts that have been detected or have otherwise come to the attention of such accountant in the course of the audit, unless the illegal act is clearly consequential.[9]

Immaterial Misstatements

Disclosure obligations under Section 10A are triggered "whether or not [the illegal acts are] perceived to have a material effect on the financial statements of the issuer."[10] Unless clearly inconsequential, an auditor is required to inform the appropriate level of management of an illegal act and ensure that the issuer's audit committee is "adequately informed" with respect to the illegal act.[11] Where the illegal act consists of a misstatement in the issuer's financial statements, an auditor is required to report that illegal act to the audit committee regardless of the impact of the "netting" of the misstatement with respect to other financial statement items.

Material Misstatements

When an auditor concludes that an illegal act may have a material effect on the financial statements and that senior management has not taken remedial action, the auditor must report to the board of directors that the failure to take remedial action is reasonably expected to warrant departure from a standard report of the auditor or warrant resignation from the audit engagement.[12] The board of directors must inform the SEC by notice not later than one business day after receipt of such a report. If the auditor fails to receive a copy of the notice before the expiration of the one-day period, the auditor is required to resign from the engagement or furnish the SEC with a copy of its report, or the documentation of any oral report given, not later than one business day following the failure to receive the notice.

To implement the Section 10A reporting requirements, the SEC adopted Exchange Act Rule 10A-1.[13] It sets forth the requirements for an issuer's and an auditor's reports filed with the SEC under Section 10A. The notice to the SEC must identify the issuer and the auditor, state the date the auditor made its report to the board regarding the illegal act, and provide a summary of the auditor's report to the board. The required summary must describe the act and its potential impact on the issuer's financial statements. The notice and report are to be treated as nonpublic in the same manner as the SEC's investigative records because they are intended to assist the SEC in its enforcement efforts.

AUDITORS' DUTY TO DETECT FRAUD

In 1997, consistent with Section 10A of the Exchange Act, the American Institute of Certified Public Accountants adopted SAS No. 82 to clarify an auditor's role in detecting fraud.[14] Under an earlier auditing standard, SAS No. 53,[15] auditors were required to design their audits to provide reasonable assurance of detecting material errors or irregularities, including intentional misstatements material to the financial statements. When risk factors indicated, auditors were to make appropriate inquiries of management concerning an entity's compliance with laws with respect to bribery.

SAS No. 82 superseded SAS No. 53. In addition to carrying on the obligations under SAS No. 53, auditors were given added responsibility in detecting and reporting fraud. These responsibilities applied to the audited statements for public and private entities as well as governmental agencies and not-for-profit organizations. Auditors were required to take on the added obligation of searching for fraud as well as reporting fraud. Auditors were required to assess the risk of fraud, document their response to those risks, and exercise "professional skepticism" in dealing with clients.

SAS No. 99 was adopted in 2002.[16] It superseded SAS No. 82. The obligations of SAS No. 82 were expanded to require heightened skepticism of an auditor's client. Auditors are not to be "satisfied with less-than-persuasive evidence because of a belief that management is honest" or because of "any past history with the entity."[17] The number of sources for identifying risks of fraud were also significantly expanded to include, in addition to management, internal auditors, in-house counsel, and others whom an auditor deems appropriate.[18] Identifying risks of fraud extends to determining whether these sources have knowledge of fraud or suspected fraud affecting the entity.

Representations of Management

SAS No. 99 also amends SAS No. 85 relating to management representations. Management is required to disclose its "[k]nowledge of fraud or suspected fraud involving (1) management, (2) employees who have significant roles in internal control, or (3) others where the fraud could have a material effect on the financial statements."[19] Management is also required to report its "knowledge of any allegations of fraud or suspect fraud affecting the entity received in communications from employees, former employees, analysts, regulators, short sellers, or others."[20]

Risk Factors

"Fraud" for purposes of SAS No. 99 is defined as an "intentional act that results in a material misstatement in financial statements that are the subject of an audit."[21] Among the risk factors to be taken into account are whether the entity has "[s]ignificant operations located or conducted across international borders in jurisdictions where differing business environments and cultures exist."[22] Risk of material misstatements due to fraud may vary among operating locations or business segments of an entity. As a result, an auditor is required to identify the risks related to specific geographic areas or business segments, as well as for the entity as a whole.

Evaluation of Compliance Programs

An auditor should evaluate whether an entity's "programs and controls that address identified risks of material misstatement due to fraud have been suitably designed and placed in operation."[23] This would include compliance programs designed to prevent, deter, and detect fraud and programs designed to promote a culture of honesty and ethical behavior. In addition, specific controls designed to mitigate specific risks of fraud must also be evaluated. The evaluation should determine whether the programs and controls mitigate the identified risks of material misstatement due to fraud or whether there are deficiencies that may "exacerbate" the risks.[24]

Material Misstatements

SAS No. 99 provides that an "auditor's interest relates to fraudulent acts that result in a material misstatement of financial statements."[25] Immaterial misstatements can be material and constitute the basis for fraudulent financial reporting.[26] SAS No. 99 requires different responses depending upon whether the misstatement is material.[27]

Disclosure Obligations

If the auditor determines that evidence of fraud may exist, the auditor must discuss the matter with the appropriate level of management. The auditor must report directly to the audit committee both any fraud involving senior management and fraud that causes a material misstatement of the financial statements. "*Misstatements arising from fraudulent financial reporting* are intentional misstatements or omissions of amounts or disclosures in financial statements to deceive financial statement users."[28] An unintentional illegal act that has a direct and material effect on the financial statement triggers the same procedures and considerations on the part of the auditor as a fraudulent misstatement.

An immaterial misstatement or misappropriation involving senior members of management may be reflective of a more pervasive problem. It may have implications about the integrity of management. "Fraud involving senior management and fraud (whether caused by senior management or other employees) that causes a material misstatement of the financial statements should be reported directly to the audit committee."[29] An "auditor also should consider whether the absence of or deficiencies in programs and controls to mitigate specific risks of fraud or to otherwise help prevent, deter, and detect fraud represent reportable conditions that should be communicated to senior management."[30]

Scope of Application of SAS No. 99

SAS No. 99 applies regardless of whether an entity is subject to the accounting and record-keeping provisions of the FCPA. Unlike Section 10A, the prospect of disclosure to the SEC is not contemplated by SAS No. 99. In all other respects, there is the same focus on detecting illegal activity and imposing obligations to report to senior management. For entities subject to the accounting and record-keeping provisions, this duty to seek out and detect fraud is enhanced by Rule 13b2-2. Officers and directors of issuers cannot withhold information from auditors or mislead them. Otherwise, they subject themselves to criminal and civil liability.

⚛ THE SARBANES-OXLEY ACT

In addition to the heightened obligations with respect to the accounting and record-ing keeping provisions of the FCPA, Sarbanes-Oxley increased obligations on officers and directors of issuers as well as their audit committees, auditors, and attorneys.[31]

Whistle-Blower Protections

Sarbanes-Oxley requires that audit committees establish procedures for the receipt, retention, and treatment of complaints received by an issuer regarding accounting, internal accounting controls, or auditing matters. It also calls for the establishment of procedures for the confidential and anonymous submission by employees regarding questionable accounting or auditing matters.[32] While the legislation does not address whether complaints are to be made directly to the audit committee as opposed to senior management, any consideration of appropriate checks and balances suggests that the prudent course is to afford some sort of alternative mechanism for information to be brought directly to the attention of an audit committee, or its staff, without any filtering by management.

In addition, Sarbanes-Oxley established a new cause of action for retaliation against whistleblowers who assist in providing information to federal law enforcement agencies, to the U.S. Congress or Congressional committees, to supervisors or those conducting internal investigations for or on behalf of the employer, or to any litigation involving various violations of federal law or any provision of federal law relating to fraud against shareholders.[33] There is short statute of limitations period of only 90 days and a requirement that there be an exhaustion of administrative remedies with the Secretary of Labor. Provision is made for reinstatement, back pay, and litigation costs.

Expansion of Criminal Sanctions

To give added impetus to the degree to which the U.S. Congress now views a violation of the U.S. securities laws, the penalties for a criminal violation of U.S.

securities laws, which include the accounting and record-keeping provisions, were dramatically increased by Sarbanes-Oxley for violating the accounting and record-keeping violations of the FCPA. Incarceration was increased from 10 to 20 years. Fines increased from $1 million to $5 million for individuals and from $2.5 million to $25 million for entities.

In addition, informants were given added protection. It is now a criminal offense for any individual or entity to knowingly retaliate against any person for providing information relating to the commission or possible commission of a federal offense.[34] "Retaliation" under the statute can consist of "interfering with the lawful employment or livelihood" of the informant.[35] Along these same lines, new criminal statutes have been added for the destruction, alteration, or falsification of records to impede a federal investigation or in anticipation of such an investigation and for the destruction of audit records in violation of rules and regulations promulgated by the SEC.[36]

Disclosure by Attorneys

Following a framework similar to that for auditors under Section 10A, Sarbanes-Oxley imposed disclosure obligations on attorneys who practice before the SEC.[37] Attorneys practicing before the SEC are deemed to be attorneys communicating with the SEC; representing anyone before the SEC; providing legal advice with respect to U.S. securities laws or the rules and regulations of the SEC concerning submissions or filings to be made with the SEC; and providing legal advice to an issuer as to whether a filing, submission, or other information is required to be furnished to the SEC under U.S. securities laws. The obligations extend to supervisory and subordinate attorneys. An attorney need not be employed or retained by the issuer in order to be subject to these obligations.

Attorneys practicing before the SEC are required to make disclosures at the highest levels of an issuer relative to material violations of U.S. securities laws. A "material violation" is defined as "a material violation of an applicable United States federal or state securities law, a material breach of fiduciary duty arising under United States federal or state law, or a similar material violation of any United States federal or state law."[38] The material violation is not limited to the entity. It extends to making disclosures relative to material violations by any officer, director, employee, or agent of the issuer.

The point of contact for a disclosure is to be made to the issuer's chief legal officer or to the chief executive officer, or to both. These officers are required to make a determination as to whether there was a material violation. The attorney making the disclosure is to be advised in a timely manner as to whether there was a material violation and, if so, what steps are being taken to address the violation. If a determination of no material violation is made, the attorney making the disclosure is to be advised in a timely manner as to the basis for reaching that conclusion. If an appropriate response is not provided to the disclosing attorney within a reasonable time, the disclosure is to be made to the audit committee, another committee of independent members of the board of directors, or to the board of directors.

If a disclosing attorney reasonably believes that it would be futile to make disclosure to the chief legal officer or to the chief executive officers, disclosures can be made to the audit committee, to another committee of independent members of the board of directors, or to the board of directors. In addition, if a disclosing attorney reasonably believes that an unsatisfactory or untimely response has been provided, those perspectives are to be brought to the attention of the chief legal officer, to the chief executive officer, or to the directors to whom the disclosure was made. A discharged attorney who reasonably believes the discharge was the result of making a required disclosure may bring that to the attention of the board of directors or a committee of the board of directors.

In the event an issuer has established a qualified legal compliance committee, disclosures may be made to that committee instead of the chief legal officer, the chief executive officer, or the board of directors. By making the disclosure to a legal compliance committee, no further obligations are imposed on the disclosing attorney to make further inquiry relative to the adequacy of the response. Similarly, by referring the matter to the qualified legal compliance committee, and so advising the disclosing attorney, the chief legal officer or chief executive officer will fulfill his or her obligation to respond to the disclosing attorney.

One of the unique and controversial aspects of the disclosure obligations placed upon attorneys is the provision allowing for disclosure of confidential information to the SEC without the consent of the issuer.[39] Disclosures to the SEC are permitted where an attorney believes it reasonably necessary to prevent a material violation that is likely to cause substantial injury; to prevent the commission or subornation of perjury or a false statement relative to an SEC investigation or proceeding; or to rectify a material violation where the disclosing attorney's services were used.

IMPLICATIONS FOR BUSINESS, EMPLOYMENT, AND CLIENT RELATIONSHIPS

The FCPA and the anti-corruption conventions have had, and will increasingly have, implications on relationships between and among private parties. Regardless of whether action is taken by enforcement officials, a growing body of domestic and international law directly bears upon the conduct of business as a result of a failure to comply with the FCPA or other legal regimes that prohibit improper inducements to foreign officials.

Public-Policy Exception to At-Will Employment

In employment contexts, the FCPA has been found in the United States to serve as a basis for the application of the public-policy exception for the termination of at-will employees.[40] For employees who are alleged to have been terminated for their refusal to condone or carry out practices that are prohibited under the anti-bribery or the accounting and record-keeping provisions of the FCPA, the practical effect is to shift the burden to the employer to show that the termination was for cause. Especially in the wake of the corporate scandals in recent years, this public-policy exception to at-will employment relationships associated with the FCPA can be expected to be followed by more and more courts.

Enforcement of Contracts

Within the context of contractual disputes, the FCPA can in certain situations serve as a basis for not enforcing a contract. In litigation in U.S. courts and in other common law jurisdictions, the "unclean hands" doctrine can bar a claim for equitable relief. But in some jurisdictions the doctrine has also been applied to bar a cause of action. This includes situations where a payment may have been made in violation of the anti-bribery provisions of the FCPA.[41] The consequence is that an individual or entity may be precluded from recovering on a contract where the individual or entity may have violated the anti-bribery provisions of the FCPA.

In the context of international arbitration, arbitral tribunals and courts in enforcing or annulling arbitral awards are increasingly confronted with situations where the enforcement of a contract or the enforcement of an award relating to a contract may be barred due to improper inducements in conjunction with the contract. Over the years, arbitrators have asserted the existence of "an international public order which makes bribery contracts invalid and contrary to *bonos mores.*"[42] Some tribunals have found national laws to also hold such contracts to be illegal.

Until the recent adoption of the anti-bribery conventions, no specific reference to international law could be made. That has now changed. There can be little question that an agreement to pay a bribe is contrary to customary international law and not simply a breach of moral standards. Arbitrators can accordingly expect to be increasingly confronted with arguments of this nature by parties challenging the enforcement of a contract where allegations of improper inducements exist.

Protected Information

The combination of management's disclosure obligations under Rule 13b2-2 and an auditor's obligation to inquire under Section 10A and SAS No. 99 may effectively eviscerate the protections of the attorney-client privilege, the attorney work-product doctrine, and other similar protections. If auditors are carrying out their responsibilities under Section 10A and SAS No. 99, audits must be designed to detect illegal conduct. Likely questions include whether management has knowledge of illegal acts and where illegal conduct is most likely to occur. Although management may learn of questionable conduct through its attorneys, management controls the attorney-client privilege. Management is presented with the dilemma of disclosing unfavorable information, and bearing the consequences, or facing civil and possibly criminal charges for violating Rule 13b2-2 for failing to make required disclosures.

All of the ramifications of Section 10A have yet to be determined. Because the legislative history is sparse, little guidance is provided as to what was really intended. Section 10A will be defined over time by what cases are brought by the SEC. But the implications can be daunting for an issuer or an auditor who fails to abide by the terms of Section 10A. Aside from the prospect of the imposition of penalties, the safe harbor from private litigation provided by Section 10A is also lost.[43] To avoid being placed in this predicament, issuers are well advised to take steps to ensure that the system of internal controls and compliance programs are adequate and actively monitored and enforced.

LIMITATIONS ON GOVERNMENT CONTRACTS AND SUPPORT

Governments often promote exports and investments by providing them with financial support in the form of credit or insurance for export or investment activities. In February of 2003, the OECD Working Party on Export Credits and Credit Guarantees agreed on an Action Statement that would assist in the implementation of the OECD Convention by precluding official export credit and insurance support for individuals and entities that refuse or fail to abide by its terms. The Action Statement urges export credit agencies to inform exporters of the legal consequences of bribery; to require a declaration from the exporter to the effect that the contract to be guaranteed or insured has not been obtained through bribery or corruption; and to threaten effective sanctions and other appropriate measures in case of violations.[44]

The United States and many of the OECD member countries have already implemented measures to carry out the Action Statement.[45] Among the ramifications in the United States is the conditioning of advocacy support for a U.S. entity and its foreign parent and affiliates. They may not pay bribes in connection with the transaction for which advocacy support is sought, and they must maintain policies that prohibit the bribery of foreign officials. The Export-Import Bank requires supplier certificates disclosing offers or other arrangements by the supplier or by third parties for any payments not already disclosed. The Overseas Private Investment Corporation precludes payments on its insurance contracts if corrupt practices by the insured are the preponderant cause of any otherwise covered loss.

ALTERNATIVE SOURCES OF ASSISTANCE

In some settings countervailing factors are likely to render useless almost any form of compliance program or procedures. In those situations, the prudent course is not to proceed with a prospective investment or relationship. But there are some individuals and entities that, to exist from a business standpoint, have no alternative but to pursue opportunities in environments where corruption is widespread. A classic example is the oil industry where sources of oil are often found in locales where businesses are subject to all sorts of extortionate demands by government officials. In such situations, thoughtful and innovative approaches to ensuring compliance need to be explored.

Nongovernmental Assistance

There is no substitute for exercising the utmost care and diligence in operating in an environment where corruption may be widespread. However, increasingly, various organizations as well as ad hoc groups have begun to explore the development of mechanisms that might enable well-intended individuals and entities to operate successfully in these difficult settings. Among the more noted examples are the work of two nongovernmental organizations, TI and TRACE International, Inc. (TRACE).

Transparency International

For some time TI has developed and begun to assist governments and entities in using what are termed "integrity pacts."[46] In general, integrity pacts are agreements entered into between a unit of government and prospective bidders on public procurement to not engage in certain prohibited activities, including the payment of bribes. These integrity pacts can be modified to adapt to the peculiarities of a particular situation. Participants refrain from bribing in the knowledge that their competitors are bound by the same rules. Typically, bidders are required to disclose commissions and similar expenditures. Sanctions can range from loss or denial of the contract, forfeiture of the bid or performance bond and liability for damages, debarment from future contracts, and criminal charges or other forms of punishment.

TRACE

TRACE works to reduce corruption in transactions involving business intermediaries, including agents, representatives, consultants, distributors, and subcontractors.[47] TRACE prepares background reports on member intermediaries who commit to its standards and makes the reports available to subscribing entities. In concept, the goal is to avoid duplication. TRACE provides a mechanism for sharing information on intermediaries and thereby reduces costs associated with the due diligence process. An intermediary that withstands the scrutiny of its due diligence process is arguably less likely to have a basis for concern. At the same time, TRACE presents distinct advantages for those intermediaries who are prepared to meet its terms.

Governmental Assistance

Especially in situations where a competitor is known to engage in improper payments for the purpose of securing business advantage in a foreign setting, the U.S. government can be a source of assistance. In the country where the improper payments are believed to have been made, U.S. Embassy or consular officials may be of assistance. In particular, the commercial attachés in those locations should be receptive to meeting with representatives of U.S. firms seeking to do business there. But regardless, the Trade Compliance Center at the U.S. Department of Commerce is specially equipped to provide assistance in these situations.[48] This can even be done over the Internet.[49]

If deemed credible, the information is apt to be directed to appropriate U.S. agencies. At times diplomatic contacts may be initiated with the government of the foreign competitor or with the government of the country where the transaction occurred. The disclosure could also lead to an investigation in the United

States or elsewhere. In addition, information on the bribery of public officials can be used within the OECD to apply "peer group pressure" on parties to carry out their obligations under the OECD Convention to take effective enforcement action.

Making a disclosure to U.S. governmental officials should never be undertaken in a cavalier manner. A false statement to the U.S. government or to a U.S. governmental official is a serious crime subject to incarceration. If action is to be undertaken by U.S. officials, every reasonable effort should be made to ensure that the information provided is credible and, to the extent possible, corroborated. Where there are uncertainties with respect to certain aspects of the information provided, appropriate caveats should be made. While U.S. officials can be expected to take all appropriate steps to ensure confidentiality as to the source of the information, no absolute guarantees can be made that the source of the information will never be disclosed.

Especially for countries that are parties to the OECD Convention, their government can be expected to provide similar assistance to individuals and entities in their countries seeking to do business in foreign settings. In addition, within the framework of procurement opportunities being offered by the multilateral lending institutions, more and more mechanisms are being put in place to bring the questionable practices of competitors to the attention of appropriate officials at these institutions. But, in all of these situations, the utmost care must be exercised to ensure that unfounded allegations are not made. Not only can an individual's or entity's credibility be put in jeopardy, it can also subject that individual or entity to legal redress.

CONCLUSION

The implications of the new international norms with respect to foreign corrupt practices in the conduct of international business cannot be overstated. With the implementation and active enforcement of the new anti-bribery conventions, the ramifications will have untold significance. The resolution of disputes and employment, procurement, and contracting practices are already being affected. It is only a matter of time before the private right of action created by the CoE Civil Law Convention will be used as a mechanism to counter the loss of business opportunities as a result of prohibited conduct on the part of competitors.

For issuers, Sarbanes-Oxley has heightened affirmative obligations to comply with the accounting and record-keeping provisions of the FCPA. The consequences for failing to comply with the accounting and record-keeping provisions have dramatically increased. Even more aggressive enforcement of their provisions can be expected to ensue from the proliferation of corporate scandals in the United States and abroad. Other countries can be expected to further develop and to more actively enforce their legal regimes with respect to accounting and record-keeping practices.

Entities can no longer limit the focus of their anti-bribery policies to the FCPA. Consideration must be given to the legal regimes now being implemented as a result of the new anti-corruption conventions. Even for entities that are not issuers, prudence dictates that compliance programs be designed to ensure the adequacy of systems of internal controls and the accuracy of records. These steps are essential to deterring and to detecting prohibited conduct.

In counseling a client on issues relating to the FCPA and the new international norms, an earnest effort to comply is fundamental. To do otherwise is to put at risk the viability of an entity. But by implementing and rigorously enforcing an effective compliance program and undertaking carefully planned and thorough due diligence with respect to transactions, retaining agents, and undertaking initiatives in unfamiliar settings, an entity puts itself in the best position to effectively engage in international business without the specter of being caught up in a scandal.

🌐 NOTES

1. *E.g.*, Lamb v. Phillip Morris, Inc., 915 F.2d 1024, 1027-29 (6th Cir. 1990), *cert. denied*, 498 U.S. 1086 (1991); J.S. Service Center Corporation v. General Electric Technical Services Company, Inc., 937 F. Supp. 216, 226 (S.D.N.Y. 1996).
2. 18 U.S.C. §§ 1961 *et seq.*
3. *See* Item 304 of Regulations S-K, 17 C.F.R. § 229.304.
4. 15 U.S.C.§ 78j-1.
5. *Id.*, § 78j-1(a).
6. *Id.*, § 78j-1(f).
7. *Id.*, § 78j-1(b)(1)(A)(i).
8. *Id.*, § 78j-1(b)(1)(A)(ii).
9. *Id.*, § 78j-1(b)(1)(B).
10. *Id.*, § 78j-1(b)(1).
11. *Id.*, § 78j-1(b)(1)(B).
12. *Id.*, § 78j-1(b)(2).
13. 17 C.F.R. § 240.10A-1.
14. AU § 316A (2003 ed.).
15. AU § 316A.05 (1997 ed.).
16. AU § 316 (2005 ed.).
17. *Id.*, § 316.13.
18. *Id.*, §§ 316.23, 316.25, 316.85.
19. *Id.*, § 333.06.
20. *Id.*
21. *Id.*, § 316.05.
22. *Id.*
23. *Id.*
24. *Id.*, § 316.06.
25. *Id.*, § 316.79.
26. AU § 312.11 provides that:

As a result of the interaction of quantitative and qualitative considerations in materiality judgments, misstatements of relatively small amounts that come to the auditor's attention could have a material effect on the financial statements. For example, an illegal payment of an otherwise immaterial amount could be material if there is a reasonable possibility that it could lead to a material contingent liability or a material loss of revenue.

In addition, AU § 317.16 provides that:

The auditor should consider the implications of an illegal act in relation to other aspects of the audit, particularly the reliability of representations of management. The implications of particular illegal acts will depend on the relationship of the perpetration and concealment, if any, of the illegal act to specific control procedures and the level of management or employees involved.

27. *Id.*, § 316.80.

28. *Id.*, § 316.04.

29. *Id.*, § 316.79.

30. *Id.*

31. *Supra* at 43 and 45.

32. 15 U.S.C. § 78j-1(m)(4).

33. 18 U.S.C. § 1412A.

34. *Id.*, § 1513(e).

35. *Id.*

36. *Id.*, §§ 1519 and 1520.

37. 15 U.S.C. § 7245.

38. 17 C.F.R. § 205.2(i).

39. *Id.*, § 205.3(d).

40. *E.g.*, D'Agostino v. Johnson & Johnson, Inc., 133 N.J. 516, 628 A.2d 305 (S.Ct. N.J. 1993); Thompson v. St. Regis Paper Co., 102 Wash.2d 219, 685 P.2d 1081 (S.Ct. Wash. 1984).

41. *E.g.*, Adler v. Federal Republic of Nigeria, 219 F.3d 869, 876–78 (9th Cir. 2000); SEDCO International, S.A. v. Cory, 683 F.2d 1201, 1210–11 (8th Cir. 1982).

42. Martin, *International Arbitration and Corruption: An Evolving Standard*, INT'L ENERGY AND MIN. ARB., MIN. L. SERIES, (Spring 2002).

43. 15 U.S.C. § 78j-1(c).

44. Action Statement on Bribery and Officially Supported Export Credits, OECD TD/ECG(2000)15 (Feb. 20, 2003).

45. For the status of implementation of the OECD Action Statement, *see* OECD, Working Party on Export Credits and Credit Guarantees, **http://www.olis.oecd.org/olis/2003doc.nsf/43bb6130e 5e86e5fc12569fa005d004c/2bee1e07e8625612c1256dbb00457365/$FILE/JT00151165.PDF.**

46. For more information on integrity pacts, *see* Transparency International, Preventing Corruption in Public Contracting, Integrity Pacts, **http://www.transparency.org/integrity_pact/preventing/ integ_pacts.html.**

47. For more information on TRACE, *see* **http://www.traceinternational.org.**

48. For additional information as to the type of assistance that the U.S. Department of Commerce can provide in these situations, see Eleanor Roberts Lewis, *What the U.S. Government Can Do to Assist U.S. Companies with Respect to Transnational Corruption* (speech, American Bar Association, Forum on the Foreign Corrupt Practices Act and the OECD Convention, San Francisco, Mar. 21, 2002), *at* **http://www.osec.doc.gov/ogc/occic/abaspeech.htm.**

49. For more information, select "Bribery Complaints & Reports" from the home page of the Trade Compliance Center, **http://tcc.mac.doc.gov.**

SAMPLE COMPLIANCE LANGUAGE*

ARTICLE X — COMPLIANCE

X.1 Compliance with Laws

X.1.1 The parties agree to comply with all applicable laws, rules and regulations, including, without limitation, those of their respective countries of incorporation or principal place of business, and of the country of operations, (collectively referred to as "applicable laws"), directly and adversely affecting the work to be performed under this contract (hereinafter referred to as "the Work") or the performance of either party's obligations under this contract.

X.1.2 Notwithstanding any provision in this contract to the contrary, the parties agree that the failure by one party, solely on account of conflict of laws, to comply with applicable laws directly affecting the Work or performance of such party's obligations under this contract shall not constitute a breach of this contract.

Optional

X.1.3 Notwithstanding any provision in this contract to the contrary, the parties agree that in undertaking the work and performing their respective obligations under this contract, neither party agrees to nor shall either party be

---

* The sample guidance language and guidance notes are, in large part, taken from the Master Service Agreements published in 2002 by the Association of International Petroleum Negotiators (AIPN). The author was one of the principal drafters of the compliance provisions. The sample compliance guidance language and the explanatory notes are published here with the permission of AIPN.

obligated to engage in any act or omission to act, which is prohibited by or penalized under the laws, or regulations of [name of country].

X.2 Compliance Policies and Procedures

X.2.1 The parties shall endeavor to ensure through the establishment, implementation, monitoring and active enforcement of pertinent policies and procedures, including, without limitation, the keeping of accurate books and records, that there is continuous and full compliance with all of the provisions of Article X.

X.2.2 The parties shall fully cooperate with each other, including, without limitation, sharing information, making necessary disclosures, and addressing concerns raised by the other party or by government officials, to endeavor to ensure that there is continuous and full compliance with all of the provisions of Article X.

X.3 Improper Government Influence

X.3.1 [name of party] shall not permit or countenance any member of its organization, or any individual or entity acting on its behalf, and [name of other party] shall not permit or countenance any member of its organization, or any individual or entity acting on its behalf, offering, promising or giving, in connection with carrying out the obligations or performing the Work under this contract, any undue pecuniary or other advantage, whether directly or indirectly through intermediaries, to a Public Official, for that official or for a third party, to act or refrain from acting in relation to the performance of official duties, to

Alternative 1

obtain or retain business or other improper advantage.

Alternative 2

obtain or retain business or other improper advantage. The prohibitions of Article X.3.1 shall also extend and apply to any facilitating or expediting payment to a public official to secure the performance of routine governmental action.

Alternative 3

obtain or retain business or other improper advantage. Notwithstanding any provision in this contract to the contrary, the prohibitions of this contract shall not apply to any facilitating or expediting payment to secure the performance of routine governmental action unrelated to the terms, award or continuation of this contract.

X.3.2 For purposes of Article X.3.1, "Public Official" means,

Alternative 1

> any individual holding a legislative, administrative or judicial office, whether appointed or elected; any individual exercising a public function for a foreign country, including, without limitation, for a public agency or public enterprise; any official or agent of a public international organization; and any political party or party official, or any candidate for public office.

Alternative 2

> any individual holding a legislative, administrative or judicial office, whether appointed or elected; any individual exercising a public function for a foreign country, including, without limitation, for a public agency or public enterprise; and any official or agent of a public international organization.

X.4 Termination for Non-Compliance

4.1 If either party breaches (*Optional* Article X.1.3) Article X.3, the other party may terminate this contract on ___ days' notice.

4.2 If either party breaches (*Optional* Article X.1.3) Article X.2, it shall be considered a default which directly and adversely affects the work or the performance of either party's obligations under this contract and termination for such breach shall be governed by the basic default provisions in Article ___ of the contract.

EXPLANATORY NOTES

Compliance with Laws

A party to an agreement generally expects the other party to comply with legal regimes that may bear on the performance of the work or the obligations under an agreement. Historically, this expectation has prompted the inclusion of language that requires there to be compliance with applicable legal regimes. Article X.1.1 reflects this general practice. However, this provision can present a number of potential problems that must be carefully considered.

Foremost among the considerations are the implications of the basic default provisions of the contract and Article X.4 and the events that would give rise to a breach of Article X.1.1. It must be recognized that a breach of Article X.1.1 is a breach of the contract and may trigger a remedy for breach at law. However, not all violations of law necessarily constitute a breach of Article X.1.1 or give rise to "default" under the basic default provisions of a contract. For a violation of applicable law to constitute a breach under Article X.1.1, the violation must be one "directly and adversely affecting the work or performance of such party's obligations under this contract." Except for this qualifying language in Article X.1.1, Article X.1.2, and Article X.1.3, any breach of contract or any violation of applicable law could give rise to "default." For example, without this qualifying language, a traffic ticket could conceivably serve as the basis for default or termination.

A related consideration is a situation in which a violation of law may, by implication, be permitted. The classic situation relates to so-called "facilitating payments". By their nature, facilitating payments are prohibited in the country of operations, yet they may be permitted by a party's country of incorporation or principal place of business, or both. Conversely, there are a number of other contexts in which a violation of law in the country of operations may be permitted but be prohibited by the country of incorporation. Article X.1.2 is designed to avoid one key "conflicts" situation in which, merely by agreeing in general terms to comply with the laws of a certain country under a choice of governing law clause, the parties thereby expose themselves to penalties under the laws of their own country of incorporation or principal place of business. In certain limited contexts, Article X.1.2 protects the parties from breach of Article X.1.1 where such breach arises because of an outright conflict of laws. For example, a conflict of laws may arise in the context of projects in many Middle Eastern countries, which may by law boycott Israel, involving companies subject to United States anti-boycott laws prohibiting them from agreeing to be bound by the boycott of Israel.

Care needs to be exercised to ensure that the implications of Article X.1.1 and its relationship to the provisions in Article X.4. While modifications may be made to meet particular needs and expectations, parties should exercise great caution in doing so. For example, one option that might be considered is the elimination of Article X.1. This would eliminate the complexities associated with its use while the essence of Article X.1 might still be implied. On the other hand, parties might be understandably reluctant to expressly agree that compliance with applicable law is not required. As drafted, Article X.1.1, together with the balance of Article X.1 and Article X.4, are designed to achieve a workable compromise that, if fully understood and considered by the parties in the course of negotiations, will minimize the likelihood of unintended consequences.

There will inevitably be situations in which conflicting rights and obligations will arise under the governing law of the contract, the laws of the country of operations, and the laws of a party's place of incorporation. Such conflict of laws situations cannot adequately be dealt with in these model forms. As noted, Article X.1.1 has been drafted to impose a general obligation on parties to comply with applicable laws. Article X.1.2 recognizes that a breach by one party on account of a conflict of laws should not entitle the other party to declare a default or otherwise declare a breach. Because of the complexities involved, specific legal advice should always be sought in any situation potentially involving such conflicts.

Compliance Policies and Procedures

Increasingly, whether through soft law in the form of corporate governance initiatives or through specific legal requirements, business entities, especially corporate entities, are being required to put in place compliance programs to ensure compliance with various legal and regulatory regimes. Article X.2.1 calls for an active and ongoing effort to implement policies and procedures to ensure that compliance obligations are being adequately discharged. Moreover, because a party may need access to the other party's books and records to prove (or disprove) compliance, this provision also includes an obligation to endeavor to ensure that accurate books and records are maintained and that there is an effective system of internal controls in place to ensure the accuracy of accounting and other records.

In dealing with Article X.2.2 compliance matters, the cooperation of the parties may prove more helpful and important than other remedies. Article X.2.2 is drafted to ensure full cooperation when questions are raised as to whether one party has adequately carried out its compliance obligations. Cooperation is thereby encouraged to facilitate access to information and disclosures among the parties as well as to governmental officials.

Improper Government Influence

Since one of the parties may be located in the country of operations, the use of "foreign" in referring to Public Official was purposely omitted. Moreover, the prohibitions apply whether a foreign or domestic Public Official is involved. This avoids confusion and coincides with the implementing legislation of most of the signatories to the OECD Convention. However, one of three alternatives must be selected. The differences relate largely to facilitation payments.

The Commentaries to the OECD Convention state that:

[s]mall facilitation payments do not constitute payments made to "obtain or retain business or other improper advantage" within the meaning of [the OECD Convention] and, accordingly, are also not an offence [under the OECD Convention]. Such payments, which, in some countries, are made to induce public officials to perform their functions such as issuing licenses or permits, are generally illegal in the foreign country concerned.[1]

Neither the OECD Convention nor the accompanying Commentaries contain a definition of a facilitation payment. At least for the near future, to the degree that there is a need for a definition, the most common definition is that used in the FCPA. Under the FCPA, a facilitating or expediting payment is defined as a payment made "to expedite or to secure the performance of a routine government action by a foreign official, political party or party official." The FCPA defines "routine government action" as

. . . action which is ordinarily commonly performed by a foreign official in (i) obtaining permits, licenses, or other official documents to qualify a person to do business in a foreign country; (ii) processing governmental papers, such as visas and work orders; (iii) providing police protection, mail pick-up and delivery or scheduling inspections associated with contract or inspections related to transit of goods across country; (iv) providing phone service, power and water supplies, loading and unloading cargo, or protecting perishable products or commodities from deterioration; or (v) actions of a similar nature [and] does not include any decision by a foreign official whether, or on what terms, to award new business to or to continue business with a particular party, or any action taken by a foreign official involved in the decision-making process to encourage a decision to award new business to or continue business with a particular party.

The Canadian Corruption of Foreign Public Officials Act, §§ 3(3) & (4), uses a very similar definition for facilitation payments. Under the Canadian statute, commonly cited examples include small payments made to an immigration official to facilitate the stamping of a passport in circumstances where securing the stamp should be routine, or a small payment to a public utility official to expedite service, such as telephone service.

British citizens and companies should note that since February 14, 2002, when sections 108-110 of the Anti-Terrorism, Crime and Security Act 2001 came into force, it has been a crime punishable by the British courts for a British citizen or company to do any corrupt act anywhere in the world and the relevant law makes no exception for facilitation payments. However, certain governments may elect not to prosecute a party for making a facilitation payment even though the applicable anti-bribery law makes no exception for them. This may be the case in the United Kingdom.[2]

Alternative 1

Alternative 1 is the "standard" provision and reflects the compromise reached in drafting the OECD Convention. Under this alternative, the parties are only bound by the prohibitions of their respective jurisdictions relative to facilitation payments. The subtleties associated with this language implicitly permits facilitation payments by parties not otherwise prohibited from making such payments. In addition, by following the express language of the OECD Convention, a party is less likely to be perceived as being an accessory to a violation in the country of operations.

Alternative 2

There may be situations where a party is prohibited from making facilitation payments, either by reason of corporate policy or applicable law. Such a party may then select alternative 2, which deletes the word "improper" and expressly prohibits "facilitating or expediting payments." If alternative 2 is selected, the payment of any bribe would be prohibited even if such a payment was not made for the purpose of obtaining or retaining business or securing an improper advantage.

Alternative 3

Alternative 3 explicitly states what is implicit in Alternative 1. By expressly permitting facilitation payments, greater clarity is provided which removes any doubt as to the permissive nature of what is intended. The realities associated with the performance of the work under the contract may necessitate the need for facilitation payments in the country of operations. To avoid confusion and unintended default situations, Alternative 3 explicitly recognizes this reality. On the other hand, the parties must be mindful that all bribes, including facilitation payments, are most likely unlawful under the laws of the country of operations. Moreover, the greater the degree to which facilitation payments are expressly authorized by the terms of the contract, the more likely that one or more of the parties could be determined to be accessories to a violation of law in the country of operations.

Choice of Governing Law

Parties must be mindful of the fact that a party cannot avoid the reach of applicable anti-bribery domestic law (either of the host government or their home government) by an express choice of governing law. A party may, however, inadvertently become subject to the anti-bribery laws of another country (e.g., a French-chartered company uses U.S. commerce to facilitate the payment of a bribe in Southeast Asia). It is unclear whether a party could inadvertently become subject to the anti-bribery laws of the country selected as the governing law of the contract. It is unlikely that such a selection would pose a problem because mere choice of law of such a country should not, in and of itself, subject the parties to the criminal jurisdiction of that country. But it may bear on seeking relief in a civil or arbitral setting. Parties who are not otherwise precluded from making facilitation payments and who may need to rely upon such payments to carry out the terms of a contract may wish to consider this as a factor when selecting the governing law of the contract.

Termination for Breach

Termination of the contract for corruption or bribery is not a requirement of the OECD Convention or the FCPA. Nevertheless, the Justice Department has taken the position that agreements should include a mechanism for termination for a failure on the part of a party to comply with the FCPA. A party subject to the FCPA may ultimately be required to terminate a relationship to demonstrate that it has taken all reasonable steps to avoid a violation of the FCPA. Given the recent implementation in many jurisdictions of the OECD Convention, other regulatory authorities may adopt a similar attitude to that adopted by the Justice Department. But regardless, to emphasis the importance of compliance a termination provision provides added leverage to ensure compliance. Accordingly, Article X.4.1 gives either party the right to terminate the contract for breach of Article X.3.

Definition of Public Official

The definition of "public official" is premised on its use in the context of the corruption of governmental officials. It is specifically designed to be used in conjunction with the compliance provisions contained in Article X.3.1 relating to improper government influence. To the extent that the definition of public official may be used in other contexts, care needs to be exercised to ensure that any revisions do not alter the intent or effectiveness of the existing definition.

The first alternative definition of "public official" is designed to extend the prohibitions on payments to foreign officials to coincide with the FCPA. The exclusion of reference to political parties, party officials, and political candidates in the second alternative definition strictly tracks the language of the OECD Convention. For parties subject to the FCPA, including parties with ADRs listed in the United States, the language cited in the first alternative should be used. Moreover, the use of the first alternative is generally a safer approach whenever the scope of an applicable jurisdiction's anti-corruption laws is unclear. As the Commentaries to the OECD Convention note:

> [u]nder the legal system of some countries, an advantage promised or given to any person, in anticipation of his or her becoming a foreign public official, falls within the scope of the offences described in the [OECD Convention].[3]

❧ NOTES

1. Commentaries on the OECD Convention, ¶ 9.
2. See FAQ No. 5 on the UK Government's Trade Partners UK Web site: **http://www.tradepartners .gov.uk/corruption_overseas/corruptionoverseas/faqsshtml#FAQs.**
3. Commentaries on the OECD Convention, ¶ 10.

PROHIBITED BUSINESS
PRACTICES POLICY

It is the policy of [name of entity], including all of its subsidiaries and affiliates wherever they may be located (hereafter collectively referred to as the "Company"), to, at all times, conduct its affairs in such a manner so as to avoid even the appearance of impropriety. This policy extends to all officers, directors, employees of the Company (hereafter collectively referred to as "personnel") and any individual or entity acting for or on behalf of the Company as an agent, representative, consultant, or in any other capacity (hereafter collectively referred to as "agents").

COMPLIANCE WITH ALL LAWS AND REGULATIONS

It is the general policy of the Company that all of its personnel and agents comply with all applicable laws and regulations in carrying out their responsibilities on behalf of the Company. Because a certain practice may be followed in a particular country, or region of a country, does not make the practice lawful. Nor is a practice lawful because other individuals and entities engage in the practice. The guiding principle must always be whether the practice is prohibited by the written law of a country or unit of government that has the power or jurisdiction to prohibit the practice that may be in question.

This seemingly simple policy can prove to be terribly complex, confusing, and difficult when one is confronted with the practical realities associated with conducting business in unfamiliar settings and in many parts of the world. There may also be situations that arise where it may not be possible to comply with the laws of one country without violating the laws of another country. When questions arise as to what may be permitted or as to how to handle a situation, it is important that advice be promptly sought.

Any personnel or agents who may have a question or a concern or need advice or assistance in addressing a situation should contact _____. Seeking assistance should never serve as a basis for any form of retaliation. Should there be a concern that seeking assistance or raising a concern may lead to some form of retaliation, contact should be made with _____.

PROHIBITED OFFERS OR PAYMENTS TO PUBLIC OFFICIALS

Except with the prior written approval of _____, no offer, promise, or payment of anything of value may be made, directly or indirectly, to or for the benefit of a public official, that is or may appear to be related to obtaining, retaining or directing business or for any other improper advantage. In addition to a government official, a public official includes a candidate or prospective candidate for political office, or anyone acting on their behalf, and an official, employee, or agent of a political party, an international governmental organization, a state-owned enterprise, or an entity owned or controlled by a unit of government.

Agents and Consultants

The use of intermediaries for the purpose of facilitating prohibited transactions is prohibited. No agent, representative, or consultant may be retained without the written approval of _____ after the satisfactory completion of specific due diligence procedures established by _____.

Political Contributions

Without prior written approval, no funds, facilities, or services of any kind may be paid or furnished to any political candidate or prospective candidate for public office, to any political party, or to any political initiative, referendum, or other form of political campaign. When any type of political contribution is being considered, the final determination in terms of amount, timing, and means of contribution shall be subject to the prior written approval of _____.

Facilitating Payments

"Facilitating payments" are small payments made to a public official necessary to expedite or secure performance of a routine governmental action. Facilitating payments can never be made to assist in obtaining or retaining business, to influence a particular decision or transaction, or for any other improper purpose. Although strongly discouraged, facilitating payments may be made in certain limited circumstances, but only with the prior written approval of _____.

Bona Fide *and Reasonable Reimbursement of Business Expenses*

Offers to reimburse and the actual reimbursement of expenses to a public official shall be documented. The amount and the reimbursement must be reasonable, and the purpose must relate directly to the promotion, demonstration, or explanation of products or services of the Company or to the execution or perform-ance of a contract of the Company with a government, government agency, or government-owned or government-controlled enterprise.

ACCOUNTING AND RECORD-KEEPING REQUIREMENTS

It is the policy of the Company that all transactions be recorded in a timely and accurate manner. Transactions must be accurately recorded in terms of amount, accounting period, accounting classification, and in terms of Company policy. Any information material to a transaction must be recorded. No transaction shall be entered into that requires or contemplates the making of false or fictitious entries or records in whole or in part.

Inquiries from Auditors

Any inquiry from the internal or independent auditors of the Company must be responded to fully and promptly. No information shall be withheld that may be material to providing a complete and accurate answer.

Accounting Practices

Each transaction and disposition of assets by the Company must have proper authorization. No secret, unrecorded, or unreported fund or asset of the Com-pany shall be created or maintained. No accounting balances shall be created or maintained that have no documentary support, that are fictitious in whole or in part, or that have no reasonable basis in fact. Without the prior written approval of _____, no third-party accounts for the Company shall be estab-lished other than in the name of the Company.

Prohibited Means of Payment

Without prior written approval of _____, no payment by the Com-pany shall be made to an individual or entity other than those with whom the Company has contracted. No payments shall be made outside the country of the principal place of business of the recipient without the prior written approval of _____.

No corporate checks shall be written to "cash," "bearer," or third-party des-ignees of a party entitled to payment. Other than fully-documented petty cash transactions, no transaction in cash that is not evidenced by a receipt bearing the signature of the recipient shall be made. In those situations, the recipient must also be the acting party in a fully-documented business relationship with the Company.

Accounting Adjustments

Adjustments to accounting records must follow established procedures. Once final-ized, documents are not to be altered. Without written approval of _____, last-minute adjustments that significantly affect financial results of a unit of the Company are prohibited.

Maintenance and Retention of Records

Access to systems of accounting or financial records shall not be permitted for individuals without proper authorization. Record destruction can be undertaken only in compliance with the Company's policy concerning the retention and destruction of records. Records in their original form shall not be removed from the Company without prior written authorization.

Disclosure Obligations

Any personnel or agents of the Company who become aware of a failure on the part of anyone associated with the Company to abide by the terms of the Prohibited Business Practices Policy shall make known the information that has come to their attention by contacting _____
_____.

EXPLANATORY NOTES

The foregoing Prohibited Business Practices Policy is designed to be placed in an entity's policy and procedure manual. It focuses on transactions or activities that are subject to the terms of the FCPA, including the accounting and record-keeping provisions, and those provisions of the anti-corruption conventions that prohibit payments to foreign officials. This policy could be expanded or combined with other policies of an entity to address other forms of prohibited practices. This could include, for example, improper inducements to nongovernmental officials in the form of kickbacks.

Clear and Understandable

It should be emphasized that there is no one way to describe or to develop a compliance policy for an entity. The overriding consideration must be whether what is written will be of assistance in deterring prohibited conduct and ensuring compliance. A policy may, from a legal standpoint, adequately address all of the relevant issues. However, the critical consideration is that the policy be one that is understandable to employees and that can be helpful in serving as a source of guidance.

Protections Against Retaliation

If an entity earnestly seeks to be made aware of questionable conduct and to assist its personnel and agents in addressing concerns, some sort of mechanism needs to be created that provides alternate means of raising issues outside the normal line of reporting. One of the serious problems that arises in the context of a compliance program is the prospect of retribution or retaliation for reporting questionable conduct or for seeking advice or assistance.

Every effort should be made to protect confidences and to protect those who seek advice or make disclosures. The result can be awkward and, at times, lead to confusion and to spurious claims that, in their own way, may be intended as a form of retribution towards more senior officials. No absolute assurances can ever be made that the source of a disclosure or the identity of the individual seeking advice will never be reported to others. What may be learned may require disclosure to others within an entity, to law enforcement officials, or even to the public. But providing a means of raising concerns and seeking assistance without the fear of reprisal can be invaluable in surfacing and addressing problems at an early stage.

There are always administrative difficulties in having a variety of means of having disclosures made or in having more than one unit serve to provide advice or to receive disclosures on compliance issues. Mechanisms for facilitating coordination without jeopardizing the concerns of those who may make disclosures or seek advice need to be developed and to be worked out over time as part of the compliance process. No easy answer exists as to the inherent tradeoffs that will be presented by whatever mechanism is put in place.

Optional Clauses

The clause relative to the use of facilitating payments should be carefully considered. Many entities subject to the FCPA prohibit all payments to foreign officials. Other entities may be subject to the prohibitions of countries that do not permit facilitating payments. In addition, the provisions relating to the accounting and record-keeping provisions may not be technically required when an entity is not an issuer subject to the FCPA. Nonetheless, prudence suggests that they, in large part, be retained. As was the case with their being added as a means of ensuring compliance with the anti-bribery provisions of the FCPA, imposing accounting and record-keeping requirements serve in a similar capacity as part of a compliance program.

Appropriate Officials

There is no legal requirement as to what officials or what units within an entity should be designated to provide approvals, furnish advice, receive disclosures, or fulfill one of the functions suggested by the blanks in the form for the insertion of names of individuals or units of an entity. In large part, it will depend upon those factors that an entity seeks to address. Consideration should be given to the structure of an organization and the various personalities that may be available and appropriate. Obviously, the more sensitive a particular situation, the more senior the official or officials should be. At the same time, there may be a preference for consistency so that the various aspects of the compliance process are centered in a particular unit or office. However, no one person should be responsible for all aspects of the Prohibited Business Practices Policy.

Under no set of circumstances should the foregoing policy on prohibited business practices be adopted in a perfunctory manner. It must be carefully reviewed and altered to meet the needs and the unique circumstances associated with an entity. The identification of officials or units to be inserted in the blanks in the form requires careful analysis to ensure that the most appropriate individuals or unit are identified. The most critical element of any compliance program is the caliber and character of the individuals responsible for its effective execution.

MEMORANDUM TO EXECUTIVES AND MANAGERS

MEMORANDUM

TO:

FROM:

DATE:

SUBJECT: CERTIFICATION OF COMPLIANCE—PROHIBITED BUSINESS PRACTICES

It is the policy of [name of entity], including all of its subsidiaries and affiliates wherever they may be located (collectively referred to as the "Company"), to comply with all laws and regulations that may apply to any of the Company's activities and operations. No officer, director, employee, or agent of the Company shall take or authorize any action that could raise the appearance of impropriety. It is therefore essential that all officers, directors, employees, and agents of the Company comply with all applicable laws in carrying out their responsibilities on behalf of the Company.

COMPLIANCE WITH ALL LAWS

Compliance with all laws includes compliance with not only the laws of the United States but also the laws of foreign countries in which the Company carries on business. An overview is provided of prohibited business practices. This overview is not comprehensive. Simply because certain business practices are not expressly addressed does not mean that they are of no concern to the Company. Good judgment must always be exercised, and advice should always be sought if questions or concerns arise.

You are requested to carefully review the summary of prohibited business practices and to sign and return the attached Certification of Compliance—Prohibited Business Practices no later than _____. Completion of this certification is an annual requirement. To ensure that all components of the Company are in compliance with its policies with respect to prohibited business practices, it will be the responsibility of the Company's _____ to verify your receipt of this certification and the return of a completed certification.

If you have any questions relative to any aspect of this certification, you should contact a member of the _____. If you have a concern as to whether a truthful answer may subject you or a member of your staff to any form of retaliation, you may contact directly _____. If, given the concerns that you may have, none of these options are acceptable, you may contact _____.

PROHIBITED OFFERS OR PAYMENTS

Except with the prior written approval of _____, no offer, promise, or payment of anything of value may be made, directly or indirectly, including through intermediaries, to or for the benefit of a public official, a political party, a party official, or a candidate or prospective candidate for political office, that is or may appear to be related to obtaining, retaining or directing business or for any other improper advantage. This includes any offers, promises, or payments that may imply an understanding that all or part of what is being offered, promised, or paid is to directly or indirectly benefit the public official. A public official includes an employee of an international governmental organization, a government-owned enterprise, or an entity owned or controlled by a government.

Consultants and Agents

The use of intermediaries for the purpose of facilitating prohibited transactions is prohibited. No agent, representative, or consultant may be retained without the express written approval of the _____ after the satisfactory completion of specific due diligence procedures established by the _____.

Political Contributions

Except with prior written approval, no funds, facilities, or services of any kind may be paid or furnished to any political candidate or prospective candidate for public office, to any political party, or to any political initiative, referendum, or other form of political campaign. When any type of political contribution is being considered, the final determination in terms of amount, timing, and means of contribution shall be subject to the written approval, in advance, by _____.

Facilitating Payments

"Facilitating payments" are small payments made to a public official necessary to expedite or secure performance of a routine governmental action, such as obtaining official documents, processing governmental papers, or providing postal or utility services. Facilitating payments can never be made to assist in obtaining or retaining business, to influence a particular decision or transaction, or for any other improper purpose. Although strongly discouraged, facilitating payments may be made in certain limited circumstances, but only with the prior written approval of _____.

Bona Fide *and Reasonable Reimbursement of Business Expenses*

Offers to reimburse and the actual reimbursement of expenses to a public official must be documented. The amount and purpose of the reimbursement must be reasonable and must relate directly to the promotion, demonstration, or explanation of products or services of the Company or to the execution or performance of a contract of the Company with a government, government agency, or government-owned or government-controlled enterprise.

INTERNAL ACCOUNTING CONTROLS AND ACCURATE RECORD-KEEPING

It is the policy of the Company that all transactions be recorded in a timely, consistent, and accurate manner in terms of amount, accounting period, and accounting classification, and be recorded in accordance with Company policy. Any information material to a transaction must be recorded. No transaction shall be entered into that requires or contemplates the making of false or fictitious entries or records in whole or in part.

Inquiries from Auditors

Any inquiry from the internal or independent auditors of the Company must be responded to fully and promptly. No information shall be withheld that may be material to providing a complete and accurate answer.

Accounting Practices

Each transaction and disposition of assets by the Company must have proper authorization. No secret or unrecorded fund or asset of the Company shall be created or maintained. No accounting balances shall be created or maintained that have no documentary support, that are fictitious in whole or in part, or that have no reasonable basis in fact. Without the prior written approval of

_____, no third-party accounts for the Company shall be established other than in the name of the Company.

Prohibited Means of Payment

Without prior written approval of _____, no payment by the Company shall be made to an individual or entity other than those with whom the Company has contracted. No payments shall be made outside the country of the principal place of business of the recipient without the prior written approval of _____.

No corporate checks shall be written to "cash," "bearer," or third-party designees of a party entitled to payment. Other than fully-documented petty cash transactions, no transaction in cash that is not evidenced by a receipt bearing the signature of the recipient shall be made. In those situations, the recipient must also be the acting party in a fully-documented business relationship with the Company.

Accounting Adjustments

Adjustments to accounting records must follow established procedures. Once finalized, documents are not to be altered. Without securing written approval of _____, last-minute adjustments that significantly affect financial results of a unit of the Company are prohibited.

Maintenance and Retention of Records

Access to systems of accounting or financial records shall not be permitted for individuals without proper authorization. Record destruction can be undertaken only in compliance with the Company's policy concerning the retention and destruction of records. Records in their original form shall not be removed from the Company without prior written authorization.

ONGOING COMPLIANCE OBLIGATIONS

Each recipient of this memorandum shall be responsible for the enforcement of and compliance with the foregoing policies within his or her area of responsibility. This includes distribution to ensure knowledge and compliance. Any personnel or agents of the Company who become aware of a failure on the part of anyone associated with the Company to abide by the terms of the Prohibited Business Practices Policy shall make known the information that has come to their attention by contacting _____. Questions of interpretation of these policies are to be referred to _____.

EXPLANATORY NOTES

There is no particular form or series of queries that are required as part of an ongoing compliance program. Nor is there a requirement that the process emanate from a particular official or unit within an entity. The foregoing Certificate of Compliance—Prohibited Business Practices Policy represents just one approach. The critical factor is that areas of particular interest be adequately covered in terms of issues as well as recipients that are key officials and units of an entity.

Tracking Recipients

This particular form is directed at more senior people within units of a larger entity. It, in effect, delegates many of the responsibilities for ensuring compliance. Identifying recipients by name or pay-grade level is normally prudent so that there is no misunderstanding in terms of intended recipients and in terms of responsibility. A means should also be established for tracking and recording the distribution and the receipt of completed certifications.

Use of Other Forms for Subordinates

This form may be used in combination with some of the forms in other parts of the appendices that are directed to individuals. For example, a recipient might well send out to subordinates a copy of the Prohibited Business Practices Policy attached to the Confirmation of Compliance in Parts 3 and 4 of Appendix III-C. The forms and procedures used should always be modified to fit the particular needs of an entity in a way that enhances the likelihood of compliance and at the same time minimizes the bureaucratic burden on staff.

Appropriate Officials

The same considerations that applied to the Prohibited Business Practices Policy in Appendix III-B in terms of officials or units of an entity being designated for providing approvals or receiving disclosures also apply with respect to the designations associated with the Memorandum to Executives and Managers. Great care must be exercised in determining who those individuals or units should be. It is essential that a memorandum of this nature be from someone at a high level within an entity who is respected and who is likely to take action if an adequate response is not received.

Optional Clauses

As is the case with the Prohibited Business Practices Policy, a number of clauses may need to be removed. Most noteworthy is the clause relating to facilitating payments. In addition, the clauses relating to the accounting and record-keeping practices are not necessarily required for entities that are not issuers. However, unless there is a well-justified basis for their removal, the prudent course is to include the clauses concerning the accounting and record-keeping practices. At the same time, there may be a desire to add clauses that may relate to various forms of commercial bribery, like kickbacks, or to practices that may, for example, relate to economic sanctions or boycott policies. Each entity must evaluate its needs and determine the most effective manner of meeting those needs.

MEMORANDUM TO CHIEF FINANCIAL OFFICER

MEMORANDUM

To: Chief Financial Officer

From:

Subject: Certification of Compliance—Prohibited Business Practices Policy

I have recently reviewed your memorandum dated _____ relative to Certification of Compliance—Prohibited Business Practices Policy. Except for what is disclosed on the back of this certification form, I hereby certify that the policies described in your memorandum are in effect at _____, which is the operating unit of _____ over which I have responsibility.

After having made specific inquiry of my staff, and anyone that may act on behalf of the business unit for which I am responsible, I have no knowledge, except for what is disclosed on the back of this certification form, of anyone having engaged in conduct that may be in violation of the Prohibited Business Practices Policy. To the best of my knowledge, the employees, agents, and consultants who report to me are familiar with and in compliance with the Prohibited Business Practices Policies.

Outside of my unit, I am also not aware, except for what is disclosed on the back of this certification, of anyone acting on behalf of _____ having engaged in conduct that would be in violation of the Prohibited Business Practices Policy.

Should I become aware of information giving me reason to believe that anyone acting on behalf of _____ has engaged in or is engaging in conduct that may be in violation of the Prohibited Business Practices Policy, I will promptly report that information to _____.

_____   _____
Signature   Name Printed

_____   _____
Title   Business Unit

_____
Date

EXPLANATORY NOTES

This form is to be used by individuals in supervisory positions. It has been designed to be used in conjunction with the Memorandum to All Executives and Managers. Some of the concerns relative to retaliation may be less pronounced than what they might otherwise be for lower-level employees. Nonetheless, even at the highest levels of an entity, the fear of retribution for candid disclosures can never be disregarded.

The breadth of the reporting and disclosures obligations in a certification of this nature should always be reviewed to ensure that it may not be counterproductive. It may be that limiting the obligation for units for which they have responsibility may engender a greater degree of compliance. Yet, especially at senior levels of an entity, there can be no excuse for ignoring or disregarding conduct or practices that may put in jeopardy the existence of an entire organization.

PART 3

CONFIRMATION OF COMPLIANCE—
SHORT FORM

TO:

DATE:

FROM:

RE: REVIEW OF PROHIBITED BUSINESS PRACTICES POLICY

I have received a copy of [insert name of company] compliance policy, which is entitled Prohibited Business Practices Policy.

I hereby certify that I have reviewed the Prohibited Business Practices Policy, and I agree to abide by its terms. This includes agreeing to report to _____ any violations or suspected violations that may come to my attention. I further certify that the Prohibited Business Practices Policy is in effect at the operating unit of _____ at which I am employed or for which I act as an agent, representative, or consultant.

Except for the situations that are set forth below or previously disclosed to _____ (identify person or persons) on _____ (insert date or dates), I am not aware of any information that has come to my attention from any source that might suggest that _____ or anyone acting on behalf of _____ is suspected of having engaged in or being engaged in conduct prohibited by the Prohibited Business Practices Policy.

_____

[Name]

Title: _____

Date: _____

EXPLANATORY NOTES

This rather straight-forward form is designed for lower-level employees. An entity's compliance policy can be attached or furnished separately. It, in effect, serves as a reminder to rank-and-file employees. It can also be slightly modified to be used with agents. It has the advantage of being less intrusive in terms of paperwork and in terms of burdening staff. Particularly where these issues are apt to be very peripheral to the day-to-day responsibilities of employees or those acting on behalf of an entity, this short form of certificate serves as reminder as to the existence of policies and as to the importance of complying with those policies.

The Drawback Associated with Brevity

Because of its brevity, this short form is less likely to force recipients to carefully review and to understand the implications of an entity's compliance policy. It is also less likely to cause useful information to be disclosed. Most employees and agents can be expected to quickly read the accompanying policy and sign the certification. The exceptions are those employees or agents who might have direct knowledge of serious violations. Consideration should always be given to whether the completion of a more comprehensive confirmation may be warranted.

Reporting on Others

Any entity must take into account the dynamics associated with requiring employees and agents to inform on others. Inherent in any compliance program is some degree of reporting with respect to the conduct of others within an entity or in some way affiliated with the entity. However, a culture of informing on others is not always conducive to a good working environment. As a result, these competing interests must be balanced in such a way so as to promote compliance without undermining the morale of an organization.

APPENDIX **III-C**

PART 4

CONFIRMATION OF COMPLIANCE— LONG FORM

TO:

DATE:

FROM:

I have received a copy of [insert name of company] compliance policy, which is entitled Prohibited Business Practices Policy.

I hereby certify that I have reviewed the Prohibited Business Practices Policy, and I agree to abide by its terms. This includes agreeing to report to _____ any violations or suspected violations that may come to my attention. I further certify that the Prohibited Business Practices Policy is in effect at the operating unit of _____ at which I am employed or for which I act as an agent, representative or consultant.

Except for the situations that are set forth below or previously disclosed to _____ (identify person or persons) on _____ (insert date or dates), I am not aware of any information that has come to my attention from any source that might suggest that _____ or anyone acting on behalf of _____ is suspected of having engaged in or being engaged in conduct prohibited by the Prohibited Business Practices Policy.

INSTRUCTIONS FOR ANSWERING QUESTIONS

In answering the questions set forth below, certainty as to what may have occurred is not required. The use of the term "aware" is meant to be interpreted broadly. You may have heard or learned through a variety of sources that some activities have occurred or are suspected to have occurred. As a result, whether it be through gossip, rumor, or sources outside of the Company, the term "aware" is meant to include any and all sources and to include information that may be rather sketchy or infirm.

The Company recognizes that a "yes" answer does not necessarily mean that anything wrong or improper may have occurred. In many instances, what may

411

have been heard or learned may be incorrect or may have been misinterpreted. In a number of situations it may not be possible to provide a "yes" or "no" answer. Some explanation may be necessary. In those situations, please provide an explanation on the reverse side of this document with the number of the specific question identified in your answer.

It should be emphasized that a failure to provide complete and truthful answers can be a basis for dismissal or for other disciplinary action. If you have any concern as to whether there may be retaliation for completing this form in a complete and truthful manner, you should not hesitate to contact _____. Anyone that may retaliate against you for providing complete and truthful answers can be subject to dismissal.

1. Are you aware of any offer, promise, or payment made, directly or indirectly, to or for the benefit of a public official, political candidate, political party, official of a political party, or official of an international organization?   Yes ___ No ___

2. Are you aware of any payments being made to an indivividual or entity outside the country of the principal place of business of the individual or entity?   Yes ___ No ___

3. Are you aware of any Company checks being made to cash, to "bearer," or to an individual or entity other than the one providing services or products to the Company?   Yes ___ No ___

4. Are you aware of an offer to reimburse or of the actual reimbursement of expenses to a public official that was not reasonable in amount or not directly related to the business of the Company?   Yes ___ No ___

5. Are you aware of any agreements to pay a commission or fee to an agent, a consultant, representative, or independent contractor that substantially exceeds what is normally paid for similar services or that does not correspond to their background, expertise, or qualifications?   Yes ___ No ___

6. Are you aware of any transaction in which the documents provided or prepared by anyone associated with the Company are not accurate?   Yes ___ No ___

7. Are you aware of the destruction of any documents not in accordance with the Company policy with respect to the retention of records?   Yes ___ No ___

8. Are you aware of any unsupported or unauthorized balances, such as reserves, or transactions, such as sales that never took place or have yet to take place?   Yes ___ No ___

9. Are you aware of any last-minute adjustments that significantly affected the financial results of your unit or any other unit of the Company?   Yes ___ No ___

10. Are you aware of any unauthorized persons having access to accounting or financial records?   Yes ___ No ___

11. Are you aware of any complaints or comments being made about questionable business or accounting practices associated with any aspect of the Company's operations?   Yes ___ No ___

12. Are you aware of the altering of any documents?

                  Yes   No

13. Are you aware of any bank or other account, domestic or foreign, in a name other than that of the Company or one of its business units?

                  Yes   No

14. Are you aware of any transaction that has not been accurately recorded in terms of amount, accounting period, accounting classification, or Company policy?

                  Yes   No

15. Are you aware of significant amounts of inventory or physical assets that are missing?

                  Yes   No

16. Are you aware of sales or other transactions being recorded or reported as being completed prior to the actual completion of the sale?

                  Yes   No

17. Are you aware of any transactions that were falsified, not accurately described, or not recorded in the accounting records of the Company?

                  Yes   No

18. Are you aware of any transactions where invoices or records sent to the Company do not set forth the true nature of the transaction?

                  Yes   No

19. Any you aware of the payment by anyone associated with Company for products or services to an individual or entity other than the individual or entity with whom or with which the Company has contracted for such products or services?

                  Yes   No

20. Are you aware of transactions in cash that are not evidenced by a receipt bearing the signature of the cash recipient who is not a party to a business relationship with the Company?

                  Yes   No

21. Are you aware of any transaction or payment entered into on behalf of the Company where any part of the funding will be used for any purpose other than that described by the documents supporting the payment or transaction?

                  Yes   No

22. Are you aware of anyone who for or on behalf of the Company has engaged in or may engage in a transaction that requires or contemplates the making of false or fictitious records or book-keeping or accounting entries in whole or in part?

                  Yes   No

23. Are you aware of any arrangements for the retention of agents, consultants, or representatives that are not based upon documentation that accurately reflects the true nature of the arrangement?

                  Yes   No

24. Are you aware of any secret, unrecorded, unreported funds or assets of the Company that have been created or are being maintained?

                  Yes   No

25. Are you aware of any shipment of product or receipt of supplies not being recorded in a time frame consistent with their actual shipment or receipt?

                  Yes   No

Except for the situations that are identified above or previously disclosed to _____ (insert name of person or persons) on _____ (insert date or dates), I am not aware of any conduct or activity, or suspected conduct or activity, that might be interpreted as a violation of the Prohibited Business Practices Policy. I am also not aware of any information that has come to my attention from anyone that might be interpreted as a violation or suspected violation of the Prohibited Business Practices Policy.

EXPLANATORY NOTES

Completing a form that is, in essence, a type of acknowledgement of compliance may not be as effective as a series of specific questions designed to elicit information that may be of assistance in identifying problems. A series of questions can prompt individuals to think about situations that may not seem as self-evident from a cursory review of an entity's compliance policy.

There is also the educational benefit as the specific issues that are likely to form a basis for concern are, on a repetitive basis, raised with rank-and-file employees. Personnel are sensitized to specific types of practices that are to be avoided. The long form can also be tailored to include the red flags that may be particularly pertinent to an entity's operations. For this reason, some questions should be deleted, and others should be added.

Unfounded Allegations

One of the drawbacks of such a searching inquiry of this nature is the likelihood of a number of issues or concerns being raised that prove to be unfounded. Affirmative answers are likely to prompt inquiries. This will prompt, in the short run, added administrative burdens. The inquiries are apt to be quite disruptive. Nonetheless, the likelihood of problems being disclosed is increased.

Optional Questions

Many of the questions posed relate more directly to complying with the terms of the accounting and record-keeping provisions of the FCPA. However, even when an entity is involved that is not subject to the terms of the accounting and record-keeping provisions, the questions still may bear on compliance with the anti-bribery provisions. By their very nature, inherent to the making of an improper inducement is the falsification of records and the inadequacy of internal accounting controls.

For these same reasons, many if not most of the questions raised would be pertinent to compliance with the terms of the OECD Convention as well as those provisions of the other anti-corruption conventions that relate to the prohibitions on offers or payments to foreign officials. Affirmative answers to any of the questions may serve as a basis for further inquiry and for prompting disclosures that are most apt to provide evidence as to whether improper inducements may have been made.

Other Considerations

An entity must also keep in mind the other considerations that have been raised with respect to the other forms included in Appendices III-B and III-C. The language contained in the forms and the manner in which a form is used must always be calibrated to meet the needs of an entity. And these needs often compete with one another. Finding the proper balance can be challenging and can take time. But at no time should the prospect of bureaucratic or other difficulties be used as a basis for failing to implement and adequately enforce a compliance program.

SPECIAL GUIDELINES FOR THE CONDUCT OF INTERNATIONAL BUSINESS

The Company, which includes [insert name of entity] and its subsidiaries and affiliates wherever they may be located, expects that all of its officers, directors, and employees will comply with all U.S. and other applicable laws and will maintain the highest ethical standards of business conduct. These expectations also apply to agents acting on behalf of the Company. Particularly in the conduct of international business by the Company, special care needs to be exercised to avoid making payments that may be or may be perceived to be improper. This includes

- *Payments to Foreign Government Officials.* No employee of the Company, or anyone acting on behalf of the Company, shall promise, offer, authorize the giving of, or give any thing of value, whether directly or through intermediaries, to any government official in order to obtain, retain or direct business or for any improper advantage. For these purposes, "government official" is intended to be interpreted broadly to apply to employees, representatives, or agents of any unit or instrumentality of government and to include foreign governments, international governmental organizations, entities owned or controlled by a government or international governmental organization, any political party or party officials, and candidates or prospective candidates for public office.
- *Cash, Third-Party, and Third-Country Payments.* To avoid even the appearance of impropriety, no payments to any third party shall be made in any situation other than as documented petty cash disbursements. No checks shall be written to "cash" or "bearer", and no payments shall be made to anyone other than with whom the Company has contracted or has a documented business relationship. No payments shall be made outside the country of the principal place of business of the recipient without the prior written approval of _____.

- *Agents, Consultants and Representatives.* No employee of the Company, or anyone acting on behalf of the Company, may retain an agent, consultant, or representative without the prior written approval of _____ certifying that sufficient due diligence has been performed to conclude with reasonable assurance that the agent, consultant, or representative understands and agrees not to promise, offer, authorize the giving of, or give anything of value, whether directly or through intermediaries, to any government official in order to obtain, retain, or direct business to or for any improper advantage for the Company.

- *Reimbursement of Expenses.* All offers to reimburse expenses of a government official must be documented. The amount and purpose of the reimbursement must be reasonable and must relate directly to the promotion, demonstration, or explanation of products or services of the Company or to the execution or performance of a contract of the Company with a government, government agency, or government-owned or government-controlled enterprise.

- *Facilitating Payments.* "Facilitating payments" are small payments to a government official necessary to expedite or secure performance of routine governmental action, such as obtaining official documents, processing governmental papers, or providing postal or utility services. Facilitating payments never include payments made to assist in obtaining or retaining business. Although strongly discouraged, facilitating payments may be made in certain limited circumstances, but only with the prior written approval of _____.

- *Political Contributions.* As a general rule, political contributions should not be made by the Company or on its behalf. When any type of political contribution is being considered, the final determination in terms of amount, timing, and means of contribution shall be subject to the prior written approval of _____.

- *Record-Keeping.* All transactions must be recorded in a timely, accurate, and consistent manner in terms of amount, accounting period, accounting classification, and Company policy. Any other information material to a transaction shall also be recorded. No transaction shall be entered into that requires or contemplates the making or the receipt of false or fictitious accounting entries or records in whole or in part.

- *Accounting Practices.* Each transaction and disposition of assets by the Company must have proper authorization. No secret, unrecorded, unreported fund or asset of the Company shall be created or maintained, and no third-party account shall be established for the Company other than in the name of the Company. No accounting balances shall be either created or maintained that have no documentary support, that are fictitious in whole or in part, or that have no reasonable basis in fact.

- *Inquiries from Auditors.* Any inquiry from the internal or independent auditors of the Company must be responded to fully and promptly. No information shall be withheld that may be material to providing a complete and accurate answer.

The failure to comply with the policies of the Company as well as these Special Guidelines will be grounds for termination or other disciplinary action. Designated personnel and agents will be asked to certify annually that they have reviewed these Special Guidelines. Any officer, director, employee, or agent of the Company with questions about these Special Guidelines, should contact _____.

EXPLANATORY NOTES

For many entities, there may be a preference to limit the dissemination of certain compliance policies to those employees or agents that are most likely to be confronted with pertinent issues. Too many admonitions can, in time, undermine their currency. As a result, the foregoing guidelines represent one approach that might be considered.

Many of the considerations that are discussed in the Explanatory Notes to the Prohibited Business Practices Policy in Appendices III-B and III-C may also apply to these Special Guidelines. Before adopting these Special Guidelines, any entity should, in particular, take into consideration (1) whether provisions need to be added to protect the recipients from retaliation for providing candid and complete answers and (2) whether the provisions with respect to facilitating payments should be removed.

Since an entity's policies with respect to accounting and record-keeping practices will extend to all aspects of its operations, it may not be necessary to include the provisions relating to accounting and record-keeping practices. One of the benefits of simplicity is a clear and focused message. On the other hand, as has been noted, following proper accounting and record-keeping practices is essential to deterring improper payments to foreign officials. Reinforcing the need for proper accounting and record-keeping obligations can seldom be harmful.

APPENDIX **III-D**

PART 2

CERTIFICATION OF COMPLIANCE WITH SPECIAL GUIDELINES FOR THE CONDUCT OF INTERNATIONAL BUSINESS

I have read the accompanying Special Guidelines for the Conduct of International Business and hereby agree to comply with all of the provisions of the Special Guidelines. Except as disclosed on the back of this certification, I have never participated in, and am not aware of, any violation of the Special Guidelines on the part of anyone associated with the Company, which includes [insert name of entity] and any of its subsidiaries and affiliates.

Should I become aware of information giving me reason to believe that anyone while acting on behalf of the Company may have in any way been engaged in conduct that violates these Special Guidelines, I will promptly report that information to _____.

_____   _____
Signature   Name Printed

_____   _____
Title   Office

_____
Date

EXPLANATORY NOTES

The proposed certification represents a very basic approach. It has the advantage of being simple and not burdensome on recipients. It serves as a reminder in terms of obligations to make disclosures concerning questionable conduct. Obviously, certain circumstances or preferences on the part of an entity may warrant or suggest alternative or additional language. This could include language used in some of the other forms contained in these appendices.

The effectiveness of the compliance process will ultimately depend on complete and candid responses. This particular form does not specifically address situations where an employee or agent may be fearful of the repercussions associated with full and truthful disclosure. No mechanism is provided to address the prospect of those situations. It is an aspect of the compliance process that should always be considered and, where necessary, appropriate provisions should be added and mechanisms put in place to address those concerns.

FROM THE ABA SECTION OF INTERNATIONAL LAW

For more information on or to order any of these books,
visit our web site at www.ababooks.org or call toll-free 1-800-285-2221

The ABA Guide to International Business Negotiations, Second Edition [PC 5210127]

Arab Commercial Law: Principles and Perspectives [PC 5210131]

Careers in International Law, Second Edition [PC 5210129]

China and Hong Kong in Legal Transition: Commercial & Humanitarian Issues [PC 5210124]

China Law Deskbook: A Legal Guide for Foreign-Invested Enterprises, Second Edition [PC 5210139]

Doing Business in Argentina [PC 5210126]

Doing Business in Brazil [PC 5210130]

Guide to Foreign Law Firms, Fourth Edition [PC 5210137]

IPDS: The Foreign Corrupt Practices Act and the New International Norms [PC 5210138]

IPDS: Joint Ventures in the International Arena [PC 5210134]

IPDS: International Lawyer's Deskbook, Second Edition [PC 5210135]

IPDS: International Trademarks and Copyrights—Enforcement Management [PC 5210136]

The Lawyers Guide to China's Technical Regulations for Imported Products [PC 5210128]

A Legal Guide to Doing Business in Russia and the Former Republics of the U.S.S.R. [PC 5210125]

Negotiating and Structuring International Commercial Transactions, Second Edition [PC 5210133]